Ezra, Nehemiah, *and* Esther

TEACH THE TEXT COMMENTARY SERIES

John H. Walton
Old Testament General Editor

Mark L. Strauss
New Testament General Editor

Old Testament Volumes

New Testament Volumes

Visit the series website at www.teachthetextseries.com.

TEACH the TEXT
COMMENTARY SERIES

Ezra, Nehemiah, *and* Esther

Douglas J. E. Nykolaishen and Andrew J. Schmutzer

Mark L. Strauss and John H. Walton
GENERAL EDITORS

ILLUSTRATING THE TEXT
Kevin and Sherry Harney
ASSOCIATE EDITORS

Joshua Blunt
CONTRIBUTING AUTHOR

BakerBooks
a division of Baker Publishing Group
Grand Rapids, Michigan

Ezra and Nehemiah © 2018 by Douglas J. E. Nykolaishen
Esther © 2018 by Andrew J. Schmutzer
Illustrating the Text sections © 2018 by Baker Publishing Group

Published by Baker Books
a division of Baker Publishing Group
PO Box 6287, Grand Rapids, MI 49516-6287
www.bakerbooks.com
Printed and bound by CPI Group (UK) Ltd, Croydon, CR0 4YY

Library of Congress Cataloging-in-Publication Data
Names: Nykolaishen, Douglas J. E., 1963– author.
Title: Ezra, Nehemiah, and Esther / Douglas J. E. Nykolaishen and Andrew J. Schmutzer ; Mark L.
   Strauss and John H. Walton, general editors ; illustrating the text, Kevin and Sherry Harney.
Description: Grand Rapids : Baker Publishing Group, 2018. | Series: Teach the text commentary series |
   Includes bibliographical references and index.
Identifiers: LCCN 2017051462 | ISBN 9780801015403 (pbk.)
Subjects: LCSH: Bible. Ezra—Commentaries. | Bible. Nehemiah—Commentaries. | Bible.
   Esther—Commentaries.
Classification: LCC BS1355.53 .N95 2018 | DDC 222/.707—dc23
LC record available at https://lccn.loc.gov/2017051462

To Cora-Fay, my faithful companion on the
journey to full restoration in Christ.
DJEN

To the *Koinonia* class of Wheaton Bible Church.
The fellowship in his Word has been nourishing, indeed.
AJS

Contents

Welcome to the Teach the Text Commentary Series

Why another commentary series? That was the question the general editors posed when Baker Books asked us to produce this series. Is there something that we can offer to pastors and teachers that is not currently being offered by other commentary series, or that can be offered in a more helpful way? After carefully researching the needs of pastors who teach the text on a weekly basis, we concluded that yes, more can be done; the Teach the Text Commentary Series (TTCS) is carefully designed to fill an important gap.

The technicality of modern commentaries often overwhelms readers with details that are tangential to the main purpose of the text. Discussions of source and redaction criticism, as well as detailed surveys of secondary literature, seem far removed from preaching and teaching the Word. Rather than wade through technical discussions, pastors often turn to devotional commentaries, which may contain exegetical weaknesses, misuse the Greek and Hebrew languages, and lack hermeneutical sophistication. There is a need for a commentary that utilizes the best of biblical scholarship but also presents the material in a clear, concise, attractive, and user-friendly format.

This commentary is designed for that purpose—to provide a ready reference for the exposition of the biblical text, giving easy access to information that a pastor needs to communicate the text effectively. To that end, the commentary is divided into carefully selected preaching units (with carefully regulated word counts both in the passage as a whole and in each subsection). Pastors and teachers engaged in weekly preparation thus know that they will be reading approximately the same amount of material on a week-by-week basis.

Each passage begins with a concise summary of the central message, or "Big Idea," of the passage and a list of its main themes. This is followed by a more detailed interpretation of the text, including the literary context of the passage, historical background material, and interpretive insights. While drawing on the best of biblical scholarship, this material is clear, concise, and to the point. Technical material is kept to a minimum, with endnotes pointing the reader to more detailed discussion and additional resources.

A second major focus of this commentary is on the preaching and teaching process itself. Few commentaries today help the pastor/teacher move from the meaning of the text to its effective communication. Our goal is to bridge this gap. In addition to interpreting the text in the "Understanding the Text" section, each unit contains a "Teaching the Text" section and an "Illustrating the Text" section. The teaching section points to the key theological themes of the passage and ways to communicate these themes to today's audiences. The illustration section provides ideas and examples for retaining the interest of hearers and connecting the message to daily life.

The creative format of this commentary arises from our belief that the Bible is not just a record of God's dealings in the past but is the living Word of God, "alive and active" and "sharper than any double-edged sword" (Heb. 4:12). Our prayer is that this commentary will help to unleash that transforming power for the glory of God.

The General Editors

Introduction to the Teach the Text Commentary Series

This series is designed to provide a ready reference for teaching the biblical text, giving easy access to information that is needed to communicate a passage effectively. To that end, the commentary is carefully divided into units that are faithful to the biblical authors' ideas and of an appropriate length for teaching or preaching.

The following standard sections are offered in each unit.

1. *Big Idea*. For each unit the commentary identifies the primary theme, or "Big Idea," that drives both the passage and the commentary.
2. *Key Themes*. Together with the Big Idea, the commentary addresses in bullet-point fashion the key ideas presented in the passage.
3. *Understanding the Text*. This section focuses on the exegesis of the text and includes several sections.
   a. The Text in Context. Here the author gives a brief explanation of how the unit fits into the flow of the text around it, including reference to the rhetorical strategy of the book and the unit's contribution to the purpose of the book.
   b. Outline/Structure. For some literary genres (e.g., epistles), a brief exegetical outline may be provided to guide the reader through the structure and flow of the passage.

c. Historical and Cultural Background. This section addresses historical and cultural background information that may illuminate a verse or passage.

d. Interpretive Insights. This section provides information needed for a clear understanding of the passage. The intention of the author is to be highly selective and concise rather than exhaustive and expansive.

e. Theological Insights. In this very brief section the commentary identifies a few carefully selected theological insights about the passage.

4. *Teaching the Text.* Under this second main heading the commentary offers guidance for teaching the text. In this section the author lays out the main themes and applications of the passage. These are linked carefully to the Big Idea and are represented in the Key Themes.

5. *Illustrating the Text.* At this point in the commentary the writers partner with a team of pastor/teachers to provide suggestions for relevant and contemporary illustrations from current culture, entertainment, history, the Bible, news, literature, ethics, biography, daily life, medicine, and over forty other categories. They are designed to spark creative thinking for preachers and teachers and to help them design illustrations that bring alive the passage's key themes and message.

Abbreviations

Old Testament

Gen.	Genesis	2 Chron.	2 Chronicles	Dan.	Daniel
Exod.	Exodus	Ezra	Ezra	Hosea	Hosea
Lev.	Leviticus	Neh.	Nehemiah	Joel	Joel
Num.	Numbers	Esther	Esther	Amos	Amos
Deut.	Deuteronomy	Job	Job	Obad.	Obadiah
Josh.	Joshua	Ps(s).	Psalm(s)	Jon.	Jonah
Judg.	Judges	Prov.	Proverbs	Mic.	Micah
Ruth	Ruth	Eccles.	Ecclesiastes	Nah.	Nahum
1 Sam.	1 Samuel	Song	Song of Songs	Hab.	Habakkuk
2 Sam.	2 Samuel	Isa.	Isaiah	Zeph.	Zephaniah
1 Kings	1 Kings	Jer.	Jeremiah	Hag.	Haggai
2 Kings	2 Kings	Lam.	Lamentations	Zech.	Zechariah
1 Chron.	1 Chronicles	Ezek.	Ezekiel	Mal.	Malachi

New Testament

Matt.	Matthew	Eph.	Ephesians	Heb.	Hebrews
Mark	Mark	Phil.	Philippians	James	James
Luke	Luke	Col.	Colossians	1 Pet.	1 Peter
John	John	1 Thess.	1 Thessalonians	2 Pet.	2 Peter
Acts	Acts	2 Thess.	2 Thessalonians	1 John	1 John
Rom.	Romans	1 Tim.	1 Timothy	2 John	2 John
1 Cor.	1 Corinthians	2 Tim.	2 Timothy	3 John	3 John
2 Cor.	2 Corinthians	Titus	Titus	Jude	Jude
Gal.	Galatians	Philem.	Philemon	Rev.	Revelation

General

cf.	*confer*, compare	etc.	*et cetera*, and so forth
chap(s).	chapter(s)	Heb.	Hebrew
e.g.	*exempli gratia*, for example	lit.	literally
esp.	especially	v(v).	verse(s)

Apocrypha

Tob.	Tobit	1 Macc.	1 Maccabees
Jdt.	Judith	2 Macc.	2 Maccabees

Mishnah, Talmud, and Related Literature

b	Babylonian Talmud	*Meg.*	*Megillah*
m.	Mishnah	*Ketub.*	*Ketubbot*
B. Bat.	*Baba Batra*	*Sanh.*	*Sanhedrin*

Greek and Latin Works

Herodotus

Hist.   Herodotus, *Histories*

Josephus

Ag. Ap.	*Against Apion*
Ant.	*Jewish Antiquities*

J.W.   *Jewish War*

Xenophon

Anab.	*Anabasis*
Cyr.	*Cyropaedia*
Hell.	*Hellenica*

Ancient Versions

LXX   Septuagint

Modern Versions

CEV	Contemporary English Version	NASB	New American Standard Bible
CSB	Christian Standard Bible	NET	New English Translation
ESV	English Standard Version	NIV	New International Version
HCSB	Holman Christian Standard Bible	NJPS	New Jewish Publication Society Version
KJV	King James Version		
NABRE	New American Bible, revised edition	NLT	New Living Translation
		NRSV	New Revised Standard Version

Modern Reference Works

ABD   *Anchor Bible Dictionary*. Edited by D. N. Freedman. 6 vols. New York: Doubleday, 1992.

DSE   *Dictionary of Scripture and Ethics*. Edited by J. B. Green. Grand Rapids:
           Baker Academic, 2011.
HALOT   *Hebrew and Aramaic Lexicon of the Old Testament*. By L. Koehler,
           W. Baumgartner, and J. J. Stamm. Translated and edited under the super-
           vision of M. E. J. Richardson. 4 vols. Leiden: Brill, 1994–99.
NIDB   *New Interpreter's Dictionary of the Bible*. Edited by Katherine Doob
           Sakenfeld. 5 vols. Nashville: Abingdon, 2009.
NIDOTTE   *New International Dictionary of Old Testament Theology and Exegesis*.
           Edited by W. A. VanGemeren. 5 vols. Grand Rapids: Zondervan, 1997.
TDOT   *Theological Dictionary of the Old Testament*. Edited by G. J. Botterweck
           and H. Ringgren. Translated by J. T. Willis, G. W. Bromiley, and D. E.
           Green. 8 vols. Grand Rapids: Eerdmans, 1974–.
TLOT   *Theological Lexicon of the Old Testament*. Edited by E. Jenni, with as-
           sistance by C. Westermann. Translated by M. E. Biddle. Peabody, MA:
           Hendrickson, 1997.

Ezra *and* Nehemiah

Douglas J. E. Nykolaishen

Introduction to Ezra and Nehemiah

The books of Ezra and Nehemiah are a faith-inspiring record of God fulfilling his promises to his people in the postexilic period. These texts say so much about the central theological themes in the Bible that by the time their story is finished, the reader has a better framework for appreciating the *New* Testament, let alone the Old. Yet that is not how these books are typically perceived. Ezra and Nehemiah do not report the kinds of miracles seen in Exodus or 2 Kings or Daniel. Instead, there are several lists that may seem tedious and a plot that may be confusing and difficult to follow at times. However, with a little orientation to the books, their powerful relevance begins to come into view. The rest of this introduction will focus on providing this necessary orientation.

Boundaries of the Text

Ezra-Nehemiah is not two books but one. There is no known Hebrew manuscript that separates the book into two parts before AD 1448. The tradition of presenting Ezra and Nehemiah as separate books in Greek Christian Bibles is no earlier than Origen in the third century AD, and even he referred to them as 1 and 2 Ezra, much like 1 and 2 Chronicles, which are to be read as one literary work. To understand the flow of the narrative and interpret any single passage correctly in context, the reader must think in terms of the whole from Ezra 1 to Nehemiah 13.

A related question involves the relationship of Ezra-Nehemiah to Chronicles. Because Christian Bibles place Ezra immediately after 2 Chronicles, and because the last two verses of Chronicles are almost identical with the first two and a half verses of Ezra, many interpreters have thought that Ezra-Nehemiah should be read as a continuation of Chronicles. But the Hebrew Bible has historically treated Ezra-Nehemiah as a work separate from Chronicles. In fact, several elements, including the slight differences between the Chronicles and Ezra versions of the "overlapping" text, are recognized by many scholars as indicating that Chronicles was probably written separately and even later than Ezra-Nehemiah. Thus, while Ezra-Nehemiah forms one continuous book, it is not joined to Chronicles.

Method of Composition

One may not read long in Ezra-Nehemiah before encountering a list of names of persons or cities, a document inserted by the narrator but written by someone else, or a change between third-person narration and autobiography. These features make the flow of the book seem less smooth than that of books like Samuel and Kings and, therefore, harder to follow. The cause of this is that the author of Ezra-Nehemiah made extensive use of source material when composing his inspired work. Most of the lists of names (e.g., Ezra 2:1–70; 8:1–14; Neh. 7:6–73; 11:3–24) were probably compiled years before Ezra-Nehemiah was written and simply inserted by the author where they suited his purpose. When the story involved decrees issued by a king, or letters sent between parties, the author chose in several instances to include the actual text of the documents rather than merely summarizing their contents (although he possibly did some paraphrasing of the wording, since that was acceptable within the conventions of ancient history writing). In Ezra 4:11–16, 17–22; 5:7–17; 6:6–12; 7:12–26, the letters are even presented in Aramaic, without translation into Hebrew. The use of documents can also be seen in the sections where Ezra and Nehemiah, although characters in the story, speak in the first person (e.g., Ezra 9:1–15; Neh. 1:1–2:20). It seems the author of the biblical book had access to records Ezra and Nehemiah had written about their activities and selected excerpts from them to include in his narrative.

The large amount of source material incorporated into the book means that the number of words originating with the author—the amount of the text in the author's voice—may be smaller than readers usually expect. However, the author usually does give enough introduction to the documents he uses that careful readers can see how they contribute to the flow of the story. In any case, readers need to think about how the documents and details chosen for inclusion relate to the message of a passage and of the book as a whole, even if the author does not always spell this out as clearly as we might like.

Another potential stumbling block involves the chronological order of events narrated in the book. In some instances it seems that events have been presented in an order different from how they happened in history. A particularly good example is in Ezra 4, and the commentary there explains why the author did this. But this can be confusing for readers, and there are several points in the book where some scholars have suggested that the historical sequence has not been preserved. Probably the most frequent suggestion along these lines is that Nehemiah 8 (and possibly 9 and 10 as well) has been moved from its original historical location after Ezra 10 (or 8) to suit the author's purpose, although similar suggestions have been made for other passages also. Such attempts to reconstruct history are subjective and speculative.

It is difficult to be sure about the complete sequence of events in Ezra-Nehemiah, but it seems the author generally intended to follow a historical order (e.g., "After these things . . . ," Ezra 7:1; 9:1). This commentary assumes that events are in chronological sequence unless the weight of evidence demands otherwise. But as far as chronology is concerned, it is even more important to recognize that the author of Ezra-Nehemiah did not intend to provide a comprehensive history of the era he described. The first event in the book happens in 538 BC, and the last event sometime between 432 and 424 BC. From this span of over a hundred years, the author has selected episodes or events that occurred within eight discrete years. This makes it clear that the story is very selective, including only those things the author thought had relevance for what he was trying to teach readers, and his aim was not to provide a complete history of this period. While the author can be trusted to be historically truthful, it is far more important to follow his didactic intention than to seek the solution to every historical question. The author has not seen fit to provide enough information to fully reconstruct the history in every case.

Author and Date

Who exactly did write Ezra-Nehemiah is difficult to say. Jewish tradition recorded in the Talmud claims it was written by Ezra. He did write much of the text included in Ezra 7–10, and he may even have been the author who composed Ezra-Nehemiah in its final form, but there is nothing in the book itself that indicates who composed it.

There are similar issues with the book's date. It must have been written sometime after the last document it used. The lists of high priests in Nehemiah 12:10, 22 end with Jaddua, who probably served between about 410 and 370 BC. It makes sense to assume that the book was given its present form between those dates. Ezra may possibly have still been alive then, but if so, he would have been very old.

It seems wisest to conclude that the author of Ezra-Nehemiah is no longer known, but that it was someone living in postexilic Judea, with access to the documents contained in the book, between about 410 and 370 BC. This person seems to have been concerned to show his fellow Judeans that the events he records are evidence of God's gracious acts on behalf of their community and to present examples of behavior from which they should learn.

Historical Setting

At the most likely date of writing, the Jewish people were dispersed in several areas of the ancient Near East. Most continued to live in the region of Babylon, where they had been brought as exiles at the fall of the kingdom of Judah in 586 BC, or in the years leading up to it. After living for several generations in that region, most families felt quite settled, and some had even become rather prosperous. Many lived in the region that came to be known as Judea (also referred to as Yehud). These were mostly descendants of those who had traveled from exile in Babylon to the area around Jerusalem during the period described in Ezra-Nehemiah. Some, perhaps, were never taken into exile. There was also a significant community of Jews in Egypt and possibly still some small communities in other parts of the ancient Near East, such as Assyria. All these Jews, except possibly those in Egypt, were under the rule of the Persian Empire, which had dominated the region since 539 BC.

The author probably writes mainly to the Jews in Judea. He expects them to know that Judea is relatively small and unimportant in the political context of the Persian Empire, and that it was like this in the days about which he writes. He also expects them to know that they occupy a location close enough to Egypt, a constant source of rebellion, to be strategically significant to the Persians. Because of this, Judea sometimes received favorable consideration from the Persians out of proportion to its size. In general, the author assumes readers know the social, economic, and political circumstances experienced by subjects under Persian rule and are familiar with the names of Persian kings. Since modern readers are not, the commentary will explain relevant background at appropriate points.

Table 1. Persian Kings over the Jews
from Cyrus the Great to Darius II

Cyrus the Great	539–530 BC
Cambyses	530–522 BC
Darius I	522–486 BC
Xerxes	485–465 BC
Artaxerxes I	465–424 BC
Darius II	424–404 BC

It is equally or even more important to understand the spiritual context of which the author assumes readers are aware. The status of the Jewish community in Babylon at the beginning of Ezra-Nehemiah can be understood from 2 Chronicles 36:15–21. Their ancestors had disobeyed God and refused to listen to the prophets God sent to warn them of impending judgment. Eventually God brought the Babylonians under Nebuchadnezzar to attack and destroy the Jerusalem temple, the city wall, and much else in the city also. Many people were killed, and others were taken into exile in Babylon.

These actions constituted the realization of one of the possible outcomes foretold by God when he made his covenant with Israel. Deuteronomy 28:1–14 describes the blessings that Israel will experience if they faithfully worship God and obey his commands, and Deuteronomy 28:15–68 and 29:25–28 describe the curses they will suffer if they disobediently turn away to worship idols. The Israelites were unfaithful to God, and the threatened punishment came in stages. The kingdom of Israel was first divided into a northern and a southern kingdom after the reign of Solomon. The northern kingdom was destroyed and taken into exile by the Assyrians in 722 BC, and the southern kingdom, the subject of 2 Chronicles 36, suffered a similar fate in 586 BC.

Interestingly, however, Deuteronomy does not leave the matter there. Deuteronomy 30:1–10 envisions a scenario in which the curses for disobedience have come upon Israel and they have been dispersed among the nations. It goes on to promise that even in such circumstances God will bring Israel back to the promised land and bless them if they turn their hearts back to him in faithful obedience. God even promises to change their hearts so they will truly love him. God elaborates on this promise of restoration in his messages through the biblical prophets, adding many particulars, including the promise of a new covenant with Israel in Jeremiah 31:31–34. More details will be given at relevant points in the commentary.

At the beginning of Ezra, then, the Jerusalem temple is in ruins and the Jewish community is in exile in Babylon because of the unfaithfulness of their ancestors. But they also know of God's promise to bring them back to the land of Judea and restore his blessing to them there if they return to him. The author tells the story against this spiritual background.

Literary Structure

Ezra-Nehemiah is composed of four main sections. In Ezra 1–6 the Judeans are permitted to return to Jerusalem and vicinity to rebuild the temple and resume worship there. They encounter considerable opposition from the surrounding people, and the project is delayed. But God enables them eventually to complete the project.

Ezra 7–10 tells about Ezra coming from Babylon to Jerusalem to ensure that the Judeans understand God's law and live by it. The surrounding people do not oppose this mission directly, but they represent a temptation that leads to some Judeans disobeying God's law. Ezra does see some progress, but the success of his mission is not completely clear.

Nehemiah 1–7 describes Nehemiah's efforts to travel to Jerusalem and lead a project to rebuild the ruined city wall. He too encounters stiff resistance from the Judeans' neighbors, but God enables him also to achieve his goal. Although the city now has a protecting wall, liaisons between the Judeans and their enemies erode the city's security.

Nehemiah 8–13 is an account of the Judean community's commitment to obey God's law and provide for worship at the Jerusalem temple. At one stage, the community's faithfulness appears to reach a level unprecedented in the Old Testament. Yet temptations arising from the surrounding peoples result in Judean disobedience that severely qualifies that impression.

The first and third sections, then, involve travel by Judeans to Jerusalem to undertake a physical building project intended to reverse destruction inflicted by the Babylonians. Opposition from outside the Judean community is encountered, but God empowers the Judeans to overcome the obstacles and clearly achieve the objective. The second and fourth sections focus on the Judeans' spiritual objective of obedience to God's law. Rather than directly opposing this, the neighboring peoples are a source of temptation toward disobedience. The Judeans' success in this matter is incomplete. In the second, third, and fourth sections, the Judeans inappropriately cross boundaries in their interactions with the other nations, leading to problems that must be addressed by their leaders.

The book thus presents the events it narrates as evidence of the fulfillment of God's restoration promises, while indicating that the promised restoration has not yet fully arrived. Readers are to learn from examples, positive and negative, how to cooperate with God as he brings about the completion of those promises. This is what readers must do with the New Testament as well.

Terminology

A question that arises when discussing the postexilic period is what to call the Jewish community that is the focus of Ezra-Nehemiah. Part of what makes this complicated is that the biblical text at various times calls them "returned exiles," "Israel," or "Jews." Arguments can be made for using each of these, but shifting among them can lead to confusion. In an effort to be consistent, this commentary will prefer the term "Judeans," since they live in the territory associated with the preexilic kingdom of Judah and that soon came to be known as Judea.

Cyrus Is Moved to Rebuild the Temple

Big Idea

God always keeps his promises, sometimes using surprising means in the process.

Key Themes

- Cyrus's decree, although generous to the Judean exiles, is intended to further his imperial agenda.
- The Lord uses Cyrus's decree for his own purpose—to fulfill Jeremiah's prophecy.

Understanding the Text

The Text in Context

Ezra 1 naturally sets the narrative plot of Ezra-Nehemiah in motion, but it also introduces the theological theme of restoration that is central to the entire book. The events of the first chapter are presented as connected to the prophetic words of Jeremiah, yet the idea that events represent fulfillment of Jeremiah's prophecy carries forward and applies to most of what happens in the book. In this sense the opening verse of Ezra 1 gives the reader a clue about how to read the story that follows. Just as the decree of Cyrus alone does not represent fulfillment of Jeremiah's prophecy, but rather sets that fulfillment in motion, so the events of Ezra 1 are part of a chain of events that together constitute the restoration Jeremiah had announced. And when the end of the narrative is reached, it is clear that the restoration, such as it is, anticipates a yet further and more complete fulfillment of Jeremiah's words. Ezra-Nehemiah thus represents an important stage in the history of salvation, and Ezra 1 begins to orient the reader accordingly.

The restoration of the fortunes of Israel begins with permission from Cyrus for previously exiled Judeans to return to Jerusalem for the specific purpose of rebuilding the temple of the Lord there. All the neighbors of those Judeans who choose to go are instructed to support them by donating a wide variety

The Cyrus Cylinder. The cylinder doesn't directly mention Israel, but it alludes to Cyrus's policy of returning exiled peoples to their homelands along with stolen sacred objects.

of goods and wealth. The Judeans would have been unable to begin this process without the permission and provision that came through Cyrus's decree.

Historical and Cultural Background

In the ancient Near East, an important way that a king could claim to be the legitimate ruler over a particular people group was by restoring the proper worship of the god of that people group. Cyrus used this same strategy to claim legitimacy as ruler over the Babylonians. On the Cyrus Cylinder, on display in the British Museum, Cyrus wrote that the Babylonian god Marduk had made him ruler of all the lands and had chosen him to restore right worship. He also mentioned that he rebuilt the destroyed sanctuaries of the gods of other peoples and allowed those peoples who had been exiled to return to their homelands as well.[1] So when Cyrus wanted to be seen as the legitimate ruler of Babylon, he claimed to have been chosen by Marduk. When asserting his rule over the Judeans, he claimed to have been chosen by Yahweh, and so on. This was political propaganda and likely recognized as such by many of his subject peoples.

Nevertheless, rebuilding a temple for one's subjects and restoring its worship usually created goodwill, regardless of whether they recognized the propaganda angle. In the polytheistic culture of the time, moreover, Cyrus probably felt it was in his own interest to curry favor with as many gods as he could. Both of these motivations likely played a role in Cyrus's decision to issue his decree.

The biblical narrator, however, sees the irony that in this case God has in fact appointed Cyrus to rebuild his temple, albeit for his own purposes rather than for legitimating Cyrus's rule.

Which Prophecy of Jeremiah Was Fulfilled?

2 Chronicles 36:22 and Ezra 1:1 are nearly identical, and both refer to the word of the Lord spoken by Jeremiah being fulfilled. 2 Chronicles 36:21 mentions "the seventy years" in connection with the fulfillment of Jeremiah's prophecy, so it is natural to conclude that a similar connection is intended in 2 Chronicles 36:22 and Ezra 1:1. Jeremiah 29:10–14 promises a return to Judah for the exiles after seventy years, so some infer that it is this return that Chronicles and Ezra refer to, with Cyrus's following instruction to go up to Jerusalem prompting the return and thus the fulfillment.

However, the seventy-year prophecy specifically refers to the period of Babylon's domination over Judah, rather than the exile (Jer. 25:11–12). Jeremiah 29:10–14 indicates that once this period is over, a new era of restoration will begin for those who have gone into exile. The features of this future restoration are described in a number of passages, including Jeremiah 30:3, 18; 31:23; 32:44, and other prophetic texts. It involves much more than the physical return to the promised land. Moreover, the usual meaning for the word translated "fulfill" (Ezra 1:1; 2 Chron. 36:22) is "complete," and the phrase could be translated "at the completion of" instead of "in order to fulfill." It seems more likely, then, that the meaning in Ezra and Chronicles is that the word of Jeremiah concerning the seventy years of Babylonian domination has come to an end now that Cyrus the Persian has assumed control. Since this has come to pass just as Jeremiah predicted, the expectation is that it will mark a turning point in God's dealings with his exiled people, initiating all the blessings of restoration also mentioned by the preexilic and exilic prophets.

Interpretive Insights

1:1 *In the first year of Cyrus king of Persia.* This connects the ensuing events to the end of the Babylonian Empire. See sidebar.

the LORD moved the heart of Cyrus. The narrator portrays the decree of Ezra 1:2–4 as the result of God's action upon Cyrus's heart. The Hebrew phrase translated "moved the heart" is the same one used in 1 Chronicles 5:26 when God causes Tiglath-Pileser of Assyria to take Israelites from the northern kingdom into exile. The picture here of the relationship between God and Cyrus is similar to the one in Isaiah. There God says of Cyrus, "He carries out my every wish" (44:28), though God goes on to say, "You [Cyrus] do not know me" (45:4–5 NABRE). Neither Cyrus nor Tiglath-Pileser knew the living God, but both were unwittingly used by him as instruments to achieve his purposes. Since God calls Cyrus his "anointed" (using the Hebrew word transliterated "Messiah") in Isaiah 45:1, some have thought Cyrus must have been a true worshiper of God, genuinely seeking to fulfill his will. But a full understanding of the concept of anointing must include the case of Hazael. God instructs Elijah to anoint him (1 Kings 19:15), but his anticipated role seems surprising (1 Kings 19:17; see also 2 Kings

8:7–10). Moreover, both Jehu and Hazael are to be anointed at God's command (1 Kings 19:15–16), yet Hazael conquered large amounts of Jehu's territory (2 Kings 10:32–33). To call someone God's anointed in the Old Testament, then, means that God has chosen and appointed him to be his agent for a specific purpose but does not comment on the anointed one's personal relationship with God.

1:2 *he has appointed me to build a temple for him.* The significance of this event for the exilic Judeans and for the narrator's audience can hardly be overstated. Destruction of the Jerusalem temple by a foreign power was understood as climactic evidence of God's displeasure with his people (e.g., Jer. 26:6). That God should now use a foreign king to rebuild the temple was surely evidence of his forgiveness and restoration of them.

Additionally, Ezekiel 37:26–28 connects the reestablishment of God's sanctuary with the restoration of his people. This may contribute to the perception that construction of the Jerusalem temple itself is a specific signal that the time of God's blessing has come.

1:3 *may go up.* Although Cyrus's main goal was to have the temple rebuilt to enhance his own authority, in the process he encouraged the Judean exiles to return to the promised land.

The God who is in Jerusalem. Coming from Cyrus, the "g" in "God" should probably be lower case. As a polytheist he acknowledged gods associated with particular localities.

1:4 *And in any locality where survivors may now be living.* The Hebrew word behind the NIV's "survivors" can just as well be translated "the rest," and a double meaning and irony may be intended by the narrator. The previous verse addresses Israelites among a wider audience ("any of his people among you"). As verse 5 indicates, the Israelites who respond to this decree are mainly people whose ancestors are from the former southern kingdom of Judah. Verse 4 can easily be read as addressing the others in the audience who are non-Israelites but who live in the same towns as the Israelites who will go up to Jerusalem (e.g., "As for the rest of you, from all the places where they [the Israelites] are currently living, you are to . . ."). The message is that the neighbors of the Israelites are to help provide for them to go, rebuild the temple, and reinstitute worship. Although a remarkable instruction, this is probably what Cyrus intended. The narrator and Judean readers, however, could also read the word as "survivor," with its theological implication of the righteous remnant referred to by the OT prophets (e.g., Isa. 10:21). The NIV translation reflects this secondary possibility. This would still imply that the surrounding peoples are to give aid to the Israelites. A third possibility is that "the rest" are those "of his people" (i.e., Israelites) who choose not to go but remain behind.

Theological Insights

The proclamation of Cyrus's decree creates an ironic situation. Cyrus claims to be carrying out God's orders but says so mostly to achieve political aims. At the same time, the narrator and reader recognize that Cyrus *is* carrying out God's orders in a way that Cyrus himself likely does not perceive. The narrator thus reiterates the view already taught in other biblical passages that God is able to influence the behavior of non-Israelite rulers for his purposes, even though they may not know it (e.g., Pharaoh [Exod. 4:21, etc.], Tiglath-Pileser [1 Chron. 5:26], and even Cyrus [Isa. 45:4, 13]). This demonstrates two important truths. First, God is able to use any people he chooses to achieve his purposes and keep his promises; such people need not be seeking to obey him. The corollary is that people can unwittingly achieve God's ends.

The postexilic readers of this book knew that the restoration envisioned by Jeremiah had not come to full fruition. Yet the account of Cyrus's decree encouraged them to remember that God does act to keep his promises, according to his timing and through the means he chooses. It encouraged them to hold on to hope in God's promises, since God could even use people they would not normally expect to bring those promises about. No matter how disappointing their circumstances may seem, God is still able to do what he said he would, at just the right time.

Teaching the Text

The narrative about Cyrus's decree highlights an irony that is quite common throughout history. On one hand, God works behind the scenes to keep his promises and achieve his purposes. On the other hand, the human actors are the visible agents, and it is easy for observers to think that God is not involved. Indeed, sometimes the actors claim to be doing God's will without realizing how they actually are doing it (compare the words of Caiaphas in John 11:49–52). This is the case with Cyrus. Although he wanted to use the rhetoric of obeying the God of Israel for his own political agenda, he was really doing God's bidding in a way he did not understand.

It is important to realize several things. Just because people claim to be doing God's will, it does not follow that they truly intend to do what pleases God. Cyrus was most concerned with legitimating and solidifying his rule over the various peoples in his empire. If his polytheistic worldview prompted some concern to curry favor with Israel's god, it was still as a means to his own ends, rather than out of sincere devotion to the Lord. Sometimes God-talk is simply calculated rhetoric.

But, just because people pursue their own agendas, trying at times to use religious words to their advantage while ignoring God's ways, it does not follow that God's plans will be thwarted. God is so wise and powerful that he can use the deeds of such people to achieve his aims. And the outcome is never in doubt. God's purposes will ultimately prevail, long after the temporary successes of humans have come to nothing.

So those who trust in God should be wise and discerning, recognizing the mix of motives that often lie behind the actions of people, including leaders. At the same time they should be confident that God will work out his plans reliably, never hindered by the actions of any human, no matter how powerful they may seem. This means that sometimes an evil action is used by God to accomplish his purposes. In one sense, the person doing the action is not doing God's will, and in another sense the person is. The supreme example of this, of course, was when the Jewish and Roman leaders crucified Jesus. Both Ezra and the Gospel accounts show readers that God can be relied on to work through human actions to bring about the restored relationship he has promised with those who will trust him.

Illustrating the Text

Not everyone who talks about God's work has godly motives.

Literature: "**Hansel and Gretel.**" Many are familiar with the German fairy tale of Hansel and Gretel, made famous by the Brothers Grimm in 1812. Offer your listeners a brief recap of the plot, in which two children are lured by an evil witch by means of a house made of cake and candy. Explain that the witch used something the kids desired to lure them into danger they hadn't ever imagined. Humans are created to hunger for God, not gingerbread houses; nevertheless, there are always some people whose talk about God will stir us but whose motives range from mixed to bad. Invite your listeners to ask: What might motivate an unbeliever to speak spiritually or attend a church? How might God show up and surprise them with the gospel, despite their motives? How can we both protect the church from manipulation *and* welcome messy people with mixed motives to encounter God?

Messy motives don't ruin God's plan.

Games: **Chess.** In chess, a grandmaster is a player who knows how to win in almost any circumstance. In fact, a grandmaster knows how to think many moves ahead and is therefore able to turn the opponents' moves against the opponents themselves, no matter how brilliantly each attack or strategy is conceived. A player making random, impulsive moves has no realistic chance of defeating a grandmaster. Our sovereign God is *infinitely* more masterful than a human grandmaster of chess. How much more can he construct a plan that turns messy motives and sinful choices upside down for his glory?

Believers must be discerning of motives yet confident of outcomes.

Sports: There is a point in many sports (like wrestling, swimming, track and field) at which a team is trailing by so many points that it becomes mathematically impossible for them to win. While individual athletes will still give their all and compete, the victory is ensured to one team and closed off to the other. Invite your listeners to imagine they are athletes on the field for the winning team in the last event. One must still size up the competition, watch out for foul play, observe the rules to avoid disqualification, and play with passion. At the same time, though, deep joy and confidence would set in as one is set free by the knowledge that no matter what, victory has already been won! This is the life of a Christian—we must still discern and play out the match before us, but we can have confidence and joy in the guaranteed victory.

Exiles and Temple Vessels Are Returned to Jerusalem

Big Idea

God graciously restores the fortunes of his people, in ways that reflect his saving actions in the past.

Key Themes

- God is the prime mover behind the events of the restoration.
- God acts to restore in ways that resemble his earlier acts of salvation, particularly in the exodus.
- Worship at the Jerusalem temple is a central feature of a restored relationship between God and his people.

Understanding the Text

The Text in Context

The first four verses of Ezra present Cyrus's decree, and the next seven give the direct results of his decree. By showing the close correspondence between decree and response, the narrator establishes the pivotal role that the decree plays. At the same time, God's role as the ultimate cause of these events is indicated by mention that he stirs the hearts of those who return just as he has stirred Cyrus's heart to issue the decree. The theme of restoration introduced in the opening verses is also extended by noting how Nebuchadnezzar's action of looting the temple vessels is directly reversed by Cyrus's action of handing them over to be taken back to Jerusalem. Attention to the Jerusalem temple as the focal point of activity and restoration continues, underlining the theme of the central place of worship in the relationship between God and his people. This theme will continue to be developed throughout Ezra-Nehemiah. A further important aspect is introduced, however, by presenting the journey of the exiles to Jerusalem as a return from exile paralleling the exodus from Egypt. This implies that God's redemptive acts in the present resemble his redemptive acts of the past. It also forges another connection with Jeremiah's prophetic expectation, since he had looked forward to a regathering of Israel from exile comparable to the exodus (Jer. 16:14–15). The many details pointing to a return to preexilic conditions prompt the reader to understand that these events inaugurate the promised restoration.

Historical and Cultural Background

It was common for kings to loot the temples of the gods of peoples they had conquered. In most cases, the idols in the temples were the main prize, but other metal vessels were frequently taken as well. When Nebuchadnezzar put the vessels from the Jerusalem temple in the house of his god, Marduk, it was seen as a statement that Marduk (and perhaps Nebuchadnezzar himself) was more powerful than the god in Jerusalem who was unable to save those who worshiped him (compare also Dan. 5:1–4, 23, 30). From Cyrus's ironic testimony in his edict, we see that in order to "take his vessels back" God took all of the nations from Nebuchadnezzar's successor and put them into Cyrus's control (Ezra 1:2). Ultimately, God is seen to be the champion in this power struggle.

From Cyrus's perspective, however, restoring the vessels is simply part of his new project of restoring the temple. Cyrus also returned sacred objects (usually idols) associated with the worship of other peoples in his empire as well. On the famous Cyrus Cylinder, after reporting that he returned idols to the temples from which they had been taken, Cyrus asked the gods those idols represented to pray to Bel (the chief Babylonian god, also known as Marduk) and Nabu (Bel's son) to give him a long life.

Interpretive Insights

1:5 *family heads of Judah and Benjamin . . . priests and Levites.* Rather than referring to individual leaders, the phrase translated "family heads" refers to the basic social unit among the Judeans in the postexilic era. It probably consisted of all living people, other than married females, descended from a person still living. Judah and Benjamin were the two tribes that made up most of the southern kingdom of Judah before the exile (2 Chron. 11:3). This group was the primary focus of Jeremiah's restoration prophecies (see sidebar), so mention of these tribes points to a fulfillment of prophetic expectation. Priests and Levites are necessary to restore the appropriate functioning of the temple as a place of worship.

God had moved. The narrator stresses that it is God himself who brought about both the decree and the response to it.

to go up. This verb is often used with reference to the pilgrimages to the Jerusalem temple required of Israelite men each year (e.g., Exod. 34:23–24). The narrator perceives the true significance of this journey in its connection to worship. The Judeans are returning to their ancestral homeland, thus reversing the exile, but the trip will find its true meaning and purpose only if it culminates in renewed worship.

1:6 *their neighbors assisted them.* In Ezra God makes provision for worship by using one of the same means he used at the time of the exodus: contributions from the surrounding people. "Articles" is the same word used for the items the Israelites were to request from the Egyptians (Exod. 3:22; 11:2; 12:35), and Exodus 12:38 mentions that the Israelites came out of Egypt with large numbers of livestock. The similarity between the exodus and the events of Ezra 1 is evident.

the freewill offerings. The Hebrew word for this is used in 1 Chronicles 29:9 of gifts for building Solomon's temple. It is also used for offerings brought by Israel in the wilderness for constructing the tabernacle. Thus, it highlights a manner in which the reconstruction of the Jerusalem temple is like the construction of the places of worship in the past.

1:8 *prince of Judah.* The Hebrew word for "prince" has a wide range of meaning and indicates a leader without necessarily implying royalty. The point in this context is that a transfer of custody of the vessels is occurring between the ruler over the Persian Empire and the leader of the community of returning Judean exiles. The word is also used for the tribal leaders who brought vessels for use at the tabernacle during the exodus journey (Num. 7:84). Sheshbazzar was probably made governor by Cyrus and was eventually succeeded after his death by Zerubbabel.

1:11 *there were 5,400 articles.* The figures in the list add up to 2,499 instead of the given total of 5,400. The list may be incomplete, it may only have specified the most valuable items, or there may have been corruption in the text in transmission. The main point is that the vessels taken to Babylon were satisfactorily accounted for and returned.

when they came up. The Hebrew phrase literally means "when they were brought up." The passive voice should be understood as implying that God is the one who brought them up, matching the point made in verse 5. This verb is often used to refer to God bringing Israel up from Egypt in the first exodus (Gen. 50:24; Exod. 3:8, 17).

Theological Insights

Every action contributing to the return and rebuilding in Ezra 1, regardless of who performs it, is depicted by the narrator as resulting ultimately from the action of God, whether directly through moving their heart or indirectly through the decree of Cyrus. Moreover, the narrator presents details that remind readers of the events of the exodus from Egypt, in order to signify that what is happening in Ezra 1 is nothing less than the fulfillment of the prophetic expectation that God would bring his exiles back to the promised land as a second exodus (Jer. 16:14–15). But the second-exodus motif itself is part of the larger promise, which has its roots in Deuteronomy 30:1–10, that God will restore his covenant with his people after sending them into exile. Together, the emphasis on God's initiative and the presentation of the events as the fulfillment of his promises encourage the postexilic community to believe that they are the heirs of what God himself has initiated, and that it is the renewal of the plan he had when he brought their ancestors out of Egypt. As God's plan unfolds throughout history, his people can be sure that he is at work, achieving his aims. This reassurance is especially relevant since, at the time when the book was written, Jews who had remained in Babylon were generally still more prosperous than Jews who had returned to Judah. This text encourages those who have returned to continue to participate in what God is doing and direct their focus to the purposes he has described in his word.

One of those purposes involves reestablishment of temple worship in Jerusalem, as is evident from its central place in Ezra 1 and its prominence in earlier Old Testament texts. This is an appropriate focus for the beginning of the restoration, since that worship is the symbol of God's presence among his people and of his covenant relationship with them. Since it is a priority for God to commune with his people as they worship him, it should be a priority for his people as well.

The numerous parallels with God's actions and purposes in the past underline the concept that God's work in the future, although new in important ways, will always be reminiscent of what he has done in the past. The expectation set for the postexilic community is that they should look to the record of Scripture for guidance about the shape of the future.

Teaching the Text

God is clearly the prime mover in Ezra 1, working in the hearts of humans to restore his people to the intended relationship with him he had revealed to them in the past. One thing this implies is that there is a genuine sense in which it is always God who brings about reconciliation and restoration in his relationships with people, rather than the people themselves. Scripture does not attempt to resolve the tensions between human freedom and divine sovereignty directly, but it is consistent in teaching that our decisions to cooperate with God and receive his blessings are a result of his work in our hearts (compare Phil. 2:12–13).

Another implication is that God's people can always look to the past both for encouragement and hope and for guidance in what to expect from God. Just as the original readers of Ezra-Nehemiah were the heirs of those who first returned in Ezra 1, so in the present day, those in the community of faith are the heirs of the work of the apostles. Some may feel that progress in achieving freedom from sin and its effects is slow, but God has begun this process in his people. They can take heart in their status in God's family and trust God to work through them to bring his objectives nearer to completion. And the place to look for insight into their relationship with God is in what he has already revealed. The Judeans who traveled back to Jerusalem had to contextualize the ancient faith even as they waited for the fulfillment of God's promises.

Similarly, believers today need to embrace the faith "once for all entrusted to God's holy people" (Jude 3) and live it out in ever-changing circumstances, while waiting for Christ's return. God does not start over with a completely new plan; he brings the plan he has already revealed to completion.

At the center of God's plan is worship. God's purpose in the exodus was not merely to release Israel from bondage to Egypt but to involve them in a relationship in which he dwelt in their midst and they worshiped him. As he works to restore the covenantal relationship with them after the judgment of exile, the restoration of worship, centered in the temple, receives highest priority. So today God's purpose in salvation is not merely to release from the burden of sin but to establish intimacy with believers and give them the opportunity and ability to worship him.

Understood in historical and theological context, this passage (or Ezra-Nehemiah as a whole) clearly does not provide a model for a modern Jewish return to the "promised land." And although it can be useful in the life of a congregation to build a new worship place, this passage does not teach that a church building is the most important way to show devotion to God, or that buildings for worship are God's highest priority in general.

Illustrating the Text

Even when we do godly works, God is the actual Worker.

History: In the past, kings, queens, and emperors used seals and signets to authorize actions in their name. These rings and other stamps were used to mark hot wax, crimp paper, or stamp ink on a page in a way that would prove that the action being taken by an agent of the crown was actually being done in the name and authority of the sovereign. Agents of the ruler would declare that their work was done "in the name of the king" or "by the queen" and show the seal or signet as a sign of this. Historical records in the Bible say that a ruler built a palace or defeated his enemies, even though they only delegated and empowered others to do the actual work on their behalf. In the same way, we may do godly works in the name of Christ, but he is the one whose Spirit's authority, commissioning, guidance, and protection have done the work.

God's past works must shape our vision for the future.

Human Experience: Ask your listeners to consider the phenomenon of family resemblance. Tell a story about a time when you met a person for the first time and knew immediately which family and/or parents belonged to them. Just as familiarity with a clan of ancestors allows you to recognize its descendants, so familiarity with God's past works enables you to recognize his faithfulness in the present and envision his faithfulness in the future. (You could take this illustration further by projecting pictures on a screen or bringing up volunteers and asking the congregation to guess which child is related to which parent or grandparent.)

Worship must be the center of a believer's life.

Human Metaphor: While a human marriage certainly includes finances, dating, child-rearing, recreation, meals, work, and chores, the center of the marriage cannot be any of these things; they are all by-products of the marriage. Rather, the center of a marriage is the willing oneness in which man and woman joyfully lose themselves in selfless love and unity. It is the same between the Bridegroom, Jesus, and his bride, the church. While Christian discipleship certainly includes study, tithing, obedience, spiritual gifts, evangelism, and more, the real core of the relationship is worship. Worship is how we express willing oneness in which we lose ourselves in love and unity with Christ. It deserves to be the center of a Christian life.

Exiled Judeans Resettle in the Promised Land

Big Idea
Those who respond to God's prompting become the recipients of his promise.

Key Themes
- The settlement of the returned exiles in Judea parallels the original settlement of Israel in the promised land after the exodus from Egypt.
- Those who respond to God's prompting through Cyrus and return to Judea are in place to inherit the restoration promises as successors of the covenant community.
- Their response is wholehearted and embraces God's terms.

Understanding the Text

The Text in Context

The idea prominent in Ezra 1 that the return of exiles from Babylon represents a new exodus in fulfillment of earlier prophecy is developed further in Ezra 2. The chapter consists mainly of a list of family groups who made the journey from Babylon to Judea, yet the details and comments included and the way they are presented seem intended to remind the reader of the journey to and entrance into the land of Canaan in the Pentateuch and book of Joshua (see Interpretive Insights for details). The climax of God's judgment had been losing the gift of the land (Deut. 28:63; 29:28, etc.). Being given the land again is thus a powerful reaffirmation of the covenant between God and Israel. It is possible that those named in the list did not all travel at one time. Nevertheless, by the end of Ezra 2, a new exodus has occurred, and it is natural to anticipate that other aspects of the prophesied restoration will follow for those who have made the journey.

There had, however, been important developments in Israel's worship since Joshua's day. The reigns of David and Solomon were understood to have brought changes, although these were consistent with God's original purposes for his people. A temple had replaced the tabernacle, and groups such as temple servants and Solomon's servants had come into existence. The fulfillment of prophecy did not expect those developments to be wiped out in an attempt to return to conditions at the original conquest. The hope seems to have been to restore conditions as they were during Israel's best preexilic days.

As with the first exodus, settlement in the land of Palestine was intended to lead to the establishment of God's sanctuary on his holy mountain (Exod. 15:17). As Ezra 1 leads the reader to expect, these two events are connected in this narrative as well. The attention given to temple personnel and the gifts given for the temple reconstruction keep the importance of the temple in view. The stage is now set for the work of rebuilding to begin in Ezra 3.

Outline

1. Introduction to the list of returnees (2:1–2a)
2. Laypeople (2:2b–35)
   a. Introduction (2:2b)
   b. Designated by family name (2:3–20)
   c. Designated by ancestral home (2:21–35)
3. Temple personnel (2:36–58)
   a. Priests (2:36–39)
   b. Levites (2:40)
   c. Singers (2:41)
   d. Gatekeepers (2:42)
   e. Temple servants (2:43–54)
   f. Descendants of Solomon's servants (2:55–58)
4. Those who could not prove Israelite ancestry (2:59–63)
   a. Laypeople (2:59–60)
   b. Priests (2:61–63)
5. Totals (2:64–67)
6. Donations for rebuilding the temple (2:68–69)
7. Settlement in towns (2:70)

Interpretive Insights

2:1 *these are the people.* The account of the exodus from Egypt includes a list of those who came out of Egypt (Num. 1) and a list of those who are about to enter Canaan forty years later (Num. 26). In the present list, those who leave Babylon are the same people who settle in Judea. Nevertheless, the presentation of such a list provides another parallel with the exodus.

they returned ... each to their own town. The narrator emphasizes the reversal of the exile event by referring explicitly to captivity, the historical connection with the actions of Nebuchadnezzar, and the geographical movements between Judah and Babylon, and by observing that everyone returns to their own town. This seems a direct fulfillment of Jeremiah 30:3.

2:2 *in company with Zerubbabel . . . Baanah.* The original intended audience did not need to read the later chapters of Ezra to find out who Zerubbabel and Joshua were. In fact, the entire group listed here were likely leaders well known to the readers. This chapter describes a situation similar to that in the original conquest, in which Israel settled in the land, accompanied by leaders, of whom two were particularly influential, and one of whom was a priest (Josh. 14:1; compare the episodes in Ezra 3–5 highlighting the roles of Zerubbabel and Joshua). In both cases, occupying the land and erecting God's sanctuary in it are closely connected (Josh. 18:1; 19:51).

people of Israel. The term "Israel" is used in this context for laymen as opposed to temple personnel (similarly in Ezra 10:25, where the word "other" is not in the Hebrew text, and Num. 2:32–33). Thus, the lists in Ezra 2:2b–35 and 2:36–58 present people belonging to nonoverlapping categories.

2:55 *servants of Solomon.* This group may have originated when Solomon subjected non-Israelites to forced labor (1 Kings 9:20–21). It is unclear what their specific duties were, but their presence seems to contribute to the sense that Israel is being restored to its preexilic shape.

2:59 *they could not show that their families were descended from Israel.* Israelite heritage is important both because Cyrus ordered Israelites to rebuild the temple and because the community must be composed of actual descendants of preexilic Israel if it is to represent the restored covenant people spoken of by the prophets (e.g., Jer. 31:16–17). The next verse indicates that only a very small number cannot prove that they meet this condition.

2:62 *excluded from the priesthood as unclean.* God had specified that only those descended from Aaron should serve as priests (Num. 16:40). Here again the community is careful to follow God's terms as they identify the legitimate heirs of his promise.

2:63 *Urim and Thummim.* These were lots used by the high priest to learn God's will on particular matters (see Exod. 28:30; Lev. 8:8; Num. 27:21; Deut. 33:8; 1 Sam. 14:41; 28:6). By seeking to handle in this way the question of those who could not prove their priestly lineage, the community explicitly leaves the matter to God to decide. In the meantime, they play it safe.

2:64 *42,360.* The total is higher than the sum of all the preceding numbers by about 11,000. It is uncertain, but possible, that women are included in the total number but not the individual counts. It would be easier for a single man to return than a married one, so a much higher proportion of men would not be surprising. The number of returning exiles is important because it is both large and small. It is large enough to be considered a genuine reoccupation of Palestine by the descendants of Israel, rather than a handful of stragglers who happened to make their way back. It is much smaller than the numbers involved in the original conquest, however, and this fits the prophetic expectation that only a remnant would return (e.g., Isa. 10:22).

2:68 *some . . . gave freewill offerings toward the rebuilding of the house of God.* Those who returned set a priority on the temple reconstruction. A lack of such care for God's temple was one of the key reasons for the judgment of exile (e.g., 2 Chron. 36:14), so this is an encouraging sign of a change of heart. The pattern of accepting freewill offerings of gold, silver, and garments from the people in order to construct the sanctuary for God to dwell among them follows Exodus 25:2–9; 35:21–29. In both cases, they apparently passed along the gold and silver given them by their neighbors before they left, but the text highlights their willingness to give to the fullest extent they were able (see Ezra 2:69). It is also in line with the prophetic expectation concerning the restoration period (Ezek. 20:40–41).

2:69 *According to their ability they gave . . . garments.* It is not completely clear how much gold and silver is referred to here, but it is clear that it is a large quantity. The amount donated represents a generous outpouring and likely reflects a willingness to give sacrificially.

2:70 *settled in their towns.* The resettlement of Judeans in the towns in which their families had lived prior to the exile is one of the important ways in which things were restored to how they previously were. Like other features of this text, it creates a parallel with the situation after the first exodus and conquest, in which Israelites, including Levites, lived in designated towns (Josh. 14–21). It also connects with the prophetic motif of restored fortunes found in Jeremiah (e.g., Jer. 30:18).

Theological Insights

By detailing the sizable number of returnees, the various families represented, the locations from which their ancestors had come and to which they themselves return, and the temple personnel available to reinstitute temple worship, this chapter establishes that the community it describes truly represents the prophesied remnant of Israel. For the original readers this is a source of assurance that God is both able and willing to do what he has said he will do. Since they are the successors of these earlier community members, they have reason to be confident that God will faithfully do among them what still remains unfulfilled in their own day.

The care taken to determine whether claims to community membership are legitimate illustrates the truth that there are conditions that must be met in order to be part of God's people. This is assumed in all biblical revelation, although the specific conditions are modified significantly in the New

Testament. It is never the case that God automatically considers all people to be part of his family.

In all periods of biblical history, one of the key characteristics God looks for among his people is that they respond to his gracious initiative with a wholehearted devotion to him and his purposes that expresses itself in generous giving of material wealth to achieve his ends. This trait is clearly visible among the returned exiles.

Teaching the Text

Although there are important differences between Zerubbabel's day and ours, those who wish to share in the benefits of inclusion among God's people must still meet certain criteria. One of the important differences between the old covenant and the new is that the old included an ethnic dimension. Those who wanted to follow the God of Israel were expected to identify with Israel and follow the practices given to it by God (e.g., Exod. 12:48–49; Josh. 6:25; Ruth 1:16). Under the new covenant, believers no longer need to follow "Israelite" practices. But the New Testament still makes use of the ideas of having to have one's name recorded in the right registry (the Lamb's book of life, Rev. 21:27) and having to be part of the right family (John 1:12–13). These conditions are attained solely through faith in Christ. In fact, faith in Christ is now the single criterion that surpasses all others, so that biological descent from Jacob is not sufficient without it (Rom. 9:6). Thus, it is important for Christians today to affirm that responding positively to the gospel call to trust in Christ is the necessary condition for inclusion in the community of God's people, but also to avoid the mistake of replacing Israelite practices with other unnecessary obstacles for those who wish to become part of the church.

The sacrificial giving of wealth seems to be part of what God expects from his people throughout Scripture, but how that wealth is used changes somewhat. In the New Testament, God dwells in his church—which is composed of people (1 Cor. 6:19; Eph. 2:21–22)—instead of in a building. While the returning Judeans rightly used their wealth to build a physical structure, Christians today need to think carefully about how best to use sacrificial donations to strengthen the church, which is "built up" through evangelism and discipleship.

It has recently become fashionable for scholars to claim that this list is part of a thematic shift in the postexilic period to give greater significance to the ordinary individual, as opposed to great leaders. Yet the list does not emphasize the individuals themselves, but rather their ancestors or the towns in which those ancestors lived. The point of the list is that these people are the heirs of preexilic Israel. It is this identity that gives the returning community its significance, and that is the narrator's intended message.

Although the New Testament is clear that Christian leaders should possess certain gifts and must adhere to high standards of conduct, it is invalid to appeal to a passage such as this to support a claim that they must also be able to point to a "divine call experience" before being allowed to serve as leaders in the church, as though that somehow replaces the genealogical requirement for Old Testament priests.

Illustrating the Text

Knowing who came before us deeply shapes who we become.

Human Experience: Many of your listeners will have had the experience of attending a graduation commencement for students. The emotional effect for Ezra's original audience in reading a list of their ancestors must have felt a lot like that. The event of the return was a momentous, transitional step for those involved. They were aware that their future would be different from their past, and they looked forward to it with great anticipation. They also knew that their forebears would be comforted and fulfilled to see their restoration. Invite your listeners to think of those who have come before them watching in the stands as they face transitions and seek restoration.

Film/Television: Many films depict a character whose quest to understand his or her past is key to shaping self-understanding and restoring the character's sense of purpose and mission. Other films depict moments when being on a particular list makes a huge difference in one's life. Older examples would be Alex Haley's discoveries about his ancestor Kunta Kinte in the TV miniseries *Roots* (1977) or the Jewish survivors' names being recorded in Oskar Schindler's list in Steven Spielberg's *Schindler's List* (1993).

Church Life: If your church has a rich history with recognizable patriarchs, matriarchs, and pastors who have served in the past and helped shape your present and future, consider including a list in the bulletin or projecting a list of names on the screen during your sermon. Ask the question, How would your church be different had these people not been part of your history and served with faithfulness? Remind your congregation that you might not know the names and people Ezra lists, but their names touched hearts and brought up memories just as the names you put in your bulletin or projected onto your screen mean a great deal to the people in your congregation.

A believer's heritage is reckoned by faith, not family history.

Contrasting Concept: In human monarchies, succession is often decided by family lineage, strategic marriages, and title. Invite your listeners to think of some examples where, either locally or nationally, in business or in politics, they have seen succession and rights handed down based on blood, names, and titles. In other systems, rights and roles are reckoned by merit and performance. In contrast, God's kingdom bases everything on something only God can see clearly: our faith in his promises. This means we can become royalty simply by virtue of gracious and undeserved adoption and God-given faith. We are God's children because of his blood, not ours.

Bible: Consider sharing some texts like Matthew 3:7–12, John 1:12–13, or Romans 8:12–17 that explore this truth.

God's house can't be built without cheerfully given treasure.

Applying the Text: Explain that God's house of worship here on earth must be built with freely and cheerfully given treasures. Invite your listeners to consider how they are contributing to the spread of the gospel by tithes and offerings, as well as by giving their gifts and talents. Point out passages like Malachi 3:7–12 and emphasize that cheerful tithing is certainly about *more* than money, but it is also never about *less* than money. Remind people in your congregation that their church would not exist today were it not for the generous faithfulness of those who came before you. Cast a vision for how their giving today will prepare the way for the generation that follows them.

The Returned Exiles Reinstate the Prescribed Sacrifices

Big Idea
Sacrificial worship deserves priority in a relationship with God.

Key Themes
- The Judean community demonstrates single-mindedness in its resolve to honor God in worship, even in the face of opposition.
- Appropriate leaders play an important role in helping the faithful community practice godly worship.
- The Judeans begin following a pattern of continuous worship by offering all the sacrifices specified by God in his word, even before the temple is restored.

Understanding the Text

The Text in Context

With the Judeans having returned from exile and settled in their towns as described in Ezra 1–2, the next important event of the restoration involves the reestablishment of worship according to God's plan. In the original exodus from Egypt, God intended to establish Israel as a holy people dwelling with him in the promised land, with this relationship perpetuated through the worship he prescribed. Since a key element of that worship was the tabernacle, which was replaced later by the temple, it is imperative that the returned community now reconstruct the temple, as Cyrus has given them permission to do.

Even before they set to work on the temple, however, they give their attention to reconstructing the altar of sacrifice. Although it is unlikely that Cyrus would object to this, we see here a slight but significant difference between his agenda and theirs. Cyrus's goal was to enhance his reputation and prestige as builder of a temple, with any benefit that might come his way from the sacrifices offered to one of many gods seen as a bonus. The Judeans' concern is to honor God as is pleasing to him, and though the temple will be part of that, the history of God's dealings with his people up to that time shows that he is more interested in the expression of reverence for him through sacrifice than through having a structure built for him (e.g., Gen. 8:20–21; 2 Sam. 7:5–7). Accordingly, they give priority to restarting the sacrificial system, and, as they have done previously in the narrative, they take care to follow God's instructions. This also continues the theme of restoring things as they were prior to the exile.

A new theme is introduced in this passage with the mention of the Judeans' fear of the other peoples around them. It foreshadows the further difficulties they will face as they try to live faithfully as God's community in the land, as well as the willingness of the surrounding peoples to use intimidation tactics.

Historical and Cultural Background

During the exile the Babylonians and Persians had the territory around Jerusalem governed from Samaria. The subsequent return of the Judean exiles and the establishment of their own local government likely upset some of the people in the area, because it took power away from them. This may be why the Judeans feel afraid. They know that building an altar to reestablish their worship practices will be seen as a further assertion of their rights in the land, which might provoke attacks. They are far from the central government in Persia, and there is no mention of specific military protection offered to them.

Texts from the ancient world reflect the importance that was placed on rebuilding or restoring sacred sites in the exact location where they were originally constructed, and archaeological excavations have found instances where particular temples were built and rebuilt as many as a dozen times on the same spot. This was an important factor in preserving the legitimacy of the sacred structure. The narrative confirms that the altar in Jerusalem meets this criterion (v. 4).

Interpretive Insights

3:1 *When the seventh month came.* The Israelites were to gather in Jerusalem to celebrate the Festival of Tabernacles from the fifteenth to the twenty-second day of the seventh month (Lev. 23:34–38). By coming to Jerusalem at this point, the returnees show their unified commitment to fulfilling this obligation.

together as one. In all eight contexts in the Old Testament where it occurs, this phrase signifies the unity of the people. The impression is that they gather of their own volition, all sharing the same intentions.

3:2 *Then Joshua . . . and Zerubbabel.* Since verse 6 states that the offering of sacrifices began on the first day of the month, the narrator probably does not mean to imply that Joshua and Zerubbabel waited until after the Judeans assembled in Jerusalem to begin restoring the altar. It is even possible that verse 6 is meant as a summary of verses 1–5, including the process of rebuilding the altar. Although the returned exiles continued to be subject to the Persians, Zerubbabel, a descendant of David (1 Chron. 3:17–19 lists Zerubbabel as the son of Pedaiah and the nephew of Shealtiel, whereas Ezra-Nehemiah designates him as the son of Shealtiel; he may have been the legal son of Shealtiel and the natural son of Pedaiah through levirate marriage), was appointed governor over them (Hag. 1:1). With this combination of lineage and political authority, he assumes, during the reestablishment of worship in Ezra-Nehemiah, the role played earlier by David and Solomon (1 Chron. 28:11–19; 2 Chron. 2–4). The fact that a priest and a Davidic leader take the initiative in this matter is further assurance that the work and its result are legitimate in God's sight.

To sacrifice burnt offerings. The festival celebration included a number of offerings sacrificed to God. In order to carry out these requirements properly, as well as continue to offer sacrifices as specified in biblical law, the leaders take the initiative to rebuild the altar of God on its earlier site. The burnt offering was the main sacrifice of the Old Testament. No one ate any of the animal, as it was completely given to God by being burnt. There was a strong conceptual connection between the animal sacrificed and the individual or community who brought it for sacrifice (see, e.g., Lev. 1:4). The implication was that those offering the sacrifice were offering themselves up to God. By burning the whole animal, the worshipers declared their complete devotion to God. Placing such priority on bringing burnt offerings to God, the returnees make a strong statement about their commitment to him.

3:3 *Despite their fear . . . they built the altar.* After the exodus from Egypt, the Israelites disobeyed God, refusing to enter the land of Canaan because of their fear of the people living there (Num. 14:1–10). In this text, the returned exiles also experience fear of the surrounding peoples, but they press ahead with obedience to God's commands when encouraged by the leaders. In this regard they are not like their ancestors, insofar as they obey God's word through Moses rather than succumbing to fear of other peoples around them.

morning and evening sacrifices. Exodus 29:38–42 and Numbers 28:3–8 specify that a lamb with flour, oil, and wine is to be offered each morning and evening, and Leviticus 6:8, 12, 13 stipulates that the fire on the altar must not be allowed to go out. The Judeans' compliance with these requirements demonstrates a high degree of commitment and consistency on their part. Their resolve to offer sacrifices was not a passing whim. These are the same as the "regular burnt offerings" in verse 5.

3:4 *Festival of Tabernacles . . . prescribed for each day.* The Festival of Tabernacles required an extensive quantity of sacrifices, and the specific numbers varied for each day (Num. 29:12–40). By following the stipulated procedure, the Judeans again show that they are scrupulous about giving what God has asked for.

3:5 *they presented the regular . . . as well as . . . freewill offerings.* The entire menu of sacrifices sanctioned by the law of Moses is reestablished by the community. All those specifically required by Scripture and any brought by an individual's choice are offered up to God. The goal is to restore worship to what God had originally intended it to be.

3:6 *the foundation of the LORD's temple had not yet been laid.* Although Cyrus naturally expected that worship, including sacrifice, would be reinstituted at the temple, his main concern was with the rebuilding of the temple itself, since that enhanced his reputation. The returnees, on the other hand, are most concerned with worshiping God as he has instructed them. Therefore they make a priority of beginning the required sacrifices, even before proceeding with temple repairs.

Theological Insights

This passage prioritizes sacrificial worship. Restoring such activity is the first order of business for the resettled community. It is recognized by all of them as so important that they all come to Jerusalem to participate. It is not an issue where some might make it a priority and others might not. They ensure that they begin the sacrificial pattern, even though it may lead to problems with their neighbors. They are willing to pay that price and the price of the offerings themselves, as demanding as that is. Although the original readers would undoubtedly be tempted at times to neglect sacrificial worship in the midst of competing priorities, this passage reminds them that God considers such sacrifice to be among the most important expressions of their commitment to him and among the most important ways they serve him.

Teaching the Text

The greatest emphasis in this text is placed on the priority that God's people give to sacrificial worship. The Old Testament describes various ways in which God's people may worship him, including some that are familiar today, such as singing and praying. These activities were carried out at the temple. Yet before the temple was reconstructed by the returned exiles, they restarted the offering of sacrifices and maintained it continuously, placing a clear priority on it. It is easy for Christians today to lose sight of the importance of sacrifice in worship. The tendency is to focus on the fact that Christ, as the atoning sacrifice for sin, has made it unnecessary to slaughter and burn animals. Of course, Christ should be at the very center of the church's worship. But as we rejoice that Christ has done what we could never do for ourselves, we may forget that the New Testament still expects believers to make costly sacrifices. These may include prayer and singing (Heb. 13:15; Rev. 8:3), but they should also include the continual offering of our material goods and our very selves to God for his purposes (1 Pet. 2:5; Heb. 13:16; Rom. 12:1; 2 Tim. 4:6). These are essential for true worship (Matt. 15:8–9).

The passage also displays the effectiveness of united, courageous obedience by God's people in achieving God's plans. The Judeans unanimously participate in the prescribed sacrifices and the celebration of the Festival of Tabernacles, even though they are afraid of what their neighbors may do to them. When Christ's church collectively places the highest priority on obedience to his revealed will, without being deflected or dissuaded by negative public opinion, it accomplishes the things that matter most to him and contributes in unimaginable ways to the future he has planned, much as postexilic Israel achieved an important step in the prophesied restoration, which itself was an important part of God's eternal plan for all mankind, with implications they could never have imagined.

Finally, although the united involvement of the whole community is highlighted, there is still an important role for leaders to play. The high priest and Davidic political ruler (who was the king during the monarchic period) were expected to provide leadership for the people in worshiping God. Joshua is the high priest, and Zerubbabel is a descendant of David and has been appointed governor of Judah (Hag. 1:1), and the narrator points out that they take initiative here, helping move God's people in the right direction. The New Testament specifies different qualifications for the church's leaders, focusing solely on character rather than lineage. But it maintains the balancing emphases of the involvement of the whole church in ministry (1 Cor. 12) and the importance of godly leaders (Eph. 4:11–12).

The reason for mentioning that the altar is built on its foundation is to show that it is located on its original site. The point is not that the foundation as they found it was somehow inadequate (even though it may have been). It is not appropriate to treat this passage as though it teaches that people need to have a solid foundation for their life, marriage, community involvement, and so on.

Illustrating the Text

There is no worship without sacrifice.

Bible: 2 Samuel 24:24 describes a scene where King David of Israel was offered free oxen, wood, and stone to build an altar and sacrifice for his sin. David insisted on buying these things, saying that he would not offer God a sacrifice in worship that had cost him nothing. Invite your listeners to consider what their worship costs them, and whether they are paying the cost willingly and joyfully. Are they personally investing in their relationship with God or riding someone else's coattails?

Quote: A. W. Tozer. Tozer, an American pastor, theologian, and author, once wrote, "I can safely say, on the authority of all that is revealed in the Word of God, that any man or woman on this earth who is bored and turned off by worship is not ready for heaven."[1] If worship seems uninteresting, or if the sacrifices required seem too costly, we have not yet fully grasped or embraced our eternal vocation.

Groups that obey together stay together.

Sports: Discuss the concept of penalties in sports. You can choose hockey, soccer, American football, or something else. The concept of interest is the idea that when a teammate breaks a rule of the game, that teammate is temporarily taken out of play or even ejected from the game. This penalizes the whole team, since they cannot continue to play the game together. Explain that when the Christian community adheres to God's law as a team and follows the rules, we experience him together. When one or all disobey God's will, the team is broken apart by penalties and consequences that set the whole team back. Encourage your listeners to make obeying God a team sport and to spur one another on to play within the boundaries. Challenge your church members to commit to blow the whistle and call a penalty on themselves or others when they see someone breaking God's rules. It is the most loving thing they can do.

Quote: John D. Rockefeller. Famous business tycoon John D. Rockefeller is often quoted as having said, "Next to doing the right thing, the most important thing is to let people know you are doing the right thing." Explain to your listeners that this is understandable from a standpoint of self-promotion, but it is not actually the heart of real obedience. Real obedience is humble and does not advertise itself, but it is most certainly contagious and appealing.

Biblically qualified leaders become catalytic multipliers.

Popular Saying: There is an old saying that asserts, "Give a man a fish and you feed him for a day; teach him to fish and you feed him for a lifetime." Invite your listeners to consider that while diligent doers may feed the flock for a day, biblically called and anointed leaders equip the flock to do the work of ministry and actually multiply the church's ability to perpetuate kingdom ministry long after individual leaders are gone. Explain that the role of church staff and office holders is not to do all the work but rather to equip and catalytically multiply the congregation's ability to do the work (Eph. 4:11–16).

The Returned Exiles Celebrate the Laying of the Temple Foundation

Big Idea

When people pursue God's presence on his terms, they have reason to rejoice.

Key Themes

- The returnees follow the precedents and instructions given through previous godly leaders as they begin rebuilding the temple and resume the worship in song associated with it.
- They rejoice in appreciation of what God has done for them and in anticipation of his dwelling among them.
- Some among them are saddened because their current state of restoration is incomplete.

Understanding the Text

The Text in Context

Ezra 1 introduces the theme of restoration for the Israelite exilic community in fulfillment of God's promise, and Ezra 2 shows that restoration indeed happens in terms of people resettling in the promised land. Ezra 3 focuses on the restoration of regular worship, with verses 1–6 describing the reinstitution of sacrifices. Verses 7–13 now move to the beginning of the physical temple reconstruction and resumption of musical and vocal worship. Each of these elements plays an important theological role, and each is an important part of showing that Israel is truly restored to its covenant relationship with God.

The very end of the passage, however, introduces the idea that the restoration is evidently somewhat unsatisfying, a theme that will recur in coming chapters.

Zerubbabel's Significance

The books of Haggai and Zechariah record prophecies that attach great expectations to Zerubbabel. Haggai frequently refers to him as governor of Judah (e.g., Hag. 1:1), and addresses him directly with a promise from God that the second temple will have glory greater than the first (Hag. 2:4–9). Above all, God says he has chosen Zerubbabel and adds, "I will make you like my signet ring" (Hag. 2:23), implying that God will invest him with divine authority. Zechariah gives Zerubbabel special prominence both in laying the foundation of the temple and in completing it, attributing these achievements to God's special enabling (Zech. 4:6–10). Such distinction was usually reserved for kings in the ancient Near East.

In Ezra, by contrast, Zerubbabel has a much lower profile. Even the title of governor is never attached to his name. Whereas Haggai and Zechariah foresee the continuation of the Davidic royal line in Zerubbabel, which will ultimately culminate in Jesus Christ, Ezra does not give as much prominence to this theme, since Zerubbabel himself never became king, and since the temple restoration narrative highlights the participation of the whole community. Yet Zerubbabel is listed first among the temple rebuilders, and he is routinely identified as the son of Shealtiel, which draws attention to his Davidic lineage. For the original readers of Ezra, Zerubbabel's prophesied role as descendant of David was significant, but many of its dimensions were not clearly fulfilled within his own lifetime.

Interpretive Insights

3:7 *gave money . . . to Joppa.* Most of this verse makes the preparation for building this temple sound exactly like the preparation for building the first temple. Solomon enlisted craftsmen, paid Tyrians and Sidonians in kind for their help, and had cedar wood shipped from Lebanon to Joppa (1 Kings 5:6; 2 Chron. 2:7–16). The effect is to show that the second temple really is a restoration of the first and therefore carries the same significance. This verse also reflects a partial fulfillment of Isaiah 60:10–13, with the cedars coming from Lebanon to adorn God's palace and a foreign king serving the Judeans. This reflects the idea that God's promises are being fulfilled in powerful ways, yet there still remains much more to be fulfilled.

3:8 *Zerubbabel.* Although the whole Israelite community takes more responsibility in building this temple than they did in building Solomon's, Zerubbabel is named first among those giving leadership. This is appropriate, since in 2 Samuel 7:12–13 and 1 Chronicles 17:11–12 God gives special importance to the role of David's offspring in constructing the temple and Zerubbabel was a prominent descendant of David (1 Chron. 3:17–19).

They appointed Levites . . . to supervise. As early as the days of the tabernacle, the Levites had the responsibility of caring for it and ensuring no one transgressed God's holy things (Num. 1:47–53). Their specific responsibility to supervise temple work is reflected in 1 Chronicles 23:4 and 2 Chronicles 34:12–13. The Judeans follow God's intentions as they assign the duty of overseeing the building project.

3:10 *the priests . . . as prescribed by David.* Many of the details here parallel the celebrations at the completion and dedication of Solomon's temple (2 Chron. 5:12–13; 7:6). This has the effect of connecting the *beginning* of this temple's construction with the *completion* of the first temple, with a couple of implications:

1. When God judged the Israelites with exile, one of the central features of that judgment was the destruction of the Jerusalem temple (e.g., Jer. 7:14–15). The fact that he has now enabled them even to begin reconstruction demonstrates that he has reversed his intentions, and it speaks as powerfully of his desire for the covenant relationship with them as the completion of the first temple ever did.
2. God's new attitude of reconciliation toward the exiles and his mighty act of redemption on their behalf make them confident that he will enable them to complete the building and will continue to bless them. The beginning of construction at this time foreshadows its completion, so it is appropriate to act now as they would at its completion.

Mention of the directions given by David (as in, for example, 1 Chron. 15:16) continues the theme of following instructions given by God through past godly leaders. It is only through faithfulness to God's directives that the community can expect to continue to enjoy their restored relationship with him.

3:11 *He is good . . . forever.* These words occur as an expression of praise nearly identically in several Old Testament passages. Once again, they are an example of continuity with preexilic worship, since they are part of a song David instructed the Asaphite Levites to sing (1 Chron. 16:34), and they are an example of fulfillment of prophetic hope, since Jeremiah said they would again be sung in the land (Jer. 33:11). But it is also very appropriate for the returned exiles to sing them. The Hebrew word translated "love" usually implies a demonstration of loyalty or faithfulness to a relationship. The Israelites broke their covenant with God through idolatry and many other acts of disobedience, and God punished them as he had warned them he would. It would have been fair for God to abandon them completely. Yet by beginning the process of restoration, he showed that he continued to treat them as his people and wanted to reestablish the relationship they had damaged. It displays his character of goodness and faithfulness.

the people gave a great shout. When the ark of the covenant was brought to Zion by David, shouting was meant to emphasize acceptance of the fact that God is king (1 Chron. 15:28). Although the ark of the covenant was not part of the second temple (see Jer. 3:16), the shout here is probably intended to endorse the idea that through the rebuilding of the temple God's kingship in Zion will be evident to all.

3:12 *wept aloud.* It is not completely clear why some of the older people are weeping. Some commentators suggest it is actually weeping for joy, but the Hebrew word used is usually connected in the Old Testament with mourning, and the context seems to contrast it with the shouts of joy. Others have thought it is because the present temple will not be as large as Solomon's, although the dimensions are likely similar. The materials used in construction and the quality of the craftsmanship were just as important to the ancients when evaluating a building as was its size, and since Solomon went to such great expense on the first temple, this structure would not be as impressive, making this a possible explanation for the weeping. In any case, it does seem that they feel it does not compare favorably with the first temple (see Hag. 2:3). Even in a climactic moment of restoration, they experience a sharp sense of loss. The mixed reaction of the people indicates that the fulfillment of expectations is only partial.

Theological Insights

The Israelites continue to try to make things "as they were" before the exile by repeating the actions of Solomon and David with respect to constructing the temple and restarting its musical worship. Just as God inspired these preexilic kings, so he enables the postexilic Judeans to return to the land and begin the reconstruction process. This is evidence that he remains committed to the covenant with Israel, providing the basis for the returned exiles to be confident of the relationship with God that the temple and its services originally stood for ("His love toward Israel endures forever," v. 11). The temple, like the tabernacle before it, was understood as God's dwelling place among the Israelites. That was important, since the foundational concept of the covenant was that Yahweh would be Israel's God and they would be his people. Thus, the temple both enabled Israel to honor and worship God in observable ways and was a tangible expression of God's presence with his people to bless them. In this way it served as a focal point of the covenant relationship itself, and the returnees' commitment to its reinstatement displays their desire for God's presence.

Teaching the Text

Whereas the first part of Ezra 3 emphasizes the commitment of the Judeans to resuming sacrifice, this section focuses on their pursuit of God's presence and their expression of praise and thanksgiving to him. As previously, the text drives home the theme that the way to experiencing God's promised restoration involves attention to what he has revealed in the past. The community is careful to rebuild the temple as much like the first one as possible, and they arrange the musical worship according to the earlier prescriptions as well. For Christians, the key to applying this is to understand that the temple was to be the place where God dwelt among the Israelites. The New Testament teaches that God now dwells within his people, both individually (1 Cor. 6:19) and corporately (Eph. 2:21–22). Thus, in order to maximize the experience of his presence, it is no longer necessary to follow the Old Testament building plans for a physical structure in Jerusalem, but rather to follow the teachings found in both testaments that reveal how to glorify God with our bodies individually and become a unified body of believers who glorify him corporately. This way of worshiping God can only occur where there is first a basic commitment to honoring Jesus as God's Son (John 5:22–23). Music and singing continue to be important features of worship in the New Testament, although once again there is no requirement to follow the Old Testament patterns exactly. What is carried over is an emphasis on praising and thanking God for his character, including the love and faithfulness he has demonstrated by his saving acts. Christians should continue to make such songs a central part of their worship.

Like the returnees in this passage, Christians have experienced God's redeeming power and should give him enthusiastic praise for what he has already accomplished for them. This enthusiasm should include an element of anticipation of the promised future—even better than the present—still in store. But this "not yet" element also has a sobering aspect. Since Christians, like the exiles, do not yet experience the full blessings promised, there are times when the awareness of what is lacking is overwhelming. The physical and emotional suffering still experienced in the present is valid reason for grieving. The normal experience of believers' worship should therefore include both sincere rejoicing and sincere grieving.

Although there is a strong emphasis on continuity with the preexilic community, the point is not merely to follow tradition. Insisting that things must continue to be done the way our grandparents did them is an invalid application. The importance of these traditions comes from their authorization by God himself.

It is unlikely that the appointment of Levites to oversee the work is intended to teach the principle of delegation of authority by leadership for the sake of efficiency. It was appropriate to give the Levites oversight because of the precedents set in the Torah and under David.

Illustrating the Text

We are created to pursue God's presence.

Outdoors: Listeners who have hunted or worked with trained dogs will understand the amazing and impressive phenomenon of watching a creature pursue the purpose for which it has been bred. Seeing a Labrador retriever swim to a downed duck, an Australian shepherd round up sheep, or a Newfoundland save a swimmer is a pleasure and delight. Generations of breeding and training have honed the instincts, senses, and habits of the animal to one purpose, and when it fulfills that purpose, the dog is more alive, invigorated, and enjoyable to be with than at any other time. The only thing better is watching the animal rest in perfect satisfaction and contentment after its work is over. Remind your listeners that believers have been born again and are purpose-built for pursuing God. We are never more alive, invigorated, and enjoyable to be with than when we are pursuing Christ. The only other thing better is when we rest in perfect satisfaction and contentment in his presence after having found him.

Real worship includes both praise and lament.

Bible: Present a sampling of verses from the book of Psalms to show your listeners the range of emotions that may be appropriately included in biblical worship. A few examples might include Psalms 28:7; 69:2; 22:1; and 31:6.

Television: In the animated series *The Simpsons*, character Homer J. Simpson once quipped, "Never Marge! I can't live the buttoned-down life like you. I want it all! The terrifying lows, the dizzying highs, the creamy middles!"[1] Explain to your listeners that, when it comes to biblical parameters for worship, we are to be like Homer. We really ought to want all the experiences God would lead us into, including amazing heights of love and joy, honest expressions of deep lament and pain, and even the "creamy middles" of mundane, everyday life. Every kind of emotion and experience can be brought to the foot of the cross and offered to Jesus.

We can learn from traditions without worshiping them.

Science: In 2015, a group of scientists at the University of Nottingham in the United Kingdom were researching the best way to treat the antibiotic-resistant bacterial infection known as MRSA. Modern antibiotics simply haven't been able to knock it out. In their quest to find new strategies, they happened to consult with Christian Lee, an English literature professor who specializes in early Anglo-Saxon texts and is a founder of a research network called "Disease, Disability, and Medicine in Early Medieval Europe." In thinking about references to cures for infection, she recalled a recipe in a particular text. It was quite elaborate and involved the boiling of leeks, garlic, wine, and oxgall in a brass pot and then fermenting the mixture for nine days. Modern scientists re-created the ancient antibiotic and found that it is actually 90 percent effective in knocking out MRSA. Scientists who started out skeptical had to admit that, while they were not ready to return to medieval medicine, this particular potion had a lot to teach them.[2]

The Rebuilding Judeans Encounter Opposition from the Surrounding Peoples

Big Idea

Those who are not committed to worshiping God as he has revealed himself interfere with the work of God's people.

Key Themes

- The enemies of the Judeans represent themselves as their supporters.
- The Judean leaders refuse to let their enemies have an integral part of their work.
- The enemies of the Judeans find ways to hinder them from doing God's work.

Understanding the Text

The Text in Context

Ezra 1–3 narrates how the returned exiles began to participate in the fulfillment of God's promised restoration by returning to the land of Palestine, rebuilding the altar, and commencing reconstruction of the Jerusalem temple. But Ezra 3:3 hints that the other people living in the area pose a threat of some kind to this process. Ezra 4:1–5 begins to make the nature of this threat clearer. The surrounding peoples act to keep the Judeans from making progress in rebuilding. By doing so, they oppose God's plan of restoration and mark themselves as the enemies of God and his people. In this way, they are comparable to the Canaanites who lived in the promised land at the time of the initial conquest under Joshua; they represent a formidable obstacle to the fulfillment of God's good promises to his people. Also, as in the original conquest, part of the danger they represent is found in the prospect of forming partnerships with them.

The immediately following narrative demonstrates that similar opposition resurfaced repeatedly during the next ninety years.

Historical and Cultural Background

In a way that can be difficult for people today to understand, the culture of the ancient Near East tended to take polytheism and even syncretism for granted. To claim that one worshiped a particular god implied nothing about whether one worshiped other gods as well. In fact, it was expected that one would also worship other gods if it seemed possible that some benefit might be gained by doing so, as, for instance, when a group of displaced people began to worship a local god along with a god associated with their original homeland. In historical context, then, the statement by the enemies of the Judeans that they worship Yahweh just as the returnees themselves do should not be taken as proof that they worship Yahweh exclusively (see the comments on "brought us here" in 4:2, below).

The dynamics of building temples is also unfamiliar to most people today. In this passage, one of the important aspects of the process is that if the labor and, possibly, expenses involved were shared among different groups, it would entail that control of the resulting temple would also be shared. This could include everything from temple finances to the way worship at the temple was conducted. The offer of the enemies to help, therefore, is also an attempt to gain control.

Taking these factors into account, we find it easier to see why the Judeans flatly reject their enemies' suggestion. Accepting it would be completely inconsistent with the care they take in Ezra 2–3 to establish pure worship.

Interpretive Insights

4:2 *brought us here.* Second Kings 17:24–42 describes how the Assyrian king brought foreigners to the land after the northern kingdom of Israel had been defeated and its residents taken into exile in 722 BC. The enemies of the Judeans describe something similar, although they seem to refer to a time a few decades later than that (about 140 years before the time of the events narrated in Ezra). The imported people of 2 Kings 17 begin the worship of Yahweh while still worshiping other gods. Something similar is likely to have happened with the ancestors of the enemies of Ezra 4 also.

seek. In this context the Hebrew word means to be a faithful worshiper and diligent follower of Yahweh. In Ezra 6:21 the Judeans allow those who demonstrate that they truly are seeking Yahweh to join them. Therefore, it

The Origin of the Samaritans

The enemies in Ezra 4 are often identified with the Samaritans of the New Testament or their ancestors. But there are significant differences between the two groups. The later Samaritans were strict monotheists, while the biblical evidence suggests that the enemies of Ezra 4 were not. The Samaritans believed that Yahweh's temple was to be on Mount Gerizim, whereas the enemies offered to join in rebuilding it in Jerusalem. There is no clear connection between the enemies and the New Testament Samaritans in the Bible itself.

The idea that they are genealogically connected comes mainly from Josephus, who was a first-century-AD Jewish historian, and the writings of the rabbis. Jews in New Testament times often called Samaritans Cutheans—that is, people originally brought to Samaria by the Assyrians from one of the Babylonian cities after the fall of the northern kingdom (2 Kings 17:24). They assumed that all of the Israelites were exiled and that any people found in the geographic area of the former northern kingdom when the Judeans returned from exile must have been descendants of these foreigners. But scholars continue to debate how reliable Josephus is for reconstructing Samaritan history, and there are places in the rabbinic literature where the Samaritans are discussed as though they are Jews, so the rabbis themselves were inconsistent. Samaritans have historically maintained that they are Israelites (e.g., John 4:12), denying a lineage like the one affirmed by the enemies in Ezra 4. And finally, biblical passages such as 2 Chronicles 30:1 assume that there were still Israelites in the territory of the northern kingdom when Hezekiah began his reign, several years after the Assyrian exile. Therefore, it is wisest to avoid assuming connections between the enemies in Ezra 4 and the New Testament Samaritans when interpreting biblical passages.

is probable that, although the enemies may have made sacrifices to Yahweh, they were known not to be exclusive worshipers of him.

4:3 *as . . . Cyrus . . . commanded us.* Appealing to Cyrus's edict may be an attempt to refuse politely, but their motivation is likely theological. The narrative has already mentioned that the Judeans are afraid of these people (3:3), suggesting that the latter are doing or saying menacing things. Since 2 Kings 17:33 mentions the syncretistic practices of at least some who were imported, it is probable that the returnees have observed this and know that they cannot enter partnership with them. They do not actually worship like the Judeans do, contrary to their claim. The Judeans knew that the exile had been caused by syncretism with pagan religions. Letting syncretists have a part in the temple rebuilding could easily lead down the same road again.

The narrator establishes a clear contrast between the enemies and the Judeans. The enemies merely hear about the temple being built for Israel's god (4:1). They acknowledge that Yahweh is the god of the Judeans (4:2). The enemies were settled in this area by another king and are therefore simply exiles themselves who have not returned home. The Judeans, however, have returned to their home and have been directly instructed by the king to rebuild the temple for their own god. The two groups are not on equal footing.

4:4 *peoples around them.* In Ezra-Nehemiah this Hebrew phrase usually seems to designate non-Jewish inhabitants of the promised land (although Nehemiah 9:30 refers primarily to Gentiles farther away, such as Assyrians and Babylonians). Using it here makes these people seem similar to those who were in the land at the time of the original conquest.

set out to discourage. This Hebrew phrase literally means "weakened their hands," and it contrasts with "assisted them" in Ezra 1:6, which is literally "strengthened their hands." Within the providence and plan of God, he sometimes causes others to help his people and at other times allows his people to be opposed. That these people are enemies of the Judeans is demonstrated beyond doubt by their response to the refusal of their suggestion.

Theological Insights

This passage highlights God's insistence on exclusivity. The enemies of the Judeans were disqualified from participation in the reconstruction process, both because they were not Israelites by descent and, even more importantly, because they were syncretistic in their religious practices. Merely adding Yahweh to the list of gods one worships is not acceptable to him and does not establish a true relationship with him. It follows that those who worship more than one god cannot be considered to be among God's people and cannot truly share in God's work in the world. Moreover, the narrator's description of the opponents as "enemies" reflects God's perspective, and the destructive response of the enemies to the Judeans' refusal to include them in the temple building demonstrates that perspective's accuracy. Those who do not worship God exclusively are in fact opposing God, regardless of how much they may protest to the contrary. There is no room for other gods beside Yahweh.

The presence of such opposition also entails an important implication. God's people are regularly faced with the choice between the expediency of theological and moral compromise, on one hand, and the maintenance of godly standards, on the other. The choice can seem difficult, because the refusal to compromise often leads to persecution—or at least interference—in varying degrees. God expects his people to remain true to him, trusting him to see them through the conflict and enable them to achieve his purposes.

Teaching the Text

In contemporary Western culture, religious exclusivism is seen by many as bigotry. The assumption is that if one cannot accept others' beliefs as being just as valid as one's own, one must be unloving and judgmental as well. This puts a lot of pressure on Christians to make compromises with those of other faiths, since, generally, no one wants to be seen as a bigot, and, specifically, an important aspect of Christian witness in the world is showing Christ's love and acceptance to others. It seems natural to assume that people will be unable to see that we love them if they think we reject them.

Yet the truth is that those who do not worship God according to his pre-scriptions in Scripture do not share the same status before him as Christians. There is no way to the Father except through exclusive faith in Jesus (John 14:6). People may claim, "We all worship the same God," but other religions, even though they contain elements of truth, are not legitimate or effective ways of knowing God. The Bible is consistent in affirming that God's self-revelation must be embraced without dilution or mixture. Jesus warned that not everyone who claims to be his follower is really one of his people (Matt. 7:21–23). As unpopular as it may be, Christians must not give the false im-pression that non-Christians have been reconciled to God.

The commitment to avoid compromise, however, raises many practical questions in the context of church outreach. How far into the life of the church can unbelievers be integrated before becoming actual believers? Can they be given any responsibility at all? While it is impossible to foresee every circumstance, and decisions ultimately must be made on a case-by-case basis, this passage suggests that God's people must be able to distinguish clearly between those who are recognized as members of the group (the church) and those who are not. The fundamental direction of the body must be determined by those who are believers, and its leaders must be from among them. Although believers should expose unbelievers to the life of the church, they need to draw thoughtful boundaries to preserve the integrity of the church.

Finally, when unbelievers are attracted to the work of the church for some reason but find that the body is unwilling to compromise with them, they will frequently be unhappy and may choose to dissociate themselves from it (1 John 2:19) and perhaps even try to cause trouble for it. Believers need to be prepared to endure this.

It may be tempting to use this passage to challenge believers to evaluate their own motives by asking them how they respond when they do not get their way. The implication would be that if they become quarrelsome and interfere with what others are doing, like the enemies, their motives must be wrong. While this is true, care must be taken, since the point in this passage is that the response of the enemies shows that they are not among God's people. Unless the intent is to question whether one has actually come to faith in Christ, it is better to avoid the comparison.

Illustrating the Text

Inclusive people must have the courage to preach an exclusive gospel.

Human Metaphor: Ask your listeners to imagine throwing a party at a beautiful venue with enough room to accommodate many people. They have invited everyone they know and are truly excited to see all of their friends and acquaintances share together in an enchanting evening. The only catch is that all the entry doors but one will be locked: the only open door will be guarded by security, and everyone who approaches will be required to show their invitation and ID for entry. If the host truly wants to be fully *inclusive* of all the guests, he or she must warn them about the *exclusivity* of the entry policy. To fail to tell them would certainly result in beloved guests being turned away. In the same way, believers who truly want to be inclusive must also be loving enough to honestly proclaim the exclusivity of salvation in Jesus Christ alone.

Testimony: Avowed atheist and famous comedian Penn Jillette speaks about a time when a man gave him the gift of a Bible after his show and attempted to witness to him about faith in Jesus. While Penn does not share the man's faith, he testifies about the love and sincerity he sensed in the man's willingness to do his best to proselytize him. Penn explains that anyone who believes what a Christian claims to believe and then *doesn't* proselytize must have a deep hatred for atheists like him.[1] In other words, the man's courage to preach an *exclusive* message about Jesus sent a very *inclusive* message to Penn's heart; he was not ready to share the man's exclusive beliefs, but he felt the man's inclusive love deeply.

The church must allow belonging without compromising believing.

Christian Book: *The Celtic Way of Evangelism,* by George G. Hunter III. Take time to look over Hunter's book.[2] In this book, Hunter explains how early Celtic churches allowed people to belong within Christian community before expecting them to believe and behave like Christians. He points out that including unsaved people in the daily life of the church is powerfully evangelistic and is the most likely way to encourage faith and works in their lives. Churches need to find safe and appropriate ways for lost people to participate without compromising church teaching or doctrine; it will be a challenge, but the results are worthwhile.

We must accept that real Christianity will irritate some people.

Contrasting Concept: Many of your listeners will be familiar with the process of encouraging a young musician. They will have suffered through out-of-tune recitals, repetitive practice, and endless wrong notes along the way. Point out that when music is done right, those irritating errors go away and the experience becomes extremely pleasant. Learning music proceeds in a way that is *opposite* to learning discipleship: when music is done right, the irritation goes away; when Christianity is done right, the irritation begins. If some people are feeling discomfort and frustration as you live out the gospel in love and sincerity, it probably means you are doing it right and God is using it to highlight truth and bring conviction.

The Opposition Stops the Rebuilding

Big Idea

At times, persistent opposition brings the work God's people are doing to a temporary halt.

Key Themes

- The surrounding peoples seek repeatedly to stop the Judeans from completing the work God has given them to do.
- Those opposing the Judeans are able to persuade the ruling authority to join in their opposition.
- The work the Judeans are doing is stopped for a time.

Understanding the Text

The Text in Context

Having described the auspicious beginning of the promised restoration achieved through the work of God and the obedient work of the returned exiles, as well as the opposition that arose when the Judeans would not compromise with those who did not share their undivided loyalty to Yahweh, the narrator now heightens readers' understanding of the severity of the opposition by including a parenthetical "flash-forward." The passage narrates events that took place during the reigns of Xerxes and Artaxerxes, who both ruled after the time of Darius (mentioned in v. 5), before returning to pick up the narrative in the time of Cyrus in verse 24 (in the introduction, see the table "Persian Kings over the Jews from Cyrus the Great to Darius II"). This was not a particularly unusual thing to do in ancient history writing, nor is it unusual even in modern history writing, but writers today would likely include parentheses or use some other means of indicating the disruption of chronological order. The ancients relied on readers to notice what was happening and interpret accordingly.

The main point of this juxtaposition of events is that the Judeans regularly encountered determined resistance from the time of Cyrus right through to

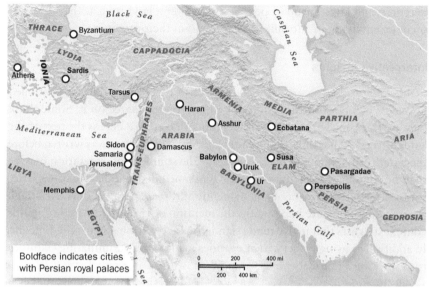

Persian Empire

the days of Artaxerxes. It also shows readers that the Judeans could not count on the support of the Persian kings, despite Cyrus's initial assistance. These factors establish the need for God's intervention to enable the completion of the temple in Ezra 5–6. Reporting the later events at this point in the narrative makes the narrator's message clearer. Finally, showing that there was resistance to restoring the city of Jerusalem even after the temple was rebuilt provides context for Nehemiah's dilemma in Nehemiah 1–2. Although he wishes to reconstruct the city's wall, he knows that the ruling king, Artaxerxes, has already issued a decree stopping all rebuilding in Jerusalem.

Historical and Cultural Background

The events of verse 6 occur between those of Ezra 6 and 7; the events of 4:7–23 occur between those of Ezra 10 and Nehemiah 1. The temple has actually been finished by the time the events of Ezra 4:7–23 take place. In fact, it has been at least eighty years since the decree of Cyrus, but the walls of Jerusalem have not yet been rebuilt. Since restoring protective walls would normally have been a high priority, this testifies to the level of immobilizing fear and discouragement the Judeans had experienced at the hands of their enemies.

The province of Trans-Euphrates covered the entire area from the Euphrates River to the border with Egypt, including what is now Israel, Lebanon, Jordan, Syria, and much of Iraq. Those writing the letter of verses 9–16 are claiming

Ezra 4:6–24

to represent a large group of people spread over a large area as they accuse a small group living in a localized region within their province.

Interpretive Insights

4:8 *Rehum . . . wrote a letter.* The relation of this letter to the one mentioned in verse 7 can be confusing, and not all interpreters agree on it. Some think they are the same letter,[1] while others think that verse 8 begins the text of the letter of verse 7 and, thus, that Rehum and Shimshai's letter was written before the letter of Bishlam and his associates.[2] The simplest interpretation may be that the content of the letter of verse 7 is not included and that Rehum's letter was written later. Ezra 4:6–8, then, mentions three separate letters. Although the text does not state it explicitly, the mention of the letter of verse 7 in this context suggests that it also made slanderous accusation against the Judeans. In addition to using bribery, their enemies made false incriminating claims to turn the king against them.

4:9–10 *Rehum . . . Trans-Euphrates.* The lengthy list of senders makes it sound as though all the important officials of the province are in this together. It also gives the impression that the Judeans, although settled in the promised land, are still surrounded and subject to domination by peoples from other lands, who now actually live in Palestine, having been brought there by an earlier Assyrian king (like the enemies in v. 2), and seem to outnumber them. The prophets' picture of the restoration, by contrast, was one in which the returned exiles would be untroubled by surrounding peoples (Jer. 30:10; 46:27; Isa. 41:11–12). Here is a clear indication that the restoration promises have not reached complete fulfillment.

4:12 *The people who came up.* The rhetoric of the letter writers minimizes the concept that the Jews have returned to their homeland and promotes instead the idea that they are merely the latest in a series of people traveling to that part of the world with royal blessing (compare v. 10). The perspective displayed is completely different from that of the narrator, who sees the Judeans' journey from Babylon to Jerusalem as the working out of God's restoration in fulfillment of prophecy.

4:13 *no more taxes . . . will be paid.* Although this is probably an outcome that the Judeans would not mind, the writers of the letter make a breathtaking leap to conclude either that this was the Judeans' actual intent or that they would have any realistic chance of getting away with not paying taxes. But the enemies want to stop the building, and, since there is actually nothing inherently seditious about the act of building itself, they must link it in the king's mind with an alarming result.

4:14 *Since we are under obligation . . . dishonored.* Like the effusive reference to Ashurbanipal in verse 10, the rhetoric here is intended to register that, unlike the rebellious Judeans, the writers are unswervingly loyal to the king. By reproducing their exaggerated tone, the narrator allows readers to conclude that they lack sincerity.

4:15 *In these records you will find.* The letter writers know that there are records of the city of Jerusalem rebelling against Assyrian and Babylonian rulers, and that the Persian kings have access to the archives that contain them. Their strategy is to have the king check for himself to see whether they are telling the truth, knowing that their statement about the past will be confirmed. Of course, the fact that Jerusalem rebelled in the past does not prove that it will again in future. But the psychological effect is that the verification of one claim they make lends credence to other claims.

4:16 *you will be left with nothing.* Once again, the connection between rebuilding the city with its walls and the king being left with nothing in the whole province seems exaggerated. However, the implication is probably not that Jerusalem and the Judeans could take over the entire area of Trans-Euphrates but rather that if this rebellious city could get free of Persian rule, others would also. During the early years of Artaxerxes's reign, Egypt revolted, and there was a general lack of stability in the western provinces of his empire. Thus, Artaxerxes may have been very concerned about the possibility of further rebellions and their potential effects.

4:19 *a long history of revolt.* This is probably a reference to the rebellion against the Assyrians in 701 BC (Hezekiah, 2 Kings 18:7, 13) and rebellions against the Babylonians in 597 (Jehoiakim, 2 Kings 24:1) and 588 BC (Zedekiah, 2 Kings 24:20–25:1). From the perspective of Artaxerxes, this makes Jerusalem seem treacherous.

4:20 *Jerusalem has had powerful kings ruling over the whole of Trans-Euphrates.* A better translation is "However, there have been powerful kings over Jerusalem who also ruled over the whole of Trans-Euphrates." The NIV translation could be understood to mean that kings based in Jerusalem (i.e., Israelite kings) ruled over all of Trans-Euphrates. But Artaxerxes is probably saying that although Jerusalem has a history of rebellion, powerful kings were able to rule over both it and the rest of Trans-Euphrates and collect taxes, and so he intends to do the same. At this point the Persian king does not seem to be a friend of the Judeans at all. In fact, his interests and intentions seem very similar to those of previous Assyrian and Babylonian rulers, who brought harsh suffering upon the Israelites.

4:24 *the work . . . came to a standstill.* Although verses 23–24 refer to different situations, their juxtaposition highlights how parallel the two situations are. In both, the enemies of the Judeans manage to stop rebuilding efforts. In Cyrus's day they effectively nullify the king's edict to rebuild the Jerusalem temple. And in the time of Artaxerxes, they motivate the king to halt reconstruction of the city of Jerusalem. The latter example also provides important insight about the Persian kings. In Ezra 1 God stirs Cyrus to issue a decree to rebuild the temple. In Ezra 4 the enemies persuade Artaxerxes to issue an order to stop rebuilding the city. The conflict is between God and those who oppose his people, and the Persian kings can be used by both to achieve their ends.

Theological Insights

Although Scripture records many examples of God's powerful work to fulfill his promises to his people, there are instances, such as those recorded in this chapter, in which the fulfillment of his promises is delayed. In fact, those opposing God's people and God's work seem to get the upper hand. God's people face opposition from unbelievers regularly, and in that struggle they can expect at times to see God bring victory and at other times to have to accept frustration and temporary (though sometimes for an extended period) defeat. In this passage the Judeans are portrayed as being in the process of obeying—not disobeying—God, but the defeat comes anyway. God is clearly willing to achieve his purposes over extended periods of time rather than always immediately, and he does not always protect his people from discouraging setbacks.

Teaching the Text

In Ezra 1–3 the Judeans' return to Jerusalem and their work of rebuilding the temple and reinstituting sacrificial worship are linked to the great prophetic promise of restoration as God's people. The former exiles are seen as striving to cooperate with God's agenda. Those who oppose them and interfere with their work, therefore, are identified as God's opponents. This passage makes plain that such people exist and that at times they will work diligently to keep God's purposes from being realized. Although these opponents may not frame the issue in their own minds as one of opposing God, in practice, that is what they end up doing. Specifically in this case, they prevent God's people from experiencing personal security (represented by rebuilding Jerusalem's walls and foundations), and they interfere with their worship (completing the temple). But there are many examples of how others interfere with the blessings God intends for his people and the lives he wants them to lead.

Opposition to God's people often involves false or exaggerated statements (or merely innuendo, as in this passage) that put believers in a bad light and make others who normally would be neutral become supportive of the opposition. The New Testament certainly warns Christians to be prepared to face this (Luke 6:22; 1 Pet. 3:16–18). Believers cannot count on a just response even from ruling authorities (e.g., Acts 24:26–27).

Seeing those who oppose God and his work get the upper hand, even when God's people are striving to be obedient, and especially after there have been initial signs of God's powerful work, can be one of the most discouraging experiences for believers to deal with. Somehow, when we know we are at least partly responsible for our difficulties, it seems easier emotionally. But when important aspects of the work of God come to a stop, at least to all outward appearances, it is easy to doubt whether God is really in control. As the end of this passage hints, God will eventually achieve all his purposes. But in real time the process can seem stuck.

The rebuff given by the Judeans to their enemies in Ezra 4:3 may possibly have contributed to the actions the enemies carried out in verses 4–24. But it would be wrong to conclude that the Judeans should have tried to be more diplomatic and inclusive. The point is that these people were opposed to the purposes of the Judeans and would ultimately have worked against them in any case. The refusal of their offer to help was nothing more than a convenient excuse for them to take offense. The narrator means to encourage steadfast obedience to God in the face of discouraging treatment rather than compromise to avoid trouble.

Also, the fact that Artaxerxes is worried about the possibility of rebellion led by the Judeans reflects his deep concern for revenue and power. It should not be misconstrued as showing that God's people have such power that, even when persecuted, they make others afraid.

Illustrating the Text

God is always in control, even when he appears to be losing a battle.

Sports: When George Foreman fought Muhammad Ali in 1974, Ali coined a phrase for the strategy he used to defeat the younger Foreman. He called it "rope-a-dope." This is a strategy in which one fighter covers up his head and leans back on the ropes, allowing the other boxer to deplete his energy and strength throughout the match. This allows the passive fighter to bide his time and wait until exhaustion or opportunity creates a weakness in the aggressor; then the fighter playing possum strikes and turns the tide decisively. God is never threatened in the ring by a younger, more aggressive opponent; however, he certainly bides his time in apparent passivity until the right moment for his will to unfold. He is not losing but simply getting ready to turn the tide. Explain that when it appears that he is on the ropes, it is a rope-a-dope in which humans are being weakened to the point of repentance, dependence, and submission to the cross. If you have the capability to do so, and if you feel it is appropriate, you might want to show a short video clip of an example of the boxing strategy.

Bible: 2 Peter 3:9 shows us that God is not slow in doing what he has said he will do—he is patient with people in process and is delaying judgment to allow time for repentance and salvation. Sometimes when he appears not to be in control, it is because he is holding back consequences and wrath for our sake!

Doing the right thing can lead to prolonged opposition.

History: For most of his adult life, Nelson Mandela worked to bring an end to the apartheid practices of South Africa. Although today most people recognize the injustice of the system he fought against, in Mandela's own day he faced considerable opposition. His efforts to change the government's inhumane treatment of its own citizens led to his arrest and trial for treason. At his trial he said, in one of the most famous speeches of the twentieth century, "I have cherished the ideal of a democratic and free society in which all persons live together in harmony and with equal opportunities. It is an ideal which I hope to live for and to achieve. But if needs be, it is an ideal for which I am prepared to die." He was jailed for twenty-seven years, eighteen of them in a prison where he lived in a small cell with no bed or plumbing, and where he was forced to do hard labor. During that time, he continued his education by correspondence, always looking for ways to work more effectively for the freedom of his people. Eventually, Mandela was released from prison and participated in negotiations to end apartheid in South Africa. But as the title to his autobiography, *Long Walk to Freedom*,[3] suggests, he had to endure many years of bitter opposition to achieve his worthy goal.

God Empowers His People to Resume Rebuilding in the Face of Continued Opposition

Big Idea

God uses his word to inspire and direct the work of his people, in spite of opposition.

Key Themes

- God's messages through the prophets motivate the leaders of the Judeans to resume temple construction.
- God providentially enables the work to continue during a period of uncertainty.
- The Judean leaders embrace God's perspective on their situation.

Understanding the Text

The Text in Context

Ezra 1–3 describes how God begins the restoration of his relationship with Israel by orchestrating their return to the promised land to rebuild the temple at Jerusalem as the symbol of his covenant presence with them. Ezra 4 then introduces the direct conflict the returned exiles encounter from the people living in the land. The narrator even provides an extended example of this conflict from the later period of Artaxerxes's reign. He makes the point that through manipulation of political power the Judeans' enemies are able to bring their reconstruction work to a halt. Ezra 5 now shows how, about sixteen years after the stoppage recorded in Ezra 4:24, God uses his word to restart the work. The effect of God's action is clearer by comparison with the account of frustration in Ezra 4. Many details of the two chapters correspond, making the situations look similar and requiring consideration of why the outcomes differ. Although the work is restarted in Ezra 5, the threat of interference remains throughout the chapter, and the stage is set for a climactic decision by the king whether the temple will be completed.

Historical and Cultural Background

In order to keep a firm grip on their sprawling empire, the Persian kings developed an elaborate system of informers. These men operated outside the provincial government structure, reporting directly to the king himself, allowing the king to spy even on his own governors and let him know of anything that could be harmful to his interests. Naturally, these informers had considerable influence over the course of events. They were sometimes known popularly as "the king's eye." The original readers of Ezra 5:5 would likely have noticed a play on words where the eye of God is said to be upon the Judean elders, countering any potential interference by Persian functionaries.

Haggai and Zechariah prophesied near the beginning of the reign of Darius. The prophecies in the book of Haggai are dated specifically to 520 BC and are variously addressed to Zerubbabel, Joshua, and the Judeans living in Judea. Haggai sought to motivate the people to finish rebuilding the Jerusalem temple, warning them that their economic difficulties would continue if they neglected the rebuilding (Hag. 1:1–11), assuring them of God's presence with them (Hag. 1:13), and promising future blessings associated with the rebuilt temple (Hag. 2). The prophecies of Zechariah 1–8 are dated to the period 520–518 BC. These were also directed to the Judeans in Judea and made mention of Zerubbabel and Joshua. Zechariah compared the people's refusal to finish rebuilding the temple to the sins of their ancestors, which had led to their eventual exile from the promised land (Zech. 1:1–6). He urged them to repent and complete the rebuilding. Zechariah also assured the people that the temple would be successfully rebuilt under Zerubbabel's leadership (Zech. 1:16; 4:9; 6:15.)

Interpretive Insights

5:1 *prophesied . . . in the name of the God of Israel, who was over them.* Just as the word of God through Jeremiah was a catalyst that began the restoration process (Ezra 1:1), so the word of God through Haggai and Zechariah restarts that process after a delay. The mention that God is over them puts the events of both the preceding chapter and this one in perspective. The enemies may be able to stop the restoration work at times, for a time. But it is God who is truly sovereign over affairs.

5:3 *At that time Tattenai . . . Shethar-Bozenai and their associates went to them and asked.* The actions of coming to the Judeans and speaking to them

Who Laid the Foundation of the Temple, and When Did They Do It?

According to Ezra 5:16, Sheshbazzar laid the foundation of the Jerusalem temple, but Ezra 3:8–10 says that Zerubbabel and those working with him did it, and Zechariah 4:9 agrees. Moreover, Ezra 3:8–10 puts the date of the foundation in the reign of Cyrus, and Ezra 5:16 seems to support that, whereas Haggai 2:18 and Zechariah 8:9 seem to place it in the time of Darius.

Although many biblical characters have more than one name, it is unlikely that Sheshbazzar and Zerubbabel are the same person. Both names are Babylonian, and it is more usual for a person with more than one name to have names derived from different languages. In addition, Ezra 5:14, 16 refer to Sheshbazzar as though he has passed from the scene, whereas Zerubbabel is currently active.

There are not enough data available to be certain, but a strong possibility is that during Cyrus's reign (Ezra 3:8–10; 5:16) Sheshbazzar is given official responsibility by the Persians to lay the temple foundation. When the work is actually done, Zerubbabel, the descendant of David, may be seen by the community as their leader, along with Joshua, doing the hands-on work under Sheshbazzar's authority. After the rebuilding is interrupted by the enemies (Ezra 4:24), Zerubbabel (who may have become governor after the passing of Sheshbazzar, Hag. 1:1) and Joshua resume the project, possibly having to redo much of the work done over a dozen years earlier and bringing the foundation laying to completion before continuing.

are reminiscent of the enemies in Ezra 4:2, and the structure of the present verse, designating specific officials supported by unnamed others, is like the structure of Ezra 4:7, 8, 9. Having seen what happens throughout Ezra 4, the reader expects more opposition to come from this encounter, especially since the phrase translated "at that time" emphasizes that the events of Ezra 5:1–2 are closely linked in time with Ezra 5:3 (compare Dan. 3:8; 4:36). Some interpreters think no hint of hostile intent on the part of the Persian officials is indicated in this chapter,[1] and it is true that the tone of the letter to Darius that follows is more restrained than the tone of the letter of Ezra 4. But the parallels to Ezra 4 and the fact that this episode comes right after it in the text lead readers to expect at least suspicion from the officials. Further details in Ezra 5 (including the request for the names of those building) and 6 (see comments on Ezra 6:6) point in this direction also.

Trans-Euphrates. See "Historical and Cultural Background" for Ezra 4:6–24.

5:5 *the eye of their God was watching over the elders of the Jews.* The reason the work is not stopped while the Judeans await Darius's reply is attributed to God's protection of his people (see this expression also in Pss. 32:8; 33:18; 34:15), not the favorable (or even neutral) disposition of the officials.

5:11 *We are the servants of the God of heaven and earth.* It is very possible that a list of the names of the leaders was sent along with this letter. As the text stands, however, this is the only identification that the leaders give of themselves in response to the officials' demand. For the leaders, at this point, this expressed the most important aspect of who they were and conveyed their devotion and dedication to God.

5:12 *because our ancestors angered the God of heaven.* This is the account of the exile found elsewhere in the Old Testament (e.g., in Lev. 26:27–45; Jer. 25:7–11; 2 Chron. 36:15–21; etc.). This verse and the preceding one show that the Judean leaders have completely embraced the view of the world and their place in it taught in Scripture. They have responded obediently, not only to the word of God coming through the current prophets Haggai and Zechariah, but to previous divine revelation as well (in contrast to the attitude displayed in Jer. 7:8–10).

5:13 *king of Babylon.* Cyrus sometimes referred to himself in writing as king of Babylon, so this is not unusual, even though he has been called king of Persia earlier (Ezra 1:1–2; 4:3). In this context it highlights the fact that Cyrus reversed the actions of Nebuchadnezzar as his successor.

5:16 *under construction.* The implication is not so much that work has been continuous as that the project currently underway is still the same one decreed by Cyrus.

Theological Insights

The community of Judeans faces fear (Ezra 3:3) and discouragement (Ezra 4:4–5). They have been blocked by political powers from continuing the work God has called them to. Into this situation God speaks his word to the community through the prophets. The result is a reversal of the inertia that had set in, and the restoration program is on track again. God's word has astonishing power to motivate and empower God's people to rise above their inner discouragement and external obstacles and pursue his plans for their lives and the world in which they live. Throughout Ezra-Nehemiah this word is presented as central to every move forward made by the Judeans. God's people must hear and heed his word.

God does not provide power through his word alone, however. He also works in unseen ways to ensure that the momentum created by his word is sustained. The people begin to build again in response to the prophetic message, but the officials could easily bring the work to a halt again. This time, however, unlike the episodes in Ezra 4, God providentially allows the work to continue while the issue is investigated. The text does not explain why God allows work to stop in some cases and ensures it continues in another. What it emphasizes is that God provides what is needed to achieve his good purposes in his time.

This chapter also reminds readers that God's work goes forward when his people embrace his perspective. The Judean elders reflect agreement with the explanation of the exile offered by the preexilic and exilic prophets. They concur that God's judgment for sin is just and that it is only by faithfully serving him that they can hope to experience the blessings of his covenant promises. Once again, the right perspective seems also to be present in Ezra 4 when the work is stopped, but it is still a necessary ingredient for the work to resume when God later adds encouragement through his word and orchestrates circumstances behind the scenes.

Teaching the Text

God's word is central to his work in the world. Ezra 5 demonstrates this in two ways. First, God's word provides motivation to his people that enables them to overcome obstacles such as fear and discouragement. As Christians go through life, they encounter many situations and people who make them afraid or otherwise deter them from being God's hands and feet in their world. Sometimes work God wants his people to do actually comes to a stop. But God has given amazing promises to meet the deepest needs of human hearts. People need to be reminded of them so they will be motivated to carry on with the deeds he has called them to do. In the days of Haggai and Zechariah, building the temple for the presence of the God of the covenant was the priority. For modern Christians it is building up the church as the body of Christ (1 Pet. 2:5).

Second, God's word shapes the understanding his people have of their identity, their experiences, and the nature of their relationship with him. Christians must embrace the teaching of the new covenant. They must agree that God's judgment on all as sinners is appropriate, and they must view their only hope of salvation as lying in becoming devoted servants of Christ and trusting in his promises. These core commitments are not only essential for salvation; they also inform all effective action by God's people and become part of their witness to the wider world (as in Ezra 5:11–12). They are instilled through encountering the word of God.

But Ezra 5 also demonstrates an important aspect of how God sends his word to his people: he has prophets speak it to them. The Judeans are told directly about God's thoughts and intentions by specific people in their community. Today we have direct access to God's word in the Bible, and it is still the responsibility of those in the church to speak it to each other. This can be carried out to some degree by all members of the body, but God equips some with the special ability to preach and teach and to explain how the word can be applied in contemporary culture. It is important for these people to do this work and be supported in it, so that the whole body will regularly receive the encouragement and instruction needed.

When God's people adopt the perspectives given in Scripture and trust God to fulfill his promises, the way is prepared for him to work powerfully through them. But God will also choose at critical times to work in unseen ways to ensure that his plans go forward, as he did when he kept the temple building from stopping while its legality was investigated. Humans cannot predict when God will do this, but they can be confident that he will when his purposes require it. The church must do what it can and entrust the rest to God.

Illustrating the Text

God's Word is our only rule for faith and life; it defines reality.

Film: The popular 2010 movie *Inception*, starring Leonardo DiCaprio, uses science fiction to explore the idea of reality and dreams. Characters in the film infiltrate other people's dreams to plant ideas and steal secrets, sometimes even to the point of creating a dream within a dream. Because the line between reality and dream gets very blurred, dream infiltrators can't always trust their senses to know whether they are awake or asleep. To fix this, each carries a small object that only he or she knows about (DiCaprio's is a spinning top). It is a way of double-checking their perceptions and proving what is real. In the same way, a believer's test of reality is the Bible. It is our "rule for faith and life";[2] it defines reality and helps us stay grounded in God's truth rather than illusion. When our sense of reality becomes confused or muddied, we set aside what we think is "reality" and cling to what God's Word teaches.

God builds things and people with his Word; believers must, as well.

Object Lesson: Put a pile of toy building blocks (plastic snap-together blocks will work, but bigger blocks make a better visual) on a table in front of your listeners. Invite a volunteer forward. Tell them their job is to build a tower out of the blocks as high as they can in under thirty seconds. Let them try. Now tell your volunteer that he or she has a full two minutes to accomplish the same task, but that there will be a twist: he or she must stand back five feet and cannot touch the blocks in any way. Don't give much time for the volunteer to react—simply say "go" and see what happens. The person will (hopefully) quickly realize that the only thing to do is to start speaking to others, giving instructions, enlisting help, and coaching with words. Explain that God builds things with words; he builds things and people with his Word. He could simply tell the blocks, "Become a tower," and they would obey. Often, though, he will tell his people about his plans and allow them the dignity of proclaiming the new things along with him.

Applying the Text: Ask your listeners to think of one person whom they could build up with a note of biblical encouragement. Challenge them to write and send that note before the sun sets.

We must do what we can but entrust the whole situation to God.

Popular Saying: Many believers say, "Pray like it all depends on God, then work like it all depends on you." This is good, but a better way to say it would be, "Pray like it all depends on God, listen like he wants you to join him, and obey like you trust him to win." God's power is not our backup plan; it is the whole and only plan.

The Recovered Decree of Cyrus Leads Darius to Ensure the Temple Is Restored

Big Idea

God arranges circumstances to overcome decisively the opposition to the obedient work of his people.

Key Themes

- God influences the course of events by bringing the pivotal document to the attention of Darius.
- Circumstances and Darius's personal beliefs and goals combine to result in a continuation of the Judeans' building work that cannot be stopped.

Understanding the Text

The Text in Context

At the end of Ezra 5, the Judeans and the local Persian officials are waiting for a response from Darius concerning whether the work of rebuilding the temple in Jerusalem had been previously authorized and will be allowed to continue. The "flash-forward" of Ezra 4:6–23 has shown that letters written to the monarch, including those requesting searches in the royal archives, can effectively shut down rebuilding work.

Thus, when the Judeans' claim in Ezra 5 that Cyrus had given them authorization to rebuild is vindicated in Ezra 6, it is further evidence of God's action on their behalf, an extension of his assistance in Ezra 5:1–2, 5. Moreover, Darius not only allows the building to continue; he provides generous government support to ensure that the project is completed. At this point there is no prospect for opposition to interfere with the Judean builders. This leads directly to Ezra 6:13–22, where the restored temple is completed.

This passage forms a chiastic structure with the letter of Tattenai in Ezra 5:7–17. A chiasm is a literary technique in which a sequence of ideas (the ideas could be called A, B, C, D) is followed by a sequence of similar ideas in the reverse order (D′, C′, B′, A′). The effect is to emphasize that, ironically, Darius's reply both was caused by and put an end to questions about whether the Jerusalem temple should be rebuilt: (1) the discovery of Cyrus's edict in 6:1–2 results from the request to search for it (5:17), (2) the text of the edict (6:3–5) verifies the claim of the Jewish elders (5:11–16), (3) Darius's explicit authorization to restore the temple (6:6–12a) answers the original question of whether the Jews had authorization (5:9–10), and (4) Darius's command that his decree be carried out with diligence (6:12b) ensures continuation of the diligent work being done by the Jews (5:7–8).[1] The structure can be represented visually as follows:

A Report of the Jews' diligent work (5:7–8)
   B Question of whether the Jews' work was authorized (5:9–10)
      C Claim by the Jews that Cyrus had authorized their work (5:11–16)
         D Request to search for an authorizing edit (5:17)
         D′ Copy of Cyrus's edict discovered (6:1–2)
      C′ Text of Cyrus's edict authorizing the Jews' work (6:3–5)
   B′ Reinforcement by Darius of the authorization of the Jews' work (6:6–12a)
A′ Command of Darius that the Jews' work continue with diligence (6:12b)

Historical and Cultural Background

Although it is impossible to know what Darius was thinking when the events recorded in Ezra 6 happened, an awareness of some historical facts may help us understand the likely motivations for his actions. Although related to the royal family, Darius was not in the direct line to inherit the Persian throne. After the death of Cambyses, a man claiming to be Cambyses's brother briefly became king. Many of the Persians accepted his claim, but many others, including Darius, believed Cambyses's brother had been killed and that this man was an impostor and a usurper. After murdering him, Darius seized the throne in 522 BC. Since there was so much uncertainty surrounding the circumstances of his rise to power, a number of rebellions flared up in various parts of the empire. After putting these down, Darius knew it was in his best interests to cultivate goodwill with his far-flung subjects, and rebuilding their religious

Questions about the Memorandum

The two versions of Cyrus's orders have noticeable differences. The decree in Ezra 1 is in Hebrew, and the one in Ezra 6:3–5 is in Aramaic. In addition, they do not cover exactly the same range of topics. But the differences can largely be explained on the basis of genre. That is, Ezra 1:1–4 is taken from a decree intended for oral proclamation and therefore containing a practical summary for mass communication, whereas Ezra 6:3–5 is from an official written record intended to be used for reference by treasury officials. It is also possible that the author of Ezra is not quoting the document in full in either case.

Moreover, the dimensions given for the temple seem strange, because they are much larger than those of the original temple, and only two dimensions are given. Since it was customary to rebuild temples in their original form to the extent possible and Cyrus and Darius both seem to have followed this practice (Ezra 5:15; 6:7), it is most likely that the rebuilt temple was supposed to have the same dimensions as Solomon's original temple, sixty cubits long by twenty cubits wide by thirty cubits high (1 Kings 6:2). The dimensions in the present text of Ezra 6:3 may have arisen by a combination of two kinds of scribal copying error, each of which is frequently observed in ancient documents.

structures was an effective way of doing this. The decision to do so was by no means automatic—hence, the inquiry by Tattenai—but it was frequently made. Historical evidence reveals that numerous sanctuaries of the gods of subject peoples were restored by Cyrus, Cambyses, and Darius. In fact, one Egyptian inscription refers to Darius as "the friend of all the gods."

One of the ways Darius tried to prove he was a legitimate king was to show that he continued the policies of earlier, respected Persian kings, such as Cyrus. Once he discovered an earlier decree by Cyrus, as in Ezra 6, it is not surprising that he would be eager to sustain and even augment it.

Typical of his time, Darius was also a polytheist. Part of the benefit he hoped to obtain from restoring the temples of various gods was favor with those gods. But sacrifices and prayers for foreign rulers were also understood in the ancient world as expressions of loyalty on the part of those making them. When they were discontinued, as those made in Jerusalem on behalf of the Romans were in AD 66, it was understood as a signal of revolt. Darius was therefore setting up a mechanism for ensuring and evaluating the loyalty of his subjects.

With this background in mind, it is easy to see that Darius is not necessarily particularly sympathetic to the Judeans' cause or their beliefs. His actions can be explained in terms of political expediency and polytheistic religion. The sovereign hand of God is seen in bringing together the circumstances of Ezra 5–6 and Darius's motivations at just the right time to ensure the temple reconstruction could be completed.

Interpretive Insights

6:1–2 *at Babylon. A scroll was found in the citadel of Ecbatana.* It is more likely that "Babylon" refers to the city, not the region. The city was an administrative center where records were usually kept for the area including Judea. A better translation of verse 2, then, would begin with "but" (as in the NRSV), since the narrator highlights the contrast between where the document was expected to be found and where it is actually found.

There is also an important switch from an impersonal active verb in verse 1, "they searched," to a passive verb in verse 2, "a scroll was found." No indication is given of the circumstances under which the scroll is found, but passive verbs of this kind are often used in the Bible to highlight God's activity behind the scenes. These two verses narrate the pivotal events by which God ensures that the temple building goes forward.

6:6 *stay away from there.* It sounds as though Darius is concerned that Tattenai has an interest in interfering with the work. Similar phrases were sometimes used in legal cases to indicate that one party had no legal claim or authority in a matter. At other times it meant that a formal accusation had been rejected. Whatever the exact nuance, Tattenai is precluded from any interference with the construction.

6:8 *expenses . . . paid . . . from the revenues of Trans-Euphrates.* The theme of taxation now undergoes a reversal. In Ezra 4:13 the opponents worry the king about losing tax revenue if the city is rebuilt, and in 4:22 he expresses a strong desire that the flow of such money from Judea to the central government should continue unimpeded. Now those same taxes are to stay in Judea to be used in support of the rebuilding and functioning of the temple.

6:10 *pray for the well-being of the king and his sons.* There is no reason the Judeans should not pray for the king as requested. Abraham prays for Abimelech in Genesis 20:17. Jeremiah 29:7 instructs the Judean exiles in Babylon to pray for the city to which they have been exiled. However, the religious worldviews of Darius and the Judeans are different. Darius believes that Yahweh is one god among many, while the Judeans believe they are praying to the only true God.

Theological Insights

The investigation in Ezra 5–6 and the investigation in Ezra 4 turn out very differently. In Ezra 4 the Persian king finds the "incriminating evidence" the officials want him to, and he stops rebuilding activity in Jerusalem. In Ezra 6, the Persian king finds the vindicating evidence that God wants him to, and he directs the temple building to continue. The temple is guaranteed restoration in order to function as it did previously in the relationship between God and Israel. Going forward, the postexilic community can be confident that God desires this relationship to be restored and that he will actively work to make it so. He is more than a match for any group of scheming government officials.

At a more detailed level, the favorable response of Darius is portrayed as the result of the combination of his own political agenda, the actions of the Persian officials, and the diligent work being done by the Judeans. The actions of the officials and the king are completely out of the Judeans' control, but they do their own part by throwing themselves wholeheartedly into the work. For his part, God takes the actions and desires of the officials and king and weaves them into a set of circumstances that gives success to the Judeans' work. God's people can invest themselves confidently in the work God has called them to in the world, knowing that he is able to take care of what they cannot in order to make their work for him a success.

Teaching the Text

Ezra 4 shows that sometimes the righteous work God's people try to do in the world is suspended by opposing forces. But Ezra 5–6 shows that this is always only temporary. Eventually God provides a way for his people to make progress. Often the decisive turning point is an event that may appear coincidental, but it turns the tide in their favor, and the efforts they are making are rewarded. There is no way to know when such a breakthrough will come, so believers should be diligently obeying God's word, as the Judeans were, knowing that the breakthrough will come in God's timing.

The "temple" that New Testament Christians are building is the church, the body of Christ, where God makes his presence known in a special way and where he is worshiped. Throughout the modern world, this work is frequently opposed in greater or lesser degrees. In more restrictive and oppressive countries, it can be greatly hindered, seeming at times practically to stop altogether. But even in more permissive countries it is often opposed in subtle ways that interfere with effective evangelism, discipleship, and worship. The opposition can come from the government or just more generally from the surrounding culture. Sometimes Christians can come to believe that the people or institutions that they perceive as opposing them need to be removed or radically changed if they are to see the church built up. But Ezra 6 shows that this is not necessarily so. Seemingly small details and events can influence the course that governments and influential people pursue. Their motivations may ultimately differ widely from those of believers. Yet God is able to bring about a state of affairs that allows or even encourages the spiritual and numerical growth of the church to advance.

At times, secular institutions may even provide support for the church's work. Christians should recognize the opportunities God is providing and be willing to make use of the assistance available to them. Ezra 3–4 illustrates the importance of refusing to compromise on what is central to the faith merely to receive goodwill or material help. But when no such compromise is entailed, there is no need for believers to reject the support or cooperation that others offer.

Many commentators think that the wording of Darius's letter reveals that he had input, whether by his request or theirs, from Jewish sources who explained key aspects of their faith. It is very possible that this happened, but the biblical writer does not make it explicit in any way. Darius is not portrayed as becoming a true believer in Israel's God or, for that matter, as becoming any closer to being one. He wants to assist their work for his own purposes. So this passage is not using Darius's response as an example of the benefits of witnessing to unbelievers.

Illustrating the Text

Breakthroughs are coming; only God knows when.

Object Lesson: Bring a latex balloon, and start to put one puff of air at a time into it while you talk to your listeners. Explain that a breakthrough is coming with the balloon, but nobody knows when. The more puffs go in, the closer the breakthrough is, and the more pregnant and suspenseful the process of waiting becomes. (You will be able to see your listeners getting more and more agitated as they wait for the explosion—you may find yourself flinching, as well! If you want, you can tease them by taking time to pause and seemingly go off track when the balloon is near popping, then bring them back to the inflation.) When the balloon pops, your listeners will all jump and laugh with the relief. Explain that in God's kingdom, breakthroughs are building behind the scenes. We never know how God is breathing into a situation, but he knows how pregnant the moment is and when it will finally pop! If you are concerned that a popping balloon might cause too much stress for some people in your congregation, you can simply explain the idea of a balloon getting bigger and bigger as it is blown up and how this causes anticipation.

God can work in, through, and around resistance to get things done.

Sports: In the martial art of judo, practitioners study the art of using their opponents' strength and momentum against them. As the two opponents grapple and circle, each seeking an advantage, a skilled student can work within the grip of the other to change directions, shift centers of gravity around, reverse momentum, and even lift and flip the other person onto the ground.

In the same way, as we wrestle with God and his plans and the nations rage against his leadership, God is able to grapple with us, working in, through, and around our resistance to him. He specializes in turning the tables and flipping his enemy's plans for destruction until they turn into blessing for his people. (You could see if your city has a judo dojo and invite them to bring some mats to church and demonstrate in the front. Or, simply show a short video that demonstrates this simple but powerful idea.)

Accepting God's help through the authorities

Human Experience: When I (Nykolaishen), a native of Canada, was making plans to study at a seminary in the United States, I was expecting that most of my financial support would come through a work arrangement I had set up with a local household. After moving a long distance to the area, and shortly before I was to begin my responsibilities, a question arose concerning the legality of the arrangement, since I was not an American citizen. With great trepidation, I contacted the immigration authorities and described the arrangement, asking whether it would be legitimate. Much to my relief, the answer came back in the affirmative. Although the government authorities had no interest in assisting my preparation for ministry, God worked through their decision to make it possible for me to get education that has helped me serve the church in various capacities for decades.

Popular Saying: People often jokingly say, "You know, just because you're paranoid doesn't mean they're not out to get you." This ironic statement is indicative of many modern people's lack of trust. Many live with an overdeveloped sense of their own importance and victimization, assuming everything negative done around them was a personal attack. And when Christians see laws being made in their country that erode moral order, it is easy for them to assume that the government has decided to become the enemy of the church. As God's people mature, they are more likely to realize that most government authorities are actually more indifferent to them than opposed to them. We ought not to be shocked that sin leads legislators at times to act more according to the world's values than according to God's. But we ought to take the opportunity to give clear and constructive input about God's good plans for society and not simply assume that lawmakers are so committed to destroying Christianity that God cannot work through them.

The Judeans Celebrate the Dedication of the Temple and Passover

Big Idea

God's people should celebrate when they recognize God has acted to fulfill his promises to them.

Key Themes

- Although the Persian kings issued decrees that the temple be rebuilt, it is the will of God that is ultimately responsible for it happening.
- The Judeans recognize that the Passover event and the completion of the temple are fulfillments of God's redemption promises, and they celebrate them with joy.
- Everyone who is committed to the covenant faith of Israel is included.

Understanding the Text

The Text in Context

The first phase of the story begun in Ezra 1 comes to a successful close here. The reference to Jeremiah's prophecy in Ezra 1:1 indicates that the time of restoration for the exiled Judeans has come, and Cyrus's decree in Ezra 1:2–4 reveals that the process is to begin with the return of the exiles to Jerusalem to rebuild the temple there. By the end of Ezra 6, another Persian king, Darius, has made a similar decree, bringing the rebuilt temple to completion. The narrative in between shows that the Judeans encounter serious obstacles as they work. But the mention of God "changing the attitude" of the king in Ezra 6:22 corresponds to the statement that he "moved the heart" of the king in Ezra 1:1 and underlines the fact that, from beginning to end, God is in control and ensuring that the temple is rebuilt. With this first phase of restoration finished, Ezra 7 will move forward in time about fifty-seven years and introduce a new phase with new challenges.

Interpretive Insights

6:14 *They finished building . . . the command of the God of Israel and . . . kings of Persia.* There are several interrelated interpretive issues in this verse. Probably the most obvious is that Artaxerxes is included, even though he does not come to the throne for another fifty years and has no recorded decree in the text to this point in support of building the temple. It is helpful, however, to note that, although the NIV reads, "They finished building the temple," the Hebrew text simply reads, "They finished building," without specifying "the temple" (as, e.g., ESV, NRSV). The account of an exchange of letters involving Artaxerxes in Ezra 4 has been seen to be a "flash-forward" to his time, showing how the Judeans' enemies persuade the king to oppose the rebuilding of Jerusalem's walls. At the end of Ezra 4:21, Artaxerxes allows the possibility that he might change his mind about this. Ezra 6:14 thus appears to be a very brief "flash-forward" indicating that he does change his mind and issue a decree promoting rebuilding, not of the already-completed temple, but of Jerusalem's walls. The details are not reported in the narrative until Nehemiah 1–6.

A further issue is hidden by the NIV translation of "decrees" and "kings" in the plural. Both words are singular in the original language. The effect is to encourage the reader to think of "Persian king" as a role within the narrative that is filled by each of the individuals named, and to notice the similarities in their function (something similar happens in Exodus with the references to Pharaoh, such that many readers never consciously realize that there must be more than one [Exod. 2:15; 4:19]). This literary device invites comparison between God's function and the Persian king's function in the story, since the "command" of God and the "decree" of the Persian king are placed side by side, and the Hebrew word is actually the same for both "command" and "decree."

Both God and the Persian king play important roles by giving commands. God's command comes through Scripture (the prophecy of Jeremiah [Ezra 1:1], the law of Moses [Ezra 3:2], etc.) and through his current prophets, Haggai and Zechariah. The command of the king comes through his decrees (Ezra 1:1–4; 6:8–12). Both God's and the king's command are effective in bringing about the temple building. But on another level, the command of God transcends the king's command, because even the king's command has been shown to be a result of God's command (see the discussion of "the Lord moved the heart of Cyrus" in the commentary on Ezra 1:1, and the comments on Ezra 6:1–2).

6:21 *all who had separated themselves . . . to seek the Lord.* "Unclean practices" often refers to idolatry in the Old Testament, but it can include any behavior inappropriate for worshipers of God, disqualifying them from his presence. The Passover is a feast that celebrates God's miraculous deliverance of Israel from slavery in Egypt. Thus, this verse says that anyone who has made a definitive break with "unclean" behavior is accepted into the community of Israel and can participate with them in remembering the salvation they have received. This contrasts with the behavior of the enemies of the Judeans in Ezra 4:2–4. Although they claimed to seek the Lord, they were likely polytheists and showed by their actions that they were opposed to God's plan. Here, the willingness to abandon unacceptable pagan practices demonstrates sincere commitment to the true God.

Non-Israelites also joined the Israelite community for Passover at the time of the original exodus (Exod. 12:44–48). The implication in Ezra 6:21 is that the return of the exiles and rebuilding of the temple have the effect of drawing outsiders to the Israelite faith, in a way similar to the exodus from Egypt. This, then, also continues the theme of the restoration as a second exodus.

6:22 *the attitude of the king of Assyria.* It was not unusual for people to refer to kings as ruling over earlier empires they had conquered (compare "king of Babylon" for Cyrus in Ezra 5:13), and the Persians had conquered the Babylonians, who had conquered the Assyrians. The Persian kings also followed some of the policies of the Assyrian kings and considered themselves their successors. But the choice of this title by the author was not random. Throughout the Old Testament, the kings of Assyria are typically regarded as enemies of Israel, used by God at times to bring judgment. There are reminders of this at Ezra 4:2, 10, in the statements that Esarhaddon and Ashurbanipal had deported foreign peoples from their homes to the territory of Judea, and in Nehemiah 9:32, which connects the Assyrian kings to the long period of hardship the Israelites have endured. The exchange of letters with Artaxerxes in Ezra 4 showed that the Persian rulers are just as apt to take sides against Israel as their Assyrian predecessors had been. So the title "king of Assyria" here underlines that the favorable treatment this king has given Israel in this case can only be attributed to God working within him.

so that he assisted them. The Hebrew syntax is slightly ambiguous in this phrase, and it could mean either that the king assisted them or that God assisted them. Either way, there is likely an intended contrast with the enemies of Ezra 4:4–5. They discouraged the Judeans (literally, "weakened their hands") by bribing officials to frustrate their plans. God and, through his prompting, the "king of Assyria" encourage the Judeans (literally, "strengthen their hands"). Officials and kings can be manipulated; it is God who overcomes the enemies of his people.

Theological Insights

The Israelites who return to Judea from exile anticipating restoration of their covenant with God are in a strange situation. They are in the promised land, but they are still under the rule of a foreign power. These are circumstances unlike the preexilic period, and it must be hard for them to imagine how they can proceed as a community focused on the proper worship of God at the temple when they cannot presume that this will even be allowed by the political powers that be. The conclusion they draw from the text of Ezra 1–6 is that God will make a way for them to have a faithful relationship with him even under these strange circumstances. If need be, he can orchestrate the intentions and motives of the people and rulers around them so that his people can accomplish what he wills them to. More than ever before, the postexilic community can see that their confidence should not be in kings or rulers, but in God himself.

Moreover, even though preexilic conditions have not been fully realized, the Judeans recognize that they are, in fact, God's people, and they can proceed confidently in their covenant relationship with him. The temple has been rebuilt, and the worship God calls for has been reinstituted. The identification of the community in this section as Israel and their sacrifice of a goat for each of the tribes of Israel point in this direction as well. As they see how God has brought the temple back into existence through them and remember how he brought their ancestors out of Egypt, they rejoice in their restored relationship with him. He continues to overcome the enemy on their behalf, and they have hope that even greater things are in store.

Finally, in the midst of the focus on the returned exiles as heirs of the preexilic community of Israel, there is a reminder that the true Israel is not ultimately determined ethnically. Rather, they are defined by their commitment to the exclusive worship of the true God as he has revealed himself. In God's sight, humans of any ethnic background are potential members of his people. He cares about the heart, not about ancestry. All who are willing to forsake other allegiances to serve him as he prescribes are welcome among his people.

Teaching the Text

The Judeans' joyful celebration has to do with both means and ends. They celebrate the way in which the temple has been completed: God has done a surprising and mighty thing by having the "Assyrian" king lend his decisive support for the project. But they also celebrate the fact of the temple's completion itself. They now have access once again into God's presence in a way that was missing during the exile. Although the full realization of the prophetic promises of restoration, including those involving the Messiah, is still in the future, an important stage in the process has been reached.

Christians still have similar reasons for rejoicing. God still brings about his sovereign will in earthly affairs so that the work of his church can go forward. He can work through rulers who help the church with its tasks, or through those who do not, as when Pilate chose to hand Jesus over to be crucified. And we can celebrate the further advances that have been achieved in God's plan of redemption, including Christ's death, resurrection, and ascension, and the sending of the Holy Spirit. Our access to God's presence is beyond what the returned exiles had. Although Christians look forward to an even greater future in which we will worship Christ in the heavenly new Jerusalem, where the temple is God and the Lamb himself (Rev. 21), in the meantime we should find ways to rejoice and celebrate together what God has already done.

The Judeans celebrated God's past acts of salvation by observing the Passover and the Feast of Unleavened Bread. Both of these were connected to the event of the exodus from Egypt, which was itself the fulfillment of a promise made earlier to Abram (Gen. 15:13–16). The Passover specifically focused on how God spared them from the plague of the firstborn and brought them out of Egyptian bondage. The Feast of Unleavened Bread emphasized how quickly they had to leave Egypt in order to follow where God was leading them. Their salvation involved rescue as well as leaving something behind. Those elements are present in Ezra 6 as well. The returnees have been rescued from exile in Babylon. But they are joined by a group of people who leave behind the unclean practices of their Gentile neighbors to follow God's leadership. The latter are considered part of the community and celebrate in worship with them. Today, those who understand what the Lord's Supper points to—the significance of Christ's atoning death on behalf of all sinners—and commit themselves to be his followers, leaving behind their old ways, should be accepted into the community of faith and join the celebration, regardless of their background.

Illustrating the Text

God doesn't just get things done; he does them remarkably.

Story: Tell a story about a time when someone vastly exceeded your expectations. Maybe it was a server at your favorite restaurant, your mechanic, a clerk at the grocery store, or the person who boards your pet. Explain what you expected from the person and share how they startled and delighted you by going outside their normal routine in order to provide the service you needed. Explain that this is a little glimpse of the heart of God—he isn't content to just meet expectations; he loves blowing us away by doing things in ways we could never imagine! That way, we know it was grace and fatherly love, not just a product from some cosmic vending machine.

Fully celebrate earthly milestones and focus forward to heaven.

Parenting: Invite your listeners to consider two different kinds of homes: In one, the parents' goal is to cling to the child and keep him or her around forever.

Milestones like first steps and birthdays are celebrated and clung to, but also mourned, since every new accomplishment brings the child closer to the day when he or she will abandon the home and leave the parents desolated. In the other home, the parents are aiming to raise a thriving and self-sustaining adult. Milestones are celebrated because they signify progress toward the goal, and the goal is celebrated because it gives purpose to the milestones. God's people are to always remember that their ultimate goal and citizenship is in heaven—the victories and milestones we have here all mark progress toward our true home, and our true home makes sense out of the milestones and glimpses of God we have here.

Salvation involves both lifting out and letting go.

Film: *Titanic*. In this iconic movie (1997) there is a scene where the lead female character, Rose, is struggling for her life in the icy waters of the North Atlantic after the ship's sinking. She is hypothermic and barely conscious, nearing death. She hears the sound of a rescue crew in a lifeboat and realizes she has just enough strength left to swim for a whistle on another passenger's life vest and blow it for help. In order to reach the whistle, though, she has to let go of the debris to which she is clinging and the frozen body of her beloved. For Rose to be saved and truly live, she has to let go of security and grief, enter the freezing water again, and risk it all to be lifted out. In the same way, the feasts celebrated by the Judeans show us that salvation means both letting go of many things and being lifted out by Someone.

Ezra Is Sent to Jerusalem

Big Idea

A restored relationship with God requires, in addition to the experience of God's presence in worship, an understanding of his instruction.

Key Themes

- God uses Ezra because Ezra has devoted himself to God's law.
- God motivates the Persian king to further the restoration of Israel from exile.
- The Persian king provides for enhancement of worship and the Jerusalem temple and implementation of God's law.

Understanding the Text

The Text in Context

Ezra 1–6 describes the first stage of the restoration of Israel from exile promised by the prophets. Thousands of Judeans travel from Babylon to Jerusalem and the surrounding area and settle there. They also rebuild the temple and reinstitute worship there as prescribed before the exile. The permission and resources needed to do this are provided by the Persian kings, acting at the unseen direction of God, who also intervenes to overcome the opposition encountered by the Judeans in the process.

Ezra 7 introduces the second stage of restoration, skipping ahead over fifty years, from 515 to 458 BC, to the reign of Artaxerxes. The events of Ezra 7–8 likely occur before the events recorded in Ezra 4:7–23, in which Artaxerxes stops construction of Jerusalem's walls. As in Ezra 1–6, God again influences the Persian king to provide assistance in the form of generous resources for temple worship. But this time the king also sends an expert in the law of Moses, Ezra, from Babylon to Jerusalem to see to it that this law is followed by those living in Judea. This sets the agenda for Ezra 8–10, in which the community's obedience to the law is the focus. Ezra also brings a group of exiles with him, reminiscent of the exodus from Egypt, as was the first group of returnees described in Ezra 1–2.

Ezra 7 gives an overview of these developments and details the relevant instructions given by King Artaxerxes. The last two verses (27–28), in which Ezra himself praises God, transition from the king's edict to Ezra 8, which narrates Ezra's response to the edict in greater detail, describing events up to and including the arrival of the group in Jerusalem.

Historical and Cultural Background

Letters and inscriptions from the reigns of Cambyses and Darius I show that Persian kings sometimes had an interest in arranging and organizing and then enforcing the traditional religious laws of some of the peoples who lived in different regions of their empire. Although likely not done for most of the peoples, it seems to have been a way to gain favor with the local population in areas of political unrest. When the kings did this, they used individuals from the people group in question who were experts in the relevant laws.

At the time of Ezra's mission to Jerusalem, the Persians had been struggling to put down a rebellion in Egypt. Because Judea was so close to Egypt, it is plausible that Artaxerxes wished to keep unrest from spreading eastward. This may also explain why he was also willing to make lavish donations for the Jerusalem temple. As a polytheist, he may have wanted to gain favor with both the local population and the god they worshiped.

Ezra knew that the political calculations of foreign kings could not be relied on to support the worship of the God of Israel. He recognized that Artaxerxes's call to provide financial assistance and enforce God's law among his people at just this time was due to the work of God himself, behind the scenes.

Interpretive Insights

7:1–5 *Ezra son of . . . Aaron.* Lengthy genealogies in the Bible were usually attached to important persons, and this is one of the longest genealogies given for an individual in an Old Testament narrative, so the reader is being signaled that the character entering the narrative here is special. As a descendant of Aaron, Israel's first high priest (Exod. 28:1), he is eminently qualified to handle affairs related to the temple, which is an important part of the mission described in this chapter.

7:6 *teacher well versed in the Law of Moses.* The other feature that makes Ezra special is his expert ability to teach God's law. This is the second major aspect of his mission. As priest and lawgiver, Ezra effectively embodies the roles of both Aaron and Moses for the community of the new exodus.

the hand of the LORD . . . was on him. As in Ezra 1 and Ezra 6, God causes the king to assist the restoration process. "According to the hand of the king" is a Hebrew idiom that refers to a king's generosity (used in 1 Kings 10:13; Esther 1:7; 2:18). By inserting "God" in place of "king" here in the context of Artaxerxes's grant, the text makes the point that it is ultimately God's generosity at work.

7:9 *He had begun his journey . . . on the first day of the first month.* There is disagreement about what the word translated "begun" means. Ezra 8:31 says that the actual travel begins on the twelfth day of the first month. Ezra 7:9 probably means either that important preparations begin on the first day of the month or that the initial plan is to leave on that day. The intention seems to be to make a connection with the exodus from Egypt, in which the Israelites leave Egypt on the first day of the first month. These preparations or plans are part of God's redemption of exiled Israel, which is patterned on the redemption from Egypt.

7:10 *For Ezra had devoted himself . . . and to teaching.* The Hebrew behind "devoted himself" could be translated "set his heart." Ezra has a firm commitment to learning God's word, applying it sincerely in his own life, and teaching it to other Israelites. The position of this verse in the present context implies that Ezra both embraces the tasks described and is aided by God because of his devotion to God's word.

7:14 *is in your hand.* This is an idiom that simply means "you possess" or "is at your disposal." It appears again in verse 25.

7:25 *appoint magistrates and judges.* This role, along with teaching the law, presents Ezra as a second Moses (compare Exod. 18:13–27).

Most historians think the intent was for Ezra to teach the law of God only to the Jewish people in Trans-Euphrates. This may be true historically, but the biblical text is somewhat ambiguous, probably capitalizing on an ambiguity in Artaxerxes's original edict. The result is a foreshadowing of the day when all, even the Gentiles, will follow God's law (Isa. 2:3; Jer. 3:17). This is an important feature of the prophesied restoration of Israel, moving beyond resettlement in Palestine and reinstitution of temple worship.

7:27 *to bring honor to the house of the* LORD *in Jerusalem in this way.* Isaiah 59:20–60:18 shares several themes with this passage: God's word known by his people (59:21); wealth of the Gentiles coming to Israel (60:5, 11), including specifically silver and gold (60:9); Gentiles supplying sacrificial animals (60:7); and foreign kings contributing to the glory of the Jerusalem temple (60:10–13). Ezra seems to recognize these parallels and draws attention to them by using the word translated "bring honor," an infrequently used Hebrew verb occurring in Isaiah 60:7, 13 (NIV "adorn"). He implies that what is happening in his own day is a foretaste of the blessings of restoration promised in Isaiah.

7:28 *extended his good favor to me.* The word translated "favor," when used of God's disposition, is typically connected to his covenant relationship with Israel. Thus, Ezra recognizes from the instructions he has been given that God is working out his covenant promises through him. As a result, he is encouraged to begin the process of fulfilling his mission.

Theological Insights

The return of another group of Israelites to Jerusalem from Babylon, the contribution of more resources to the temple and its worship, and the teaching of the law to Israel together present another iteration of the second-exodus theme with its implication that prophecies of restoration are beginning to be fulfilled. The leader of this new exodus is a new Moses: Ezra. He qualifies for this role because he has determined to study God's word thoroughly, practice in his own life what it teaches, and then teach it to others. Accordingly, God directs him through Artaxerxes and provides everything he needs to fulfill his mission, and Ezra is able to recognize God's activity behind the king's decision and take appropriate action. Those who make a priority of knowing and understanding God's revealed word, aligning their thoughts and behaviors with it in every area of life, and being prepared to share it with others and explain it to them clearly, will have the greatest chance of being used effectively by God to help others be restored to relationship with him.

Ezra's mandate to teach the law represents a big step forward in the restoration process. The return and rebuilding of the temple in Ezra 1–6 demonstrates God's desire to follow through on his promises and establishes the special place where he will be present among his people and where atoning sacrifices can be offered. But God intends for his people to respond to his gracious forgiveness by living lives characterized by true righteousness, and they cannot do that without knowing and following the instructions he has revealed. So God provides people like Ezra, who by teaching and appointing judges will try to realize this aspect of restoration. God considers this work central to achieving his purposes.

Teaching the Text

Ezra's devotion to God's word illustrates an approach to be emulated by all believers. The three ways he is said to interact with it remain applicable today. First, there is no substitute for careful study. Much damage has been done within the church because of careless reading and interpretation. Second, study is not merely for the sake of knowledge but must translate into personal application. Scripture is intended to change our lives, including our thoughts, attitudes, and actions. Finally, what is learned and practiced must also be communicated. The New Testament commands believers to encourage one another with Christ's truth, and it broadens this with the call to share the gospel with unbelievers to the fullest possible extent.

Some specific results of Ezra's devotion to God's word are evident in this text. Because of his familiarity with Isaiah's prophecy, Ezra is able to recognize how events occurring around him contribute to the fulfillment of God's promises. This, in turn, leads him to see that God is and has been at work in his own life, preparing him and providing for him so that he can play a major part in the restoration. This realization motivates him to invest himself in the opportunity placed before him. It is a great example of the sovereignty of God and human responsibility working together. The better believers understand God's intentions for his people and the world, the better they are able to discern God's activity in their own setting and cooperate with him. Finally, Ezra is able to gain perspective on the king's actions. His cultural knowledge enables him to understand the political reasons why Artaxerxes might give the support he does. But his biblical knowledge lets him understand that God is behind this, working out his own purposes. Ezra knows he can benefit from Artaxerxes's decree without making the mistake of identifying God's agenda with the king's. Christians should not see government support for the church's goals and values as the ideal to pursue. When governmental policy advances the work of the church without requiring compromise, it is welcome. But political complexities do not allow governments to become reliable partners in God's work. All of these important perspectives and motivations result from the priority of God's word in Ezra's life.

The giving of the law at Mount Sinai and the special attention given to teaching the law as part of the postexilic restoration underline the importance of obedience to God's instruction on the part of his covenant people. Indeed, it continues to be prominent in the new covenant, according to Jeremiah 31:33. Of course, there are significant differences between a New Testament believer's relationship to Old Testament law and that of a pre-Christian Israelite. But the entire Old Testament, including the law of Moses, continues to have an important function in preparing individual Christians to do good work (2 Tim. 3:16–17). Throughout the Bible, God's salvation progresses toward the fundamental ideal of complete obedience to his word, reversing the disobedience in the garden of Eden.

Ezra's lengthy genealogy contributes to his portrayal as a special character uniquely suited for his roles as priest and teacher of Torah. Since the reinstitution of temple worship and the reintroduction of Torah at the center of the life of the Judean people are central themes of God's restoration of his people, Ezra's entrance onto the narrative stage is evidence that God is carrying out his sovereign plan. While it is true that God has made each person unique and therefore able to contribute to the achievement of his purposes in special ways, it is probably straying from the author's purpose to derive that lesson from this text.

Illustrating the Text

Scripture is meant to be studied, applied, and communicated to others.

Biography: Mary Jones was a young Welsh girl who had no Bible of her own. Jones lived at the turn of the nineteenth century. She was the daughter of a weaver and professed Christianity at the age of eight. Having learned to read, she resolved that she would find a Welsh Bible of her own to read and study. She saved for six years to have enough money, then walked barefoot over twenty-six miles of rough terrain to another town where she knew she could buy one from the Reverend Thomas Charles. Charles told her story as the inspiration to call the Religious Tract Society to supply Wales with Bibles. Her passion for the Word of God inspired the founding of the British and Foreign Bible Society and made her a Welsh national hero. Modern believers need to cherish God's Word and work to ensure that all those who need a Bible can obtain a copy in their own heart language.[1]

Studying the Bible helps us interpret our times and circumstances.

Nostalgia: Many listeners will recall the toy decoders with a red lens that one uses to look at a scrambled red-and-blue image. The red lens matches the red parts of the scramble, and hidden words or pictures that are written in blue ink can suddenly be discerned. If you can find one, show it or pass it around to your listeners. Explain that reading the Bible has a similar effect as we look at the jumble of ideas, situations, attitudes, and events going on in the world around us. When we interpret the Bible correctly, it acts as a lens that cuts through the clouds of confusion and reveals the clear purposes, truths, and instructions that God intends for us to see but that have been covered up or lost in the static of life.

Discipleship must always include obedience.

Devotional Classics: *"So Send I You" / "Workmen of God": Recognizing and Answering God's Call to Service,* by Oswald Chambers. In this classic volume Chambers speaks about the need for real discipleship that includes ordinary obedience, rather than spectacular feats: "The 'show business,' which is so incorporated into our view of Christian work today, has caused us to drift far from our Lord's conception of discipleship. It is instilled in us to think that we have to do exceptional things for God; we have not. We have to be exceptional in ordinary things, to be holy in mean streets, among mean people, surrounded by sordid sinners. That is not learned in five minutes."[2] Real discipleship is not about doing something amazing to impress God once or twice; it is about full obedience to his Word in a million mundane things over the course of a lifetime.

Ezra Leads a Group of Exiles to Jerusalem

Big Idea

As believers seek to follow God's revealed pattern for restoration, God provides what is needed.

Key Themes

- Ezra understands that the postexilic restoration is to be patterned after the exodus from Egypt and intentionally structures his journey that way.
- God provides everything necessary to accomplish the present stage of restoration.

Understanding the Text

The Text in Context

Ezra 1–6 tells of the Judean exiles who were the first to return to Jerusalem from Babylon. In several ways, their journey is depicted as similar to the exodus from Egypt centuries earlier. This is to be expected, since the prophets predicted that the restoration from exile would resemble the exodus. The features reminiscent of the exodus that appear in these chapters are mainly orchestrated by God himself, often through the decrees of the Persian king.

Ezra 7 begins the story of a later period, in which the Persian king once again approves the return of a group of exiles from Babylon to Jerusalem, and which introduces the character of Ezra, a Judean devoted to God's word. Ezra's familiarity with Scripture enables him to recognize the king's plan as a tool being used by God to further the Judean restoration. Ezra 8 proceeds to tell how Ezra organized and led the group's return. This time the recognizable similarities to the exodus from Egypt are a result of Ezra's understanding that the restoration is to be like the exodus and the actions he takes to make them seem similar.

When the journey ends successfully, the stage is set for the second part of Ezra's mandate from the king, which is to ensure that the Judeans observe God's law.

Historical and Cultural Background

Economically and socially, there may have been little to attract people to go to Jerusalem with Ezra. Living conditions were probably better for them in Babylon, and this may be why the numbers given for this group are much smaller than those for the group recorded in Ezra 2 (about five thousand, compared to about forty-two thousand). This makes Ezra's attitude all the more remarkable. He discerns that God is behind the opportunity presented to him and understands that he is uniquely positioned to lead an "exodus" as part of the prophesied restoration.

Interpretive Insights

8:2 *descendants of Phinehas . . . David*. The families of Phinehas and Ithamar represent the line of priests (Exod. 28:1; Num. 25:11–13). The family of David obviously represents the royal line with messianic associations. These families are important in order to make the group of returnees representative of all Israel and their journey thus eligible to be considered a new exodus.

Within Ezra and Nehemiah, the Davidic descendants never become kings independent of Persian rule. Since the promised restoration includes a Davidic king ruling over Israel (Jer. 23:5–6), it is clear the restoration has not fully occurred by the end of this narrative and more fulfillment is yet to come.

8:3 *the descendants of Parosh*. The family names listed in Ezra 8:3b–14 match almost identically those in Ezra 2:3–15. Since the earlier returnees were found to be genuine descendants of preexilic Israel (compare Ezra 2:59–63) and heirs of the restoration promise, the same can be said for these.

8:9 *of Joab*. The descendants of Joab are listed separately from the descendants of Pahath-Moab (v. 4), although Joab's line is listed as part of Pahath-Moab in Ezra 2:6. This arrangement allows the number of nonpriestly and nonroyal families here to be twelve, a number used throughout this chapter to mark the returnees as representative of the twelve tribes of Israel (compare Jesus's decision to choose twelve disciples in the New Testament [e.g., Mark 3:14–19]).

8:15 *no Levites there*. Ezra believes the group is unable to begin the journey without Levites. Their presence will allow the trip to match the first exodus, in which Levites were given specific tasks, including carrying sacred vessels for the tabernacle (Num. 10:13–28).

8:22 *I was ashamed to ask the king for soldiers*. Some have thought that Ezra's approach is irresponsible, suggesting that he has backed himself into a corner by saying things he perhaps should not have. But it is hard to say with confidence that he acts wrongly, especially in light of the fact that God hears the prayers of the group and gives them safety. What Ezra demonstrates is a faith in God that is much stronger than his faith in what a king could provide. He recognizes God's hand at work in bringing about Artaxerxes's decree, the donations for the temple, and the arrival of Levites to participate in the trip. It is entirely appropriate for him to testify before the king as he does. On further reflection he sees what may be perceived as a conflict between his trust in God and requesting military protection from the king, and so he refrains from the latter. It should be noted, however, that it seems such protection is not provided or even offered by Artaxerxes. If the king is unconcerned, Ezra's quandary seems more understandable. He might appear to have less faith in his own God than Artaxerxes has. Given his awareness of God's hand upon him, he chooses to rely on God for safety. He may also have felt that there was a specific promise to rely on. Isaiah 52:12 promises that those going out of Babylon carrying the Lord's vessels will have God himself as their protector.

8:24 *priests, namely, Sherebiah.* Many scholars agree that "namely" reflects an error in the transmission of the text and should instead be "and." Numbers 3:8, 31; 4:5–15 show that the priests were to handle the sacred objects and the Levites were to carry them on the journey through the wilderness. So both priests and Levites were necessary for the task on the trip from Babylon, and Ezra designates twelve priests and twelve Levites (Sherebiah, Hashabiah, and ten others; see Ezra 8:18–19) in particular.

8:28 *You as well as these articles are consecrated.* In effect, Ezra pronounces the priests and Levites, as well as the items they are carrying, holy. This gives them a status similar to that of the tabernacle personnel and furnishings on the wilderness journey from Egypt. The priests and Levites on Ezra's journey would likely not have been functioning as such in Babylon, so Ezra inducts them into these roles anew.

8:32 *we rested three days.* The three-day rest after arriving at Jerusalem may correspond to the three-day rest at the end of the exodus journey before crossing the Jordan (Josh. 3:2).

8:35 *Then the exiles who had returned from captivity sacrificed.* The narrative changes here from first person to third person, and the effect of the change is to shift focus from Ezra and the temple personnel to the whole group that returned and their representation of the entire nation of Israel. Most of the numbers of sacrificial animals are a multiple of twelve.

Just as the exodus from Egypt was intended to result in worship (e.g., Exod. 7:16; 15:17), so the present journey represents travel to the land of promise resulting in worship.

8:36 *gave assistance to the people and to the house of God.* The response of the surrounding people is quite different here compared to Ezra 3–5. Whereas in the earlier narrative the neighboring peoples and officials sought to interfere with work on the temple and discourage the returnees, this time the edict that

God prompted from Artaxerxes precludes opposition from even beginning and, in fact, elicits helpful support. The accomplishment of God's purposes seems to humans to come more smoothly at some times than at others.

Theological Insights

Throughout Ezra 8, Ezra and ultimately the returnees as a whole take care to follow the expectations God has for his restored people. Among other things, Ezra carefully structures the trip from Babylon to Jerusalem to conform to the pattern of the original exodus from Egypt. In so doing, he seeks to honor God's intent to restore Israel from exile in a way recognizably similar to the way he redeemed their ancestors as described in Exodus.

When Ezra notes that no Levites are present among the group to carry the articles intended for temple use, he delays departing and sends carefully chosen men with scripted instructions to persuade some Levites to join them. With respect to the safety of the group as they travel without military protection through areas where they may encounter thieves, Ezra chooses to depend on God rather than troops from the king and proclaims a fast to pray for protection. He assigns the temple money and articles to the care of the priests and Levites, appointing twelve of each to this duty as a way of identifying with Israel of old. He helps ensure proper stewardship of God's holy belongings by scrupulously measuring and counting the items at both beginning and end of the journey (the Hebrew verb meaning "to weigh" occurs in vv. 25, 26, 29, 30, 33, 34). He even rests three days on arrival at their destination in Palestine, just as Joshua did. Finally, the group as a whole identifies itself as God's covenant people Israel through the number and type of sacrifices they offer.

God's response to this careful attention to his will is to provide them with a safe and successful return. He brings them capable Levites (v. 18). He gives them a safe journey (vv. 23, 31). All the donated items are accounted for in Jerusalem (v. 34). The king's orders result in assistance from the government officials.

The unmistakable lesson is that God provides at every step of the way as his people seek the blessings he has promised according to his terms.

Teaching the Text

The pattern that Ezra followed for the return from Babylon was appropriate for his circumstances and time in history. Believers today have patterns to follow that are connected to God's saving acts in the Old Testament but modified and transformed by the life, death, and resurrection of Christ. Just as Ezra was careful to follow the pattern set out for him, so believers today need to be equally conscientious, for redemption occurs on God's terms.

Ezra knew from Scripture that the restoration of Israel would be similar to the exodus from Egypt. Christians know that their salvation comes through following the pattern set forth by Christ. The Lord's Supper, although not in and of itself conveying salvation, points to the death of Christ on behalf of sinners. By eating the bread and drinking the wine, participants symbolize their reception, by faith, of the life Christ's sacrifice imparts. Similarly baptism reflects the death and resurrection of Christ. One who is baptized professes death with Christ to his own selfish ways and the values of the present world and "resurrection" to new life lived for God by Christ's power. The life and death of Christ provide the pattern for the believer to follow in order to experience the redemption Christ brought. Someday believers will even participate in Christ's physical resurrection. The life of Christ, then, which was foreshadowed in numerous ways by God's acts in the exodus and postexilic restoration, takes precedence for modern Christians.

Ezra's reliance on God through prayer and fasting instead of on soldiers provided by the king reflects not so much a connection with the exodus as a timeless principle that it is better to trust in God than in the might of earthly rulers. This is consistent with a theme that runs throughout Ezra-Nehemiah, that it is God who is at work for the benefit of his people, even when that benefit comes through earthly rulers. The trust of God's people is rightly placed only when it is in God himself and not primarily in human power. The specific actions Christians take will depend on the details of their situations, and sometimes the assistance of secular authorities may be accepted, as seen in Ezra 1–6, and even when Ezra himself accepts the king's donations in Ezra 7. The point is not to try to make it through all dangerous situations by prayer alone; the point is to keep faith in God primary and express that faith in action.

Ezra's careful handling of the temple materials is also exemplary. The modern "temple," the church as the body of Christ (Eph. 2:21–22), still deals with money, and it is important that those in leadership handle it with the kind of transparency and honesty that Ezra displayed, ensuring that it is used for God's purposes.

When God's people follow the patterns he has set out for them, they can be confident that he will provide all that is needed to bring about his redemption in their lives.

Illustrating the Text

Christ is our pattern for faith and life.

Object Lesson: Invite a tailor or seamstress from among your listeners to bring a bolt of cloth and a sewing pattern up front. Interview them and tease out the way a pattern works. (It may seem a little obvious, but don't let that stop you from drawing out the information for people to hear. The simplicity is part of the point!) The simple effectiveness of a pattern is remarkable; one needn't know the measurements of the pattern or be able to draw it oneself. One simply needs to pin it onto a piece of cloth and cut it out. The pattern does its work by being joined to the cloth and then marking what needs to be removed and what can remain until the cloth matches it perfectly. In the same way, Christ serves as our pattern for faith and life when we are joined to him; his example marks the boundary between what must be removed from us and what may remain. Being patterned after him restores the full image of God with which men and women were endowed at creation.

It is better to trust in God than in earthly might.

Testimony: Interview someone from your congregation who has experienced miraculous healing after doctors indicated they had no hope for a cure. Invite the person to explain how relying on human medicine was helpful but, in this case, failed to heal. In contrast, ask them to tell what happened when God's power intervened and how his divine power brought about a result that human strength could not.

Classic Sermon: In 1619, before the Pilgrims left Leiden to sail on the Mayflower, John Robinson preached a sermon on Ezra 8:21. In it, he encouraged them to trust God for safety as they were embarking on a voyage that they believed to be accomplishing the very will of God.

Worship Tradition / Liturgy: Many of your listeners may be familiar with the *votum* from liturgical tradition. Most often, the *votum* is from Psalm 124:8, which says, "Our help is in the name of the LORD, the Maker of heaven and earth." This short little verse has begun Christian worship for centuries, reminding us that it is better to trust in God for help and salvation than in any earthly power or might.

How we handle God's money matters.

Church Government: Point out that one needn't look too far to see examples of how embezzlement, carelessness, and fraud have ruined the reputations of nonprofits and religious organizations. Financial misconduct in church not only discredits the perpetrator's ministry; it harms and degrades the reputation of the whole faith. With this in mind, take this opportunity to mention some of the financial controls, accountability procedures, and boundaries your organization observes to ensure that gifts consecrated to God are handled with the highest standard of ethics possible. If you have many unbelievers or new believers present, you may also want to explain the concept of how generous giving is related to God's material blessing (2 Cor. 9:6–12).

Ezra Prays about the Sin of the Israelite Community

Big Idea

Confession of sin to God, accompanied by appropriate remorse, is essential in order to experience his promised restoration.

Key Themes

- God's covenant with Israel included expressing faithfulness to him through their family life.
- Disobeying God's expectations puts the Judeans at risk of being destroyed instead of experiencing the completion of the restoration he has promised.
- Ezra displays the appropriate response to the awareness of sin by confessing it to God with deep remorse.

Understanding the Text

The Text in Context

After God uses the Persian kings to overcome the obstacles faced by the returned exiles in Ezra 1–6 so they can complete the temple, and after the generous support and cooperation from the Persian authorities in Ezra 7–8, the process of restoration after exile appears to be gaining momentum. The reader expects Ezra to further this by implementing God's law in Judea as Artaxerxes has instructed him to.

Surprisingly, the most serious crisis so far occurs at this point. Whereas previous obstacles have been created by the surrounding peoples opposing the Jerusalem temple reconstruction, this crisis arises from among the Jews themselves, as some of them marry non-Israelite women. Recognizing the threat this poses to the restoration process, Ezra responds first by making humble confession of the sin to God. His actions set in motion a wider response among the people that is described in Ezra 10. Although there is no mention of Ezra teaching the law at this point, his actions strive to prompt Israel to observe it (compare Ezra 7:26).

Interpretive Insights

9:1 *have not kept themselves separate from the neighboring peoples.* The people allowed to participate in the Passover celebration at the dedication of the rebuilt temple in Ezra 6:21 include all those who have "separated themselves from the unclean practices of their Gentile neighbors in order to seek the LORD, the God of Israel." This potentially includes people not of Israelite descent who have made a decision to worship Yahweh alone according to his covenant with Israel. In Ezra 9:1 the leaders report to Ezra the opposite case, in which people of Israelite descent have married Gentiles who are not worshipers of Yahweh, thereby compromising their commitment to the covenant. In addition, "neighboring peoples" is the same Hebrew phrase as "peoples around them" in Ezra 3:3, used to describe the enemies of the returned exiles. In Ezra 9:14 the same group is designated "peoples who commit such detestable practices," emphasizing that the problem has to do with their attitude toward God and his wishes. The point is that a number from the Israelite community have effectively joined those who oppose God's purposes.

detestable practices, like those of the . . . Amorites. The first four and the last of the peoples listed here probably no longer existed in the postexilic period. This detail highlights the fact that the major concern was not race or ethnicity but religious practices contrary to faith in Yahweh.

When the Israelites first journeyed to the promised land after the exodus from Egypt, God commanded them not to intermarry with the surrounding peoples, specifically because the latter worshiped other gods and would likely turn the Israelites away from worshiping the true God (Exod. 34:11–16; Deut. 7:1–4). The surrounding peoples in that context included those listed in Ezra 9:1. The point of mentioning them in Ezra, then, is to make the connection with the situation at the time of the exodus, implying that marrying foreigners continues to be as it was previously, and for the same reason, namely, the danger of syncretism or apostasy.

9:2 *holy race.* The Hebrew phrase is better translated "holy seed." The descendants of Abraham through Jacob were chosen by God to be a holy people for him (Exod. 19:6). The intent was that they would function like priests mediating between God and other nations (Deut. 4:5–8). The purpose was for other nations to be drawn to a relationship with the true God like the one Israel possessed. In order to achieve this, Israel needed to remain a nation distinct from other peoples, maintaining the beliefs and practices given to them by God.

9:3 *I tore . . . appalled.* Tearing clothes, pulling out one's hair, and sitting in silence were all behaviors associated with mourning in Israelite culture. Ezra recognizes that the community deserves destruction by God because of the intermarriages, and he demonstrates his anticipation of that result. His mourning is sincere, but by carrying it out in public he also shows the community how it should begin to respond to the situation. Ezra leads by example.

9:6 *our sins.* The extent of Ezra's identification with those who have married foreign women is conditioned by the corporate nature of Israel's covenant with God. In Joshua 7, for example, Achan takes for himself some of the items to be set apart for God. As a result, Israel is unable to defeat Ai in battle. God explains to Joshua that it is because "Israel has sinned" (Josh. 7:11). Later in its history, the whole nation experiences exile because of disobedience, although there are faithful people among them, such as the prophets. While the New Testament continues to emphasize that the actions of individuals within the body of the church have important implications for the whole, there is a shift in the direction of individual responsibility before God. Compare, for example, the letters to the churches in Revelation 2–3, each of which ends with a promise "to the one who is victorious"—that is, the one who trusts in and remains faithful to Jesus despite suffering.

9:8 *the Lord our God.* The shift from second to third person in reference to God is an indication that Ezra intends his prayer to be heard by those around him as much as by God himself. Davies calls this a "sermon-prayer."[1] Ezra is modeling the appropriate response for the community, implicitly inviting them to join him.

brief moment . . . remnant . . . firm place . . . light . . . little relief. The language used by Ezra in this verse emphasizes the provisional nature of the restoration up to this point. The "brief moment" refers to the eighty years since Cyrus's edict allowing the Jews to return and rebuild the temple. It seems short compared to the longer preceding period of oppression by Assyrians and Babylonians. In Ezra's mind the promised restoration has not yet been underway long.

The Hebrew word translated "remnant" is an important word used by the Old Testament prophets to refer to those who would survive the exile and experience God's restoration of Israel. Although thousands had returned to Israel, many more had been killed at the hands of the Assyrians and Babylonians. The survivors were expected to return to faith in God and function as his holy people (e.g., Isa. 10:20–21).

The translation "a foothold," in the NIV margin, is better than "a firm place." The Hebrew word actually means "tent peg." It could allude to how nomads would stake a claim to a plot of land for the tents of their families. Ezra sees the rebuilt temple in Jerusalem as an important prerequisite for the full restoration of Israel.

"Gives light to our eyes" is actually "makes our eyes brighten." It refers to the change in the appearance of one's eyes when they begin to feel a little stronger, as happened with Jonathan's eyes in 1 Samuel 14:27.

Ezra makes a pointed comparison between the present condition of the community and the slavery of the ancestors in Egypt by stating that they are in bondage. The Hebrew word he uses appears also in Nehemiah 9:17 to refer to the slavery in Egypt. Although the ancestors were released from this bondage by the exodus, Ezra's community has experienced only a little reviving.

This verse is a clear statement that the present situation is seen as the beginning of restoration, with much more expected that has not yet come. The accomplishments of Ezra 1–6 and the lavish support of Ezra 7 are just a start.

9:9 *a wall.* The Hebrew word for "wall" is used metaphorically, referring to God's protection in reestablishing the community in Palestine. Psalm 80:12 and Isaiah 5:5 use it to picture God removing his protection of Israel in order to punish them. The literal sense of the word refers to fences or hedges that were often temporary.

9:15 *you are righteous.* Ezra acknowledges that God has been just in punishing Israel for its sin and in nevertheless leaving them a remnant as he had promised. He also acknowledges that God would be just in destroying the remnant if they continue to be unfaithful to him.

Theological Insights

Ezra's prayerful response to the leaders' indictment of the people reflects a key aspect of God's nature. God is both just, therefore judging sin, and merciful, therefore forgiving sin. Although these attributes may seem to conflict, they are both continually relevant to the human situation.

Ezra's awareness of the sin in the community leads him to confess it before God. He is acutely aware that they cannot presume upon God's mercy. Although God has shown mercy in leaving a remnant among the Israelites, the strong possibility exists that he will bring their survival as a people to an end if they continue to rebel against him. At the same time, the fact that God has shown mercy in allowing the remnant to survive and return to the promised land means that he may be open to forgiving them. If Ezra believed that judgment was inevitable, there would be no point in praying at all.

When God's people commit sin, they must recognize its seriousness before God and how it grieves and angers him. But they can also have hope that true contrition will lead to forgiveness. That is why repentance has an indispensable role in the ongoing relationship of God's people with their God.

Teaching the Text

The time and energy spent by Ezra to express remorse over the community's sin strike many modern readers as strange or at least excessive. While his actions were certainly ritualistic, the point of the ritual was to focus attention on the awful result of sin and outwardly express a remorseful inner attitude toward it. It is not necessary to adopt the stylized penitential practices of some groups, but it is necessary to have genuine contrition for sin. Our current culture tends toward an approach to repentance that advocates "saying sorry" to God and trying (at least for a while) not to repeat the particular sin. The truth is that without an understanding of the seriousness of sin that affects us on an emotional level, we are unlikely to be truly repentant and may be unable to receive full reconciliation with God.

The experience of living between partial and complete fulfillment of God's promises is another theme that resonates with believers today. Ezra recognizes ways in which God's restoration has already begun to occur for the returned exiles, but his knowledge of Scripture makes him aware that there is still much more to come. It is interesting that while confessing sin, he does not presume that somehow judgment will be averted and the community will necessarily receive God's blessing, even though a case could be made from the prophets that this is a sure thing. Instead, he holds open the possibility that persistence in unfaithfulness will result in destruction. It is similarly wise for believers today not to jump to the conclusion that just because they have "tasted the heavenly gift" (Heb. 6:4), there is no danger to fear from persisting in sin (e.g., Heb. 3:7–19).

The commitment to Christ required of a believer today is no less than the commitment to God required of an Israelite in the Old Testament. Now as then this commitment has implications for every part of life, including the choice of a marriage partner. In the Old Testament, the nation of Israel represented the people of God. In the New Testament, it is the church, defined as those who believe in Christ, who are God's people; biological descent and ethnicity are no longer factors (Acts 15). But the principle is repeated that marriage outside God's family is to be avoided (2 Cor. 6:14–18; 1 Cor. 7:39). Unfortunately, this is often overlooked by Christians today. In anticipation of Ezra 10, however, it should be noted that the New Testament does not recommend that a believer divorce an unbelieving spouse (1 Cor. 7:12–15).

Sadly, this passage has been misused by many to claim that God wants to preserve purity among what they see as various human races. They imply, for example, that marriage between people of European and African ancestry is wrong. This completely misses the point that the reason for forbidding intermarriage with the nations surrounding Israel was to avoid idolatry. As mentioned above, the New Testament repeats this principle and shows no misgivings about interracial marriage.

Illustrating the Text

Reconciliation and restoration only happen after real repentance.

Object Lesson: Bring a padlock or a safe to the front. It should be one that has a rotary dial or some other type that uses a numerical combination. Even a cell phone with an access PIN would work. Invite a volunteer to the front and tell them that their job is to open the lock. Then, give them the digits of the combination, *but do so out of order*. Simply say, "The numbers of the combination/PIN are ___, ___, and ___." They will most likely assume that you gave the digits in order and proceed to fail repeatedly. They may ask you to repeat the numbers. Give them back in a different *incorrect* order. Eventually, the volunteer will catch on and realize the order is wrong. Once they do, give them the proper order and let them succeed. Explain to your listeners that the various works of God belong in their God-ordained order. When it comes to healing relationships, knowing that repentance, reconciliation, and restoration are all good gifts is not enough to unlock healing. They need to be put in their proper order, and repentance always comes first. We can never put things back together between people until they turn away from sin and back toward God.

We have only just begun in our call to hate sin and flee from its effects.

Popular Saying: Many listeners will be familiar with the popular saying "Moderation in all things." This is a great concept when it comes to a balanced diet, work versus play, and so on, but it doesn't apply to everything. Hating sin, for example, is something in which we are to show *no* moderation. We are to hate it and flee from it with zeal and passion that will make us feel and look excessive and weird when compared to our past selves and our culture. If we are not feeling immoderate and excessive in our quest to be free of sin, we must press further.

Quote: **John Paul Jones.** Many are familiar with the military quote "I have not yet begun to fight!" Few will recall who said it. It was the reply of American captain John Paul Jones as he was asked to surrender during a battle with a British frigate off the northern coast of England in 1779, during the height of the American Revolutionary War. His reply showed defiance, courage, and undaunted resistance. When it comes to our pursuit of holiness, the devil often presses us to dial down our efforts or even surrender. May we cry with courage, "I have not yet begun to fight!"

Whom we love and marry affects our beliefs.

Film: In James Cameron's movie *Avatar* (2009), the protagonist, Jake Sully, finds himself in a quandary. Although he has been tasked with finding information that will enable his employer to gain access to a valuable mineral on the moon Pandora, he soon learns that his employer's plans will endanger the way of life of a group of human-like beings, the Na'vi, who live there. Jake meets and falls in love with a female Na'vi, Neytiri, and as the story progresses, it becomes clear that his attachment to her is an important factor in his increasing sympathy for the Na'vi's welfare. He is eventually initiated into the tribe and marries Neytiri. The differences between Jake's employer and the Na'vi develop to the point where it becomes clear that he will have to choose to support one or the other. By then the audience expects that he will support his wife's people, which he does, even praying to the goddess they worship. Although it is science fiction, we as viewers recognize that the effect his romantic attachment has on his beliefs and commitments is realistic.

The Judeans Decide to Send Away Their Foreign Wives

Big Idea
God's people must deal thoroughly with sin in order to experience his promised restoration.

Key Themes
- The initiative to send away the foreign wives comes from a layman.
- The community treats the mixed marriages as a serious threat to their well-being.
- Virtually the entire community agrees to discontinue the mixed marriages.

Understanding the Text

The Text in Context

After the account of the initial resettlement of the exiles and rebuilding of the temple in Ezra 1–6, Ezra 7–10 focuses on the mission of Ezra to further the postexilic restoration, especially by ensuring that the returnees observe God's law. In Ezra 9 the Judean leaders tell Ezra that some of the men have disobeyed God by marrying non-Israelite women. Ezra mourns this as potentially ending the restoration. In Ezra 10 the Judeans decide that the mixed marriages should be terminated so that the community can be faithful to their covenant with God.

The result is in line with Ezra's mission, since the community's behavior has been conformed to God's law. Also, by reversing their sinful behavior, the community has overcome the latest obstacle to complete restoration. This one was of their own creation, whereas previous obstacles consisted of opposition from outside the community. The way is now open for fulfillment of the restoration promises to continue.

Historical and Cultural Background

Modern readers often feel that the actions of the community toward the foreign wives and their children in this passage are heartless. But while divorce and separation of family members are always heartrending, it is helpful to realize that some contemporary associations with divorce probably did not apply at this time.

Marriage contracts discovered from this period often included terms in the event of a divorce, something like modern prenuptial contracts. Divorces seem to have been fairly common and executed without much bitter wrangling. In most cases the mothers and children would have found a stable living environment with extended family. There would also be the possibility of remarriage. The contemporary single-parent scenario was virtually unheard of. Since the poorest people in the community do not appear in the list of those with foreign wives, these marriages were probably contracted among the upper socioeconomic classes. Once again, this does not ease the severing of emotional ties, but it does suggest that the women and children expelled by the Judeans may not have faced extreme financial hardship.

Interpretive Insights

10:3 *let us make a covenant.* Although Ezra is sent to teach the law to any who do not know it (Ezra 7:25), the narrative does not report any such activity in the four months after his arrival (compare Ezra 7:9 and 10:9). Thus, Shekaniah appears to make his suggestion based on his own understanding of the law and the prophetic promises of restoration. His choice of words is suggestive: by making a covenant (with each other) in God's presence to bring their behavior in line with God's law, they will, in effect, be renewing their commitment to the covenant God made with them at Sinai.

Although it is obviously discouraging that some members of the community have committed this sin, it is surely a good sign that one from among the people takes the initiative to correct the problem and that the broader leadership present in the land before Ezra's arrival support it. This is a much different scenario from that of previous covenant renewals in the Old Testament, in which a single leader, such as Moses or a king, took all the initiative. In this context, Ezra only mourns and prays (Ezra 9; 10:1, 6), administers an oath (10:5; he is the appropriate person to do this, consistent with the authority given to him by the king), exhorts the community according to their previous decision (10:10–11), and chooses a committee to make judgments (10:16). The identification of the problem (9:1–2) and the initiative and proposal to solve it (10:2–4, 12–14) come from others.

The implication is that, while not yet perfect, there is a greater desire among the postexilic Judean community to obey God's law than there was among preexilic Israel and Judah. The promise of a new covenant seems closer to realization (compare Jer. 31:31–34), which may be the basis for Shekaniah's hope (Ezra 10:2).

according to the law. There is no requirement in the law to divorce foreign wives or send away their children. But Deuteronomy 24:1–4 allows divorce if a man finds "something indecent" about his wife. Under the circumstances, the community seems to feel that the threat of the introduction of idolatrous practices qualifies as an indecency.

In the ancient Near East it was common for divorced wives to have custody of their children, which explains why they are sent away as well.

10:8 *forfeit.* The Hebrew word used here usually refers to something being given over irrevocably to God, implying either destruction or exclusive use for temple purposes (e.g., Lev. 27:21). Its presence here is somewhat surprising and connects with the story of Achan in Joshua 7. Because of his unfaithfulness to God (compare Josh. 7:1 and, e.g., Ezra 10:2, which use the same verb for "to be unfaithful"), Achan and his possessions were given over to God by destruction. The Judeans have likewise been unfaithful to God, and individuals stand to lose their possessions and be cut off from the community as a result. The way in which they will be removed from the community is less harsh than in Achan's case, but the punishment is appropriate in that the individual has not separated from the ungodly peoples and will now be separated from God's people.

There is also a further parallel to the Achan event. Just as Achan's unfaithfulness shortly after entering the promised land put the inheritance of Canaan at risk for all Israel, so the unfaithfulness of intermarriage shortly after the return to Canaan puts the restoration at risk. The threat of excommunication is extended even to those who will not attend the meeting to deal with the situation.

10:11 *honor the* LORD. The meaning is to honor God by agreeing that his judgment in the matter is right, thereby effectively confessing one's sin. A very similar expression is used in Joshua 7:19, strengthening the connection between the two passages. Confession of sin is a necessary step in dealing with it appropriately.

10:44 *and some of them . . . these wives.* The Hebrew in the final half verse of the chapter is extremely difficult to understand. The NIV gives as good a guess as any translation, but it is impossible to be sure what was meant, or, if the text has been corrupted in transmission, how it originally read.

Thus, it is possible that, although the community is virtually unanimous in agreeing to divorce all foreign wives, the account ends with no clear statement that they do so, contributing to the ambiguity noted above concerning the fulfillment status of the new-covenant promise.

Theological Insights

The exclusive nature of the relationship God desires to have with his people is given stark expression in this passage. The Judean men who have married foreign women must choose between God and their wives. Being faithful to God, honoring him, and avoiding his anger require a willingness to place more importance on one's relationship with him than on any other relationship.

Looked at in the context of contemporary Western culture, this can make God seem unreasonably demanding, selfish, and even cruel. In response it should be pointed out that it is inappropriate to judge God as though he were merely another human being, albeit an extraordinary one. As God he is a being far above humans and deserving of complete devotion from his creatures in a way not applicable to any other entity in existence. The Judean community assumes, however, and Scripture elsewhere also makes clear, that God is ultimately the only source of joy and blessing in life. To the extent that humans compromise their relationship with him, they compromise their prospects for true fulfillment and satisfaction, regardless of how tempting alternatives may seem. Complete faithfulness to God, then, is not only pleasing to him; it is good for people.

While it is perhaps not difficult to see the logic of this, it can be difficult to remain enthusiastic about it when faced with the realities of life. The necessity of backtracking on the life-altering decision of marriage, faced by the Judean men in this chapter, illustrates how gut-wrenching faithfulness to God can be. Yet it is finally for our good.

Teaching the Text

It is easy to lose the focus of this passage if distracted by the divorce issue. The New Testament advises that even if a believer disobediently chooses to marry an unbeliever (2 Cor. 6:14–18), the believer should not divorce their spouse but should try to win them over with a godly lifestyle (1 Cor. 7:12–16; 1 Pet. 3:1–2). This passage must be put in its Old Testament context, in which nationality was a defining characteristic of God's covenant people: they were Israelites. Therefore, marrying outside Israel constituted unfaithfulness to God and his covenant, and since divorce was permitted, it was a possible remedy.

The real point of the passage concerns the danger presented by unfaithfulness to God and the urgency to prevent such a state from enduring. It is easy for Christians to become inappropriately comfortable with the awareness of sin in their lives, thinking that God will ultimately forgive everyone who has made a profession of faith in Jesus. It is important to remember that New Testament teaching is based on the belief that Christ ushered in the fulfillment of the new covenant as prophesied in Jeremiah 31:31–34 (Heb. 8:6–13; 10:15–18; Luke 22:20). This new covenant was to be characterized by God's people having a deep desire to obey him. The New Testament consistently affirms this expectation and warns of serious consequences for those who do not practice obedience to God (e.g., Heb. 3:13; 1 John 2:11; 3:8, 15; Eph. 5:5). Without debating "eternal security," it can at least be said that believers who persist in sin are severely limiting their experience of the effects of salvation.

Inspired by the vision of the pure body that Christ desires it to be, the church should use its influence to move its members in the direction of holiness and righteousness. It is possible that there was a shortage of women available for marriage within the Judean community and that there were distinct social and economic advantages to be gained by marrying some of the foreign women. Nevertheless, the Judean community threatened their members with expulsion if they would not deal thoroughly with known sin. A similar approach was ultimately advocated by Jesus and Paul (Matt. 18:15–17; 1 Cor. 5:13). Of course, there are prior steps to be taken in hopes of rendering such drastic action unnecessary, and there is room for discussion about what removing a believer from the church entails. But the point is that the church owes it to the body as a whole and to the specific individuals involved in sin to work together to use its influence to encourage obedience to God and discourage disobedience, even if disobedience seems to provide some cultural advantages.

When God's people deal thoroughly with the sin in their lives, the sacrifice of Christ (foreshadowed by the ram given for a guilt offering, Ezra 10:19) takes away their guilt and extends to them the full fellowship of the family of God.

Illustrating the Text

We must be willing to adjust our lives to match God's instructions.

Human Experience: Invite your listeners to think of a time when they bought something or were given it as a gift, but the seller or giver had lots of strong opinions about how they should use it. Perhaps a grandparent gave a grandchild a cherished possession but then said, "Let's just keep it at my house to be sure it's safe," or a homeowner sold a house but made the buyer feel pressure not to alter it. In such cases, the buyer/recipient might rightly wonder if the seller/giver really understands the idea of personal property and ownership. Point out that Christ has purchased his people with his own precious blood. We are his, bought and paid for. We have no right to say, "Thanks for buying back my life from the power of sin and death and hell, but I think I'll just keep managing it for now to keep it safe." Nor can we say, "Thanks for saving me and my household from certain destruction—but please don't rearrange anything or move around the furniture of our lives." Christ owns us. We are his and can be used however he sees fit for his glory. We must adjust to him.

Holiness matters; it isn't just an abstraction.

Medicine: Invite your listeners to think of a surgical room in a hospital. Use words or pictures, but point out the many steps taken to ensure a sterile and clean environment. Every aspect of the room—nonporous surfaces, clothing, hands, instruments and tools, and even the temperature and purity of the air itself—is arranged to keep infectious diseases and bacteria away from the patient. Ask your listeners: If you or your loved one is the one on the table being cut open, do you care if the surgeon washes his or her hands? Are you OK with the nurses coming straight from garden work or taking out the garbage? Thus, cleanliness is not an abstraction in surgery—it matters. In the same way, keeping our lives and witness free from the infection of sin is not abstraction—it truly matters for spiritual health.

Church discipline is essential to the purity of the church.

Church Governance: This would be a great time for your church to explain how you handle restorative church discipline. Make available any bylaws, handbooks, or policies that explain how refusal to conform with biblical standards for morality and conduct is to be addressed between laypersons, between leaders and staff, and even between your congregation and its denomination.

Take time to point out that *everyone* in the church is accountable directly to Christ, and yet we are *also* all accountable to the authority and order his Word establishes in the home, in the church, and even human governments. Assure them that no one is above the law, and that the law of love will always guide church discipline at your church.

Christian Book: *Manual of Church Order*, by John L. Dagg. In this book,[1] written over 150 years ago, Dagg asserts that "when discipline leaves a church, Christ goes with it."[2] When the church fails to discipline unrepentant sin as part of its effort to establish true discipleship, it utterly undermines its own witness, its preaching, and its power in the Spirit.

Testimony: It might be very powerful to have a loving testimony from someone about the cost of an unevenly yoked marriage between a believer and an unbeliever. The ideal candidate would be a couple that started that way and then became evenly yoked through conversion; they could offer a "before-and-after" without recrimination and bitterness. Use video to ensure the ability to edit properly and ensure good boundaries. (Be careful not to invite a testimony that will encourage "missionary dating," bring division, or drag the congregation into the bitterness of a divorce battle. This could be challenging and redemptive if you choose your testimonial with discernment.)

Nehemiah Prays for God to Help Him Overcome Jerusalem's Trouble

Big Idea

God's people should ask him to continue his promised work of restoration and to enable them to help.

Key Themes

- Nehemiah learns that the state of Jerusalem's walls reflects a major outstanding need in the restoration of Israel.
- He prays about the restoration on the basis of God's promises in Scripture.
- He asks God for success in the role he anticipates playing.

Understanding the Text

The Text in Context

The ending of Ezra 10 does not strike the reader as completely satisfactory. Although there is every indication that the members of the Judean community who have married foreign wives intend to divorce them, the text stops just short of clearly saying that they do so. There is no community celebration or report of success as there is in previous episodes (Ezra 3:10–11; 6:16). It is not at all clear what the ultimate effects of the community meeting in Jerusalem are. It seems the goal of a restored community observing God's law may not have been fully achieved.

In Nehemiah 1, the narrative jumps ahead about thirteen years. Although Ezra 1–8 reports the rebuilding of and provision for the Jerusalem temple, the city's wall is in ruin. This may still be due in part to the destruction done by the Babylonians in 586 BC, but it is likely that the decree of Artaxerxes to stop rebuilding the wall has also played a part (Ezra 4:12, 21–23). This means both that the wall needs extensive repair and that repairing it is prohibited.

The narrative so far has highlighted a connection between the Judeans' unfaithfulness to God and their experience of destruction and shame (Ezra 5:12; 9:7). Nehemiah makes the same connection as he responds to the news about Jerusalem's wall with a prayer of confession of Israel's unfaithfulness to God. His expectations are likely conditioned by prophecies implying that Jerusalem's wall will be rebuilt as part of Israel's restoration (e.g., Jer. 31:38; 33:7; Amos 9:14) and by statements such as 2 Chronicles 6:36–39, which asks God to forgive his people if they confess their sin when praying in exile. Thus, Nehemiah confesses Israel's sin so that God will forgive their unfaithfulness and continue the restoration by restoring Jerusalem's wall.

At the very end of his prayer, Nehemiah asks for God to give him personal success and reveals that he is the king's cupbearer. How this relates to the rest of his prayer is clearly understood only in the following chapter.

Historical and Cultural Background

For a city to be without a good wall on an ongoing basis was unthinkable in the ancient Near East, since it was actually the principal element in a city's defense. If the wall was broken down, the city was vulnerable to attack, and this was a source of shame to the city's residents.

This explains Nehemiah's reaction when he hears about the state of Jerusalem's wall. The possibility of further attack and destruction and the associated shame experienced by the Judeans were the opposite of the peace and security associated with restoration. Thus, Nehemiah perceives a need for further action by God to fulfill his promises.

Interpretive Insights

1:2 *the Jewish remnant.* This refers to the same group the narrative has been following in Ezra—namely, those Judeans who returned from exile to Judea and all those who have joined them by committing themselves to follow the terms of God's covenant with Israel (Ezra 6:21). They are the expected recipients of God's blessings associated with restoration (see, e.g., Isa. 10:20–22). Therefore, Nehemiah is able to gauge the progress of restoration by observing their situation.

Jerusalem. As the site of God's temple, Jerusalem became the focal point for Israelite aspirations for prosperity and well-being in the preexilic period, and this carried over into the postexilic period as well (Pss. 137:5–6; 122:6–9). Thus, the status of Jerusalem is particularly important to Nehemiah for understanding the progress of the restoration.

1:4 *I mourned and fasted and prayed.* In Ezra 10, Ezra fasts while mourning over the sin and resulting judgment of his people, whereas in Ezra 8, Ezra's fasting reflects complete dependence on God to provide needed safety on a long and dangerous journey. Nehemiah's fasting combines these purposes: he, too, mourns Israel's sin and resulting judgment, and he depends on God to provide a solution to the predicament of the ruined wall, which is itself a result of God's judgment.

1:8 *the instruction you gave . . . Moses.* The ideas and many of the phrases in verses 8–9 come from Deuteronomy 30:1–5, and these themes are also present in other prophecies of restoration, including Jeremiah 31:31–34 and Zechariah 1:2–6. God's promises in Scripture shape Nehemiah's requests and his expectation of what God may do in the present situation, and they also bolster his confidence that there will be restoration after judgment and repentance.

1:9 *return to me.* Keeping God's commands is given prominence in this prayer, but standing behind that is the idea of being in a personal relationship with God. When Israel disobeyed him, it was a symptom of turning away from that relationship. On the other hand, those committed to the relationship experience the covenant blessings. Returning to God is a metaphor for seeking God in relationship again.

and bring them to the place . . . for my Name. By making direct allusion to Deuteronomy 30, Nehemiah implies the teaching it contains, as well as the teaching of similar prophecies elsewhere in the Old Testament, that God will bring his people back from all the nations where he has scattered them. So although some Judeans have already returned from exile to Jerusalem, Nehemiah anticipates that this gathering and return is not yet complete. Also, the prophecies of return indicate that restoration has much more to it than a simple movement from the place of exile to Palestine, including a life of peace and confidence for God's people (e.g., Jer. 30:10). That is why he prays as he does, even though it could be argued that this specific promise has already been fulfilled.

The place where God chose to put his name, which means the place where he chose to have a temple built as his dwelling, was Jerusalem (1 Kings 11:13). Although some Judeans have physically returned to Jerusalem, their distress on account of the ruined wall (Neh. 1:3) and the fact that relatively few of them actually lived in Jerusalem (Neh. 7:4) make the situation less than satisfactory. Once again, Nehemiah prays as he does because he has reason to believe that God intends to improve their circumstances considerably.

1:11 *Give your servant success . . . I was cupbearer to the king.* Nehemiah apparently thinks there is some way that he can help the distressed situation in Jerusalem, but it will require intervention by God as Nehemiah deals with a specific man, who turns out to be the king of Persia. At the very end of the verse, he reveals that he is one of the king's cupbearers. Tasting the king's wine (to ensure it contained no poison) and often being assigned other duties such as managing financial accounts, cupbearers held a very important position in the kingdom. They had direct access to the king himself and had his confidence. Thus, they could be very influential.

Knowing this, we see Nehemiah's prayer take on another dimension of significance. Although he probably has some influence with the king, his first priority is to ask God for help. He is more confident of having favor with God as an Israelite with a repentant heart than of having favor with the king as his cupbearer.

It is also unusual that he refers to the king as "this man." In the context, though, it highlights the contrast between the power of God and the power of the king, who is a mere human being. Nehemiah demonstrates trust in God's love and power as being far greater than the favor or power of the most powerful king on earth. If Nehemiah receives any help from the king, it will be because God has answered his prayer.

Theological Insights

A number of the dynamics of relating to God are illustrated in this chapter. As has been evident throughout Ezra and can be seen in the rest of the Old Testament, God judges those who are unfaithful to him. He also promises to restore those who return to him and are willing to obey his instructions. Nehemiah draws on these truths in his prayer, but he also counts on God's willingness to use his great power in the process of restoration. Nehemiah recognizes that bringing the Judean community back to a position of respectability in the ancient Near East will require dramatic intervention by God, and God's promise to Moses motivates Nehemiah to trust that God will do so.

In addition to repentance, obedience to God's commands, and trusting in God's promises, however, the process of restoration also involves connecting with God in prayer and involvement in activities that will help bring the restoration about. Nehemiah does not ask God for anything that God has not already promised, but he does ask. And the end of his prayer reveals that he is already intending to help build the future that God desires for his people. He sees a specific and significant way he can contribute, but this too will require God's help.

God wants his people to trust him submissively, but he also wants them to talk directly to him and ask him about what they are trusting him for. He also wants them to dream creatively about how the abilities and opportunities he has given them might be leveraged to produce results that line up with his stated purposes.

Teaching the Text

The gap between Nehemiah's situation and the situation of modern believers presents a challenge when one teaches this text. The restoration Nehemiah was longing for and monitoring the progress of had primarily to do with the identifiable community of the descendants of Israel in Palestine. It involved their faith in God, expressed mainly through obedience to the Mosaic law, and the material prosperity and peace that God would give them. For believers today, God's covenant promises have more to do with the church throughout the world, not limited to any ethnic or cultural group, and involve faith in God that is expressed mainly through a personal relationship of trust in Jesus and the experience of God's spiritual blessings. It is important for God's people to monitor the spread of the gospel and the production of God's character and deeds in their lives more than the material blessings they receive. While they should still pray for physical needs to be met and be involved in meeting them, it is more important, for example, when a church building is destroyed, that the congregation continue to exhibit the character of Christ than that enough money is received to rebuild the building quickly. The concerns and prayers of believers must be adjusted to the priorities outlined in the New Testament.

The priority of prayer itself, however, has not changed. It is no less tempting today for Christians to place their trust in the power of political forces or money or technology or other things to realize God's purposes than it was for Nehemiah to place his trust in his influential position with the Persian king to see the wall of Jerusalem rebuilt. Yet he believed it was God alone who could bring to pass all the good that God intended for his people. Believers today need to follow his example and develop a deep conviction that only God himself can accomplish his will in the world.

When God's people adopt such a perspective, it becomes natural for them to place prayer at the top of the agenda and to adopt the attitude Nehemiah displays in his prayer. God should be recognized as all-powerful, loving, and faithful (Neh. 1:5). Those who pray should see themselves as God's humble servants (vv. 6, 10, 11), whom he has graciously redeemed (v. 10), and they should continue to appreciate how the fulfillment of God's purposes is linked to their own confession and repentance of sin. Christians stand in closest fellowship with God and are most effectively involved in his work when they turn away from disobedience and purify their love for God (e.g., Rev. 2:5; 3:3, 19).

Praying like this from the heart prepares the way for individual believers to see more clearly how they can be directly involved in God's work of fulfilling his promises to those he has called to be his people. They are then in a position to make such specific requests in faith (John 15:16).

Illustrating the Text

Believers should be invested in the story of Christ's church.

Popular Culture: Research and gather information on some current pop culture icons and trends. Of special interest would be any celebrity romances or breakups, sports teams headed for the playoffs, or royalty headed through life transitions. (Have some teens help you, if need be.) Ask your congregation for a show of hands: "How many of you have heard the name _____? How many of you were sad that he/she broke up with _____? Who is rooting for such-and-such a team? Do you think Princess _____'s baby will be a boy or a girl?" If you researched right, you will see many hands go up and down with these questions. Now ask something more obscure about the worldwide church or persecuted Christians: "How many think pastor _____ will get out of jail soon? Is there going to be an opening for preaching to the _____ tribe this decade?" Humbly suggest that we are more invested in the story of popular culture than the story of Christ's kingdom and we need to make it a high priority to learn about and pray for our brothers and sisters around the world.

Hymn Text: The great old hymn "I Love to Tell the Story"[1] speaks about the joy and wonder a believer should have in knowing salvation and the gospel. Consider reading it during the message or singing it during the service, especially the lyrics, "I love to tell the story, for those who know it best seem hungering and thirsting to hear it like the rest. And when, in scenes of glory, I sing the new, new song, 'twill be the old, old story that I have loved so long." Believers need to fall in love with the gospel story and never fall out of love with it.

Prayer changes things; it trumps all earthly advantages.

Games: Pick a card game or board game your listeners and you know well. Describe a hand of cards or token in the game that is unbeatable. (For example, a royal flush in poker, a lay-down hand in euchre, or a 300 in bowling.) Explain that prayer is an unbeatable play for the Christian; there is no earthly power or advantage that comes close. It is unbeatable not because it gives us magical powers but because it unites us in purpose and desire with the sovereign King of the universe.

Testimony: Have someone in your congregation who has experienced amazing answers and freedom in prayer share their experience. They can tell their story, pass on wisdom about prayer, and even lead the congregation in a time of intercession.

Don't use prayer as a last resort; humbly make it your first response.

TV: Many listeners will be familiar with *Power Rangers* and other shows where there is a formulaic battle with a transforming foe. The fight always starts small, and then the monster transforms into giant size, requiring the good guys to use giant robots to fight back. It looks like they will fail, until they pull out their most powerful weapon at the last minute. Many a fan has asked, "Why didn't they just use that weapon in the first place?" This cliché illustrates the ridiculous way many Christians approach prayer: they battle the problem in their own strength until it reaches epic proportions, and only then do they pull out their most powerful weapon as a last resort. Admonish your listeners not to pray like a Power Ranger fights but to instead use their best weapon first.

Applying the Text: Offer your listeners a time of response after the message in which they can pray immediately. Challenge them to plan a season of prayer and fasting over the issues in their lives and communities.

Nehemiah's Bold Request Is Granted

Big Idea

God supplies his people with what they need to accomplish his purposes when they act in faith that he will do so.

Key Themes

- Nehemiah finds himself in a dangerous situation.
- He responds by pursuing what he perceives God wants done.
- God supplies him with everything he needs to begin the task.

Understanding the Text

The Text in Context

After four months of mourning, fasting, and praying about the disgrace of Jerusalem's ruined wall, Nehemiah receives an answer from God. Having understood that the promised restoration of Israel is under way, as evidenced by the Judean remnant reinhabiting Judea (Neh. 1:2–3), he has confessed sin on behalf of his people so that God's promises may move further toward fulfillment. The example of his prayers over that period ends with a hint that he expects to be directly involved in God's action (Neh. 1:11) and that it will also involve his own interaction with the Persian king, Artaxerxes, whom he serves as cupbearer and whose earlier decree contributed to Jerusalem's hardship (Ezra 4:17–23).

In Nehemiah 2:1–8 God's answer comes through an encounter Nehemiah has with the king in the course of his duties. Nehemiah is encouraged that God is providing for him, and he receives everything he needs to begin to address the problems in Jerusalem. The next episode describes what he encounters when he actually arrives there.

Interpretive Insights

2:1 *the month of Nisan.* During the four months between the time when Nehemiah heard of Jerusalem's condition and the time of this episode, the king may have been at one of the other royal residences, or he may have been served by another cupbearer. Even if Nehemiah were serving him all this time, he did not perceive an opportune moment for bringing up his concern.

2:2 *Why does your face look so sad . . . ?* While it is possible that Nehemiah is looking sad on purpose to catch the king's attention, the text does not say he is, and it is as likely that on this occasion the grieving of recent months just happens to show through. The Hebrew words translated "sad" and "sadness" in this verse and in verse 1 are related and have a wide range of meaning. It is possible to understand the king's question as somewhat vague and less sympathetic, along the lines of "Why do you look so out of sorts today?" His follow-up statement could be taken as "It must be an evil heart," which is the way the same idiom is meant in 1 Samuel 17:28. It is no wonder, then, that Nehemiah is very much afraid. To begin with, those serving in the king's presence were expected to be cheerful, or at least not despondent (compare Esther 4:2). But Artaxerxes might be interpreting Nehemiah's demeanor as indicating he has a malicious plot he intends to carry out. Either way, Nehemiah could be in serious trouble. At this moment the king's attitude is ambiguous at best, and Nehemiah has no confidence that he can count on the king to be sympathetic to him.

2:3 *the city where . . . lies in ruins.* Instead of seeking clarification of the king's meaning or denying malicious intent, Nehemiah takes the initiative by answering the king honestly, but shrewdly. His reply explains his appearance with reference to the destruction of the city of his ancestors' graves. Ancient Near Eastern kings are known to have had a special interest in the preservation of ancestral tombs. By answering this way, Nehemiah maximizes the personal element and minimizes the political. He deflects attention away from the decree Artaxerxes had made earlier and the possible implications for the prosperity of the returned exiles. This is his best chance of both protecting himself and inducing the king to support the reconstruction of Jerusalem's wall.

2:4 *Then I prayed.* Given the opportunity to make a request, Nehemiah requests from God before requesting from the king. He understands that it is ultimately God who provides, even if it is through the king.

the God of heaven. It seems that it became typical, when speaking to non-Judeans, for Judeans living under Babylonian or Persian rule to refer to God with the phrase "God of heaven" (e.g., Ezra 5:11–12; 6:9–10; Neh. 2:20; Dan. 2:37, 44). One hypothesis is that such a title was part of an effort to make Yahweh sound acceptable to the polytheistic Persians by portraying him as a god who would side with their chief god, Ahura Mazda, in his perennial struggle against the forces of evil. This would still not explain why Nehemiah uses it when speaking as the narrator. Perhaps he has become so used to the phrase in the context of the Persian court that he continues to use it, even when merely narrating events that occurred there. Later in the book, when addressing Judeans in Judea, he simply refers to "God," "my God," or "our God."

2:5 *and I answered the king, "If it pleases . . . I can rebuild it."* Nehemiah again replies honestly, yet tactfully. Rebuilding the wall of Jerusalem is exactly what he wants to do, but he is careful to show proper deference to the king, and he again does not mention the name of Jerusalem. His request is bold, because rebuilding a city always had political consequences and could be seen as seditious, depending on circumstances. Nehemiah has no way to be sure how Artaxerxes will respond to this request.

2:6 *How long will your journey take . . . ?* The king's questions show that he is open to Nehemiah's idea. It is at this point that Nehemiah can breathe a sigh of relief. The discussion would never get this far if Artaxerxes were suspicious of Nehemiah's motives.

2:8 *the gracious hand of my God.* Reflecting on everything recorded in this passage, Nehemiah marvels that he received everything he asked for. He has everything he needs that the king can supply. It has all turned out so well because God has intervened in answer to prayer and in accordance with his promises. The language he uses is the same as was used to describe Ezra and the people he leads in Ezra 7:6, 9; 8:18. This highlights the theme of God's sovereign intervention on behalf of those who seek him.

2:9 *The king had . . . sent . . . cavalry with me.* There is no indication that Nehemiah requested an escort, but in the context this appears to be one more provision that God supplied through the king. Given that the building in Jerusalem had previously been stopped by force (Ezra 4:23), it made sense to send a military escort with someone coming to restart it. And even if Artaxerxes did not realize that he was effectively overriding his earlier decree, the subject of building city walls was always politically sensitive.

Nehemiah's situation is different from Ezra's in Ezra 8:22, where he and his company fast and pray for a safe journey because he does not want to ask the king for military protection. Ezra might have encountered bandits along his journey, but, unlike Nehemiah, he had no reason for concern about possible opposition once he arrived in Jerusalem. Some interpreters have suggested that Ezra shows more faith in God than Nehemiah does, but Ezra is not offered a military escort, and Nehemiah does not ask for one. Within the larger context of Ezra-Nehemiah, the point is more likely that God provides in different ways in different situations.

Theological Insights

In a dramatic way, Nehemiah's concern for Jerusalem's distress, his understanding of God's promises, his consistent prayer, his eagerness to give hands-on help, and his creative thinking about how to do so culminate in God taking a potentially dangerous situation and producing a decision by the Persian king to help bring about the very thing Nehemiah has been hoping for.

Many passages in Ezra-Nehemiah emphasize the high degree of commitment God calls for in those who would be in relationship with him, but this one draws attention to the gracious response God gives to those who do trust him. Having devoted himself to prayer that God would advance the restoration of Israel another step, Nehemiah finds himself at a precarious moment in the king's presence. At that instant he decides to take a risk motivated by his faith in God. But in the split second before he makes his daring request of the king, Nehemiah prays to God one more time. God answers his prayers, and the king grants him what he asked for.

This episode displays several important truths about God. Perhaps most obviously, it demonstrates God's power. The most powerful king of the day in the ancient Near East is portrayed as subject to God's intervention in his decision-making process. But the passage also illustrates God's presence with his people in the midst of the turbulence of life. When Nehemiah perceived that he might be in danger, his emotions and his adrenaline were likely running high. God was aware of Nehemiah's situation and responded effectively to what must have been a very brief prayer. In a related way, then, this event also implies that God is accessible to his people at any moment. Nehemiah does not have to step away from Artaxerxes to pray, and his prayer does not have to be eloquent. God is ready and, indeed, eager to display his kindness to his faithful servant.

Teaching the Text

Nehemiah provides an outstanding example for contemporary believers, but, as with the preceding passage, there are some important differences between his setting and that of believers today. God's new covenant does not involve Christians building a physical city but rather building the church, valuing the spiritual qualities that give it meaning over any merely physical qualities (Heb. 12:22–24). But with that essential adjustment in mind, there is much in this passage for believers to imitate.

Nehemiah's foundational commitment to God's plan cannot be overemphasized. His response in the middle of a crisis was shaped by his understanding of and dedication to what God wanted and his trust that God would bring it about. God's people need to think carefully about his revealed plans for the world and what he wants to accomplish in it. And they need to adopt those plans as their own agenda for life, looking for ways to be personally involved in them. Then when difficult and frightening circumstances arise, they will be more likely to move in the best direction.

Christians should also learn from the tact and respect Nehemiah displayed. Pursuing God's purposes often involves dealing with unbelievers. Christians should always be honest and sincere, and not pushy, critical, or whining. But honesty does not always necessitate exhaustive disclosure. Nehemiah was completely honest with Artaxerxes but did not mention that the city's name was Jerusalem and probably did not explain to him at any time that God planned eventually to have a son of David rule the whole world. God's people are not to deceive, but they are to use good judgment about what information to share and when to share it. Matthew 10:16 urges Christians to be as shrewd as snakes and as innocent as doves.

It is also important to remember that there is no guarantee in Scripture that things will always turn out just the way believers envision. God's will often looks different from how they imagine it. This was certainly the case with Christ's life on earth, which was a surprise to many devout Jews. The concept is not that God will do just what his people ask but that as they align themselves with his intentions and trust him, he responds in powerful ways.

It is popular to use Nehemiah's story as a training manual for leadership. While leaders can learn many important things from Nehemiah (as they can from every part of Scripture), leadership training may not be the main thrust of much of his story. In this passage, for example, it is unlikely that the intention is to teach leaders that they should plan ahead so they can ask for what they need when the opportunity presents itself. Making lists may be a good idea, but the point of the story is to show the depth of Nehemiah's commitment and how that shaped his thoughts, behavior, and speech. As he acted in faith, God brought the good results, beyond what he could have foreseen.

Illustrating the Text

Understand God's ways and plans first, then model yours after them.

Military: Military commanders operate within a clear chain of command. Lower-level leaders wait for so-called marching orders from the officers above them before making their own, subordinate plans. It would make little sense for a lower-ranking soldier to formulate a battle plan that didn't match what their commander had in mind for the battle. In fact, it could lead the small battle group to actually end up in opposition to the rest of the force. In the same way, we need to model our plans and vision after God's; it makes little sense for us to march off on our own without listening to him and his Word first.

Be both innocent and shrewd when dealing with unbelievers.

Nature: Anyone who has worked with large animals like horses or cattle knows something about being both innocent and shrewd in dealing with them. A horseman cares for his horse, works in close proximity with it, and deals with it gently in a relationship of kindness and trust. However, the good horseman never forgets that the horse has a size and power that put him or her in potential danger at all times while working around the animal. A frightened, moody, or panicking horse can easily kick the teeth out of his handler, and a falling horse can crush a man. Likewise, a rancher is kind and caring to his cattle, but he knows not to get boxed into a trailer with a bull or to attempt certain medical care without the proper enclosure to keep the animal at bay. Unbelievers are certainly not animals—they are image bearers of God, like us. Nevertheless, we must be innocent and genuinely kind in our interactions with them, while also remaining shrewd enough to set proper boundaries and recognize the potential for harm if we are improperly yoked with them.

Align your desires with God's intentions—amazing things will happen.

Human Experience: Your listeners will most likely be familiar with escalators. As a child (or maybe as an adult), many will have had the experience of trying to run up the down escalator or down the up escalator. Some may even have had bumps and bruises to show for it. Explain that when we go against God's desires, we are taking on an exhausting and unwinnable battle, an unfinishable task like running up an infinite down escalator. On the other hand, when our desires are formed by Scripture and in line with God's, it is like running down the down escalator toward blessings—there is a catalytic multiplication of our desire with God's, and amazing things may start to happen at a miraculous pace!

Nehemiah Prepares to Begin despite Opposition

Big Idea
When facing opposition to God's work, God's people must endure necessary inconvenience as they continue to rely on God's provision for the task.

Key Themes
- Politically influential people are fundamentally opposed to the benefit Nehemiah wants to bring to his people.
- This makes Nehemiah's preparatory work much more difficult.
- Nehemiah articulates his faith that God will ensure the completion of the project.

Understanding the Text

The Text in Context

Nehemiah has obtained permission from the king to rebuild Jerusalem's wall and has been given access to the necessary supplies. He has traveled to Jerusalem to begin this important work, which he understands to be part of God's promised restoration of Israel. Upon arrival, however, it becomes clear that the theme of opposition to God's work and God's people is again present (compare Ezra 3:3; 4:1, 4–24, etc.). If Nehemiah has been careful about what he discloses to the king concerning his plans because he was unsure of what the king's attitude would be, he has all the more reason to proceed in near-complete secrecy at Jerusalem, given the overt opposition. Thus, Nehemiah is forced to carry out his preparatory work under rather difficult conditions. Nevertheless, God's amazing answer to prayer in supplying his needs through Artaxerxes continues to bolster Nehemiah's confidence. By the end of the passage, the people of Jerusalem are eager to work on reconstructing the wall, which is the focus of the following chapters.

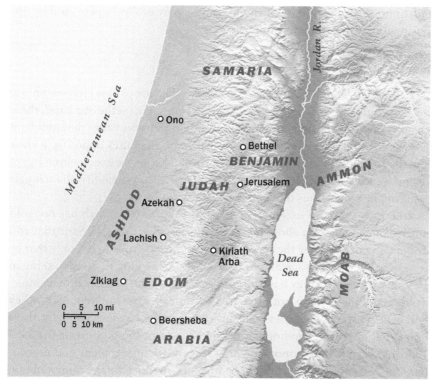

Judea in the postexilic period

Historical and Cultural Background

Papyri from the fifth century BC recovered from Egypt indicate that the Sanballat mentioned in this passage was possibly already governor of Samaria, to the north of Judea, by Nehemiah's time. He may have been given authority over Judea also after the decree that stopped the Jewish building project in Ezra 4:21.

Tobiah was probably a Samarian official subordinate to Sanballat, although of Ammonite descent. Since his name is Jewish, not Ammonite, he may have been of mixed descent.

Geshem the Arab ruled a league of Arabian tribes that controlled territory to the east, south, and southwest of Judea. While it is uncertain precisely what authority or interest these men had with respect to Jerusalem and Judea, they effectively surrounded the area. Since Nehemiah has been given authority to oversee construction in Jerusalem, they are likely to see him as interfering with their influence in some way. This helps to explain why they would be unhappy that he has come to promote the Judeans' welfare. However, while it is understandable that they would be unhappy that their personal interests

Nehemiah 2:10–20

are diminished, the welfare of the Judeans is part of God's plan, and by opposing it they are effectively opposing God.

Interpretive Insights

2:10 *When Sanballat . . . heard about this.* The use of this Hebrew phrase here and again in verse 19 suggests a parallel between, on the one hand, these enemies opposing Nehemiah and the Judeans in Jerusalem after the latter have returned from Babylon and, on the other, the Canaanites opposing Joshua and the Israelites during the conquest of the land after the exodus from Egypt (compare Josh. 9:1–2; 11:1–5). Readers anticipate the possibility of a struggle resulting in a victorious outcome brought about by God.

2:12 *I set out . . . I was riding on.* To this point Nehemiah has not told anyone outside of Susa about his plans. It is possible that even Sanballat and Tobiah do not yet know the specifics of what he has come to do, only that he is to be given safe passage and has been sent by the king to do something in Jerusalem. But since they have connections among the Judeans (for example, Tobiah and his son are both married to Judean women, Neh. 6:18), they will hear whatever Nehemiah tells his own people. He does not want these influential opponents finding out before he obtains the support of the local Judeans, because the opponents may spread discouragement and make it hard for Nehemiah ever to obtain the Judeans' support. But he cannot obtain their support before he has surveyed the state of Jerusalem's wall for himself. Therefore, Nehemiah concludes that he must initially operate in secret. He does not disclose the purpose of his actions to anyone, and he carries out his actions in such a way that the fewest people possible will know about them. This requires inspecting the walls at night, possibly with no illumination other than the moon. There are only a few men with him and only one riding animal among them. He emphasizes twice more (vv. 13, 15) that he carries out the inspection at night. Such is Nehemiah's determination that he carries out the necessary preparatory work in a short time, even under difficult conditions. His motivation continues to be that his plan has come from God.

2:15 *so I went up the valley.* A large amount of rubble probably remained on the east side of Jerusalem from the destruction of the city by the Babylonians in 586 BC. This could have made it impossible for Nehemiah to ride through the area, and he may have been able to continue only on foot. But the point is that he does continue and perseveres to see what he needs to see.

2:17 *let us rebuild . . . no longer be in disgrace.* Having done the difficult reconnaissance, Nehemiah is now able to ask the other Judeans to participate with him in his plan. He presents the problem in the terms in which he first understood it himself (Neh. 1:3). He highlights the sense of shame reflecting the punishment of exile, contrary to a state of restoration of the relationship with God. And he does not ask for the people's opinion nor directly order them to take up the work but invites them to join in the task God has laid on his heart.

2:18 *and what the king had said to me.* The fact that the same Persian king who had ordered reconstruction of the walls to stop is now ordering that it be completed functions as evidence that God's hand is indeed upon Nehemiah (compare Ezra 6:13–18; 7:6). Testifying in this way helps Nehemiah to transfer his confidence in God's sufficiency to the people.

So they began this good work. A wooden translation of this clause would be "And they strengthened their hands for the good." The meaning is not that they begin to work but that they encourage each other to do this good work. It is the exact opposite of the idiom in Ezra 4:4, where the enemies of the Jews discourage them from building ("weaken their hands").

The Hebrew idiom here is also used in Ezra 6:22 to describe the effect God had on the Judeans through changing the attitude of the "king of Assyria" (the Persian king; see comments on Ezra 6:22). Throughout Ezra-Nehemiah when God's people overcome opposition to restoration, it is in part because of the encouragement God gives them through the actions of Persian kings and their own Judean leaders.

2:19 *they mocked and ridiculed . . . "Are you rebelling against the king?"* Any attempt at defensive fortification, such as building a wall around a city, could be interpreted as an attempt to gain a measure of independence. So the Judeans' opponents raise the question of rebellion as a veiled threat that they will make an accusation against them. It was a similar accusation in Ezra 4:11–16 that eventually brought construction to a standstill (4:21–23). At the same time, the rhetorical force of their question is that the Judeans could not possibly rebel successfully. Thus, the enemies are combining mockery with threat in order to try to discourage the Judeans from building.

2:20 *The God of heaven will give us success.* Nehemiah prayed for God to give him success in 1:11, and he saw God's answer in 2:1–9. Now he reaffirms his faith that God will give success to the whole group as they participate.

you have no share . . . historic right to it. Nehemiah also ignores the suggestion of rebellion. At this point he is not aiming for political independence for Judea, seeking only to further the restoration by rebuilding Jerusalem's wall. The city's future political status is not presently an issue.

But he does make a significant statement about the future *status quo.* "Share" probably refers to a political voice or interest, as when the seceding northern tribes stated that they had no share in David (1 Kings 12:16). "Claim" likely signifies legal jurisdiction, and "historic right" probably refers to participation in religious ceremonies, since the same Hebrew word is used to describe celebrating the Passover (Exod. 12:14; NIV "commemorate") and the Feast of

Unleavened Bread (Exod. 13:9; NIV "reminder"). Nehemiah is confident that, as a result of the work about to be done, Jerusalem will be established and those who disparaged the rebuilding will be on the outside looking in, unable to receive the social and spiritual blessings God will give his people. The exclusivity is reminiscent of the temple building in Ezra 4–6 (especially in 4:1–5).

Theological Insights

As this portion of narrative follows Nehemiah's actions and speeches, it indirectly provides testimony to God's trustworthiness to achieve his purposes by working behind the scenes. In Nehemiah 1, Nehemiah responded to God's promise of restoration by praying for God to bring it about and to give him success as he contemplated taking part in the process. Nehemiah now discloses that one way God has been at work is by giving him a specific plan to address Jerusalem's ruined wall. It is God himself, not Nehemiah, who has bridged the gap between the general idea of rebuilding and a concrete strategy.

Nehemiah also testifies to his fellow Judeans about what the reader has been shown in Nehemiah 2:1–9: how God intervened in his encounter with the king, causing the king to grant Nehemiah's requests. His declaration then leads naturally to his confident statement to the enemies that God will give the Judeans success in their efforts. Nehemiah anticipates many challenges ahead and has not witnessed a miracle in the usual sense of an obviously supernatural event. But God's direction and intervention have given him confidence to press forward against any obstacle. God tells his people what they need to know, and the evidence of his timely help grounds their faith.

Teaching the Text

The reality of opposition to God's people as they do God's work appears again, as it did earlier in Ezra. The New Testament affirms that this is something Christians should expect regularly (1 Cor. 16:9). The motivations that people have are extremely varied, and sometimes even those who self-identify as believers end up interfering with the blessing God wants to give his people. This may have been the case with Tobiah, with his Jewish name (which means, ironically, "Yahweh is good"). The critical factor in determining "the good" is not personal desires or preferences but what God has defined as good and what he instructs his people to pursue. Those who work against "the good" defined in this way are ultimately opposing God, whether they realize it or not, and believers need to be prepared to encounter such resistance.

It is important for Christians to remember that all the opposition they face has a spiritual source (Eph. 6:12). In one way this complicates matters, because those who stand against the church's progress may not fully understand what they are doing or why they do it. But it also simplifies things, because the way forward has less to do with overcoming individuals and everything to do with embracing the spiritual values Christ wants his followers to pursue. Nehemiah did not try to win an argument with those ridiculing him; he simply affirmed faith that God would give success as his people did his work.

Opposition always makes things harder, and Christians need to be prepared to go the extra mile often. Reaching the world with the truth and love of Christ will involve inconvenience and personal sacrifice at the best of times, but especially so when others are creating obstacles. Sometimes God allows things to proceed relatively easily, as when Nehemiah makes his requests to Artaxerxes, but other times it is more of a struggle.

The greatest need is for God's people to maintain faith that God will give them success as they pursue his stated purposes. Nehemiah is locked onto removing Jerusalem's disgrace by rebuilding its wall and demonstrates his confidence in God's provision by his actions as well as his words. His ability to respond to challenges flows from his inner state.

As with the previous passage, it is best to avoid teaching it as a management seminar. The fact that Nehemiah examines the wall for himself before asking the Judean people to work on it is simply logical. It is unlikely that the text intends to teach a leadership technique. Rather, the text shows that Nehemiah's determined faith prompts him to do the obviously necessary thing, even under difficult conditions.

Illustrating the Text

When we're risking for God, earthly resistance often signifies heavenly favor.

Human Experience: Many of your listeners may have had the experience of wearing team colors at a sporting event and ending up surrounded by people dressed in the other team's colors. Opposing fans may have joked, taunted, booed, or even thrown things. Representing the opposing team in hostile territory means you will sometimes stand out or be mocked. When we stand for God in this world, we will face the same persecution and misunderstanding that Jesus did. It just means we are loved by him and hated by the world. (Consider putting on the jersey of a team or brand opposed by most of your listeners; when they boo or laugh, it will add to the point.)

The best response to impersonal resistance is personal persistence.

Classic Sermon: During his tenure as chaplain at Hope College (Holland, MI), the Reverend Ben Patterson was fond of pointing out that soldiers during a great war don't jump up from their trenches with hurt expressions and ask the other side, "Was it something I said?" The spiritual battles we face, according to Patterson, are not always really about us—our enemy is raging against Christ in us and is opposing him and his church by leveraging myriad weapons and human obstacles against us. Our task is not to take it personally and wonder if we did wrong—our task is to suit up in spiritual armor, show up on the battlefield, and persist for Christ, knowing that resistance is just part of the story when you are doing the right thing.

An inner state of faith helps sort out an outer state of chaos.

Bible: Mark 4:35–41 recounts the story of Jesus and his disciples in a boat during a storm. Jesus slept calmly on a cushion in the storm, unfazed by the chaos around them. When they asked if he cared or not, he spoke and the storm ceased. His inner faith and peace with God were able to give him rest *and* make a difference in the chaos around him.

Christian Music: Christian songwriter Scott Krippayne wrote the song "Sometimes He Calms the Storm" (1995), in which he teases out this concept. The song reflects on the fact that while God can certainly use his power to still storms around his children, more often he uses his miraculous power to calm the storms *within* his children. Consider playing a recording of the song or asking a musician to perform it live—it is an older song, but many will remember it or enjoy discovering it.

The Judeans Rebuild
the Wall around Jerusalem

Big Idea

God's work is achieved as all of God's people take part, with each contributing according to their unique circumstances.

Key Themes

- Every segment of the Judean community in Palestine was represented among those working on the wall.
- Many people worked on segments of the wall that had personal significance to them.

Understanding the Text

The Text in Context

The return of Judeans to Judea and their rebuilding of the temple in Ezra 1–6 and the further provision for the temple and reestablishment of observance of the Mosaic law in Ezra 7–10 are all presented as important elements in the restoration of the covenant relationship between God and his people (see comments on Ezra 1:1; 7:27; 10:3). Nehemiah 1–2 establishes the rebuilding of the wall around Jerusalem as another component of this process. Therefore, Nehemiah 3 should be seen not as merely a list of people involved in a mundane project but as a record of those involved in fulfilling God's promises on earth.

The chapter comes between the decision of the people in Jerusalem to rebuild (Neh. 2:18) and the narrative of events that occurred during the rebuilding (Neh. 4 and following). But it views the wall building as already complete, referring to the setting of the doors in place (Neh. 3:3, 6, etc.), even though Nehemiah 6:1 states that the doors have not yet been hung. Nehemiah 3:1 seems initially to continue the narrative from the previous chapter, in that the people follow through on their decision and actually begin to rebuild, but it then carries on with a full account of who worked on which part of the wall before returning to a chronological description of the process.

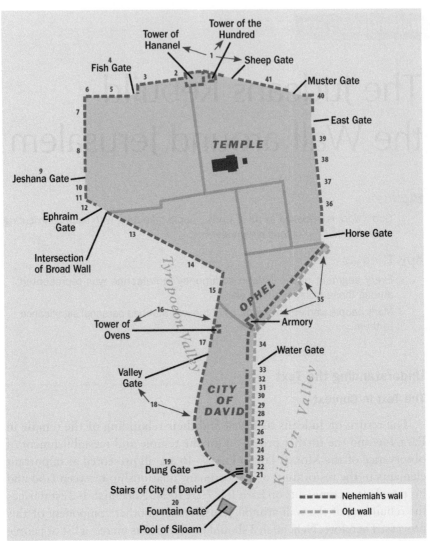

Jerusalem at the time of Nehemiah with approximate locations of the worksites listed in Nehemiah 3

1. Eliashib and priests
2. Men of Jericho
3. Zakkur
4. Sons of Hassenaah
5. Meremoth
6. Meshullam (son of Berekiah)
7. Zadok (son of Baana)
8. Men of Tekoa
9. Joiada and Meshullam (son of Besodeiah)
10. Melatiah and Jadon
11. Uzziel
12. Hananiah (perfume-maker)
13. Rephaiah
14. Jedaiah
15. Hattush
16. Malkijah (son of Harim) and Hasshub
17. Shallum and daughters
18. Hanun and residents of Zanoah
19. Malkijah (son of Rekab)
20. Shallun
21. Nehemiah (son of Azbuk)
22. Rehum and Levites
23. Hashabiah
24. Binnui and Levites
25. Ezer
26. Baruch
27. Meremoth
28. Priests from surrounding region
29. Benjamin and Hasshub
30. Azariah
31. Binnui
32. Palal
33. Pedaiah and temple servants
34. Men of Tekoa
35. Priests
36. Zadok (son of Immer)
37. Shemaiah
38. Hananiah (son of Shelemiah) and Hanun
39. Meshullam (son of Berekiah)
40. Malkijah (goldsmith)
41. Goldsmiths and merchants

By stepping out of strict chronological progression, Nehemiah 3 serves as a kind of "flash-forward" that functions in a way opposite to the "flash-forward" in Ezra 4:7–23. The Ezra passage displays the nature of later opposition so that God's overcoming power in the present can be appreciated. Nehemiah 3 assures the reader that the work on the wall is completed, so that the opposition to it in coming chapters may be anticipated as futile.

Historical and Cultural Background

Modern scholars are uncertain about many of the locations mentioned in Nehemiah 3, although the original readers would have been familiar with all of them. The description appears to proceed from the northeast corner of the city in a counterclockwise direction and follows a full circuit back to the starting point.

Interpretive Insights

3:1 *the high priest and his fellow priests went to work.* The working involvement of the priests and their position at the beginning of the list gives the impression that this is seen as a project with spiritual significance. This is consistent with how Nehemiah has been presenting it to this point (Neh. 1:3–4; 2:8, 12, 20).

They dedicated it . . . which they dedicated. The dedication, or, better, consecration, of their work contributes further to the impression that there was spiritual significance involved. The verb used here, at the beginning of the project, is different from the one used in Nehemiah 12:27–30, at the end of the project, when the entire wall is dedicated, so it is likely a different kind of ceremony.

A parallel may thus be seen between the work of Joshua in Ezra 3:2, 8 and the work of Eliashib here. The leadership of a priest is obviously appropriate in rebuilding the altar and temple, but the fact that a priest takes a leading role in rebuilding Jerusalem's wall suggests that the wall building is seen as holy in a way parallel to temple building. Eliashib is Joshua's grandson (Neh. 12:10–11).

Tower of Hananel. Jeremiah 31 looks forward to a time of postexilic restoration in which there will be a new covenant between God and Israel (v. 31) and the city will be rebuilt, including the Tower of Hananel (v. 38). Its mention here marks the current project as part of that anticipated restoration.

3:4 *Meshullam son of Berekiah.* Meshullam's daughter is married to Tobiah's son (Neh. 6:18). This work may be done in spite of considerable family tension.

3:5 *the men of Tekoa.* The involvement of these and other people from outside Jerusalem shows that Jerusalem has an importance for the Judeans beyond a mere administrative center. Many prophecies of covenant restoration involved Jerusalem (e.g., Jer. 31:38; 33:7; Amos 9:14; Mic. 7:11), and the restoration of the city therefore symbolizes reconciliation between God and his people.

their nobles would not put their shoulders to the work. This metaphor portrays not a half-hearted effort but rather an uncooperative refusal to participate in the work at all. The motive is not stated, but possibilities include fear of reprisals (since Tekoa is close to the area controlled by Geshem, who was hostile to the building project [see Neh. 2:19]) and simple pride. Not everyone among the Judeans takes part.

their supervisors. This should be translated "their lord" and be understood as a reference to Nehemiah as the one in charge of the project. Compare Ezra 10:3, where Shekaniah addresses Ezra as "my lord."

3:16 *tombs of David.* This does not imply that David's bones were contained in more than one tomb but rather refers to the tombs of David and his descendants.

3:20 *Baruch . . . repaired another section.* While it seems that Baruch is not listed elsewhere as repairing any other section, it is possible that he is also part of one of the groups without a named leader (vv. 22, 28).

3:28 *Above the Horse Gate.* On the east side of Jerusalem, the reconstructed wall was west of the preexilic wall. It was therefore higher up the hill, which slopes down to the east. The Horse Gate was part of the old wall and was therefore not repaired, but the priests mentioned in this verse make repairs directly up the hill from, or above, the Horse Gate.

3:31 *the temple servants and the merchants.* This section of the wall is near the temple. It is easy to see why the temple servants would take interest in this part, but the merchants also have an interest in this area, since they sold supplies necessary for sacrifice to those coming to worship at the temple.

Theological Insights

Since God is not mentioned in this passage, any conclusions reached about him must be arrived at indirectly, but for a text that appears to be little more than a list, it contains a surprising amount of theological teaching. Perhaps the most important feature of all is how the building project is portrayed as involving the entire community of Judeans in Palestine. Numerous segments of the population are mentioned, and the groupings are identified in a variety of ways. Sometimes it is by family, sometimes by occupation, sometimes by geographical location of residence, sometimes including women. The picture that emerges is that there is representation from across the whole people. Although he is able to bring about whatever he wants simply by willing it into existence, most of the time God seems to achieve his ends through the cooperation of people. And although at times he uses select individuals to accomplish great things, he seems to prefer to involve as many as possible. God does not intend his work for only a few. It is for all.

Along with this we see that God arranges his work in the world such that every contribution to it has meaning and significance. A comparison of the list of workers with a map of Jerusalem reveals that not everyone works on the same length of wall. Also, some work primarily on gates as opposed to the wall itself. Yet the structure of the list gives the impression that each contribution is as significant as every other. In a real sense, all work done for God's cause is vital in order to achieve the ultimate goal. The work would be incomplete if even a small part were missing.

Looked at from the other side, although all contributions are vital, that does not imply they are identical. Some do a greater quantity of work than others, with some working on more than one section of the wall. God is not bound by a theory of egalitarianism. He is free to assign different roles to different people and equip them accordingly. He uses variety and diversity as he employs people in his service.

Diversity typically presents a considerable challenge in getting people to work together. But God's greatness is demonstrated in his ability to overcome the obstacles diversity can present. The list of workers reflects social and economic diversity. This means that they cannot possibly be in agreement on everything and undoubtedly have different preferences concerning various issues. Yet they are able to work side by side on what they understand God's will for them to be. They put aside what is of secondary importance to achieve what God wants them to achieve. God does not expect his people to share the same perspective on every life issue. While God is aware of the diversity of opinions that exists on various topics, he views his priorities as transcending other concerns and rendering such differences relatively insignificant.

Also, the list does reveal that there is not complete unanimity of purpose concerning this project within the Judean community. Some of the Tekoite leaders refuse to take part (v. 5). The metaphor used to describe them implies that they should join in but do not. Although complete unity of purpose and participation in God's work is desired, it is seldom attained. Yet God's purposes are not ultimately thwarted by those who oppose him. He is able to see his projects through to completion through those who do cooperate with him.

Teaching the Text

In order to communicate the meaning of this text effectively, it is important to establish the spiritual significance of the wall building. It is only then that the bridge can be built to the contemporary setting and application made concerning doing God's work in the present. Nehemiah and the Jews working with him connected the reconstruction of the city walls with the gracious removal of the disgrace that had come upon them because of their disobedience to God. Christians understand that the whole world is in disgrace because of sin (Rom. 3:23). The death of Christ makes it possible for that disgrace to be removed, and believers are called to live new, unashamed lives. They are to demonstrate the love and holiness that are part of their identity as God's people, shunning the shameful deeds that brought disgrace previously (Eph. 5:1–6). It is this sort of "work" (Eph. 2:10) that provides the Christian's parallel to the building in this chapter.

As believers share God's love with the world around them, it is vital that all segments of Christ's body be involved. It is not just the clergy, or the educated, or the white- or blue-collar worker, but believers from any and every demographic who are to be engaged in this project. No one can claim an exemption. This makes perfect sense, because the different kinds of contributions they are able to make are each vital to the effectiveness of the whole (1 Cor. 12:15–21). This is true even though the contributions may not initially seem to be of equal value.

A big challenge for contemporary Christians relates to diversity within the church. It can be hard for those with different views on political or social issues to put those differences aside in order to cooperate in displaying God's love. This is true both within and between individual congregations. Yet the New Testament example is seen in Acts 2:5, 43–47, where Jews from various countries, undoubtedly holding divergent opinions about many things, function as a remarkably unified group. Christ's causes need to eclipse all others that believers may have commitments to.

There is plenty to learn from what appears to be the author's intent in this passage without straying into more speculative interpretations. Many have noted that this project would not have been completed in this way without careful planning and organization on Nehemiah's part. This is certainly true, but there seems no intent within the text to highlight this. Leaders in Nehemiah's day, as in ours, can learn from many sources, including personal experience, that planning and organization are important. The narrator of Nehemiah seems to take for granted that organization is necessary; he has other truths that he is interested in teaching God's people.

Illustrating the Text

Within the body of Christ, every individual's role matters.

Sports: Invite your listeners to think about the sport of baseball. Some positions don't seem to matter as much as others, but imagine how the game would proceed if there were nobody playing second base. What if the team had no catcher? The game might possibly go on in some cases, but the results would be lopsided.

Story: Pick an unsung hero or two from your church's list of volunteers and tell a story or two that honor them and their unseen work. Emphasize that while pastors get lots of airtime, elders face lots of responsibility, and singers get heard, the church could not function without these persons' quiet contributions and care.

A single shared effort can only flow from a single shared love.

Metaphor: Some groups of people are bonded like a popcorn ball—every piece is stuck to one or two beside itself. These bonds aren't very durable, and even a slight blow can break the whole ball apart into pieces. Other groups of people are like a wheel, where all the spokes share part of the load and tie into the same hub. If these are churches, the first kind has a hard time making a concerted effort in mission, since the only common bonds are about sticking together. The second kind has amazing potential, because of a single, shared love and a common sharing of burdens and bumps in the road. When we all share one love and carry one load as a team, we can do amazing things for the Lord.

Nature: The biblical picture of a vine and branches (John 15) gives us a clear picture of this concept. Good fruit is produced only when all the branches are tied into the soil by one, healthy root and sharing the life-giving sap and sun together.

Applying the Text: Consider challenging your listeners to join you in partnering with another local congregation of differing ethnicity or culture on a common project in your city. Explain that the one love that binds you demands that you work in one harvest field as partners.

Nehemiah Leads the Judeans in a Successful Response to Their Opponents' Tactics

Big Idea

When God's people come under attack as they do his work, they need protection and encouragement in order to continue the work.

Key Themes

- The Judeans' enemies become very angry when they hear of the progress the Judeans are making, and the enemies try to stop the work.
- Nehemiah and the Judeans pray and trust God to thwart their enemies' schemes.
- Nehemiah implements a plan to protect the people and speed their work on the wall.

Understanding the Text

The Text in Context

Nehemiah 3 listed those involved in reconstructing Jerusalem's wall and all the specific areas in which they ultimately worked. In this way, Nehemiah 3 actually reached forward to the end of the rebuilding project. Nehemiah 4 now returns to the period when the wall is under construction to provide a glimpse of what life on the ground is like for those involved.

The theme of opposition to the Judean restoration, seen in Ezra 4 and Nehemiah 2, continues. The Judeans' enemies hear about the progress Nehemiah and the Judeans are making in rebuilding Jerusalem's wall and respond with anger and mockery initially, and then with more anger and threats of mortal attack. As the opposition intensifies, Nehemiah finds it necessary to adopt military measures in response. The escalation of hostility climaxes in

Nehemiah 4. Although the enemies will continue to try to make trouble, they cannot interfere with construction of the wall.

The Hebrew verb for "were equipped" (v. 16), "held" (v. 17), and "holding" (v. 21) is the same as that for "repaired" used throughout Nehemiah 3 and constitutes a wordplay that connects the two passages. It helps show that the Judeans found that being prepared to defend themselves turned out to be an important part of rebuilding the wall.

Overall, Nehemiah 4 functions as a picture of the back-and-forth struggle waged over the removal of Israel's disgrace, which was embodied in the rebuilding of Jerusalem's wall. The opposition was real and required a concerted response.

Interpretive Insights

4:2 *Will they offer sacrifices?* It is not completely certain what Sanballat means by this question, nor what the immediately preceding or following questions mean either. What is clear is that the string of rhetorical questions is intended to portray the Judeans as incapable of rebuilding Jerusalem's wall. Sanballat vents his anger through ridicule, and he hopes the Judeans will be demoralized.

4:4 *Turn their insults back on their own heads.* Nehemiah's motivation from the beginning has been to help fulfill God's plan of restoration by removing the disgrace the Judeans are experiencing (Neh. 1:3). Since their opponents are seeking to hinder the rebuilding project and perpetuate the Judeans' shame through ridicule, Nehemiah asks God to do to the opponents what they are hoping will be done to the Judeans. In this way the enemies will be paid back for opposing God's plan and people. The request that the enemies be given over as plunder (Heb. *bizzah*) is, through a play on words, seen as an appropriate payback for their contempt (Heb. *buzah*; NIV "despised") toward the Jews.

4:5 *Do not cover up their guilt.* It is easy for contemporary readers to read more into this verse than they should. The Old Testament context focused on reward and punishment within the present world, not in an existence after death. Nehemiah is asking for justice and that God not overlook or forget what his enemies have done. His intention is unlikely to have included a concept of eternal damnation.

4:8 *They all plotted together.* After declaring that the Judeans will be ineffective, Sanballat and company are embarrassed by the Judeans' progress and become angrier still. The Hebrew verb translated "they plotted" has a wide range of meanings that generally relate to joining or connecting in some way. In this verse it refers to the enemies' joining together in conspiracy. A more formal translation of the Hebrew of verse 6 would include that the whole wall was "joined together" (using the same verb; compare ESV, HCSB)

Christians and Imprecatory Prayers

Christians are often uncomfortable with so-called imprecatory prayers, which ask for harm to come to one's enemies. They seem in direct conflict with Jesus's teaching in the Sermon on the Mount and his own example on the cross of forgiving those killing him.

One of the important factors to consider is that in all imprecatory prayers, the call is ultimately for God to vindicate himself. In every case the one praying has been mistreated by his enemies, who have disobeyed God's righteous expectations in the process. Also, in most cases, part of the reason for the mistreatment is that the petitioner seeks to be faithful to God. By association, the shameful mistreatment has brought God's own name into disrepute. The prayer thus asks for God to preserve justice and protect his reputation by judging those who have acted in this way.

A second consideration is that, by praying, the one who has been mistreated is not taking justice or revenge into his own hands. Although the one praying has specific suggestions about what appropriate punishment might be, it is left entirely to God to bring it about.

Similarly, Romans 12:19 instructs Christians not to take revenge but to leave vengeance to God. In so doing it implies that there will be a day of vengeance. At that point God will vindicate his name, just as Nehemiah and others in the Old Testament had prayed. In the meantime Christians can still pray for God's justice and for evil plans to fail, but since Christ has paid for the sins of all, believers should pray for the preferred outcome for their enemies, which is salvation (see, e.g., Ezek. 18:23, 32; 2 Pet. 3:9).

and reached half its height. The play on words underlines how the activity of one group prompts the response of the other.

4:10 *the people in Judah said.* The reported speech that follows is in poetic form, suggesting that this became a common saying among the Judeans. It seems that those clearing away debris from the destroyed wall were overwhelmed with the magnitude of the task, making it impossible for new construction to go forward.

4:12 *ten times over.* This is an idiomatic way of saying that something happened repeatedly or frequently.

Wherever you turn, they will attack us. This part of the verse is difficult to translate, and there is significant disagreement among interpreters over its meaning. The most likely meaning is reflected in a translation that reads, "You should return to us."[1] The Judeans living near the enemies may have caught wind of their plan to attack and are repeatedly urging their relatives and friends to leave Jerusalem and return to their home towns to avoid danger.

Together verses 10–12 show that the enemies were planning deadly aggression and the Judeans had become discouraged and fearful, perhaps close to abandoning this project vital to the restoration. This sets the stage for Nehemiah's following actions.

4:13 *behind the lowest points of the wall at the exposed places.* Nehemiah's strategy is to have the enemy see Judeans in Jerusalem armed and ready for conflict. The point is for them to conclude that their plan has become known and that there may well be similarly armed forces in places behind the wall that they cannot see.

4:14 *fight for your families . . . and your homes.* Since their families and homes were in many cases not in Jerusalem, Nehemiah's point is that by standing firm against the enemies' attack and seeing the wall-building through to completion, the Judeans will be doing a greater benefit to their families than they would by fleeing danger and going home to them as was suggested in verse 12.

4:20 *Our God will fight for us.* Throughout the Old Testament, an important part of the relationship between God and Israel is that God will fight for them if they are faithful to him (see, e.g., Exod. 14:13–14; 1 Sam. 17:37). Nehemiah frames the present conflict in those terms, implying that the Judeans are obediently doing God's will by rebuilding the wall and can therefore count on his protection.

4:23 *even when he went for water.* This clause is extremely difficult to translate, and it is possible that the text has been corrupted in transmission. While the exact details may remain unclear, the point being made is that just as the Judeans in general were required to commit themselves full-time to building the wall and guarding the city, so Nehemiah and the people closest to him also dedicated themselves to the task, accepting hardship in the process.

Theological Insights

Even as God begins the process of restoring his people from the disgrace accompanying judgment, they continue to experience ridicule from their enemies. And the very progress they make as they cooperate with God's plan provokes increasing anger from those opponents, which in turn can lead to more serious forms of attack. Although God can and often does shield his people from abuse, he does not guarantee it. Scripture makes clear that the compensations God offers render the assaults his people endure worthwhile. But it teaches equally that he allows believers to face attacks, even as they obey him.

In the midst of intense opposition, the temptation to be discouraged and give up can be extreme. While God expects the leaders among his people to provide appropriate practical resources to equip them all for the battles they may face, it is also an opportunity for them to be reminded that God himself is their source of strength and protection. Ultimately, God wants his people to engage him in prayer even more than he wants them to devise clever strategies.

Teaching the Text

Although the Judeans are prevailing against their enemies at the end of the chapter, the story it tells is not a pleasant one. The Judeans' enemies do their best to shame them and make them feel discouraged about the work they are doing. While the Judeans initially persevere, they eventually come to see the task as overwhelming, and when their enemies introduce threats to harm them, they are tempted to abandon the work altogether.

This aspect of the text can apply quite directly to Christians today, and the opportunity should be taken to explore the variety of negative emotions that believers experience when actively trying to achieve God's purposes in the world. Serving God is often presented as exciting and meaningful, which it is, but believers need to be prepared for the feelings they experience when unbelievers express disdain for their work and even for them personally. Doing God's will on earth also often seems overwhelming and even dangerous. It is good for the church to realize that this is a normal and regular part of the process.

After acknowledging the reality of the difficulties connected with God's work, one should focus on how to respond. Here Nehemiah's actions can guide church leaders. The priority response is prayer. The leaders must pray and must encourage the rest of the body to pray as well. Prayer will renew a healthy perspective on the situation, helping the church form an accurate interpretative framework within which to understand what is happening. And those under attack should pray for God to intervene against evil. But leaders also need to think of other practical steps that can be taken to help their people fend off enemy attacks.

In Nehemiah's setting he provided the people with weapons and stationed them in strategic places so the enemies would realize that their plans had become known. The Christian context, however, recognizes a shift in emphasis from the physical realm to the spiritual (Luke 12:4–5; 2 Cor. 10:4–5). Believers differ over the extent to which they should use force to defend themselves from physical aggression, but there should be no disagreement that protection within spiritual warfare is essential. Leaders need to equip God's people to overcome temptations, discouragements, and other kinds of attacks that their real enemy, Satan, will make against them.

Again, knowing what to expect is an important part of being prepared. The Judeans ended up working with one hand and holding a weapon with the other, and working long hours without returning home. The church needs to understand that making the difference that God calls it to make will often involve great inconvenience and sacrifice. The comfortable lifestyle that many Christians crave does not allow room to make the kind of impact God desires.

In an attempt to make Nehemiah's imprecatory prayer (Neh. 4:4–5) seem more acceptable to Christians, some interpreters have argued that it could actually be a prayer that ultimately intends good for the enemies, since God's judgment can have the effect of leading people to repentance. The theme of judgment leading to repentance is certainly present in both the Old and New Testaments, but there is no indication in this passage that this is what Nehemiah has in mind.

Illustrating the Text

If discipleship feels uncomfortable and costly, it could be a sign that you're doing it right.

Fitness: Your listeners will be familiar with the concept of exercise and weight training. Bring two weights up with you, one very small and light—the other heavy and quite challenging for you. Ask, "If I do bicep curls with this small weight, it feels great and it's really easy; if I do them with this heavy weight, I feel blood rush into the muscle, it burns with activity, and I can't do more than ten repetitions. Which one should I use if I want to grow?" They will answer that the larger weight is more effective. Explain that the exercise is going *correctly* when it gets difficult and muscles get tired. In the same way, faith may feel difficult or fatiguing precisely because we are doing it right. God has a plan to strengthen us in those moments!

Work with one hand and wield the sword of the Spirit with the other.

Creative Media: Enlist help from a creative person in your congregation to create a video slideshow of people from your congregation doing their work with a Bible in their hand or in their pocket. Get a variety of shots: moms feeding their babies while reading Scripture or praying, farmers listening to the Bible on tape while harvesting, a family doing devotions at dinner, students in class with a Bible peeking out of their backpack, and a truck driver with memory verses taped to the dash would all be good examples. Add some music and show this as a creative visual on doing one's work while being prepared to wield the sword of the Sprit.

Applying the Text: Challenge your congregation to learn Scripture by heart. Give them a list of essential verses to start with and offer accountability and incentives. Explain that the best way to be ready to be guided by the Bible in season and out of season is to have it memorized.

Nehemiah Relieves the Economic Hardship of the People

Big Idea

Godly leaders use their authority to alleviate the suffering of those they lead, even if it costs them personally.

Key Themes

- The Judean nobles and officials follow practices that create intense distress for the other Judeans.
- Nehemiah intervenes to stop these harmful practices on the basis of godly ethics rather than relying solely on existing law.
- Nehemiah also makes significant personal sacrifices in order to make the people's lives more bearable.

Understanding the Text

The Text in Context

In Nehemiah 4 the Judeans overcame external opposition to construct the wall of Jerusalem and thereby furthered God's program of removing Israel's reproach. In Nehemiah 5 a new threat to the returned exiles' dignity and prosperity is identified, and its source is within the community itself. It is not completely clear whether the events of Nehemiah 5 occur chronologically between those of Nehemiah 4 and Nehemiah 6, and therefore take place during the construction of the wall, or whether they take place at a later time. Either way, their placement in the narrative at this point draws attention to important contrasts. Whereas Nehemiah 3–4 emphasized the solidarity of the Judeans as they supported each other in the rebuilding effort, it now emerges that some of them are exploiting others for economic gain. This is contrary to the expectations of the restoration period, in terms of both the lack of unity displayed within the community and the hunger and family breakup experienced by those exploited. It highlights the fact that the potential for disrupting the restoration lies as much in the conduct of the Judeans themselves as in the actions of the surrounding peoples.

Historical and Cultural Background

The Persians assessed the tax on a field on the basis of what the field was expected to be able to produce. In most years it was difficult to actually achieve the projected level of production, and when crops were poor, it was impossible. It is not surprising, then, that many have to borrow in order simply to pay the tax (Neh. 5:4; compare v. 3).

Also, once a landowner pledged his land as security in order to "borrow" food, the normal procedure was for the produce of the land to be used to pay off the loan. But documents discovered from this time period show that the interest rate on grain was very high. Thus, those needing to pay taxes and pay off loans of food frequently found themselves in situations from which it was impossible to recover (Neh. 5:5).

Interpretive Insights

5:1 *raised a great outcry.* There may be an intended connection here to the exodus from Egypt (the same Hebrew word for "outcry" is used in Neh. 5:6, and the verb form is in Exod. 14:10–11). In that situation the Israelites feared for their lives, since, although they had left slavery, Pharaoh and his troops were advancing on them. Now, the community has "left" the slavery of exile by returning to the promised land, but, ironically, the slavery has intensified, and they again fear for their lives, this time at the hands of fellow Judeans who have reduced them to starvation and bondage. This is not what restoration was supposed to be like, and the Judeans should not be their own enemies.

5:7 *charging your own people interest.* Although some of the most popular English translations refer here to charging interest, there is actually considerable disagreement among interpreters over the exact meaning of the Hebrew (the same uncertainty is present in v. 10). NET refers to seizing collateral, and NJPS, more generally, to pressing claims on loans. While the exact meaning is uncertain, the point seems to be that many of the Judeans have made secured loans to other members of the community and are now insisting on enforcing the terms of their agreements, even though that will result in the borrowers losing the security they offered for the loans. Whether interest is a key factor in these agreements or not, the problem is ultimately that as the borrowers surrender real property of various kinds, they become increasingly unable to ever get out of debt and risk losing absolutely everything, including their personal freedom and that of their family members.

I called together a large meeting to deal with them. The difficulty in knowing whether interest is specifically in mind in this verse also contributes to uncertainty over whether Nehemiah has strict legal grounds for intervening in the economic arrangements. Biblical legislation did allow for securing loans with pledges (e.g., Deut. 24:10), so the creditors may not be violating the letter of the law. As governor, Nehemiah could potentially impose a solution to the crisis, but instead he brings the whole community together in an assembly. By doing so, he deals with the matter in an open manner, and although he is clearly providing leadership to the process, he allows input from others as he establishes the facts and determines a satisfactory course of future action.

5:8 *you are selling . . . sold back to us.* Redeeming an Israelite sold to a foreigner was something normally done by a blood relative (Lev. 25:47–49). Nehemiah and some others were using money to purchase the freedom of Judeans who had been sold as slaves. In doing so they were appropriately acting as family to them. The creditors he is confronting, although also Judeans, have been involved in selling these Judeans into slavery, therefore acting just the opposite of how family would. It is not hard to see how selling fellow Judeans to foreigners is reminiscent of Joseph's brothers selling him into slavery in Egypt (Gen. 37:25–28) and a reversal of God's redemption accomplished through the exodus.

5:9 *avoid the reproach.* The Hebrew word translated "reproach" is used also in Nehemiah 1:3 and 2:17 (translated "disgrace" both times). Being in such a state is associated with enduring God's judgment connected with exile, which is expressed in Jerusalem's ruined walls. Here, however, it is not what the nations have done to the Judeans that is the potential source of disgrace but the actions of the creditors in enslaving their fellow Judeans. The implication is that people who become wealthy by forcing others into poverty are bringing God's judgment upon themselves.

5:11 *the interest.* From this verse it is clear that the creditors are demanding various forms of percentage payments. Once again the point is that all debt claims creating undue hardship should cease to be pressed, whether involving the seizure of collateral or the payment of interest, and what has already been taken should be returned.

5:13 *shook out the folds of my robe.* Nehemiah's action represents what will happen to those who do not do as they swore. Other examples of such prophetic actions are found in 2 Kings 13:15–19 and Jeremiah 19:10–13. In this case, the folds of robes were the ancient equivalent of pockets, so shaking them out symbolized the loss of all one had. It is an appropriate judgment for any who seek to gain possessions at the cost of others' suffering. By thus invoking God's conditional judgment, Nehemiah seeks to ensure that the people will really do as agreed.

5:18 *I never demanded the food allotted to the governor, because the demands were heavy on these people.* Since the governor's food allowance was ultimately provided by the local population through taxation, Nehemiah is sparing them by paying for all the provisions himself. Rather than loaning money to those needing food and then seizing their securities, as others were doing, he gives food away at his own considerable expense. Doing so, he demonstrates love for the Judeans.

5:19 *Remember me with favor, my God.* Nehemiah is not afraid that God might literally forget what he has done. This is simply a way of saying that he wants to receive an appropriate reward from God for his actions. He has not taken opportunities to benefit personally from the hardships of others or from his position as governor. He seeks only that benefit God would choose to give him for righteous behavior. Nehemiah's expectation may be connected to promises like those in Exodus 20:6 and Deuteronomy 7:9, where God promises to bless those who love him and keep his commandments.

Theological Insights

The passage provides important theological insights in connection with both the actions of the creditors and the actions of Nehemiah. The efforts of Sanballat and his allies to stop work on the Jerusalem wall were ineffective partly because the Judean community remained united (compare Neh. 3). This unity is related to an important concept lying behind Nehemiah 5—namely, that the Judeans should consider one another as brothers and treat one another accordingly (in Hebrew, the word for brother occurs in vv. 1, 5, 7, 8; the concept is found elsewhere in the Old Testament also, such as in Lev. 19:17; Deut. 19:18; 23:19; where the NIV's "fellow Israelite" translates the Hebrew word for brother). When the creditors leave the debtors destitute by seizing their property, however, they destroy this essential unity.

Nehemiah provides an important contrast to the creditors. He takes action to protect those facing cruel hardship, reflecting the spirit of the Pentateuch, even if not clearly the letter. To bring about the necessary changes, he is willing to call the wealthy and influential to account. But he also uses his own resources sacrificially. The fact that Nehemiah acts out of the fear of God (Neh. 5:9, 15) means that he embodies God's values when he gives what it takes to protect the economically vulnerable because of his love for his fellow Judeans.

Community is an important value to God. The primary venue in which it is expressed is the biological family, but God intends that a similar community be expressed among the "family" of his people. It is an essential element of his plan to achieve his purposes in the world through his followers. He values it so highly that he expects believers to make personal sacrifices to preserve it and will punish those who threaten it (v. 13).

Teaching the Text

As God's people live in the world, economic needs invariably arise. This passage illustrates that the proper response is not to take advantage of the needy but to do what can be done to help them. The New Testament is as clear as the Old Testament in teaching that believers should do what they can to help other believers in need (e.g., 1 John 3:17). But Nehemiah helps readers understand in a unique way that this expectation outweighs legal considerations. His critique of the creditors does not suggest that the loan contracts were improperly executed, nor does he clearly cite specific statutes from Mosaic legislation. Instead he appeals to the spirit of God's instructions to Israel, which expect them to treat each other as family above all. Christians are also to act as the family of God toward one another, so at the very least they should not contribute to another's suffering by exploiting one another's needs for their own economic advantage. Whether a contract has been signed is irrelevant. Christians cannot hide behind law while they inflict suffering on others.

Nehemiah also goes beyond this minimum, however, doing all within his power to alleviate his people's hardship. As a leader he uses his influence to bring about change. He does this by delivering a well-thought-through (v. 7) appeal to the consciences of the creditors (vv. 7–8), followed by a bold exhortation to drop all claims and repay what has already been taken (vv. 10–11). When he obtains the desired response, he tries to ensure future compliance by having the creditors swear an oath and enacting a conditional judgment against them (vv. 12–13). It is probably possible to find modern parallels for the specific actions just listed, but it is most important to grasp the larger principle, which is that Nehemiah gives his best and fullest effort to ensure that the suffering of the poor will be relieved. Believers today need to put all their creativity and resourcefulness into the same endeavor, especially with respect to the poor among the body of Christ.

Besides using his influence to change practice, however, Nehemiah gives his own wealth to relieve the suffering of the poor as well. He both relinquishes income he is due and bears expenses for which he is not obligated. He is not content to find clever ways to help the poor that cost him nothing personally. He invests both ability and treasure in this undertaking, because it is an expression of his relationship with God. Contemporary Christians should seek to put these principles into practice as well. Like Nehemiah, they should look for the reward God has promised them rather than seeking earthly wealth.

It would be a mistake, however, to conclude that this passage prohibits charging interest on a loan, any more than it prohibits requiring security for a loan. Because of the economic crisis, such practices are stopped, but it is not the intention that loans should never be secured again.

Illustrating the Text

Legal rights never excuse exploiting our brothers and sisters.

History: History is filled with instances of laws that have been enacted, changed, or repealed to stop people from taking unfair advantage of others. Famous examples with this intent include the 13th, 15th, and 19th Amendments to the US Constitution, the Civil Rights Act of 1964, and the English Magna Carta of 1215, but there have been many thousands of others as well. In each case, prior to the legislative action taken, it was legally permissible to do something that was ultimately recognized as unfair. What this proves is that the fact that an activity or action is legal at a given time does not make it fair or right. If an act were automatically good and right simply because it was legal, there would never be need to change laws. While the legality of their actions is important for Christians to consider, it is far more important to evaluate whether their actions meet God's standards of justice and generosity.

Relieving the suffering of the poor deserves our best and fullest effort.

Literature: *A Christmas Carol*, **by Charles Dickens.** In this classic story, Ebenezer Scrooge is asked to give charitable help to the poor in his city. He replies by asking, "Are there no prisons? . . . And the union workhouses? . . . Are they still in operation?"[1] His hard heart believes that helping the poor is someone else's problem and that some institution out there will solve it. He ignores the possibility that using his God-given wealth to serve the poor in his city deserves his best and fullest effort.

Biography: Many are familiar with Santa Claus, but not as many are aware of the historical person, Saint Nicholas, behind the myth. Nicholas was born in the late 200s AD to very wealthy parents in the area of modern-day Turkey, then under Roman control. He had been raised a devout Christian, so when he lost his parents in a plague, he decided to obey Jesus's instructions to sell all you have and give to the poor. He used his whole inheritance to help the needy, the suffering, and the ill. He dedicated his life to Christian service and was made bishop of Myra when he was still quite young. He was known for his generosity, love for children, and care for sailors and ships. He was persecuted under the Roman emperor Diocletian and, after having suffered for his faith, was exiled and put in prison. In 325, after he was released, he went to the council of Nicaea, which produced the Nicene Creed. He died in 343 on December 6, and celebrations commemorating his death (St. Nicholas' Day) eventually became merged into Christmas traditions. Saint Nicholas truly gave care for the poor his fullest and best efforts.

Sharing our wealth with others brings fellowship with God.

Family Life: If one wants to grow closer with a new acquaintance who is a parent or grandparent, all one has to do is strike up conversation about the kids. Pictures will come out, stories will be told, and smiles become broad. In fact, to really connect with such a person, join them in a family activity or assist in the care and education of these children. Put simply, investing in someone's kids unites you quickly to that person. Sharing our wealth (which is really already God's) with others he loves is a great way to grow closer to him. Take an interest in helping his other kids, and you will see his smile often!

Nehemiah Resists His Enemies' Attempts to Intimidate Him

Big Idea

The leaders of God's people can overcome intimidation by trusting God for strength to complete the tasks he has given them.

Key Themes

- The enemies of the Judeans try various schemes to intimidate Nehemiah so he and the rest of the Judeans will not complete the Jerusalem wall.
- Nehemiah's trust in God is evident in his responses to the enemies' efforts.

Understanding the Text

The Text in Context

Nehemiah understands that the rebuilding of Jerusalem's wall would be a major step forward in the fulfillment of God's promise to restore the Judean people after exile. He has been leading the Judeans on this project since Nehemiah 1. The enemies of the Judeans, however, perceive the repair of the wall as leading to a reduction of their influence in the region. With the Judeans' internal problems of Nehemiah 5 resolved and the project nearly completed (there are no more gaps left in the wall [Neh. 6:1; compare Neh. 4:7]), the enemies make a few final attempts to sabotage it. Their earlier efforts to interfere targeted the entire community (Neh. 4), but now they focus on Nehemiah, the leader. His resistance to their attacks results in the completion of the wall, which is an important indicator of God's blessing, and which leads to the next stage in the restoration process.

Historical and Cultural Background

The precise location proposed by the enemies for a meeting with Nehemiah in 6:2 is uncertain. Where the NIV has "villages" (following the reading of the Septuagint and Vulgate), Hebrew manuscripts have the name of a currently unknown town, "Kephirim." The plain of Ono itself was probably at the edge or just outside of the Judean territory where Nehemiah was in charge (Ezra 2:33). It was close to Samaria. A meeting there would have required a day's journey for Nehemiah. Thus, accepting their proposal would have been time consuming and might have made it easier for them to harm him physically.

Interpretive Insights

6:3 *I am carrying on . . . go down to you.* Although Nehemiah perceives that the enemies intend to harm him (v. 2), his response attributes to them neither that motive nor a desire to stop the work. Instead he simply and honestly states that his priority is to continue the work without delay.

6:5 *an unsealed letter.* The point of the unsealed letter is to ensure that the rumors contained in it become public knowledge and that Nehemiah knows they will. The hope is that he will be alarmed enough to meet with the enemies to try to stop the rumors from reaching the king.

6:6 *It is reported.* The Hebrew word translated "is reported" is the same word translated "came" in verse 1 and "get back" in verse 7. The enemies have been informed of the progress on the wall, but in response they launch a misinformation campaign to get Nehemiah into trouble. The point is to use lies to put a false and damaging spin on what actually is true. They intend that when others, including the king, hear that the wall has been rebuilt, it will make the falsely slanted impression that serves the enemies' purposes.

Although Nehemiah has obtained support from the king for this project, attempted rebellions within the Persian Empire were not unusual. The satrap of Syria had even led a revolt not more than five years before Nehemiah traveled to Jerusalem. It would have seemed at least possible that Nehemiah was leading a revolt.

6:9 *Their hands will get too weak.* This idiom refers to inner state rather than physical strength. The enemies expect that the Judeans will become discouraged and unmotivated. The same expression was behind "discourage" in Ezra 4:4, where the enemies of the Judeans were successful in preventing them from rebuilding. The enemies hope to stop the process once again.

But I prayed. These words are not in the Hebrew text, but since the words of Nehemiah that follow sound as though they are addressed to God, most English translations indicate in some way that Nehemiah prays at this point. The parallel structure of 6:1–9 and 6:10–14 also favors this interpretation.

Each begins with a general description of the situation, followed by a report of the enemies' scheme, Nehemiah's response, and a statement that the point of the scheme was intimidation. Nehemiah 6:14 then concludes its section with a prayer. A prayer at the corresponding place in 6:9 maintains the pattern.

strengthen my hands. Nehemiah asks God to produce the exact opposite of the result the enemies seek. This idiom denotes motivation and determination. Instead of being intimidated, Nehemiah wants to have courage. This continues the theme of the Judean community needing to be strong as they carry out their role in the process of restoration (Ezra 6:22; Neh. 2:18). Ezra-Nehemiah teaches that God will give his people the strength they need to do their part in fulfilling his plans.

6:11 *Should a man like me run away?* Nehemiah is the governor of a Persian province, with his own armed bodyguard (Neh. 4:23). For him to run into the temple and hide in response to a mere rumor of a death threat would be embarrassingly inappropriate and would discredit him in the eyes of all.

should someone like me go into the temple . . . ? Nehemiah is not a priest and is therefore not allowed to go into the temple (Num. 18:7; 2 Chron. 26:16–18). The right to seek asylum from a feared killer (1 Kings 1:50) was connected to the altar in the temple courtyard and not to the temple interior, behind closed doors. Nehemiah is unwilling to disobey God's commands.

6:12 *I realized that God had not sent him.* It appears that Shemaiah is presenting the message he speaks to Nehemiah as a prophecy from God. But Nehemiah recognizes that the advice Shemaiah is giving him is contrary to God's commands in Scripture and therefore not from God and not to be heeded. He then catches on that Shemaiah has been put up to this charade by Tobiah and Sanballat.

6:13 *to discredit me.* The word translated "discredit" is closely related to the word translated "disgrace" in Nehemiah 1:3; 2:17, "insults" in Nehemiah 4:4, and "reproach" in Nehemiah 5:9. This episode is part of the larger struggle for the people of Israel to be free of the shame they suffer as part of their judgment for unfaithfulness to God. The rebuilding of the wall finds its true significance in the removal of disgrace from the returned exiles. Their enemies, however, not only oppose the rebuilding; they seek opportunity to perpetuate the shame any way they can. Scaring Nehemiah into sin would fit their intentions particularly well.

6:14 *Remember . . . what they have done.* When Nehemiah asks God to remember the actions of several people, he implies that God should pay them back for what they have done. It is similar to his request in Nehemiah 5:19 for God to remember him with favor for the good things he has done. Both kinds of requests are based on the expectation that God will be faithful to his covenant with Israel in which he promises to bless them when they obey and fear him (e.g., Deut. 6:24) and to be an enemy to those who are an enemy to his obedient people (Exod. 23:22). As in Nehemiah 4:4–5, Nehemiah's prayer leaves it up to God to bring appropriate judgment on those doing evil, as opposed to Nehemiah trying to take matters into his own hands. (See the sidebar "Christians and Imprecatory Prayers" in the unit on Neh. 4:1–23.)

the rest of the prophets. In Ezra 5–6 the prophets Haggai and Zechariah furthered God's plan by playing an important role in encouraging the Judeans to finish rebuilding the temple, which is what one might typically expect prophets to do. But here it is clear that a number of prophets worked against Nehemiah as he tried to do God's work. Even those designated as prophets can oppose God's will. This provides a hint that threats to the success of the restoration will not be removed merely by completing the wall. Even some within the community are surprisingly ready to cooperate with the enemy.

Theological Insights

The Jewish community has made considerable progress on the wall, the completion of which represents a significant indicator of the restoration of their relationship with God. But there are those who continue to oppose their endeavors. These opponents try to intimidate the Judean community in general, and the leader, Nehemiah, in particular (6:9, 13, 14). Whereas they used open threats of force in Nehemiah 4, they use subtler tactics in Nehemiah 6, including veiled threats, explicit threats of accusation before the king, and messages purportedly from God himself. In this last strategy, they even enlist to their cause those among the Judean people who should be spiritual leaders. Once again, the narrative reveals that God regularly does not intervene to prevent his people from facing attack. While we might prefer a plotline of straightforward progress toward the goal, God allows the complication of opposition and is not threatened by it.

Nehemiah's response to these attacks is effective. He does not fight back with aggressive counterattacks. He uses only enough words to decline dangerous invitations and deny false accusations. Above all, he trusts God. He continues with the task God has given him and refuses to disobey his commands. He prays that God will give him the necessary courage and punish his enemies justly. And he prevails in the struggle. God brings glory to himself not by an overwhelming display of power as at the Red Sea but by quietly enabling one who openly trusts him to endure in the midst of battle.

Teaching the Text

Working to advance the kingdom of God does not necessarily involve building physical structures today, as it did for Nehemiah (although sometimes constructing buildings can be an important part of it). The kinds of "construction" more relevant for Christians are the building of relationships, the establishment of local churches, and the development of Christian character in the lives of disciples. Yet there are still many people who, although they may not think they are opposing God, see a conflict between something the church is doing and how they want things to be. Consequently, they sometimes try to stop that work by intimidating the church and its leaders. In some parts of the world, the intimidation regularly involves physical force. But in the West it is usually subtler. A popular tactic is to hold out the threat of damaged reputation. If the enemies of the church can bring the public at large or church members to believe that the church's leaders have acted dishonorably, they know that the effectiveness of the leaders will be diminished and that the effectiveness of the church as a whole will therefore also be dimished. The enemies can achieve this through putting a false and negative spin on things the church is actually doing ("You are about to become their king," v. 6). Another approach is to exaggerate the likelihood of an undesirable event in order to make an otherwise objectionable and desperate solution seem like a good plan ("Let us meet ... inside the temple ... because men are coming to kill you," v. 10). If the desperate plan is adopted, the leaders end up looking foolish or worse. All the ploys used by the enemies in Nehemiah 6 involve intimidation of some kind, and all enhance the danger that Nehemiah will be driven by fear to make an adverse decision. This sort of psychological warfare is common today.

There is no simple way to deal with intimidation. Sometimes it is important to dialogue even with those who truly are opposed to God's work. But godly wisdom requires the ability to discern the right response in a particular case, and leaders are wise to include among their options the approach Nehemiah uses in this passage. Having good evidence that Sanballat, Tobiah, and company mean only to disrupt his work (Neh. 2:10, 19; 4:1, 7–8), he avoids lengthy interaction with them. He does not make counterattacks or launch public relations campaigns to win public opinion to his side. On the contrary, he focuses on God's will as it has been revealed in Scripture, which includes both the rebuilding of postexilic Jerusalem as part of the promise of restoration and the command for laypeople not to enter the temple. He also prays, both for himself, that God would strengthen him, and about his enemies, that God would deal justly with them. Such courageous, practical expressions of faith in the midst of real-life complexities will usually provide the best way forward for Christian leaders faced with intimidation.

It is important to see clearly that the reasons Nehemiah knows Shemaiah's message does not come from God are that it tells him to do something Scripture says not to (enter the temple as a layman) and, secondarily, that it involves a failure to act in line with the responsibility and authority he has been given as governor (run away). To conclude that the passage teaches that people should avoid becoming overly busy or taking on duties that do not fit their personalities is to stray from the author's intent.

Illustrating the Text

Intimidation of believers takes many forms.

History: Through the centuries, those attempting to live faithfully for Christ in the world have faced much intimidation, and those seeking to frighten them have often been imaginative in their methods. During the era of the Soviet Union, for example, Soviet authorities often tried to turn public opinion against Russian pastors by labeling them as foreign spies and subversive terrorists. Many were arrested and held for long periods in prison. Some were even tortured and forced to pose in photographs staged to give the impression that they were involved in sexual immorality. At times the government made it illegal for parents to teach their children about religion or to bring them to church services. It was even against the law for clergy to make religion popular by personal example! Believers persevered through such opposition only by prayer and commitment to faithfully following Christ.

Worrying about personal reputation is a snare.

Human Experience: How often have you made decisions that were based on a desire to have other people think of you (or not think of you) a certain way? How often have those decisions turned out well? Young boys often accept dares because they don't want their peers to think they're afraid. The great irony is that their acceptance of the foolish dare shows how afraid they are of their peers' judgment. As we get older, we can see more clearly that some of the decisions we made as children were unwise. Yet we never outgrow the desire to be liked and accepted by others. Those who use the threat of rejection or slander to try to control us, however, demonstrate that they do not have our best interests at heart. As Christians we need to remember that compromising our faithfulness to Christ to try to protect our reputation is no wiser than giving in to a childish dare.

Advice that contradicts God's instructions is worthless.

Outdoors: Many secure the services of a guide when attempting a mountain climb or wilderness trek. A good guide can tell you the best way to use the skill and resources you have to get up the mountain safely and is there to steer you around obstacles you might not see and that might otherwise defeat you. On a mountain climb, for example, a guide can advise you on how much to pack, how fast to go, what route to take to the summit, and how to avoid avalanches. If you hired a mountain guide who advised you to free-climb Mount Everest in a bathing suit or who questioned the very existence of mountains and had never climbed one personally, you would deem his or her advice to be worthless. Likewise, other believers who actively obey Christ can help us apply God's instructions in our lives, prioritize steps in our faith, or accelerate in our discipleship process. If they contradict the Bible or have no experience in obedience, however, their advice is utterly worthless.

Nehemiah Is Prompted to Prepare to Repopulate Jerusalem

Big Idea

For God's people to live as he has planned, responsibilities must be assigned among them thoughtfully.

Key Themes

- In the struggle to remove shame through rebuilding the wall, the Judeans emerge victorious by God's power.
- Although an important stage of the restoration has been completed, mixed allegiances among the Judean leaders weaken the security of the community.
- Nehemiah and his brother make wise decisions, assigning important responsibilities to various people to help the community function.

Understanding the Text

The Text in Context

The rebuilding of Jerusalem's wall, the focus of Nehemiah 1–6, comes to a successful end. The opposition presented by the enemies (Neh. 2, 4, 6) and the internal problems of the Judean community (Neh. 5) have been overcome. Having a restored wall around Jerusalem is a significant part of restoring the Judeans from the judgment of exile to the experience of God's blessing. Yet in this passage, it becomes clear that the repaired wall alone is insufficient to ensure the security of Jerusalem. Awareness of the need for guards to protect the city then leads to awareness of the need for a larger population in it generally. At that point God gives Nehemiah the idea for his second project in the book, the repopulation of Jerusalem. Like the wall-building project, Nehemiah's new project has a tangible component, relocating individuals to the city. But since it focuses on people, it provides an appropriate transition to the concerns of the last part of the narrative, which are the spiritual condition of the Judeans and Jerusalem's status as a holy city.

The transition is highlighted by the list in Nehemiah 7:6–73a, which is virtually the same as the list in Ezra 2:1–70. By repeating the list in full, the narrator of Ezra-Nehemiah forms a kind of envelope around Ezra 3:1–Nehemiah 7:5, a little like opening and closing credits for a movie, and defining it as a discrete section of the narrative. That larger unit tells of the major return journeys and reconstruction projects that signaled the restoration and in which these people were the major actors. The ensuing narrative will give less attention to physical rebuilding and more to the character of the people who make up the Judean community.

Interpretive Insights

6:15 *the wall was completed . . . in fifty-two days.* Although this is a remarkably short time, the builders were not starting from scratch, and portions of the wall were probably relatively intact, so this does not represent a miracle. On the other hand, a similar project had earlier been forced to stop (Ezra 4:12, 23), and the builders faced considerable opposition this time as well (Neh. 4; 6). The fact that they are able to finish so quickly is evidence that God is working through them to remove the shame that the broken-down walls represented.

6:16 *When all our enemies heard . . . the help of our God.* The pattern so far in Nehemiah has been for the enemies to hear about plans or progress made by the Judeans and respond aggressively, requiring a counterresponse from Nehemiah (Neh. 2:19–20; 4:1–9; 6:1–9). The pattern now comes to an end, since the response from the enemies is fear. This part of the struggle has ended in a decisive victory for the Judeans. It is an appropriate outcome also, because the enemies have been trying to make the Judeans afraid (Neh. 6:9, 13–14). Nehemiah helped bring about this result by trusting God to strengthen him and to bring upon the enemies what they sought to do to others (see comments on Nehemiah 6:1–14).

6:17 *Also . . . sending many letters to Tobiah.* Immediately after reporting the great achievement of building the wall, Nehemiah states that there is an ongoing correspondence between Judean nobles and Tobiah. This shows that those Judeans' allegiance is compromised (v. 18) and poses an internal security threat (v. 19). The restoration is far from complete.

6:19 *his good deeds.* It is possible that Tobiah's family ties to the Judean community had led to business contracts (perhaps the oaths mentioned in v. 18) that brought economic benefits to those involved. Whatever the actual details were, it seems that some of the Judean nobles saw Tobiah as helping their personal interests and tried to get Nehemiah to see him more favorably.

Nehemiah, on the other hand, continually received Tobiah's intimidating letters, and so knew that Tobiah did not have the community's best interests at heart.

7:1 *the gatekeepers . . . were appointed.* The roles mentioned in this verse were normally associated with the temple. But since Tobiah's tactics and the sparse population of Jerusalem make it vulnerable, these groups are probably assigned to protect the whole city. Placing temple personnel around Jerusalem also has the further effect of portraying the city itself as the holy temple of God, something Jeremiah prophesied it would become (Jer. 31:38–40).

7:3 *The gates of Jerusalem . . . shut the doors and bar them.* There is some uncertainty about the correct translation of this part of the verse. It could be saying that the city gates are not to be opened until the hot part of the day (as the NIV and some other translations have it), thus probably opening around noon, or it could mean that they should not be opened during that part of the day (so, e.g., the NLT), thus, not open during the early afternoon. The reasoning in the second case would be that the guards might be on siesta then and the city would be more vulnerable. The intent of the next statement is also uncertain. The NIV states that the gates should be shut before the gatekeepers go off duty, but it could also mean that the gates should be kept shut even while the guards are on duty or that they should be kept shut until the guards come on duty. The intended meaning was probably unambiguous to the original readers, and, whatever it is, it seems that the point is to take unusual steps to ensure the city's security. Such measures make sense in light of the efforts made by the enemies of the Judeans in preceding chapters and the continuing intimidation tactics of Tobiah mentioned at the end of Nehemiah 6.

7:4 *there were few people in it.* Having a sparse population in Jerusalem highlights two problems: (1) the city is more vulnerable to attack, since there are fewer people to be aware of attackers entering, and (2) God's promised restoration remains unfulfilled, since the prophets predicted that the streets of Jerusalem would be filled with people again (Zech. 8:5; compare Jer. 30:18–19). In this weakened state, the city is still an object of reproach to some extent, which is the situation Nehemiah has been seeking to change (e.g., Neh. 2:17).

the houses had not yet been rebuilt. It is clear from the end of the preceding verse, as well as from Nehemiah 3:20, 29, that there are houses in Jerusalem at this time. It may be better to translate "houses were not (at that time) being rebuilt," since the Hebrew allows it.

7:5 *my God put it into my heart.* Nehemiah made a similar statement in 2:12 about the idea of rebuilding Jerusalem's wall. Just as that activity was an important part of God's restoration of the Judean community, so, by implication, the idea he is about to describe will also contribute to it.

to assemble . . . for registration by families. The purpose of conducting a census becomes clear only in chapter 11. Nehemiah intends to solve the problem of Jerusalem's underpopulation by having some of the Judeans relocate to the city. To do that he must first know how many there are and where they are.

the genealogical record of those who had been the first to return. The numbers on this list are not current in Nehemiah's day, so initially it seems strange that he considers it useful. It provides a list of clans and local communities where returnees had originally settled, giving him a helpful starting point for organizing the registration of the population by family groupings. But there is a more important factor also. Given the centrality of Jerusalem in the promises of restoration and the concerns about enemies described in the preceding narrative, it is essential that only the true people of God be chosen to repopulate it. Nehemiah wants to know that all who move into Jerusalem are descendants of the Judean exiles who returned in response to Cyrus's decree, referred to in Ezra 1. When the list was used in Ezra 2, it demonstrated continuity between the returnees and preexilic Israel, showing they were the rightful recipients of God's restoration promises. Connecting the new residents of Jerusalem with the initial returnees here extends that continuity and guarantees they are the right people to advance the restoration further.

7:6 *These are the people of the province.* For comments on the significance of the list and its internal details, see Interpretive Insights in the unit on Ezra 2:1–70. There are some discrepancies between the text of this list and its version in Ezra 2:1–70, but most of them probably arose in the course of textual transmission. Also, when the original government document was copied into Ezra-Nehemiah in either place, the writer may have felt free to summarize some details; compare especially Ezra 2:68–69 with Nehemiah 7:70–72.

Theological Insights

God enables his people to overcome any and all opposition to achieve his purposes. Sometimes circumstances are such that even those working against God's people can recognize his intervention. But even at times like those, it does not necessarily follow that God's opponents will stop resisting him and trying to carry out their own agenda. Moreover, there are often those among God's own people who act with mixed allegiances and motives. God's people must prepare for a long struggle as they seek the fullness of the restoration God has promised.

Although God is ultimately the one who ensures the success of his plans, he regularly chooses to work through the thoughtful decisions of those to whom he has assigned responsibility. Many times the decisions he favors are those that might be described as pragmatic common sense. In this passage, those with experience guarding the temple are the first appointed to guard duty for the city, and people are asked to keep watch near their own houses. But even more important to God are spiritual considerations. Nehemiah delegates authority on the basis of a man's integrity and fear of God, and only true Israelites will be recruited to move to Jerusalem. God's highest concern is whether people make decisions according to his revealed values; common sense can and should be used when it does not conflict with these.

Teaching the Text

The action of this passage takes place in the context of the recent completion of the Jerusalem wall by the Judeans. They have worked diligently and sacrificially, and their intense labor has been evident to everyone. Yet at the same time it is plain that they have finished it so quickly because God has helped them. While the planting of a new church or the establishment of an effective ministry may not seem like a supernatural event, in a very real way it stands as testimony to divine enabling.

The completion of the wall does not mean the end of opposition to the Judeans, however. In addition to attempts at intimidation, Tobiah also cultivates relationships within the Judean community that result in divided loyalties among them. Christians often face this too. Living in the midst of unbelievers, some of whom are antagonistic toward the things of God, they form various kinds of relationships and even interdependencies. But it is important for God's people to manage those relationships to prevent their loyalty to the cause of Christ from being compromised. It can be a delicate issue, because both those within and those without the church typically have mixed motives, and it is important to try to see all sides of a disagreement. But siding with one who makes attacks against a fellow believer is inappropriate.

Given, then, that opposition to the Judeans of Jerusalem continues, it is necessary for them to appoint people to specific responsibilities to provide for the city's security. Nehemiah and the leaders with whom he works take practical considerations into account, like using the experience people already have and assigning tasks people will likely be motivated to carry out (like guarding the wall near their own homes). But they give priority to spiritual and moral qualifications. Similarly, it is necessary to entrust ongoing responsibility in the church to those who demonstrate the kind of character a Christian should have. This is really the principle behind the criteria given in the New Testament for selecting elders (e.g., 1 Tim. 3:2–12). The goal is to reduce the possibility of compromise among those doing God's work.

At the most general level, Nehemiah perceives the need for more people to live in Jerusalem. But God's promises concerning Jerusalem are part of his broader promises to his people, so the city must function as God's city.

It is necessary, therefore, to have God's people, the recipients of his grace in the return from exile, living there. Membership in the church is not based on biological descent or geographical location. It is based on the experience of God's grace through faith. It is not always possible to be completely certain who is and who is not a believer, but the church must do its best to be sure that the benefits and responsibilities of membership are given only to those who have been given life by the Spirit. Otherwise the church will not function as it should (Eph. 2:19–22).

Illustrating the Text

Even when we work hard, God's miraculous power shines through.

Information: Many amazing inventions were what we call "flukes," meaning unintended positive benefits that resulted from another process. People were working hard on important goals, and inventions emerged that were far more remarkable than the original project. One example is the chocolate chip cookie! Ruth Wakefield, owner of the Toll House Inn, was trying to bake regular chocolate cookies, when she ran out of baker's chocolate. She broke sweetened chocolate into chunks and added it to the dough at the last minute, hoping it would melt in. The chunks stayed separate, and the chocolate chip cookie was born. Another example is the microwave oven. Percy Spencer was working as an engineer at Raytheon researching new vacuum-tube technologies when he noticed the candy bar in his pocket had melted. He put popcorn into the machine next, and when it popped, the microwave "radar range" was born. These flukes are examples of how hard work and miracles are not incompatible; God still finds a way to show his brilliance, even when we are working hard.

We must love the lost and stand united with the bride of Christ.

Christian Trends: Many authors and speakers who claim to be Christian are working hard to show their love for the lost by being highly critical of the church. Such people write articles that elicit approval from unbelievers by confirming their complaints about the bride of Christ. Explain that such efforts are misguided; we need to show the lost that we love them *and* that the body of Christ presents them with a viable community of refuge and safety in this world. Claiming to love Jesus and then impressing people by complaining about his bride is a highly flawed and offensive plan.

Those who most live like Christ are most qualified to lead with Christ.

Everyday Life: There are many careers that require a high level of training and aptitude, such that only a very small percentage of applicants make the cut. Examples include certain medical specialists, special forces soldiers, elite athletes, and professional musicians. We understand that these positions are not for everyone, and that only those with the proper aptitudes and training should attempt them. In the same way, while all believers should follow Christ and grow in leadership, there are certain levels of church leadership that aren't for everyone. Often, the aptitude and experience needed are related to character and selflessness. In the end, those who most resemble Christ in life are most qualified to lead in his name.

Popular Saying: There is an old saying, "It takes one to know one." When it comes to Christian leadership, this is certainly true. Those called to lead have to live out and experience a living relationship with Jesus; only then can they spot and nurture that hope in others.

The Israelites Rejoice after Understanding and Obeying God's Law

Big Idea

Both the understanding of and the obedience to God's teaching produce joy for God's people.

Key Themes

- All the Judeans take initiative to obtain knowledge and understanding of God's law.
- The leaders of the people help them to understand the law.
- When the people understand and obey the law, they have great joy.

Understanding the Text

The Text in Context

When God judged the nation of Judah for unfaithfulness and disobedience to him, he sent the people into exile and allowed the Babylonians to destroy the temple and wall of Jerusalem. These physical circumstances were a source of shame to the Judeans. In Ezra 1–Nehemiah 6, each of those judgments is reversed as an indication that God's promised restoration of the Judeans is under way. Nehemiah 7 reminds the reader that the Judean community is composed of descendants of those who experienced God's grace in the return from exile. Beginning in Nehemiah 8, greater emphasis is given to the spiritual condition of the Judeans. God's promise of restoration included a new covenant with Israel in which his people internalize his instructions and obey him sincerely (Jer. 31:31–34). In this chapter the people hear God's instructions and respond with joyful obedience. This leads to further steps to be taken in the ensuing narrative, such that Nehemiah 8–10 resembles a covenant renewal between Israel and God, a taste of what the new covenant should be like.

God also promised that in the restoration Jerusalem would become a holy city (Jer. 31:38–40; Ezek. 48:35). Nehemiah 7:4–5 gives an advance indication that Jerusalem is about to be repopulated, so the covenant renewal of Nehemiah 8–10 appropriately ensures that the city's new inhabitants, who are determined in Nehemiah 11, will be suitably holy.

Historical and Cultural Background

It may seem strange to modern readers that the assembly gathered to hear Scripture read aloud. In contemporary culture it is taken for granted that a text is something easily accessed, and therefore something all can read privately. In the ancient Near East, however, relatively few copies of written texts were available, and many people had practically no access to them. Literacy itself was also lower in those cultures. Thus, the quickest way to satisfy the people's desire to know God's word was through a public reading.

The people's request to hear the law read also sits well against the background of Deuteronomy 31:9–13. In that passage Moses commanded that the law be read to Israel every seventh year during the Festival of Tabernacles. It is not clear whether the events of Nehemiah 8 occurred during a "seventh year," but even if they did, the people clearly asked for the law to be read even before the Festival of Tabernacles, indicating their eagerness.

Interpretive Insights

8:1 *as one.* During the seventh month the people were to observe the Festival of Trumpets (on the first day), the Day of Atonement (the tenth day), and the Festival of Tabernacles (fifteenth to the twenty-second day). For Tabernacles, all the men were to travel to Jerusalem. The fact that all the people came to Jerusalem at the beginning of the month and without any mention of anyone calling them indicates an unusual eagerness on their part and an uncommon degree of unity.

they told Ezra . . . to bring out. The initiative for reading the law comes from the laypeople, not from Ezra or the priests. This is somewhat similar to, but perhaps even more impressive than, Ezra 10:2–4, where laypeople initiated action about the mixed marriages. There was no requirement in the Pentateuch for the law to be read at the Festival of Trumpets, and this fact highlights the people's desire and initiative all the more.

8:9 *"Do not mourn or weep." For all the people had been weeping.* It is not stated why the people are weeping. When Josiah heard the law read, he wept in repentance of sin (2 Chron. 34:27), so that is likely why the people weep here. However, the leaders instruct them to rejoice instead of mourning. The reason is that the occasion is a festival, and all festivals were to be

The Missing Day of Atonement

One of the important events God instructed the Israelites to observe was the Day of Atonement (Lev. 16; 23:26–32; Num. 29:7–11). Since it was to occur on the tenth day of the seventh month, readers have frequently wondered why there is no mention of it in Nehemiah 8. Pondering this question may actually make it easier to observe the writer's purpose in this chapter.

Nehemiah 8 focuses most on the actions of the people as a whole rather than on the actions of the priests. It shows that the people gathered together in Jerusalem and were eager to obey God's law, even if that meant they needed to change behavior they were used to. It also emphasizes the joy that came from understanding and obeying the law. By contrast, the Day of Atonement mainly involved the actions of the priests, especially the high priest. The people were not required to gather in Jerusalem. The community may already have been observing the day according to God's regulations, so there may have been no need to make changes. And it was not a day of celebration. Since the narrator's message centered on the features noted above, there was no reason to include mention of the Day of Atonement in this chapter. In addition, however, the ark of the covenant had a central place in the activities of the Day of Atonement (e.g., Lev. 16:11–17), and since the ark was destroyed at the time of the exile, it is also possible that the people felt they could no longer observe the day properly.

observed with rejoicing and fellowship offerings (Num. 10:10; Deut. 12:7, 12, 18). Modern readers might expect that a day designated as holy would be observed with solemnity, but the Old Testament expectation was that such days would be full of rejoicing. The people's joy was to come from remembering the blessings they had as God's people. So the leaders are simply reminding the people how to obey God on this occasion.

8:10 *the joy of the LORD is your strength.* The phrase "joy of the LORD" is by itself ambiguous. It could refer to the joy the Lord has or supplies, or it could refer to joy that someone has concerning the Lord. The people are told several times in the context to rejoice, and the cause for their rejoicing is the relationship they have with the Lord and the blessings he brings. The phrase probably refers, then, to joy the people have concerning the Lord. The word translated "strength" may more accurately be rendered "fortress" or "refuge," implying a source of protection. Thus, the message is that when people rejoice over the Lord, their rejoicing protects them (see further in Theological Insights below).

8:15 *as it is written.* The proclamation reported in this verse is not a quote from any part of the law of Moses. It seems instead to be a summary of what the community leaders understand the law to be telling them to do in light of their study of it (vv. 13–14). Leviticus 23:2 states that all the appointed festivals are to be proclaimed, which may be the basis for the proclamation here. Leviticus 23:40 tells the Israelites to gather branches from several specific types of trees but also from leafy trees in general. This is likely the basis for directing the people to gather branches from types of trees that were not specified in Leviticus but were available to them. Finally, Leviticus 23:42 instructs the people to live in temporary shelters for seven days, and this is why the present passage tells the returned exiles to build such shelters. By understanding the intent of the Leviticus text, determining how to apply it in contemporary circumstances, and sharing these insights with the people, the leaders feel confident that they are guiding the people to do what Scripture says.

8:17 *From the days of Joshua . . . had not celebrated it like this.* The Festival of Tabernacles had been observed in Solomon's day (2 Chron. 7:8–10; 8:13) and in the time of Zerubbabel (Ezra 3:4), at minimum. Therefore it must be that the *manner* in which it is celebrated here has not been matched since the time of Joshua. The narrator emphasizes building shelters and living in them. Although this is instructed in Leviticus 23, the instructions for this festival in Numbers 29:12–38 do not include this aspect, and the descriptions of the celebrations in Solomon's and Zerubbabel's times do not mention it either. It is quite possible, then, that the Israelites had neglected to live in temporary shelters during this festival between Joshua's time and the events of Nehemiah 8. Their eager discovery of this requirement and willing obedience to it illustrate an attitude to God's Torah that is unusual in Israel's history.

Theological Insights

This passage helps the original readers to visualize what the fulfillment of Jeremiah 31:33–34 should look like. God's ideal relationship with his people is one in which he protects and provides for them, and all of them obey him wholeheartedly. Nehemiah 8 emphasizes the Judeans' eagerness to hear the word and understand it, as well as their obedient response. The whole community acts this way, not just some.

Mention of the joy of the Lord leads to another important insight. What people are attached to and value affects their emotions. When the Judeans listen to God's word, they hear both stories of how he has chosen, saved, and blessed their ancestors and commands they are to keep. As they listen, they are able to recognize that God has similarly delivered and blessed them by bringing them back to the promised land. They understand that his commands are intended for their good. They begin to grasp that the covenant relationship they have with God is the most wonderful possession possible, and they mourn the ways that they have been unfaithful to him. But the leaders in Nehemiah 8:10 remind them that God wants them to rejoice, not mourn. He promises to forgive and restore them. If they truly value their relationship with him enough that the prospect of returning to mutual covenant faithfulness makes them rejoice, then they already have the attitude God desires, and he will not judge them. Such joy in the Lord is a refuge for them.

Teaching the Text

The entire Bible highlights the connection between God's word and the ability to be in relationship with him. Israel understood God's love for them and his plans for them through the revelation preserved in the Old Testament. The New Testament reveals that eternal life can be received only through hearing the word of Christ (Rom. 10:17). Because God's word plays such a central role in connecting his people to him, it is only natural that they have a deep desire to know it and order their lives by it. And since the church participates in the new covenant as inaugurated by Christ, its members should have an even greater desire for God's word than pre-Christian Israel had. They should be encouraged to see this desire as normal.

But although knowing, understanding, and obeying the word of God are natural impulses for believers, sometimes their interest in it can be dulled. The list of possible interferences is long, but this passage sheds light on a particularly subtle one. The Bible contains answers to many problems and needs people have, and in self-centered, modern Western culture it is easy for Christians to fall into the trap of seeing Scripture as a set of solutions for the troubles we identify. But Nehemiah 8 tells the story of a people hungry for God's word to set the agenda for their lives, whatever that agenda may be. God's people today need to develop the same attitude. The point is not to ignore their felt needs but to give highest priority to letting God's word establish the goals they aim for, not only the means to achieve them.

Another obstacle can be difficulty understanding the Bible. Western society suffers increasingly from biblical illiteracy, and the vast differences between the cultures in which Scripture was written and contemporary culture make it seem like alien literature. Like the Levites of Nehemiah 8, believers should take whatever role they can in helping one another interpret and apply the Bible correctly. Postmodern relativism encourages the idea that one person's interpretation is as valid as the next person's, but such approaches ultimately empty Scripture of its meaning. A different idea that leads to a similar outcome is to downplay the gap between the culture in which Scripture was written and the current culture, implying that knowledge beyond the ability to read the Bible in one's own language is unnecessary for correct interpretation. The obvious refutation of this latter opinion is to invite those who hold it to interpret a passage of Scripture as it was originally written—that is, in one of the biblical languages. At that point, their absolute dependence on those with specialized knowledge becomes clear.

It is especially important for church leaders to provide guidance. With so many avenues of ministry in demand, the teaching of the Word itself can be neglected. Yet it is vital, and it is unsurprising that Paul placed such importance on this (2 Tim. 4:2–4).

The result of earnestly seeking to know God's Word, receiving the necessary help to understand it, and then actually applying it in the real world is joy. Of course, it is important to remember that believers have a relationship with Christ and are not merely following a book of rules. But the relationship will never produce its intended happiness unless God's people desire to do his will. Christians will experience the highest heights of joy only when their true heart's desire is for God's kingdom to come and his will to be done on earth as it is in heaven.

Illustrating the Text

The Bible reveals God's goals, not just tips on how to achieve our own.

Military: Imagine that a new recruit goes to basic training and is told by a raging sergeant to run a mile and do one hundred push-ups. The recruit tells the sergeant, "Thanks for taking time out to train me, but I was really hoping to work on my abs and biceps today; I feel like I'm good on cardio and triceps." How would that go for the recruit? The army is ready to shape new soldiers to fit its plans and needs; the recruits' goals may be well and good, but the army isn't there to coach them through personal goals—it is there to prepare them to defend the best interests of the country. In the same way, the Bible isn't there to give us helpful tips in reaching our own goals; it is there to reveal God's goals and to strengthen us to serve his interests.

To understand the Bible well, we need the Spirit and one another.

Popular Saying: Many of your listeners will be familiar with the African proverb "If you want to go fast, go alone; if you want to go far, go together." When it comes to studying the Bible and applying it faithfully in everyday life, we can go fast and single-mindedly alone, but we go deeper, further, and richer when we read together.

Applying the Text: Invite your listeners to join a small group Bible study. Explain that the best way to read the Bible is in community with others who can help you pray for illumination, listen for God, understand, and apply what is being taught in the pages of Scripture.

Doing demands understanding, and understanding demands doing.

Family Life: Many parents will have had the experience of admonishing their child about a certain bad manner or behavior, only to hear the child reply,

"I know." For example, a child who just left his coat on the floor is told, "Remember—we need to pick up our own things around here." The child responds with indignation, "I knooooww!" The irony that is maddeningly obvious to the parent is that the child really doesn't know that truth; if he or she did, the coat would have been picked up in the first place. Moments later, that same child can push down a sibling, be asked why, and respond with indignation, "I don't knooooww!" Knowing that never takes the form of doing is just meaningless data on file. Doing that never involves knowing is empty impulse. Healthy knowing bears fruit in doing, and healthy doing finds its direction and meaning in knowing.

The Israelites Acknowledge God's Constant Mercy in Response to Their Rebellion

Big Idea

No matter how rebellious people have been, they can count on God to keep his gracious promises, because he has shown himself faithful.

Key Themes

- God has more than fulfilled his good promise to Israel.
- In spite of God's goodness to Israel, they have repeatedly rebelled against him.
- Although God has punished Israel because of their rebellion, he has compassionately rescued them whenever they have called out to him.
- Based on God's demonstrated character, the Israelites trust that God will deliver them from their present distress.

Understanding the Text

The Text in Context

Ezra-Nehemiah highlights the reestablishment of the remnant of Israel in the promised land as a partial fulfillment of the prophetic promise of restoration of the relationship between God and Israel. An important facet of the promised restoration is the new-covenant prophecy of Jeremiah 31:31–34, which looks forward to the time when Israel will obey God from the heart. Nehemiah shows that he understands that reestablishment in the land and new-covenant obedience belong together in his prayer in Nehemiah 1:7–9.

With the temple and wall of Jerusalem rebuilt and thousands of exiles re-settled in Judea, it is appropriate for the narrative focus to shift from their physical reestablishment in the land and concentrate on spiritual renewal, a theme that was previously introduced in the mixed-marriage incident in Ezra 9–10.

The structure of Nehemiah 8–10 follows a pattern recognizable from a number of covenant renewals in earlier parts of the Old Testament (Exod. 34; Josh. 24; 2 Chron. 15; 29–31; 34–35)—proclamation of God's law, confession of sin, renewal of commitment to obedience. Whereas Nehemiah 8 records the reading of God's law and the community's joy in knowing and obeying it, Nehemiah 9 relates their confession and mourning over sin. This leads to the renewed commitment to obedience in Nehemiah 10. The actions of the remnant seem to anticipate the new covenant.

Since God has brought his people back to their land from captivity and they are returning to him sincerely, the prayer in this chapter expresses hope for another promised aspect of restoration, that they will be freed from ser-vitude to foreign rulers (e.g., Isa. 49:22–23).

Historical and Cultural Background

One of the ways in which ancient Near Eastern culture differed from con-temporary Western society was in the concept of corporate identity. Whereas modern Westerners think of themselves primarily as individuals, the ancients took their identity just as much, if not more, from the community with whom they shared a common ancestry. The community was represented by all of its members, including those of the past and future. What happened to one member was considered to some extent to have happened to all, and what one did was considered to have consequences, either positive or negative, for all.

This helps to explain why God expected his people to confess the sins of their ancestors (Neh. 9:2; compare Lev. 26:40). For the people to be reconciled to God, they have to address the history of their relationship with him.

Interpretive Insights

9:2 *Those of Israelite descent had separated themselves from all foreigners.* The separation mentioned here would involve at least avoidance of marriages with non-Israelites, thus representing an improvement over the situation in Ezra 9:1. The point is not to be antisocial but to avoid participating in activi-ties that violate God's law (see Neh. 10:28).

9:7 *who chose Abram.* God took the initiative in beginning a relationship with Israel. He is the subject of all the verbs in verses 6–15. The emphasis is on his gracious acts that benefit his people.

9:8 *you made a covenant with him . . . the land.* This prayer tells the story of the relationship between God and Israel, and that relationship was founded on the covenant with Abraham. Since the status of Israel's possession of the land is a major concern to the community in Nehemiah 9, as well as throughout Israelite history, God's gift of the land receives greatest attention among his covenant promises.

9:9 *you heard their cry.* In verse 4 the Levites cried out to God. The Hebrew word for "cry" in verse 9 is the noun form of the verb used in verse 4. The implied hope is that God will hear the present community's cry as he heard their ancestors' cry at the Red Sea.

9:16 *But they . . . became arrogant and stiff-necked.* The first part of the prayer has portrayed God as giving blessing after blessing to Israel. In response, however, Israel was not humble and thankful, as they should have been. They are contrasted with their faithful God, acting arrogantly, like the Egyptians of verse 10, and being stiff-necked, which draws on the image of an animal struggling to resist a yoke placed on its neck. They refused to cooperate with God in spite of his goodness to them.

9:17 *But you are a forgiving God.* A key theme of the prayer is introduced here. The Israelites behaved ungratefully and rebelliously toward God, but instead of punishing them, he forgave and continued to provide for them. It is God's consistent demonstration of his willingness to forgive that inspires confidence in the returned exiles that he will do so again.

9:19 *By day the pillar of cloud did not fail.* Verses 19–21 list several acts of God that correspond closely to his actions of verses 12–15. Even after the insulting rebellion and idolatry of the Israelites in verses 16–18, God still treated them as compassionately as he had before.

9:24 *You subdued before them the Canaanites.* The prayer makes continual reference to God overpowering other peoples for the benefit of the Israelites, including Pharaoh and the Egyptians (vv. 10–11), various kingdoms (v. 22), Sihon and Og (v. 22), and the Canaanites. This sets up an expectation that God will deliver the current generation from the domination of the Persian kings.

as they pleased. The identical phrase is used in verse 37 to describe the control the Persian kings exercise over the Judeans. The Israelites of Joshua's day both settled the land and controlled it, but the returned exiles have only been able to settle it.

9:25 *they reveled in your great goodness.* The enjoyment of blessing that the Israelites experienced after the conquest contrasts with the situation described in verse 36. The same goodness cannot now be enjoyed by the community because they live as slaves in the same land. Once again, the current generation is depicted as enduring inferior circumstances.

9:26 *But they were disobedient . . . awful blasphemies.* This entire verse describes the insulting behavior of the Israelites. Ignoring God's law implied that his instructions were unimportant. By sending prophets to warn the people, God was graciously going the extra mile to avoid judging them, but they simply killed his prophets. The prayer underlines the Israelites' insolence and ingratitude to the point where no one could expect God to tolerate it.

9:27 *So you delivered them . . . rescued them from the hand of their enemies.* To this point in the prayer, only God's actions that benefited Israel have been recounted. Here it is recalled that he punished their behavior by placing them under oppressors. Even then, however, when the Israelites cried out to him, he compassionately delivered them. It would have been just for God to ignore their cries, but the extent of his mercy is illustrated by his response. As the prayer progresses, God's character shines brighter and the Israelites' looks worse.

9:32 *do not let all this hardship seem trifling.* This is the only actual request in the entire prayer. Its significance is closely related to the structure of the preceding context. Verses 26–27 present a cycle of Israelite disobedience, God's judgment through oppression by foreigners, the Israelites' call to God, and God's deliverance. The entire cycle is repeated in verse 28. The cycle then begins again in verses 29–31, but only includes the first two steps, bringing the account to the present time. Thus, verse 32 represents the call for help made by the community. Given that God has so consistently acted mercifully and powerfully in the past, the implication is that the Judeans can expect him to deliver them from their current foreign oppression as before.

9:36 *we are slaves today.* The Judeans' description of their situation recalls the time of slavery in Egypt. It is also a way of saying that the oppression brought on by the Assyrians and extended by the Babylonians continues under the Persians. The Judeans are once again in need of God's deliverance from subjugation.

slaves in the land you gave our ancestors. The cruel irony is that, whereas the ancestors left Egypt and inherited the promised land as freed people, this generation has entered the land but continues to be slaves to the Persians. The sense of slavery likely arises from the heavy taxes imposed by the empire (Neh. 5:4) as well as the right of conscription for military duty and forced labor and the requisition of cattle (9:37). As long as these circumstances persist, the covenant has not been fully restored (compare, e.g., Jer. 31:12–14).

Theological Insights

The Israelites' prayer shows God they understand that in the history of their relationship with him he has consistently been righteous and they have consistently been wicked. They recognize his many benevolent acts of provision, compassion, and forgiveness. They see that he has always kept his word and even been better than his word. They agree that when he has judged them for disobedience, they have deserved it. They marvel at his patience.

All this is accentuated by their own history of rebellion and proud disregard for God's law. He has maintained his impeccable character even though they have acted so insultingly toward him. Therefore, since the community is demonstrating its own desire to be faithful to the covenant through its actions in Nehemiah 8–10, it confidently requests that God act in mercy yet again to forgive and complete the promised restoration.

For the original readers of this book, this was a strong encouragement to believe that, regardless of past disobedience, God is ready to extend forgiveness to those who honestly confess sin.

Teaching the Text

The attitude illustrated by the prayer in Nehemiah 9 is as appropriate for Christians today as it was for Judeans in the postexilic period. Indeed, it is the only attitude that allows for a healthy relationship with God. It is based on the recognition that God, as the creator and sustainer of all, is the one who has brought every good thing into our lives. We realize that we owe him an enormous debt of gratitude, even before considering the effects of our sin.

But the picture comes into sharp contrast when sin is considered. Honest reflection on both human history in general and one's personal history leads to the conclusion that all are guilty of responding to God's good gifts with shameful disobedience and rebellion. This is difficult for many people to accept. The tendency in contemporary culture is to minimize the wrongness of one's own actions or to assign blame for them to others, even to God. Yet without the frank acceptance of responsibility for disobedience, it is impossible to proceed to reconciliation with God.

Once one's sinfulness is authentically owned, it follows that God has already responded with grace, even if only because he has not yet terminated one's life. The Israelites understood that God could justly have brought them to an end as a people (v. 31). The very fact that a person has the opportunity to repent is proof of God's mercy. The more one comprehends one's own sin, the more wonderful—even shocking—God's grace appears.

The conclusion to be drawn from history, with Scripture's help, is that when people understand the story of their lives in this way, they can be confident that God is willing to forgive them and restore their relationship with him. The prayer's expression of the bottom line is that God is righteous and faithful, while humans act wickedly (v. 33). But, amazingly, the realization of these facts leads to the expectation of forgiveness and reconciliation rather than to despair.

God's gracious forgiveness leads to inclusion in the blessings of his covenant, the new covenant in the case of believers today. The New Testament describes these blessings, and most will be experienced in full only when the present age passes away. Like the Judeans in Nehemiah 9, Christians do not know when all of God's promises will be fulfilled for them, but they can be confident that those promises will be fulfilled for those whose faith resembles the faith that characterizes this prayer.

The important difference between the situation of the Judeans in Nehemiah 9 and Christians today has to do with the way God's people express their faith in and submission to him. One of God's great gifts to the Israelites was his law (v. 13). By following it and ordering their lives around it, they demonstrated their devotion to him. The even greater gift God has now given is Jesus Christ. Since his coming to earth, it is by devoting their lives to following him that people express faith in God.

Illustrating the Text

Recognition of sin unleashes appreciation of grace.

Apologetics: Apologist and evangelist Ray Comfort uses this metaphor to explain why recognition of sin is the entry point to the gospel: Imagine that you are boarding an airplane and someone offers you a parachute, telling you it will improve your flight. You will quickly shed the clumsy, ugly, and lumpy backpack when you realize it is not delivering on the promise of an enhanced flight. On the other hand, if the person offering you the parachute had explained that the plane would be crashing and that wearing the backpack would save your life, you would wear it gladly no matter the discomfort! In the same way, unless we first recognize our sin and understand its destructive consequences, we won't properly appreciate and cherish grace or pay the cost of discipleship.[1]

Appreciation of God's grace unleashes confidence in forgiveness.

Human Experience: Motion sickness occurs when one's senses send the mind conflicting messages and the nervous system reacts with nausea. In the same way, when our hearts base salvation on our own works, it is like a person on a ship who is rising and falling on feelings of worthiness and worthlessness as they come and go. Resting on the mixed message of emotions leads to distress. On the other hand, when we recognize God's consistent graciousness to us, it is like a person standing on the shore. God's forgiveness does not rise and fall with the waves of our emotions! Salvation that rests on him gives great comfort and confidence—we know we are forgiven based on his promise, not our feelings.

Confidence in forgiveness unleashes inclusion in blessings.

Christian Book: In C. S. Lewis's book *The Horse and His Boy*,[2] a young, mistreated foundling named Shasta discovers he is actually a lost twin son of a king. Once this is discovered, he gains an identical brother, a title and promise of the throne, wealth, an education, a loving family, and a home. Once he is assured that he is truly the king's son, all of these gifts are his inheritance, whether he is ready or not. Similarly, once a Christian is assured of his or her forgiveness and adoption into the family of God, all the benefits and blessings of heaven become his or hers, all at once, ready or not!

The Israelites Commit to Honoring God through Obedience

Big Idea

Devoted obedience is an essential feature of the relationship of love and blessing God offers people.

Key Themes

- The Israelites are confident in God's willingness to forgive and restore them, based on his actions throughout their rebellious national history.
- The reliability of God's graciousness motivates the Israelites' desire to obey him.
- They determine what obedience requires by applying the intent of Scripture to their circumstances.
- They pay special attention to areas where obedience will be countercultural, and therefore likely difficult.

Understanding the Text

The Text in Context

The process begun in Nehemiah 8–9 is completed in Nehemiah 10. According to Jeremiah 31:31–34, the restored Israelites will experience God's forgiveness and have a genuine desire to obey his law. Nehemiah 8–9 depicts the people as joyfully eager to hear God's word and obey it, aware of the mercy God has already shown them, and desiring a more complete fulfillment of his promises to them. They now declare that they are committed to the type of relationship envisioned in the new-covenant prophecy, in which their role involves submissive obedience to God's instructions.

The structure of events in Nehemiah 8–10 is the same as that described briefly for the confirmation of the Sinai covenant in Exodus 24:7 and repeated in subsequent covenant renewal ceremonies. The people hear God's word and then respond with commitment to obey. This portrays the actions of this section as another renewal of the covenant, further enhancing connections with the new-covenant prophecy.

The restoration begun with the return of the exiles to the land in Ezra 1 would be incomplete without the spiritual renewal of the people described here. Nehemiah showed that he understood this in his prayer in Nehemiah 1. A rededicated Israel creates the expectation of greater blessing from God in the future.

Interpretive Insights

9:38 *In view of all this.* This section continues directly from 9:1–37. The setting in time is the same, and the flow of thought is logically connected. Because the community recognizes their history of sin and God's history of mercy toward them described in 9:1–37, they will make the commitments outlined in 10:29–39.

we are making a binding agreement. Although the speakers in 9:5–37 were the Levites, they were leading the whole community in prayer and speaking on their behalf. The pronoun "we" continues to represent the community.

The Hebrew word for "agreement" likely does not have bilateral implications, as a covenant would. The only other use of this word in the Old Testament is in Nehemiah 11:23, where a formal translation could be "a *regulation* was over the singers' daily activity." The people are making a rule for themselves to follow—namely, that they will obey God's law. They are expressing their degree of determination to be obedient. Yet the Hebrew word in 9:38 for "making" is the verb usually used for making a covenant. The combination of the familiar verb with the rare noun suggests that the similarities to a covenant-renewal ceremony should be recognized, while stopping short of asserting that the new covenant has fully arrived. The choice of the noun may also be influenced by the reference to Abraham's faithfulness in 9:8. The Hebrew words for "faithful" and "agreement" are from the same root. The community is expressing their determination to be faithful to God as Abraham was.

affixing their seals to it. A wax or clay seal, imprinted by a stamp bearing the name of the owner, was often used to keep a rolled document closed. Here the seals represent their owners' legal assent to the document's contents, like a signature would today.

10:28 *The rest of the people.* This verse lists various categories of people in order to emphasize that all of the people join in. This is not merely a decision made by their leaders. The only conditions for inclusion seem to be ability to understand God's law, willingness to avoid compromising relations with the surrounding peoples, and, of course, desire to participate in the agreement itself. The new covenant is explicitly for people from all walks of life (Jer. 31:34).

10:29 *a curse and an oath.* The people took an oath with a curse attached to it as a consequence if they did not keep their word. This was common in the ancient Near East and demonstrated that the people were serious about their decision.

follow the Law of God . . . the commands, regulations. The ancestors shamefully ignored and disobeyed God's laws, commands, and ordinances (Neh. 9:29). They did not turn from their evil ways even when they were enjoying God's goodness in the promised land (9:35). The returnees pledge that, although not yet enjoying God's goodness to the extent the ancestors did (9:36–37), they will do the opposite of what the ancestors did and obey God's instructions ("ordinances" in 9:29 represents the same Hebrew word as "regulations" in 10:29).

10:30 *not to give our daughters in marriage . . . for our sons.* The returned exiles had already struggled with this issue (Ezra 9–10). Passages such as Exodus 34:11–16 and Deuteronomy 7:1–4 had warned against marrying non-Israelites. Since true converts to faith in Yahweh, such as Rahab and Ruth, were allowed to marry Israelites (see Matt. 1:5), the prohibition against intermarriage was not racially or ethnically prejudiced. The intent was to avoid being drawn into idolatry, as happened to Solomon (1 Kings 11:1–4). The earlier biblical laws listed specific nations the Israelites were not to intermarry with, but here the community expresses and follows the principle behind those laws.

10:32 *the commands to give a third of a shekel each year.* Exodus 30:11–16 instructs each Israelite male age twenty or over to pay a half-shekel during a census. The money is to be used for the operation of the sanctuary. No annual payment is stipulated in the Pentateuch. By the time of Nehemiah 10, the ancient Near Eastern economy had become more money based than previously. It would have been harder for all the needs of the temple to be met solely by offerings of animals and grain. It appears that the Judeans recognize the new need resulting from new circumstances. They honor the principle of the old law that cash should be given for the sanctuary. But they modify it by disconnecting it from censuses and reducing the amount from one-half to one-third of a shekel but also by making it an annual payment. The net result would be more money given for the temple under the new version.

10:34 *have cast lots.* There is no direction given in the law about organizing the provision of wood for sacrifices at the sanctuary. The community considers everyone eligible for this obligation and then casts lots to determine assignments. This is a way of letting God decide the responsibilities rather than letting the influential people place the burden on others.

as it is written in the Law. Since there is no command to bring a wood offering in the Pentateuch, it is likely that the community is referring to the commands that the fire on the sanctuary altar must never be allowed to go out and the priest must add wood to it every morning (Lev. 6:12–13). The Torah command implies that wood must be supplied regularly, so the people are making the implicit explicit.

10:36 *the firstborn of our sons.* The Israelites were to give the first of every kind of blessing they received to God. In the case of sons, they were to pay a "redemption fee" in lieu of donating the child to work at the sanctuary (Exod. 34:19–20). The firstborn of unclean animals were similarly redeemed, but the firstborn of clean animals were brought for sacrifice. These are ways of affirming God as the source of all blessing and placing priority on worshiping him.

10:39 *We will not neglect the house of our God.* Throughout Chronicles the attitude a king of Judah takes toward the temple is an important indicator of his spiritual character. Those who provide for its services and upkeep are considered godly and are blessed. Those who do not are not (e.g., 2 Chron. 24:18). The returned exiles realize that it would be very easy to become lax about the responsibilities that God had given them for the temple and its personnel. They therefore give special prominence to these obligations.

Theological Insights

This passage illustrates an essential aspect of being in relationship with God. He always stands willing to forgive, but he actually forgives only those who understand their own sinfulness and appreciate his willingness to forgive them. Going forward, such people have a strong desire to obey him and consciously commit to doing so. As we understand from human relationships, genuine reconciliation with God takes place only when we are honest about how we have harmed the relationship with him and are sincere about investing ourselves in it appropriately, which means, in the case of a relationship with God, on his terms.

An important principle of how God communicates through Scripture underlies the activity of this passage. The community discerns the intent of the individual laws in their original setting and seeks to produce the same effect in the current setting, even if some details must be modified to do so. The resulting standards are at least as high as those set by the original laws. The reason they are able to follow this procedure is that God's word to the original hearers was a statement of his timeless principles expressed in specific examples relevant to their setting. Although the details of people's historical circumstances change, God's principles do not change.

In contemporary Western culture, which promotes the concept that every system of values is equally valid, one of the more challenging aspects of God's nature is his insistence that distinctions be drawn between right and wrong, implying precisely that not every system of values is equally valid. Rejecting mixed marriage, honoring the Sabbath, and maintaining temple worship in strict adherence to God's instructions would strike many today as arbitrary demands and were seen that way even by many in preexilic Israel. Yet the distinctions God draws cannot be ignored. Those who do not correctly apply the principles in his Word to the setting in which they themselves live set out on a course that ultimately leads away from him.

Teaching the Text

It may appear at first sight that there is little application for Christians to make from this passage. Yet the attitude of obedience it portrays is as relevant for God's people today as ever. Romans 6 (especially vv. 13, 19) echoes the thought that all who have received God's grace and forgiveness should be as obedient to God as possible. Whether individuals or groups wish to make written declarations of their intentions to obey God like the Judeans did is optional, but the same resolve should be evident in their lives.

Figuring out how to apply God's teachings in the contemporary world—a challenge to an even greater degree for the church than it was for the postexilic Judeans—is just as necessary now as it was then. The cultural differences between today's world and the worlds of the Old and New Testaments are larger than the gap between the world of the Torah and the world of the Persian Empire. But the approach is basically the same: the principle behind the original teaching must be understood. God gave specific commands to specific people in specific circumstances. Those commands illustrate time-less principles that God wants to teach his people. Once the principles are understood, it becomes possible to envision what it would look like to live by them in contemporary settings. Seeking to keep the spirit of the law over its letter will frequently lead to a higher standard of ethics (e.g., Matt. 5–7).

As believers seek to live obediently, they will identify areas of life where it seems particularly difficult, as the Judeans found. Although Christians are not constrained by ethnic barriers to marriage (though God still expects them to marry only other Christians; see 2 Cor. 6:14), nor required to provide for the Jerusalem temple as the Judeans were, nor even expected to keep the Sabbath with the same stringency as the Judeans (Col. 2:16), they are still called to a lifestyle that many find difficult to maintain. As the Judeans understood, some of the hardest areas of obedience are those that preserve the distinctiveness of faith in God from the unbelieving culture.

Of many possible examples, one suggested by this passage involves the high priority God's people should place on the corporate aspect of faith. The Jerusalem temple was the center of worship for Israel and represented God's presence among them. Everyone was required to worship there at least three times a year. It was impossible to maintain a private faith in God that did not involve other believers. Modern Western culture places a high value on privacy and personal convenience, and many Christians are tempted to disengage from the church, believing they can worship God just as effectively alone. However, the New Testament affirms the importance of the church functioning as a body, with members vitally connected to one another. As in postexilic Israel, this calls for conscious prioritization of the contributions required, in terms of time, effort, and money. Neglecting the church is not acceptable.

Illustrating the Text

We must discern the spirit of God's commands to reapply them well.

Human Experience: All of us have gotten into situations where a rule we received does not exactly apply. For example, a parent may tell a child never to drive a favorite car. In the case when someone is injured and only that vehicle is available, the child must decide whether the spirit of the rule was to prevent *frivolous* use of the car or *absolutely any* use of the car. The practice of interpreting biblical literature and understanding the context and spirit behind God's commands is called *hermeneutics*. It is the study of the assumptions and reading rules we bring to the Bible. We are called to discern carefully what the Spirit of God was saying to the ancient readers so we can apply that same meaning in our context. God's word can never *mean* what it never *meant*. We need the indwelling Spirit and one another to do this well.

The hardest areas of obedience are those that make believers stand out.

Story: Your listeners will all recall the immense pressure to fit in and conform during the awkward years of middle school. Show some pictures of your awkward preteen years and the fashions you used in order to fit in and be cool. Share a story about a particular clothing item, hairstyle, or habit you used to try and blend into the crowd. Share something that made you stand out in an embarrassing way. Share how doing anything that would have made you stand out from the crowd would have been excruciatingly difficult for you at that time. The truth is that, while we grow up, we continue to struggle with things that cause us to stand out from the crowd and draw special ridicule, persecution, or embarrassment because of our commitment to Christ. Challenge your hearers to stick together and encourage one another in such moments and to take a stand as a team.

Christian worship can be more than just corporate, but never less.

Everyday Life: Some people say that they don't need to go to church because they feel closer to God in nature than in a pew. The sentiment of feeling close to God in nature is totally appropriate. Applying it as a reason to skip church is not. Worship can be varied and flexible in its forms; in fact, all of life ought to be worship for us. However, while worship can be more than just corporate, it is never less than corporate—all the other variations are founded on corporate gatherings and cannot therefore replace them.

The Laypeople and Temple Personnel Implement God's Plans for Settlement and Worship

Big Idea

The fulfillment of God's promises emerges in greater visible detail as his people faithfully obey and worship him.

Key Themes

- Many people relocate their homes to Jerusalem in a sacrificial act of obedience.
- The rest of the people establish their presence in the land promised to them by God.
- The priests and Levites maintain worship according to God's revealed design.
- Each individual's role within the community of God's people is important.

Understanding the Text

The Text in Context

Having finished building the Jerusalem wall, Nehemiah realized the city was underpopulated and formed a plan to correct the situation (Neh. 7:4–5). While the vast majority of the people were still residing in their ancestral towns (Neh. 7:73), they gathered in Jerusalem at the beginning of the seventh month and requested that God's law be read to them. Hearing the law resulted in a joyful celebration of obedience to it (Neh. 8), a prayer of confession and affirmation of God's covenant faithfulness (Neh. 9), and a renewed commitment to faithfulness to God's commands in return (Neh. 10). Part of that commitment was the pledge to provide a tenth of their produce for the Levites and priests (10:37–38). Continuing in the spirit of chapters 8–10, without further prompting from any leader, the people now address the problem of Jerusalem's underpopulation themselves by contributing a tenth of the community to live there. Their goal seems to be for their settlement pattern in Judea to conform to God's promise and plan. Moreover, Jerusalem, which was to become a holy city (Jer. 31:40), will now be inhabited by people committed to holiness.

The lists of 12:1–26 confirm that worship at the Jerusalem temple, reestablished in Ezra 3 and committed to as part of the pledge of Nehemiah 10, continued, led in the appropriate way by appropriate people.

Outline

1. Action taken to repopulate Jerusalem (11:1–2)
2. New settlers in Jerusalem (11:3–19)
   a. Introduction to list (11:3–4a)
   b. Men from Judah (11:4b–6)
   c. Men from Benjamin (11:7–9)
   d. Priests (11:10–14)
   e. Levites (11:15–18)
   f. Gatekeepers (11:19)
3. Dwelling places of people not assigned by lot to live in Jerusalem (11:20–36)
   a. Introduction to list (11:20)
   b. People living in Jerusalem for various reasons (11:21–24)
      i. Temple servants (11:21)
      ii. Levites (11:22–23)
      iii. Royal official (11:24)
   c. Locations inhabited by Judeans throughout the region (11:25–36)
      i. Villages inhabited by men of Judah (11:25–30)
      ii. Villages inhabited by men of Benjamin (11:31–35)
      iii. Note about relocation of some Levites from Judah (11:36)
4. Priests and Levites who returned with Zerubbabel (12:1–9)
   a. Introduction to list (12:1a)
   b. Priests (12:1b–7)
   c. Levites (12:8–9)
5. Succession of high priests (12:10–11)
6. Heads of priestly families in the time of Joiakim (12:12–21)
7. Notes on the times when the heads of families were recorded (12:22–23)
8. Heads of Levitical families in the time of Joiakim (12:24–26)

Historical and Cultural Background

In the ancient Near East, a holy city was one believed to be founded, defended, and ruled by the god who resided in that city's temple. The Old Testament parallels this idea by stating that God chose Jerusalem as his dwelling place (1 Kings 9:3) and showing that he defended it (Isa. 37:32–35). Nehemiah 12 expands the concept of a holy city further, as noted below.

Interpretive Insights

11:1 *cast lots.* As in Nehemiah 10:34 (and elsewhere in the Old Testament, e.g., the settlement of the land in Josh. 14:2), lots are cast as a way of leaving a decision to God. This way the choice of who will move to Jerusalem is not potentially affected by the wishes of influential people.

the holy city. This is the first place in Ezra-Nehemiah where Jerusalem is called holy, and it is an important fulfillment of the prophetic expectation of God's restoration of Israel. The main reason it can be seen as holy is that the temple there has been restored to proper function, making it possible again for God to dwell in it among his people. The city's holy status is also enhanced by the fact that, since the ark of the covenant was destroyed at the time of the Babylonian exile, the city itself, rather than the ark, is to be understood as God's throne (Jer. 3:16–17). As well, the people have repented and committed themselves to obeying God, so the city will be appropriately inhabited by holy people. A holy God living among his holy people is the ideal established by the Old Testament (Exod. 19:6; Lev. 11:44, etc.). Thus, this verse reflects hope for the people's future.

11:2 *volunteered to live in Jerusalem.* The Hebrew verb translated "volunteered" is elsewhere used to describe a material donation voluntarily given to the temple (Ezra 1:6; 2:68; 3:5). English translations may make it sound as though there are two groups of people: those who are chosen to live in Jerusalem by lot and those who volunteer to do so. This may be the case, or the text may be stating that those chosen to move to Jerusalem do so willingly. Either way, in the context of the tithing theme already noted (10:37–38; 11:1), the implication is that the people moving to Jerusalem are effectively presenting themselves at the holy place as an offering to God.

11:6 *men of standing.* The Hebrew word translated "standing" has a wide range of meaning. In this context it is more likely to mean "military ability" (given that concern for the safety of Jerusalem was one of the reasons for adding to its population in Neh. 7:1–5) or "ability" more generally. While it is hard to be sure of the exact nuance, it seems to indicate that some of Judah's finest are living in Jerusalem. The same semantic consideration applies in verse 14.

11:30 *they were living . . . Valley of Hinnom.* This statement summarizes the message of verses 25–30a. Most of the villages listed in these verses are in areas not under the control of the governor of the Judean province at this time, and most were not listed among the cities in which the first returnees settled in Ezra 2 or Nehemiah 7 (see the map in the unit on Neh. 2:10–20). Some may be in Arab or Edomite territory, and some may simply be in territory directly administered by a Persian governor, known as a satrap. Yet all of them were part of the land settled by the Israelites during Joshua's conquest. The point is that even though the Judeans do not have full control of this territory, they are occupying it in anticipation of the day when they will (compare Neh. 9:36–37; Jer. 29:10–14). Beersheba was traditionally the southernmost boundary of Israel, and the Hinnom Valley was just outside Jerusalem. The villages of the Benjamites (vv. 31–35) extend this occupied territory further north beyond Jerusalem. In line with this theme is the verb translated "living," which actually means "camping." The choice seems intended to recall Joshua's conquest, during which the Israelites camped in various places as they did battle to take the land. The narrator presents the people as in a similar transition phase, having reentered the land promised to them by God and anticipating its full restoration to their control.

12:9 *stood opposite them.* The references to standing opposite (here and v. 24) probably refer to an arrangement where two choirs face each other and sing alternate lines or verses of a song. Since David instituted this format (v. 24), mentioning it here implies that the Levites are conducting worship as God wished.

12:24 *the man of God.* In the Old Testament, this phrase usually refers to a prophet. By referring to David here as a man of God rather than as the king, the text emphasizes that the reason his directions continue to be followed is that God spoke them through him. That was more important than the political authority he had as king.

Theological Insights

It is easy to think of God fulfilling his promises through mighty global acts at the end of time, or even by intervening in smaller, but equally miraculous, ways in the lives of individuals today. This passage, although perhaps uninteresting at first glance, emphasizes that God works out the details of his promises through the mundane efforts of his people. In a striking way, it draws attention to the necessity of many people taking part in the outworking of God's plans. The repopulation of Jerusalem and the settlement of Judeans in towns throughout territory historically belonging to Judah and Benjamin are both significant features of the prophesied return. So, too, is the maintenance of worship in the Jerusalem temple according to God's prescriptions.

But each of these outcomes depends on the actions of many individuals. Many ordinary people, with appropriate lineages, have to leave the towns where they have already settled and move to Jerusalem for the city to have enough people. At this point in history it is less attractive as a place of residence than the places they are moving from (few houses had been rebuilt, Neh. 7:4), so they have to sacrifice in order to help fulfill God's plan. Settling outside the boundaries of the contemporary Judean province (11:25–35) also takes courage. Many priests and Levites have to honor their ancestry and take up the duties God prescribed for their families through Moses and David (12:1–26), since these roles are hereditary. As they do, the future God promised his people takes on greater concrete shape.

God can and will perform miracles on a grand scale. But more often he prefers to construct his promised future out of the mosaic of the ordinary, yet faithful, courageous, and sacrificial, lives of thousands of his people.

Teaching the Text

Moving one's residence or attending a regular church worship service are not activities people usually think of as important accomplishments for God's kingdom. Miraculous answers to prayer, rescuing people from addiction, and leading others to put their faith in Jesus seem to fit the description better. But this passage shows that even relatively unspectacular acts of obedience are important parts of God's plan.

For the ancient Judeans, moving to Jerusalem is probably more an inconvenience and a lot of hard work than anything miraculous. Donating a tithe of their income is one thing, but "donating themselves" to be new residents of Jerusalem takes sacrificial giving to a new level. Although there is no direct parallel to this relocating to Jerusalem for Christians, the New Testament example is of believers who give themselves to God first before making decisions about giving other things, such as money (2 Cor. 8:1–5). All believers should give of themselves in whatever way will help to do what God wants done in the world. This will often not be convenient or pleasant.

Those Judeans who settle in towns where they are a minority will not have an easy time of it either. They may well encounter persecution of various kinds, but their presence in the land promised to Abraham's descendants is an important phase in the land's restoration to them. Christians are not called to claim real estate in the same way. Instead, they anticipate God's kingdom coming in his will being done on earth as it is in heaven. To that end they seek to be salt and light wherever they are. That may involve anything from going to live in another country to just going to work. No matter where, they should provide an effective witness of Christ and his plans for the world, even when that may be unpopular.

The lists of priests and Levites may seem uninspiring, but they confirm that godly worship continues at the Jerusalem temple from the return from exile down to the narrator's time, and that this is an essential feature of the restoration of God's relationship with his people. Many of the detailed prescriptions for this worship no longer apply to the New Testament church, but worship itself is still central in the life of God's people. To enjoy his presence and praise him is among the greatest blessings God has given to believers. As Christians worship, they are already receiving God's promises, even as they look forward to a greater experience of his presence in the future. It is no coincidence that many of the scenes of heaven in Revelation have worship as a major theme.

This passage is a great reminder of the value of living as believers wherever we are and making worship a priority, even if these can seem very mundane at times. The future God promises is increasingly fleshed out as the whole church adopts this lifestyle.

The lists in these chapters certainly present a structured and ordered worshiping community. The author's intent, however, is to indicate that the structure of the community matches the design given by God in Scripture, leading toward the fulfillment of God's plan and purposes. To see a message about the need for order within the context of renewal is likely departing from the authorial intent.

Illustrating the Text

We must give our whole selves sacrificially to the Lord.

Marriage: Ask your listeners to imagine a marriage in which one spouse agreed to promise only one half of himself or herself to the other. Half their time, half their affections, half their earnings, half of their children, one arm, one leg, one ear to listen, and so on. What kind of marriage would that be? How would the other spouse feel about that arrangement, giving all and getting half? If we cannot imagine that working on a human level, then how can people do that to God? We are the bride and he is the bridegroom. He deserves all we have and all we are, and we cannot pick and choose which parts of ourselves he has purchased by his blood. If we want all of ourselves to be saved, then he should receive the sacrifice of our whole selves in sacrificial worship.

Bible: Romans 12:1–2 is a great text to support this concept. Consider challenging your congregation to learn it by heart.

Earthly worship is a preview and a foretaste of our heavenly vocation.

Popular Culture: Many cartoons depict people in heaven as floating on clouds; wearing a halo, white robe, and wings; and playing a harp. Many people joke and say that it looks monochromatic, boring, and silly to spend eternity floating and strumming a golden harp. Ask your listeners to think of a date or party they wished had never ended, a meal they wish had gone on forever, a wedding dance that should never have stopped, or a story they wished had never run out of chapters. Explain that worship isn't about music or standing still—it is about hungering for God and never growing tired of him. Assure them that they are purpose-built to glorify him and enjoy him forever, and that when they see him face-to-face, the question won't be, Will I get bored? but rather, Can I stand this joy for eternity without being exhausted by the intensity of it?

Making worship a priority is central to the Christian life.

Family Life: Many families would say that they long to have a close and healthy relationship together. However, the myth of quality time (without quantity time) tears away their ability to truly achieve the closeness they desire. Without planning and intentionality that lead to quantity time, the quality just doesn't materialize. In the same way, worship has to be a priority deserving of planning and intentionality that lead to quantity time. Attendance in church, regular devotions, plentiful prayer time, and rich moments with God won't happen by themselves; they need to be prioritized and nurtured consistently. Challenge your listeners to face both these challenges by prioritizing family worship. Then, they can build family time and worship time into one habit. It might be an interesting experience for families to go back over the previous month and identify how much time they spent together in recreation, in watching TV or movies, in working and doing chores, and in worship and seeking the face of God. Encourage families to reflect on how important worship is in their family life and then to raise the bar!

The People Celebrate the Dedication of the Wall of Jerusalem

Big Idea

God's people should rejoice as they devote every aspect of life to him for his use.

Key Themes

- The wall of Jerusalem is treated like an object to be used for divine purposes.
- The people of Judea rejoice that God has restored his covenant relationship with them.
- The faithful service of the priests and Levites motivates the rest of the people to follow through on their own previous commitment.

Understanding the Text

The Text in Context

The narrative prior to this passage has described a series of events that together give evidence of God's fulfillment of his promise to restore a remnant from Israel after the judgment of exile. He has brought people back to the land he promised to Abraham's descendants (Ezra 1–2; Neh. 7), restored the altar of sacrifice and the temple in Jerusalem (Ezra 3–6), provided an effective teacher of the law in the person of Ezra (Ezra 7–10), enabled the rebuilding of Jerusalem's wall (Neh. 1–6), and given his people knowledge of his law and the desire to obey it (Neh. 8–10). Each of these acts of God corresponds to earlier promises he made. Such renewal of divine blessing represents a major milestone in Israel's relationship with God and holds the promise of more to come in the future. It is fitting, then, for Israel to celebrate what the achievements recorded in Ezra-Nehemiah signify. God has worked on their behalf to restore them.

The book does not end here, however, and the closing chapter shows that, as real and good as the fulfillments narrated so far are, in important ways the restoration is not yet complete.

Interpretive Insights

12:27 *the Levites were sought out.* The Levites' special role was to assist the priests in leading the worship activities of the community. They helped in the care of the temple, provided music and singing for worship, and taught the people God's word, among other tasks (1 Chron. 23:26–32; 2 Chron. 35:3). The fact that they are intentionally included in what is to follow shows that it is not merely a civic ceremony but has spiritual importance.

songs of thanksgiving. Thanksgiving is a major theme in this passage. It appears again in verses 31, 38, 40. In verses 31, 38, the Hebrew word translated "choir" refers specifically to a "thanksgiving choir." One of the main purposes of this event is to express thanks to God for all he has done to restore the community. The rebuilt wall is seen as part of his work and plan.

12:30 *they purified . . . the gates and the wall.* Purification in the Old Testament has predominantly to do with making someone or something ready for holy action or holy use. Most objects that are purified are connected with the temple, such as utensils used in worship. This is the only place in the Old Testament where a city wall is purified. It confers a special status on the wall, comparable to that of the temple itself and the people who have also been purified. In addition, the only other object in Ezra-Nehemiah said to be dedicated is the temple (Ezra 6:16–17). Together, all this suggests that the wall and the city it contains are set apart for God's use, as in the prophecies of Jeremiah 31:38–40 and Zechariah 14:20–21.

12:31 *I had the leaders . . . go up on top of the wall.* The completed wall was probably about eight feet wide, so it would have been easy to have a procession on top of it. When the wall was under construction, the Judeans' enemies taunted them that even a fox jumping on it would break it down (Neh. 4:3). It is a satisfying part of their celebration to have a large company of people walking around the city on the wall.

12:36 *with musical instruments prescribed by David the man of God.* David's directions concerning musical instruments were specifically for worship at the temple (1 Chron. 25:1–6). Their inclusion here is further evidence that this procession should be understood to share characteristics of a temple worship service. The reference to David's instructions also shows that the Levites are following the commands given by God in the preexilic period, since David, as a man of God, or prophet, was speaking for God when he issued these directives. A similar point is made by the references to David, Solomon, and Asaph in verses 45–46.

12:40 *The two choirs . . . took their places in the house of God.* The procession culminates at the temple. The scene thus connects the temple, the people, and the Jerusalem wall, each of which has been a focus in the restoration of the Judean community (temple, Ezra 1–8; people, Ezra 9–10 and Neh. 8–10;

wall, Neh. 1–6). There are also other specific connections with the earlier narrative. Like this text, the account of the founding of the temple in Ezra 3:8–13 includes priests with trumpets (Ezra 3:10; Neh. 12:35, 41), Levites with cymbals (Ezra 3:10; Neh. 12:27), thanksgiving (Ezra 3:11; Neh. 12:27, 31, 38, 40), and expressions of joy so exuberant that they can be heard far away (Ezra 3:13; Neh. 12:43). Similarly, the report of the dedication of the completed temple in Ezra 6:16–22 shares the features of enthusiastic joy attributed to God's activity (Ezra 6:16, 22; Neh. 12:43) and large numbers of sacrifices offered (Ezra 6:17; Neh. 12:43). Thus—surprisingly—the wall seems to be treated as virtually an extension of the temple, reinforcing the concept of the entire city of Jerusalem being holy.

12:43 *God had given them great joy.* With temple, people, and wall brought together on this day, it is likely that the rejoicing is not merely for the construction of the wall. It is rather that God has restored the temple and walls to their proper state and the people to the land, and that all three have been dedicated to him for his service. Great joy comes from both receiving God's gifts and devoting them to him to use as he pleases.

The sound of rejoicing in Jerusalem could be heard far away. This recalls the similar report in Ezra 3:11–13 at the founding of the temple, but there is an important difference. In the earlier scene, the crowd had a mixed reaction, with some shouting for joy and some weeping. Now there is no evidence of sadness. This is further proof that any doubts that God has been restoring his people should be put to rest. The process seems to have arrived at completion.

12:44 *men were appointed to be in charge of the storerooms.* In Nehemiah 10:35–39 the Judeans had pledged to contribute the prescribed tithes and offerings for the Levites and priests and have them kept at the temple storerooms as part of their commitment to obey God's law and care for the temple. Now they take a further practical step by designating individuals to organize the process and ensure it is carried out. Enabling and facilitating obedience are themselves part of obedience.

for Judah was pleased with the ministering priests and Levites. The temple personnel were carrying out their duties according to the instructions given by David and Solomon (see v. 45). The faithful, obedient work of the priests and Levites had a motivating influence on the rest of the people. They moved forward with previous obligations because the temple workers were meeting their own obligations.

12:47 *They also set aside the portion.* The Hebrew verb translated "set aside" implies that the object is being set aside for a holy purpose. In contributing these portions, the people and Levites are not just meeting practical needs; they are using their means to do God's work in the world. This continues the theme, present throughout the passage, of committing all resources to God.

Theological Insights

Two striking main thoughts run through this passage together. One is that God's holiness extends beyond the area normally thought of as sacred—the temple and its courts—to include the wall of Jerusalem and thus the city itself and its people. The other is that this extension of God's holiness to what is ordinarily perceived as common is greatly welcomed by his people.

God made it clear at Mount Sinai that he intended Israel to be a nation embodying his holiness among the other nations of the world (Exod. 19:6). The purity laws, which determined the conditions under which an individual could be in the presence of sacred things, had the particular effect of reminding the Israelites about God's holiness daily, in connection with certain everyday experiences. Yet for much of their history, Israel did not even honor God's temple as holy, let alone reflect his holiness through their daily behavior and attitudes. Now, however, among the returned remnant committed to obeying God in the postexilic period, there is a new understanding that the whole city, not just the temple, partakes of God's holiness. In other words, God intends every aspect of life to be dedicated to him as holy, for his use.

The correct response by God's people to the spread of his holiness is illustrated in this passage. Rather than seeing it as a limiting inconvenience, they mark the event with celebration and rejoicing. They understand that this has been God's purpose from the beginning and that participating in God's holiness is a great blessing, the capstone of his provision for them.

Teaching the Text

Christians today often misunderstand what leads to the experience of the greatest good in life. It is relatively easy to see that God's forgiveness and the promise of eternal life in his presence are great blessings. The same goes for the peace in our relationships and improved material prosperity that may come as a result of following God's instructions. But when it is not so clear how dedicating every part of our lives to God's purposes will bring recognizable blessing, we are tempted to act in selfish and unholy ways, just as preexilic Israel was.

This passage shows God's people getting it right. They thank God for the tangible blessings they have been given, like the return of their ancestral property and the repair of the broken-down city wall. But they realize these gifts are part of something even bigger. The very things God gives to his people are themselves to be set apart for him to use for his purposes. This extends to everything, even those things that our culture considers secular. It is a big challenge for Christians to think through what it would mean to devote every part of the life God has given us to his use.

When we understand the value of God's holiness, however, the process of committing our lives to his purposes becomes a joyful one. Rather than seeing this as sacrificing the blessings God has given us, we view it as learning to live the life we were created for. Using our abilities and resources in godly ways produces fulfillment and satisfaction that can come in no other way. Like the Judeans, we rejoice when we see God's work in our lives result in holiness in the everyday. But many Christians may have experienced this only seldom, and the connection may be hard to see. It is important, therefore, that spiritual leaders take the initiative in bringing the holiness of all of life to the church's consciousness. Worship leaders, like the Levites, need to guide public celebrations of the intersection of God's holiness with our lives, in addition to prompting thanks to God for gifts we are more naturally inclined to be grateful for.

Once we embrace and desire God's holiness in every facet of our lives, we actually motivate other believers around us to do the same. The Levites and priests were faithful in the work of serving God and purifying the community, and this stimulated the rest of the people to ensure the framework was in place for Levites and priests to receive their appointed food and to donate it faithfully. The laypeople saw their contributions as a holy responsibility given to them by God. As believers today faithfully seek to be holy in all they do, they provide stirring examples to other believers to be equally dedicated.

Illustrating the Text

God's gifts aren't payment for past obedience; they are resources for new obedience.

Film: In the 2000 movie *Pay It Forward*, a young boy seeks to make the world a better place by repaying debts forward; that is, rather than reciprocating kindness back to someone who showed it to you, you pass it on to a third party and invite them to do the same for a fourth, and so on. This concept is one way of looking at what God does when he gives gifts to us. His gifts are not a payment given to us in exchange for our own past goodness. Nor are they a loan that he wants back for himself, since it has always been his to start with. He is giving us blessings so that we can be a blessing to the world while knowing, enjoying, and proclaiming him. When we get good things, then, we ought not to ask, What did I do to deserve this? but rather, How can I obediently use this to spread God's gospel and kingdom?

There is meant to be no division between faith and the rest of life.

Christian Book: *Making Room for Life*, by Randy Frazee. Frazee shares about the concept of crowded loneliness. [1] Whereas, a century ago, people would only meet around one hundred people in a lifetime and would interact with them in all spheres of life, now we interact with hundreds in a day but in separate spheres of life. For example, we used to go to church, buy groceries, play softball, and date the same, small group of people. Now, the people from those activities represent different groups that seldom commingle. We start to become a different person in each sphere, until we are divided into compartments of life that are inconsistent. Eventually, some spheres will not include our Christian discipleship or witness at all—we will be hypocrites in a growing number of compartments. We know many people but may feel very broken and lonely. The remedy is to relink all the spheres of our lives and make faith part of all of them.

Dedication to God can be contagious—pursue holiness together.

Fitness: Runners know the power of running alongside faster, more competitive runners. Changing your running partner can vastly improve your speed and energy. Subtly, imperceptibly, the natural desire to match rhythm, stay together, and keep up starts to stretch your abilities, and the next thing you know, your times and stamina are improving. Christian discipleship is similar—running our race alongside motivated, sincere Christ-followers inspires us and subtly raises our game until we hunger for God more profoundly and pursue him more passionately. Choose (and be) good running partners for this great race!

Testimony: Have a group of young people in the church share about how friendships in youth group have helped spur them on to love and good works in their everyday lives. Have the congregation pray a prayer of blessing over the youth and youth leaders.

Nehemiah Restores the Purity of the Judean Community

Big Idea

Maintaining a faithful relationship with God requires vigilance to avoid the temptations to compromise presented by unbelievers.

Key Themes

- Influenced by unhealthy associations with foreigners, the Judean community fails to keep its commitments to obey God.
- Nehemiah confronts those responsible for the sin.
- Nehemiah also acts to reestablish obedient behavior.

Understanding the Text

The Text in Context

Ezra-Nehemiah tracks the restoration of the Judean community from exile. The people's return from Babylon, the rebuilding of the temple and the Jerusalem wall, and the commitment of the people to faithful obedience to God's law are all presented as evidence that God is working to accomplish what the prophets foretold. In this final section, however, the community fails repeatedly to follow the very commands of God they earlier committed explicitly to follow. The gap between expectation and their actual performance shows that the new-covenant promise of obedience from the heart has not yet been completely fulfilled.

The time markers in this section can be confusing. "On that day," in verse 1, sounds as though it is describing further action occurring at the time of the events in 12:44–47. The Hebrew phrase, however, often refers to a more general period of time, not necessarily connected to the preceding context. "Before this," in Nehemiah 13:4, is probably better translated "Despite this," rather than as a time marker. "While all this was going on," in verse 6, is ultimately what provides the key to understanding the temporal order. The events of

13:1–5 take place after Nehemiah leaves Jerusalem, whereas the events of 12:27–47 take place before he leaves. Once that is established, the chronological sequence of Nehemiah 13 becomes clearer.

Interpretive Insights

13:1 *no Ammonite or Moabite . . . into the assembly of God.* Deuteronomy 23:3–6 is the passage being read to the people. The point is not that true converts to Yahweh's covenant (which were extremely rare in ancient times) could not be allowed to worship with Israel. Rather, the behavior of Ammon and Moab is used as an example to show that foreign nations ultimately pursued an agenda different from Israel's, making them willing to even harm Israel. The rare exceptions were when a person came to identify so thoroughly with the worship of Yahweh that they changed national identity to become an Israelite (as did Ruth; see Ruth 1:16).

13:3 *they excluded from Israel all who were of foreign descent.* The Hebrew noun behind "foreign descent" is closely related to the verb translated "mingled" in Ezra 9:2, so the focus here is actually on those of mixed Israelite and non-Israelite descent. Still having a foot outside Israel's camp, these people are not to be included among the Jerusalem temple worshipers. Since all the surrounding nations showed themselves hostile to the Judeans in a way similar to Tobiah the Ammonite (Neh. 4:7; 6:1, 16), it makes sense to extend the exclusion of the Ammonites and Moabites to all of them.

13:5 *he had provided him with a large room.* Eliashib's action is wrong in at least two ways. First, he allows the temple storeroom to be misused, displacing the food and worship materials that were to be stored there, interfering with the community's commitments recorded in Nehemiah 12:44 and 10:37–39. Second, he allows an Ammonite (Neh. 2:10) access to the temple area, the center of worship, conflicting with the action just taken in Nehemiah 13:1–3.

13:10 *all the Levites . . . had gone back to their own fields.* Levites were not supposed to own land. Since they were to serve in the temple worship, they were supposed to receive their living from the offerings brought by the Israelites (Deut. 18:1–5; Neh. 12:44). But with the Judeans no longer bringing their contributions, reversing the practice of Nehemiah 12:44, 47, the Levites are forced to find other ways of supporting themselves, with the result that personnel are unavailable for temple service.

13:11 *I rebuked the officials.* The Hebrew verb translated "rebuked" is a key word in several complaints or disputes God raises with disobedient Israel in preexilic prophetic texts (e.g., Jer. 2:5–9; Hosea 2:2–23; 4:1–3; Mic. 6:1–8). Nehemiah is taking the role of the prophets in speaking for God as he confronts the leaders about the community's lack of obedience. He uses the same verb in verses 17 and 25.

Why is the house of God neglected? Nehemiah's question directly recalls the commitment made by the community years earlier (Neh. 10:39). They have done the very thing they said they would not.

13:13 *they were considered trustworthy.* The Hebrew word rendered "trustworthy" is closely related to the term used in Nehemiah 9:38 to describe the "binding agreement" the community made, which included provision for the Levites. In one sense it would be obvious to appoint trustworthy people to oversee the distribution of food. But there is also a contrast here with the rest of the community, which had not been trustworthy in keeping its promise to provide the tithes for the Levites.

13:14 *what I have so faithfully done.* The Hebrew word behind "faithfully" refers to deeds done out of devoted loyalty in a relationship. Ancient Near Eastern covenants created expectations that the parties involved would show loyalty to one another even beyond the strict terms of their agreement, somewhat like family members. By caring for God's house and its personnel, Nehemiah demonstrates his deep commitment to God. It is the faithful and loving attitude behind his deeds that is the basis of his relationship with God, and which he wants God to be sure to remember. The same word is used for God's "love" in verse 22 and is connected there with God's mercy to Nehemiah. This sheds light on the dynamics of the relationship, in which Nehemiah acts out of faithful loyalty to God, and because of God's loyalty to Nehemiah, God is merciful to him.

13:18 *Didn't your ancestors do . . . and on this city?* Nehemiah may have in mind Jeremiah 17:19–23, 27, which threatens destruction for Jerusalem in response to people carrying loads into the city on the Sabbath. Although the city and its wall have been rebuilt, Nehemiah sees the difficulties of the community as ongoing, since they are still subject to Persian rule; compare Nehemiah 9:32, 36–37.

The behavior of the people here stands in stark contrast to their pledge in Nehemiah 10:31.

13:22 *I commanded the Levites to . . . guard the gates.* The Levites were typically responsible for guarding the temple gates, not those of the city (1 Chron. 9:26–27). Enlisting their service to guard the city shows that there is a spiritual purpose in mind (ensuring that the Sabbath is respected) and continues the theme of the city of Jerusalem being viewed as an extension of the temple itself (see discussion of Neh. 12:30).

13:24 *Half of their children . . . did not know . . . the language of Judah.* If the children do not know Hebrew, they will be unable to understand the Scriptures—since the Scriptures have not been translated into any other language at this time—and will find worship at the Jerusalem temple irrelevant. They will also feel that they belong with others who speak their language rather than with the Judeans. Obviously, their participation in the restored covenant with God is threatened.

13:25 *pulled out their hair.* This should not be seen as an angry outburst from Nehemiah. Inflicting bruises and plucking out hair was a culturally recognized way of dishonoring men (2 Sam. 10:4; Isa. 50:6). Nehemiah wants to display visually that intermarrying with foreigners is an act with shameful consequences.

I made them take an oath in God's name. The oath Nehemiah administers matches the oath the people swore in Nehemiah 10:30. Again it is obvious that the people have failed to do as they said they would.

13:26 *he was led into sin by foreign women.* Polytheism was taken for granted by most people in the ancient world. By intermarrying with people who worshiped gods other than Yahweh, the Israelites were inevitably tempted to commit idolatry, and they were seldom able to resist. The danger of unfaithfulness to God, rather than ethnic or racial prejudice, is the real reason for avoiding intermarriage.

13:28 *I drove him away from me.* This expression probably means that Joiada's son is exiled from Judea, the province where Nehemiah is governor. Since intermarriage and subsequent idolatry were understood to be major contributing factors to Israel's exile many years earlier, it seems fitting to exile someone embarking on the same path now.

Theological Insights

Throughout this passage Nehemiah is continually focused on the purity of the Judean community and the Jerusalem temple (vv. 9, 22, 29, 30). Although the community understands the dangers present (vv. 1–3; Neh. 10:30–31), Nehemiah documents how the Judeans repeatedly allow their obedience to God to be compromised as they cross paths with foreigners. The narrative shows that the people in general seem unable to uphold God's law in the way envisioned in the new-covenant prophecy; they need God to do a further work in their hearts. God has promised that he will do this work (Deut. 30:6–8; Jer. 31:33), but its completion remains in the future, even for New Testament Christians, who have received a further step in the fulfillment of this promise by being given the Holy Spirit. Although God expresses throughout Scripture his eagerness for his people to obey him, his intent is for them to learn obedience by trusting him in the midst of this world, rather than for him to "zap" them into a perfect state.

Teaching the Text

Christians are often taught that the Old Testament shows that people are unable to keep God's law. This is true, and Nehemiah 13 provides a good example. According to Christ, the new covenant was instituted only at his crucifixion (Luke 22:20), and the Holy Spirit was poured out on believers after Christ's ascension (John 16:7; Acts 2:1–4). But even with God's help to resist sin (1 Cor. 10:13), Christians still struggle with temptation and often fail. In many of his letters Paul takes a role similar to that of Nehemiah in this passage, working with seemingly resistant church members to set them back on the right path (1 Cor. 5:1–2; 11:17–22; Gal. 1:6–10; 3:1).

Believers need to understand that God still expects his people to be pure, although it is moral, not ritual, purity that he desires (1 Pet. 1:14–16). This requires continual vigilance. While there is no longer a need to keep unbelievers from attending our worship services, and we should actively be seeking to reach them for Christ, we still need to be aware of the danger of compromise that our relationships with them present. An unbeliever is ultimately a rebellious enemy of God until coming to faith, no matter how friendly they may seem.

Nehemiah's response to what he found when he returned to Jerusalem illustrates how urgent it is for church leaders to confront and correct sin within the body. This is a delicate topic in Western culture because of the widespread assumption that no one should interfere with another's personal choices. While it is inappropriate to pluck out hair or call down curses, it is appropriate to communicate the seriousness of sin in culturally suitable ways. The leader's role also goes beyond this to finding ways to help believers return to and maintain the right path. Again, cultural differences do not allow imposing the same kinds of restrictions that Nehemiah did. But with dedication and creativity, leaders can help believers see where appropriate behavioral lines should be drawn. Finally, it is important to be clear about how, when dealing with sin in the church, the biblical view of the responsibilities of leaders differs from the expectations of our culture.

Although the principle of maintaining purity before God continues to be valid, none of the examples in this chapter should be applied directly to Christians today. There is no need to avoid interracial or interethnic marriage, but Christians are to avoid marrying outside the faith. The specific requirement to donate a tithe is no longer in force, but believers are expected to financially support those who do the work of the ministry for a living, and to support them generously, which in many cases will amount to giving more than a tenth of one's income. Observance of the Sabbath is not expected as it was in the Old Testament (Rom. 14:5), but believers should still recognize that Christ is Lord of our time. The temptation to bend God's instructions in order to make more money still needs to be resisted.

Illustrating the Text

God demands moral and spiritual purity of his people.

Bible: In Leviticus 11:44–45 and 19:2 (texts quoted by Peter in 1 Peter 1:14–16; compare also Lev. 20:7), God says to his people, "Be holy, because I am holy." He requires that we resemble him in his purity and righteousness.

Theological Reference: Theologians talk about God's communicable and incommunicable attributes. These are qualities that we can either "catch" or "not catch" from our relationship with him. For example, we will never possess aseity (self-existence) or immutability (unchangeableness), as these are characteristics proper only to God. However, there are many traits of God that we can grow toward by his grace (even if we never fully embody them the way God does): we can become more loving, more wise, and more righteous. As for holiness, there is some debate about whether this is a communicable or incommunicable attribute. It is sort of a hybrid. In one sense, no one is truly holy as God is holy-holy-holy. He is the epitome of purity and set-apart-ness in a way we shall never be. However, he demands that we be holy as he is holy (see Scripture references above), and he certainly wouldn't demand it without making a way for us to obey. This means that, by his good pleasure and his indwelling Spirit, somehow he gives us grace to share in his holiness. What an amazing thing that the holy God of the universe allows us to share in his utter set-apart-ness and purity, washing us and re-creating us to be more like himself!

Godly leaders must courageously and humbly confront sin.

Applying the Text: Nobody wants to confront sin. It is an uncomfortable mess every time, like poking a hornets' nest. However, the person who ought least to have wanted to was Jesus. He knew the joys of a sinless and safe heaven, hated the scent of evil, and had no guilt of his own that would have required him to come anywhere near impurity and pain. His love for his Father's ways and will, however, meant that he couldn't ignore sin or abandon the wretched people under its control. It meant he wouldn't stand by and watch as we suffered deservedly and God's creation was ravaged by demons and deceptions. If Jesus can find it in himself to confront sin, then we who are called by his name can as well. We need to step up and remove it from our lives and fight to make sure others around us are set free as well. Invite your listeners to battle sin through confession and repentance, admonition, discipline, and purity. Invite them to preach the gospel that can snatch others from the fire as well.

Grace frees us from obligation, but then takes us further in love.

Film: In *The Patriot* (2000), a movie about the American Revolution, a slave discovers that if he serves long enough in the colonial militia, he will be set free. Other white soldiers in the militia initially show prejudice and disdain for him, but he perseveres. Late in the film, at the start of a momentous battle, a fellow soldier points out that he no longer needs to fight—he has served his time and is a free man. The former slave refuses to leave and asserts, "I'm here now of my own accord." When grace frees us from our need to earn God's approval, we are liberated to serve him out of love of our own accord. Love and freedom take us further and with more courage than guilt and obligation ever could.

Esther

Andrew J. Schmutzer

Introduction to Esther

Author

The book does not identify its author, though the book's title, like Ruth, comes from the name of its heroine. Jewish tradition considers Mordecai the possible author, based on 9:20 and 9:32, but Ezra was also considered.[1] Josephus claims that the Jewish Scriptures were written from the time of Moses "until Artaxerxes" (464–424 BC).[2] In other words, canonical books were still being written.[3]

The Greek historian Herodotus (484–420 BC) records much in his famous *History of the Persian Wars* that sheds light on the historicity of Esther. Traveling throughout the Persian Empire after the Peace of Callias (449 BC), Herodotus records valuable information about Median and Persian life.[4] It is likely that Herodotus was in contact with ruling families throughout western Asia Minor. His knowledge of Mesopotamia, Egypt, and Scythia is also invaluable. His records of the battles of Thermopylae and Salamis, for example, have been confirmed by archaeology, topographical surveys, and linguistic studies.[5]

In the final analysis, some Persian Jew—possibly a court "recorder" from the capital of Susa—is most likely the author.[6] This assessment is based on statements of written documents (2:23; 6:1–2; 10:2), firsthand knowledge of administrative practice, broad acquaintance with Persian custom and law (e.g., Esther's orphan status), the tone of Jewish nationalism, and a large number of Persian words in comparison to the number used in other Old Testament books (about 60 Persian words in the book's 165 verses).

Date

There is no clear date of writing. A probable time, however, is around 460 BC, after the reign of Ahasuerus (486–465 BC) and before Alexander's conquests. Dates that help orient the story, however, are references to the third (1:3) and seventh (2:16) years of Ahasuerus's reign. In 465 BC, Artabanus, the captain of the bodyguard, assassinated Ahasuerus.

The governorship of Zerubbabel was past, and the temple was already being rebuilt under the prophets Haggai and Zechariah (516 BC; Ezra 3–6). The events of the book of Esther also appear to have happened before Ezra's return to Jerusalem (458 BC; Ezra 7:9). Regardless, Esther mentions nothing of these events concerning Jewish life and well-being in Palestine. If Esther were written after the Persian period (559–330 BC), one would expect to find Greek terms. The Persian Empire lasted until 331 BC.

Table 1. Persian Kings

King	Reign
Cyrus the Great	559–530 BC
Cambyses	530–522 BC
Pseudo-Smerdis (imposter)	523–522 BC
Darius I Hystaspes	522–486 BC
Xerxes I (Ahasuerus)	486–465 BC
Artaxerxes I	464–424 BC
Xerxes II	425–424 BC
Darius II	424–404 BC
Artaxerxes II	404–358 BC
Artaxerxes III	358–338 BC
Arses	338–336 BC
Darius III	336–333 BC

Audience

The Hebrew language is postexilic, as some phrases show. The Diaspora—geographic and cultural spread of the Jewish people after Babylon defeated Judah (597 BC)—must also have been the core audience who first encountered the book, as a part of the broad postexilic community.

The earliest audience observing the Festival of Purim intentionally celebrated with a view toward future generations. As the Jews lived in the international theater of powers vying for control (i.e., Babylon, Persia, Greece, Rome), the synagogue audience heard a two-pronged message: First, be encouraged if you are being oppressed by a hostile nation—Esther and Mordecai modeled savvy relationships. But second, be warned if you wield harsh authority over the weak—Haman showed how contemptuous the arrogant can be in the eyes of the powerless.

Purpose

The core purpose was to record the background and establishment of the Festival of Purim. At the forefront of this festival was the great deliverance of the Jews during the reign of Ahasuerus. The book recounts the historical initiation and social obligation of that festival for all Jews in every country of residence (9:26–32). Outside Esther, the Festival of Purim is first mentioned in 2 Maccabees, where it is called "Mordecai's day" (15:36).

In terms of ethical living, Diaspora Jews are challenged, "Seek the peace and prosperity of the city to which I have carried you into exile" (Jer. 29:7). Moreover, Jews in Persia should consider that *post*exilic life is a respectable station for a Jewish transformation of the nations (Zech. 8:19–23).

In terms of everyday life, Esther shows that God can still accomplish his will through "coincidences" and frail human agents as he can through the grandest of miracles. God uses everyday people who live amid class discrimination and ethnic tensions to further his cause. In Esther, God delivered the Jews from Haman's "edict of death" (9:20–22). God's presence need not be overt to be effective. At times the book feels decidedly *secular*, but beauty contests, harems, banquets, and a small army of eunuchs advance the program of God—even in exile! God also works from *within*.

Occasion

The book of Esther recounts Persian intrigue and intense court drama during the reign of King Ahasuerus of Persia (486–465 BC). By this time, the kingdom of Persia controlled the entire Middle Eastern world. Unfortunately, there is no historical record that confirms Esther was the queen of Persia.[7] The book falls between the two halves of Ezra, but deals with the Jews in the Persian capital of Susa, not the Jews in Jerusalem. In the prior generation, Sheshbazzar (538 BC), the first Babylonian governor of Judah, oversaw the return of fifty thousand Jews from their Babylonian captivity (Ezra 1:1–8; 2:64–67). However, a large contingent of Jewish families, skilled workers, and trained court officials remained behind. This included Esther's family. The book of Esther is distinctive, in that its setting and occasion are entirely outside Palestine. But as in Daniel, the key characters are largely foreign rulers and governments.[8]

Esther in the Megilloth

In the Hebrew Bible, the book of Esther is part of the *Megilloth* ("the five scrolls"). Each of the five books was historically used in the celebration of a particular festival:

- Ecclesiastes → Feast of Booths
- Song of Solomon → Passover
- Ruth → Feast of Weeks
- Lamentations → Ninth of Av (remembrance of the temple's destruction)
- Esther → Purim

While Lamentations and Song of Songs are entirely poetic and Ecclesiastes is mostly poetry, Ruth and Esther are narrative. What ties Ruth and Esther is their brevity and their connection to a Jewish festival. In a practical way, Israel used these festivals for (1) historical memory, (2) intentional theology, and (3) a stable ordering of their celebration.

These connections integrated the Old Testament Scriptures with the religious behavior of people. Ritual practice and sacred calendar merged.[9] Purim answered questions the Jews had about their future identity, scattered in foreign lands. Like the Passover, Purim celebrated God's strong arm, ever capable of rescuing his people.

In the Christian canon, these five books were "distributed" through the Scriptures on a *historical* rather than *liturgical* basis. The book of Esther is never alluded to in the New Testament, nor is it found among the extensive Dead Sea Scrolls. It is possible that Esther was kept out of the Essene collection of biblical texts because the ancient celebration of Purim acknowledged a time of greater ethnic integration among pagan peoples. Additionally, the Dead Sea community appears to have not observed Purim because it conflicted with their 365-day calendar and would have consistently fallen on the sacred Sabbath.[10] The calendar now used in modern Judaism guarantees that Purim will never conflict with Sabbath observance. The Christian liturgical calendar revolves around the three great celebrations: (1) Christ's birth (= Christmas), (2) Christ's resurrection (= Easter), and (3) Christ's gifting of the Holy Spirit to inaugurate the church (= Pentecost).

Key Theological Themes

1. Purim within Israel's Festivals

The name *Purim* receives a storied explanation in the scheming of Haman. From the Babylonian word *pûru* ("lot, fate"), *purim* is a Hebraicized word.[11] Esther recounts how the offended Persian official Haman "cast lots" to determine the best day to exterminate all the Jews (Esther 3:7; 9:24–26). The statements of yearly "custom" (9:19, 27–28) imply that the festival has already been established and some time has passed. The festival was fixed in the Jewish liturgical calendar (Adar 14) and commemorated the Jews' deliverance.

The festival tradition reaches back to lively occasions in Israel's social life. Festivals were a combination of popular cultural environment and self-conscious theological interest. These two forces were endlessly reconfigured throughout Israel's history. Still celebrated, Purim now includes the memory of the Holocaust, marking the resilience of the Jewish people.

The purpose of festival occasions was to give public, dramatic demonstration to the identity of Israel as the people of God and of YHWH as the protector of Israel.[12] Purim became a communal embodiment of the book of Esther itself. Purim in festival includes reading of the book of Esther, exchanges of food, gifts to the poor, and a large meal. Jewish celebrants historically dress in costume, engage in role-play, use noisemakers, and whip up a well-inebriated atmosphere. The Talmud actually instructs celebrants to imbibe so much wine that they can no longer distinguish between the phrases "cursed be Haman" and "blessed be Mordecai."[13] The secular tone of "carnival" surrounding Purim has led Messianic Jews to draw deeper (typological) connections to Yeshua within the canon of Scripture.

More broadly, three major festivals were "codified" around major events: (1) *Passover* dramatized the exodus and incorporated new generations into the identity of Israel (Exod. 12–13); (2) *Festival of Weeks* and (3) *Festival of Booths* were tied to Israel's cycle of agriculture but were drawn in the liturgy of historical memory.[14] For all three festivals, God was celebrated as the benevolent sovereign over the rhythm of "nature" and the deadly crises of history. Less significant were *Yom Kippur* (a day of reconciliation, Lev. 23:26–32) and *Purim* (which Moses never commissioned), a celebration of Jewish identity in the face of perennial risk.[15]

2. God's Providence

God is famously absent from the book of Esther, a fact not lost in its history of detractors. However, the hand of God is evident on numerous occasions where mere coincidence strains the imagination. Such moments include Esther's superiority in the beauty contest (2:1–18), Mordecai's hearing of assassination plans (2:19–23), Ahasuerus's sleepless night and Haman's early visit to secure Mordecai's execution (6:1–6), and Haman's unfortunate "fall" on Esther's couch that fixes his own death (7:8).

God's sovereignty never outruns the will, thought, or complex interactions of Esther's characters. Significant in the book is the degree to which human agents—usually unknowingly—flesh out the hand of God. On numerous occasions, the Hebrew text uses *divine passives*, phrases that hint at God's presence working though human events. So when Esther "was taken" (2:8) or "the Jews got relief" (9:22), the eyes of faith see more than dumb luck or good fortune. When Esther asks Mordecai to gather support and asks, "Fast for me," she appeals to a sacred ritual but omits the prayer to God, typically found as "prayer and fasting" (Neh. 9:1–3). Even though no person mentions God—even in expected places like 4:14—God is present and working, rather creatively.

3. Haman's Connection to the Amalekites

It is significant that Haman is immediately linked to the house of Agag, the king of Amalek (Esther 3:1; 1 Sam. 15:32–33). The Amalekites were the paradigmatic enemy of Israel. God said there would be war with Amalek for generations (Exod. 17:16) and that his name would be blotted out (Deut. 25:19; 1 Sam. 15:17–18). Though Samuel would later kill King Agag, Saul took plunder and also spared his life. So Haman, Agag's descendant, resurfaces to provoke the Jews again (cf. 1 Chron. 4:43). Similarly, Mordecai's genealogy mentions Kish (Esther 2:5), Saul's father. There may be a form of *telescoping* happening here. Biblical texts could say "father(s)" without insisting on exhaustive genealogy (see comments on 2:5–6). The reason for mentioning Shimei and even Kish goes beyond biography to act as reminders of a prior time when David himself was opposed—under great duress—yet God spared him. Additionally, Mordecai fulfills God's command to dispose of the Amalekites, the instruction originally given to Saul. This helps explain why the Jews in Esther refuse to take any plunder (9:10, 15–16; cf. 1 Sam. 15:21).

4. The Absurdity of Evil

Throughout Esther, evil and malice are always present. In fact, behind every key movement in the plot, some wicked plan, driven by scheming dialogue, is mounting. The prime case is Haman's devilish ruse to exterminate the Jews (3:6–14), driven by hatred of *one* man (3:5). The book illustrates how moral evil requires *agency* and *volition*.[16]

In Esther, evil colonizes itself, especially in the halls of power. Personal rage becomes bald hatred, leading to an empire-wide death sentence. Haman's ploy is all the more insidious because he never identified the Jews to the king when he proposed his edict of death. Evil penetrates all corners of Persia, concocted by a Persian noble, stamped by the king's ring, sanctioned by Persian law, and carried by a famous Persian carrier-system (1:22; 3:13; 8:10). The application to contemporary corruption, ethnic hatred, global genocides, and urban violence is obvious.

Outline

1. The banquets of Ahasuerus (1:1–2:18)
   a. Vashti is deposed (1:1–22)
   b. Esther is made queen (2:1–18)

2. The banquets of Esther (2:19–7:10)
   a. Mordecai foils a plot (2:19–23)
   b. Haman devises a plot (3:1–15)
   c. Mordecai pleads with Esther (4:1–17)
   d. Esther's appeal to the king (5:1–8)
   e. Haman's pride and rage against Mordecai (5:9–14)
   f. Mordecai is honored (6:1–13)
   g. Haman is destroyed (6:14–7:10)
3. The banquets of Purim (8:1–10:3)
   a. Esther secures an edict for the Jews (8:1–17)
   b. The Jews kill their enemies (9:1–19)
   c. Purim is established (9:20–32)
   d. Mordecai's effective rule (10:1–3)

Ahasuerus, a Narcissistic King

Big Idea

Wealth and power used without a moral compass create egotistic leaders and selfish relationships.

Key Themes

- The great power of Ahasuerus[1] displays a king who is stunningly powerful yet utterly inept.
- Multiple banquets and layers of political leadership make a mockery of the wisdom and understanding that Persia really needs.

Understanding the Text

The Text in Context

Chapter 1 sets a dramatic stage in the Persian court—decadence is mixed with protocol. Three banquets occur at the outset: for the ruling aristocrats (1:3–4), the male populace (1:5–8), and the women (1:9). King Ahasuerus is introduced as a drunken fool amid an outlandish display of his wealth and absolute power. Other feasts will be offered in the middle (5:4–8; 7:1–9) and end of the book (9:16–32). Here is a banquet "that exceeds all imaginable criteria for extravagance."[2]

Through the opening pericope (a set of verses that communicate a coherent unit or thought), key characters, groups, and themes are introduced. These people illustrate how honor is tied to status, and both are defined by relationship to royalty (*malkut*).[3] Everyone in attendance is expected to respond with personal gratitude and political loyalty. In verses 1–8, the author communicates with dense description. The absence of dialogue serves to combine the first two banquets.

Historical and Cultural Background

Son of Darius I Hystaspes (522–486 BC), Ahasuerus ruled as king from 486 to 465 BC. A king was honored by delineating his geographical control.[4]

It was Darius who had organized the empire into provinces extending from India to Cush, or southern Pakistan to northern Sudan. The 20 to 30 larger divisions of the empire were subdivided into 127 smaller provinces (*medinah*),[5] which may have represented different ethnic groups (cf. Ezra 2:1; Neh. 1:3).[6] These larger divisions were responsible to collect taxes, conscript troops for the Persian army, and keep the peace in the local areas (cf. Ezra 4:10–11).[7]

Susa (*shushan*) was one of four capitals of Ahasuerus. Other palaces were at Babylon, Ecbatana, and Persepolis, and these were occupied on a seasonal basis. Susa functioned as the king's winter palace.[8] Its walls were about 350 feet long. There were seventy-two stone columns, some eighty feet high.[9] The "third year" (v. 3; 483/482 BC) marked the end of revolts in Egypt (485 BC) and unrest in Babylon (484, 482 BC). This prompted both celebration and new military planning aimed at invading Greece. One scholar even claims that the Susa banquet doubled as a "war counsel."[10] This is reasonable, since Herodotus claims that Xerxes declared his intention to destroy Athens.[11] Hindsight, ironically, tells of the Persian army that was defeated by the Spartans at Thermopylae (480 BC).

Ancient historians speak of Persian banquets (*mishteh*; lit. "drinking parties"), wealth, ornate goblets, and excess.[12] Interestingly, many of the rare elements of royalty listed in verse 6 also occur in lists of building material and ornamentation for the tabernacle and temple (cf. Exod. 26–27; 1 Kings 7; 1 Chron. 29:2).

Interpretive Insights

1:1 *This is what happened.* This is the standard Hebrew phrase (*wayhi bimey*) of historical narrative or the sphere of the past. Other books begin similarly (e.g., Joshua, Judges, and especially Ruth).

Xerxes. Ahasuerus (*'ahashwerosh*) is the Hebrew name (see NIV text note). Xerxes was translated by the Greeks and related to the Persian, *xshayarsha*. The Septuagint and Josephus misidentify the king as Artaxerxes.

127 provinces. This was a practical division, enabling more efficient governing by as many as 31 satraps (3:12) or governors of the king. These various divisions formed political subdivisions within the kingdom.

from India to Cush. In general terms, this is southern Pakistan to northern Sudan in contemporary geography. The east-to-west span of territory that Ahasuerus inherited from his father, Darius I (521–486 BC), would have reached from the northwestern region of the Indus River to the Upper Nile region (i.e., Ethiopia).

1:2 *At that time.* This characteristic expression (*bayyamim hahem*) of historical narrative is used over thirty times in the Old Testament (cf. Exod. 2:11).

citadel of Susa. A more literal translation of the Hebrew would be "the fortress of Shushan." Susa was not only the name of the city (cf. 3:15; 8:15); it was also the name of the royal fortress that occupied a portion of the city. The phrase refers to the lower portion of the city (also v. 5), not to a mere building. Translations struggle to express this. So "citadel" (*birah*) is translated "fortress" (HCSB), "capital" (ESV), "fortified part of Susa" (CEB), "[royal] citadel" (NRSV), and "court" (NAB). *Birah* is used ten times in Esther alone. In 1 Chronicles 29:1, 19, the same word is used to refer to the Jerusalem temple.

1:3 *in the third year of his reign.* These events that are described begin around 483 BC. At the time of these events in Esther, the first return under Zerubbabel (538 BC) has already occurred. The second return, led by Ezra (458 BC), is yet to happen.

he gave a banquet . . . military leaders . . . princes . . . nobles. "Banquets" and "drinking" form a theme powerfully used throughout the book. Such banquets are used to signal new directions in the story. Having put down several rebellions in his empire, the king now seizes on the opportunity to celebrate and strategize with the empire's elite. Those in attendance are representative of military officers and aristocrats, identified by dress, seating, and gesture.[13] Though all the right dignitaries are present, the carnival atmosphere combined with the snub from his queen (v. 12) reveals something different. This banquet is really a parody of the Persian institution of the "king's table."

1:4 *a full 180 days.* Various kinds of activities occurred in alternating form. No one group suspended their duty for six months but possibly rotated attendance in and out.[14]

vast wealth . . . splendor and glory of his majesty. In Hebrew, several phrases are stacked to communicate what Ahasuerus *displayed.* In some ways, the entire "endgame" of the first banquet was a spectacle of the wealth and wonder of King Ahasuerus. It is a small wonder that Ahasuerus would also soon "display" (v. 11) the "beauty" of Queen Vashti. In the pompous environment of the king, there appears to be little distinction between property and people. Whether this is fact or fantasy, ancient historians speak of the legendary Persian banquets (similarly, the 120-day feast of Jdt. 1:16).[15]

1:5 *for all the people.* The second banquet was tailored to the people of Susa, "from the least to the greatest" (i.e., nobles to commoners). It was held in the ten-acre citadel courtyard, within an open colonnaded pavilion.[16]

1:6 *garden had hangings . . . couches of gold and silver.* Persian palaces were famously surrounded by elaborate gardens.[17] The longest verse in the book (twenty-one Heb. words) describes the opulent environment. Verse 6 alone uses three different terms for "fine linen." In Israel, such words for fine linen were almost exclusively used in connection with royalty and religious personnel. The colors represented include white, violet, and purple. Later,

King Ahasuerus will give to Mordecai a "purple robe of fine linen" (8:15). In stunning detail, the narrator describes multicolored linen hangings that were suspended throughout the royal gardens and fastened by ornate cords to silver rings on marble pillars. In the opening scene this pageantry of colors, mosaics, marble, and mother-of-pearl forms a list of rare and exquisite terms that heighten the exotic splendor of the royal surroundings. These terms read like a description by breathless guest, trying to take it all in.

1:7 *goblets of gold . . . the royal wine.* The visual parade culminates with the wine and the goblets (vv. 7–8), and no two gold goblets are the same!

1:8 *command. Dat* is a significant word in Esther, meaning "edict, decree" or "law" (cf. 1:13, 19; 2:8; 3:8, 14; 4:3, 8, 11, 16; 8:13, 17; 9:1, 14).[18] Aramaic forms also occur in Ezra 7:12, 14. A comparable form can be found in the earlier Hebrew expression "Law of Moses" (*torat mosheh*, Josh. 8:31; cf. *m. Ketub.* 7.6). Life in Persia is lived by edicts that come from the royal palace. Later, Haman will manipulate this same process of "law" (*dat*, 3:8). Occurring twenty times in Esther, *dat* is from a Persian loan-word (*data*, "law") and can include "custom," "law," or "practice."

to serve each man what he wished. Persian drinking approaches an art form in the book. By the royal decree in 1:8, guests are allowed to drink as each person desires. Unending drinking matches the king's pretense of absolute power. Without compulsion or restriction, this banquet in the royal court shows that even getting drunk can, ironically, comply with an edict. The only rule seems to be "more is better"—What else could the king possibly want?

Theological Insights

It is God who raises kings to rule (Prov. 21:1; Dan. 2:20–23) and lends the ability to make wealth (Deut. 8:18–20). The cosmic King deserves all glory, but earthly rulers notoriously encroach on God's splendor. The wealth of Ahasuerus (1:4–7) illustrates a vital theme of Wisdom literature and Scripture as a whole: the hubris of kings is a prelude to their own humiliation (e.g., Eccl. 2:1–11; Dan. 3 and 5 of the related era).[19] Wealth and power are always invitations to disgrace when riches are gathered in arrogance (Ps. 49:6–7, 13; Esther 5:11; Luke 12:16–21).

Teaching the Text

This text offers much reflection on key vices. First is the danger of acquisition and power, whenever it defines a culture. "Got it, flaunt it" may be a pop-culture mantra, but money and vanity are nothing new. Solomon—another powerful king—was taken down by his own extravagance, powerful alliances, and following "after other gods" (1 Kings 11:4). This link between theology and economics is sharply critiqued in 1 Kings 11:1–18. Like Solomon's sin, our "lust for more" can be a violation of the first commandment ("no other gods") in the form of coveting, a violation of the tenth commandment.[20]

Second, pride is particularly tempting for those who are wealthy or powerful or who tie their ego to status (Prov. 3:34; James 2:1–7). Among CEOs, senior pastors, movie stars, and athletes there is often a palpable air of superiority. In truth, society at large "crowns" such figures with more money and influence than they can handle, calling them "stars," "heroes," or even "icons". Because we want their accolades, we also hand them out, but "loyalty cannot be bought for long, and true respect comes from an admiration of a person's character, not from being dazzled by a three-karat diamond ring or a million-dollar house."[21] Part of the reason Ahasuerus flaunted his "splendor and glory" is that he had no sense of proportion (e.g., "180 days"). The antidote includes the ancient prayer: "neither poverty nor riches" (Prov. 30:7–9).

Third, Ahasuerus was a "divine sovereign" who went off the rails in a more-is-better philosophy (seven-day feast, v. 5). Similarly, there is the ongoing danger of linking wealth with faith and divine approval. Those who have wealth are viewed as deserving, and those without it deserve that, too. The church, however, has been given different *types of currency*: wisdom, vision, communication, experience, and teaching. When prominence is given to the elite, other forms of currency are marginalized, including the principles of humility (Phil. 2) and leadership as "slaves of all" (Mark 10:42–45; Luke 22:25–27).

Illustrating the Text

Love of money and power is idolatry and leads to grief.

Bible: 1 Timothy 6:10 illustrates this truth exceptionally.

Mythology: In the ancient Greek myth of King Midas, avarice and lust for money destroy the life of the king. Midas, a king already rich but greedy and miserly in his wealth, is offered a chance to wish for any gift. He asks that everything he touches be turned to gold. Though warned to reconsider, he insists and begins to touch everything in his palace and is overjoyed to see it turn to gold. It seems wonderful until he tries to grasp and smell a rose, consume a grape, eat a slice of bread, and drink a glass of water. He suddenly realizes his gift is actually a deadly curse that will consume him. Just then, his beloved daughter enters the room. He embraces her in his panic, only to find her turned into a gold statue. In the end, he is offered a chance to wash off the curse in a river and finds his household restored. From then on, he resolves to share generously with others. Point out that, though the story is pagan, the moral is timeless and undeniable: idolatry of wealth dehumanizes and curses us.

Love and respect cannot be bought for long.

Music: The Beatles' song "Can't Buy Me Love" (1964) could provide a classic rock reference to this concept. While lighthearted and playful, the tune and words will quickly help many listeners remember the concept and apply it to Ahasuerus's relationship with Vashti. Another great example is Willie Nelson's popular version of the country song *"If You've Got the Money, I've Got the Time"* (1976). Fun, companionship, and enjoyment are all promised as long as the money holds out—but not a second longer!

Money is not the most valuable currency in God's economy.

Economics: Talk about the various kinds of currency with which your listeners are familiar. Many will understand the use of paper or coins to stand in place of more valuable things. Talk about how little that paper could really be worth in a situation where the society that backs the currency collapses. Point out that in such a case, values would suddenly become very different (bartering, food sharing, hunting skills, etc. would surpass money, gold, and stocks). Explain that someday the so-called gold standard will be replaced by the God standard. Then commodities like wisdom, vision, teaching, edification, love, worship, and so on will surpass the things that bring power and prestige in this world.

Vashti Defies a Self-Centered King

Big Idea

At times, people must take a stand against manipulation and exploitation, even though it may provoke a backlash.

Key Themes

- Court leadership blindly supports Ahasuerus, creating layers of dissension.
- Physical beauty is a trust to be stewarded and guarded, not something to be flaunted as a commodity.

Understanding the Text

The Text in Context

In 1:9–12, a third banquet is held by Queen Vashti (v. 9; cf. vv. 3–4, 5–8). Several significant themes are introduced here that will develop later in the book: (1) segregation, (2) queen's banquets, (3) court eunuchs, (4) and the king's anger. Later, it is the Jews who are singled out (3:8–15a); Esther will have banquets (5:5b–7; 7:1–7); the eunuchs Hegai (2:8), Hathak (4:5), and Harbona (7:9) perform duties of life and death (6:14); and the king will be enraged (7:7). Additionally, Haman's character will emerge as an extension of Ahasuerus's.

Queen Vashti's banquet (1:9) culminates three feasts of the *ceremonial* type in which the inviter and invited celebrate their mutual solidarity.[1] A contrast is struck between the bloat and bluster of the king's banquet and the silent modesty of Vashti's. Ironically, the deeper message that emerges is hardly "oneness." Vashti refuses a "show and tell," and the pericope culminates with the king's anger (1:12). This scene has overtones of impropriety.[2]

Historical and Cultural Background

Hebrew *saris* can mean "official" or "eunuch." The eunuchs of Esther 1:10 were castrated males, a standard servant class in the ancient royal court.

Without the same libido—and aspirations for the throne—eunuchs were prized for court responsibilities as tutors, personal attendants, and caretakers of royal harems. Herodotus records that when rebellions were put down in the Ionian cities, the best-looking boys were imported to Persia, castrated, and made eunuchs.[3] Occasional references early in the Old Testament (e.g., Gen. 37:36; 40:2, 7) are simply to "officials." Both terms become more common in the Israelite court (1 Kings 22:9; 2 Kings 23:11). But in the Medo-Persian culture, "eunuch" is overwhelmingly in view (Jer. 29:2; 34:19; 38:7; 41:16; cf. "young men without any physical defect, handsome," Dan. 1:4).

The ancient Greek writer Plutarch, in his *Advice to Bride and Groom*, gives counsel that sheds light on Vashti's situation: "The lawful wives of the Persian kings sit beside them at dinner, and eat with them. But when the kings wish to be merry and get drunk, they send their wives out and send for their dancing girls and concubines. They are right in what they do because they do not concede any share in their licentiousness and debauchery to their wedded wives."[4]

Interpretive Insights

1:9 *Queen Vashti also gave a banquet.* Culturally, this is unusual. Literarily, however, this separation is a plot device. The reader is led to ask, How will they associate again, and under what circumstances?

in the royal palace of King Xerxes. "Royal" (*malkut*) is used two ways in Esther: as the noun "kingdom" (3x) and the adjective "official" or "public" (6x). Vashti's banquet for the women is not in the "harem quarters" (*bet ha-nashim*, 2:3) but the "royal hall" (*bet hamalkut*, 1:9). But because the queen's "banquet" is tied to the king's "royal palace," she is also property for public viewing. The narrator combines her royalty as a contingent status with the location of the king's exhibition.[5] Whether women were obligated to feast separated from the men is not clear. While Persian custom excluded royal women from drinking-type parties,[6] Esther will invite both Ahasuerus and Haman to her own banquets (cf. 5:5b–7; 7:1–7). The logistics of size and service might have required a separate banquet for the king's concubines (over 360; cf. 2:9, 11, 13, 14; Dan. 5:1–3).[7]

1:10 *on the seventh day.* This temporal phrase marks a profound change in the social and political atmosphere of the "royal palace." Multiple uses of "seven" so close to one another are no coincidence (e.g., "seventh day," "seven eunuchs"), and signal a key change (cf. the seventh plague [Exod. 9:13–35], seventh trumpet [Rev. 11:15–19]). It is possible that Ahasuerus highlights the climactic seventh day of the feast by sending these seven named eunuchs. Such eunuchs often played an important role in political and administrative events (cf. Jer. 29:2; Dan. 1:7; Acts 8:27). While the scenery has been luxuriant, there

Vashti

Both the meaning of the name and identity of the person Vashti are uncertain. The Hebrew *washti* may reproduce the Persian *vahishta*, "the best" or "the beloved,"[a] possibly making Vashti an honorific title for the most prized wife. Ancient records only cite Amestris with Xerxes.[b] Maybe Vashti was her Persian name and Amestris either the Greek name or the name of another wife altogether.[c] While some scholars see a credible connection between Amestris and Vashti (with certain phonetic changes to make the name association), others view the testimony of Herodotus to that effect (7.61, 114) as doubtful and think Amestris may even refer to Esther.[d]

The Jewish Talmud links Vashti with the granddaughter of Nebuchadnezzar and daughter of Belshazzar (*b. Meg.* 10b). Of course, neither king treated the Jews well. One talmudic rabbi claimed that Vashti was struck with leprosy and that this was the reason she refused to obey the king's command (1:10–12). Jewish tradition also views Vashti's banquet (1:9) as an occasion of serious political intrigue in which the nobles' wives are being held as captives. Their detainment was for "in-

surance" so that their husbands would think twice about breaking loyalty with Ahasuerus.[e]

The biblical text does offer an intriguing portrait of Vashti in a *decrescendo* of power. She is initially described as "Queen Vashti" six times (1:9, 11, 12, 15, 16, 17), then once as "the queen" (1:18). Finally, she is merely called "Vashti" (1:19), when a royal edict is drawn up to banish her. She exits the story when her title is withdrawn.[f] In fact, the narrator places Vashti *outside* the racket of drunk nobles, preserving her from the mocking characterization of Persian leaders and a foolish king intent on making a spectacle of her beauty (1:11). Though she is banished by paranoid officials (1:17–18), the narrator evaluates Vashti positively.

Vashti may have been deposed in 484/483 BC, with Esther not assuming the role of queen until five years later (479/478 BC). If Vashti is Amestris (according to Greek historians), then she may have returned to power later as queen mother, with her son Artaxerxes, until her death around 424 BC (cf. Ezra 7:1, 7, 11–12, 21; 8:1; Neh. 2:1; 5:14; 13:6).

---

[a] Clines, *Ezra, Nehemiah, Esther*, 278, citing views of Haupt and Gehman.
[b] Herodotus, *Hist.* 7.61, 114; 9.109–13.
[c] Smith, *Ezra, Nehemiah, Esther*, 231.
[d] Yamauchi, "Vashti," 827.
[e] Branch, "Vashti," 1353.
[f] Laniak, *Shame and Honor*, 43n26.

---

has been no social drama to this point. Now dramatic action begins and the plot takes off.

in high spirits from wine. The Hebrew reads literally "the heart was good" (cf. Judg. 16:25; 1 Sam. 25:36; 1 Kings 8:66; Prov. 15:15). Literarily, this is an ominous note of vulnerability and potential exploitation: compare with Noah (Gen. 9:21–25), Lot (19:30–38), and Nabal (1 Sam. 25:36). Especially illustrative are the raucous Philistine party ("While they were high in spirits, they shouted, 'Bring out Samson to entertain us'" [Judg. 16:25]) and the imbibing King Belshazzar ("He gave orders to bring in the gold and silver goblets . . . , so that the king and his nobles, his wives and his concubines might drink from them" [Dan. 5:2]).

Mehuman . . . Karkas. Eunuchs are mentioned forty-five times in the Old Testament, with twelve of these in the book of Esther. These names are Persian or Iranian in origin, with a few mirrored in verse 14. Some, like Karkas, have even been found in ancient administrative records (e.g., *Persepolis Treasury Tablets,* xxii). When "King Ahasuerus" (v. 10) commands seven named eunuchs to fetch his wife, and "Queen Vashti" (v. 11–12) refuses to come, the scene has become charged with the tension of political office and personal egos.

1:11 *bring before him Queen Vashti . . . to display her beauty.* Using the same verb, the narrator illustrates how the king's self-glorification makes no distinction between the "display" (*l*har'ot,* v. 4) of his wealth and the "display" of his wife (v. 11). While the entire chapter "reeks of drunken indulgence, royal incompetence, and sexual innuendo," this command has a disgusting voyeuristic tone.[8]

1:12 *Queen Vashti refused to come.* No motive is given as to why the queen refuses the king. It is probably not her commitment to royal protocol,[9] even for his honor. Jewish tradition suggests that Vashti was to appear only in her "royal crown" (Megillah, Targums). It is more likely that Vashti refuses to be reduced to the status of a concubine, just for the sport of (and possible violation by) inebriated men. The combination of king, wives, concubines, drinking, and flaunted display in Daniel 5:2 is a significant parallel. Regardless, her refusal is a stunning dismissal of Ahasuerus's presentation of power.

furious and burned with anger. Anger will flare up with several characters (3:5; 5:9; 7:7, 10), and no good ever flows from it. Between the queen's refusal to appear and the king's subsequent anger, the reader is given needed insight into the character of Ahasuerus.

Theological Insights

God is *always* at work. Even in a disaster, God is already unfolding the next steps. When Vashti refused to play along in the king's little drama (1:12), God was preparing an entirely new cast of characters to take center stage. When commitments are lived out—whether personal or secular in nature—God incorporates human actions and commitments as the "building blocks" for the next phase of his plan. It's almost paradoxical how we can see God's hand, once we round the corner of crisis and catastrophe; he was working the whole time.

Teaching the Text

This pericope has several negative elements that must be taught carefully. This text needs to be culturally explained, not morally justified. The main character,

Ahasuerus, issues commands that even his own wife disobeys. His power is not impregnable, nor is his kingship wise. Vashti's choice illustrates how cultural *systems* can place impossible demands on people who are (1) defined by skewed social traditions, (2) caught in huge power differentials, and (3) then punished for not complying with the demands of power (cf. 1:13–22). Christian maturity helps us to think carefully about our specific traditions, eliminating elements that are destructive to others. Our strategic leadership can be a force for positive change and justice, embracing accountability. Public awareness teaches us to be "wise as serpents, and harmless as doves" (Matt. 10:16 KJV), no longer naïve to the ways that unfair laws or aggressive business practices can crush simple people who have few resources or no constructive options.

Contemporary audiences—who largely live by the values of individualism, self-expression, and empowerment—will struggle with this text. Vashti was caught between a husband's command and social expectations. Systems don't create easy options. So it's simplistic to moralize Vashti as the "poster-wife" fighting against male domination, in search of her own power. Neither *victim* nor *manipulator* are gendered words. Potophar's wife played power-games with Joseph in Egypt (Gen. 39:7–20). It's also wrongheaded to use this text to defend obedience to one's husband or manager, under the pretense that "God placed them in authority." Too much abuse has happened to missionary children, uneducated minorities, and obedient wives under this theological banner. While the mighty work of the gospel doesn't submit to our timetables, Christ's work does *purify* culture; it does not destroy culture. Consider new ministries to support and boards to serve on that are facing *systemic* issues today (e.g., mission work in Muslim areas, trafficking children, community action programs).

Illustrating the Text

Don't let cultural systems fool you—all power will be subject to accountability.

History: Eliot Ness and his crew of so-called untouchables sought to bring Al Capone and his entire organized-crime family to justice during the 1920s in America. Capone seemed to elude them at every turn, and it appeared that he would escape accountability for his crimes, until Ness and his crew were able to finally bring him to justice. Ironically, it was not the murder, theft, bootlegging, bribery, or any number of other illicit activities that brought Capone to accountability in the end—it was income-tax evasion. All of the strong-arm tactics and measures of law enforcement were ineffective against him, but accounting was his undoing. Invite your listeners to consider that though there may be people in this world like Capone and Ahasuerus who seem to be an untouchable law unto themselves, accountability is always coming for every human power. It may not come when we expect it, and systems of this world may seem arrayed to protect them from judgment. But there are other systems at work, and God's justice is not mocked.

Hymn: **"This Is My Father's World," by Maltbie Babcock.** In one stanza of this great hymn, we hear the testimony of a pastor who loved to walk in God's creation in Lockport, New York. In contrasting the majesty of God the creator with the evils of this world, he proclaimed,

> This is my Father's world,
> O let me ne'er forget
> That though the wrong seems oft so strong,
> God is the Ruler, yet!
> This is my Father's world:
> The battle is not done.[10]

Jesus will be satisfied and history will prove that, no matter how much the systems and powers of this world seem to win in the short term, God rules and always wins.

Fighting cultural systems in your own strength will cost you.

Stories: Take time to share a moment in your life when you attempted to fight against a cultural system; it could be a time when you were young and took a stand against a system of social castes in your school, a time you tried to protest your parents' discipline or rules, or a time when you went toe-to-toe with a school administrator, authority figure, or tradition. The key to the illustration is that it must be a time when you *lost* and paid a price for it. It will work even better if it was a time when you were clearly wrong or comically misguided in your youthful ideals and enthusiasms. Either way, the point is *not* in the particular details of the battle you chose, but in the way you fought the system and became aware that you were not in charge and could not win the fight. Point out to your listeners that, right or wrong, cultural systems have an amazing momentum, and when we fight them alone and in our flesh, we often lose epically.

Ahasuerus and His Nobles Overreact

Big Idea
Leaders often overreact to external threats while ignoring their "blind spots" and internal problems.

Key Themes
- Though possessing absolute power, Ahasuerus seeks advice from his court and impulsively implements it.
- The greatest dangers to the Persian Empire actually come from inside the palace, not outside.

Understanding the Text

The Text in Context

The pericope of 1:13–22 is a flurry of legislative activity. The king galvanizes Persia's judicial experts (v. 13) to figure out how they should respond to Vashti's disobedience. By no law is Vashti ever found guilty, she is just declared "wrong" (v. 16) in order to preserve the honor of the king and banish the problem. The massive overreaction to the queen in this scene, all to avoid an insurrection in the kingdom, creates a parody of Ahasuerus's court. When dialogue finally occurs in the book, it is dedicated to justifying a "royal decree" (v. 19), written for every language and province of the kingdom (v. 22; cf. 3:8–15). The final verse, 22, returns the reader to the reign and reach of Ahasuerus that began in 1:1.

Various elements of the pericope support the narrator's parody of the Persian leaders. The king's use of the "seven nobles" (1:14) reenacts the drama of the "seven eunuchs" (1:10). In fact, comparing the lists, the name Memukan plays off Mehuman and Admatha with Abagtha—much like the literary sound-play of Bifur and Bofur or Kili and Fili in *The Hobbit*.[1] Here is the first of three "dispatches" sent throughout the kingdom (cf. 1:22; 3:12–13; 8:10–14). And ironies abound. Vashti does not wish to appear before the king, and her punishment grants her that wish.[2] Every man is to rule "over his own household"—except the king (v. 22)!

Interpretive Insights

1:13 *experts . . . law and justice.* These experts were professionals who understood the spectrum of local to royal law (Heb. *dat wᵉdin*, "law and justice"). Custom may have required checking with imperial advisers,[3] but the image of Ahasuerus as a highly suggestible king also emerges.

wise men who understood the times. These phrases are in parallel ("experts . . . ; wise men . . ."), making it unlikely that the latter are astrologers.[4] Rather, these are advisers who understand common law, based on precedent (cf. 1 Chron.12:32).

1:14 *Karshena, Shethar . . . seven nobles.* The same kind of group or "Counsel of Seven" is also mentioned in Ezra 7:14 and Jeremiah 52:25, and also by some ancient historians (e.g., Herodotus, Xenophon).[5]

These seven close advisers were available for assistance but had limited access to the king. Any violation was punishable by death (cf. 4:11). Darius, who preceded Ahasuerus, used a similar counsel. The advisers were allowed to enter the king's presence at any time, except if he was with a woman.[6] The use of special messenger eunuchs began in the reign of Deioces and continued into the reign of Darius. It is a particular messenger eunuch (Hathak) that Esther uses in chapter 4. Esther's concern that she had not been summoned to the king by a messenger for thirty days (4:11) shows that the same court customs were still in play in her time.

had special access to the king. Proximity to royalty serves two purposes: it heightens the very access that Vashti is about to lose—that of those who, literally, "see the face of the king"—and draws on the vested interest of Memukan, one of the nobles (v. 14) who fears "disrespect" (v. 18) spilling over into other domestic arenas.

were highest in the kingdom. Literally, these people "sat first in the kingdom." The detail in Memukan's speech (vv. 16–20) reveals a fear of losing their second-to-none position.

1:15 *what must be done . . . ?* Interestingly or pathetically, the first dialogue of the book is used to elevate a domestic dispute into a national crisis—for which there is no law on the books! The reader is right to wonder whether an excess of wine has also left Persia's wise men, as well as the king, a little "in high spirits" (cf. 1:10). That one woman's decision requires an immediate conclave of Persia's "wise men" (v. 13) is absurd and begs for the laugh of a dinner theater.[7]

1:16 *Memukan replied.* In verses 16–18, Memukan becomes the collective voice for all seven advisers on behalf of aristocracy throughout the kingdom. Memukan's response grossly overcompensates. Using "nobility" language four times to emphasize a number of points: he (1) expands the offense to include his rank of nobility (v. 16), (2) anticipates widespread "discord" among noble wives (v. 18), (3) recommends the queen be banished by "royal decree" (v. 19), (4) and proposes that another fill her position (v. 19), (5) for the desired result that "all the women will respect their husbands" (v. 20). Like the political maneuvers between Ahab and Jezebel (cf. 1 Kings 16:31), Memukan's logic may have precedent, but his motive is self-serving. In short, Memukan fears that wives will act like Vashti whenever their husbands act like Ahasuerus.[8]

1:17 *they will despise.* Elsewhere, biblical texts do equate disobedience with despising (cf. Prov. 14:2; 15:20). But this does not justify Memukan's conclusion that a kingdom-wide insurrection is inevitable.

1:19 *laws of Persia and Media, which cannot be repealed.* A few biblical texts show that royal documents can become fixed law (Esther 8:8; Dan. 6:8, 12, 15). However, neither Persian nor Greek texts portray their own laws this way. The emphasis may rather be to adherence without exception or that rescinding would shame the king. Regardless, the reality of unchangeable laws is a significant theme in the book of Esther, moving the plot along.

The strained logic behind Memukan's recommendations will be repeated in Haman's extreme anger over Mordecai's indifference (3:6)—which will also result in a new law for all of Persia! Regardless, the notion of "fixed law" is used within the plot to create a moral tension between harsh legalism and timely justice.

Vashti. In the space of one speech, "Queen" has been formally dropped (cf. "Queen Vashti," v. 16). In verse 19a, her access to the king is formally suspended. Since Vashti refused a royal audience, she is now permanently denied one.

someone who is better than she. Does "better" have in view "respect" (CEV), "worthy" (HCSB), "deserving" (NET), "beauty," or some combination of these? Regardless, beauty takes the focus as the plot now anticipates Esther (1:11; cf. 2:2–3, 7). This is an intertextual echo of Saul, who lost his royal status to David: "The LORD . . . has given it to one of your neighbors— to one better than you" (1 Sam. 15:28). This phrase in 1 Samuel and Esther contrasts two pairs: Saul/David with Vashti/Esther. The replacement is one who will please the Lord.[9]

1:20 *king's edict.* The word translated "edict" (*pitgam*) is a Persian loanword that entered the Hebrew Bible through Aramaic. This term highlights a message that enters the public domain. Once written, the new decree must then be publicized. In the portrayal of the book of Esther, the Persian Empire is obsessed with royal decrees and the preservation of records (6:1; cf. Dan. 6:8–9). However, there is much irony in a royal document that publicizes the king's personal domestic problems.[10]

1:22 *in their own language.* Aramaic was the official language of international diplomacy. However, isolated pronouncements were made in the scores of languages represented in the Persian-Median Empire. This required distribution to "each province in its own script" (cf. Ezra 6:3–5). The Persian communication system was famous for distributing important messages.[11] One of the enviable resources of the Persian kingdom was its empire-wide communication system. A fresh horse was used for each leg of the day's journey. Each day, a letter could cover around 250 miles. "A letter would travel over the Royal Road from Susa (in modern Iran) to Sardis (on the western coast of what is now Turkey) in a week via 111 relay posts."[12] Information could be quickly and efficiently distributed to all the provinces, using a special fleet of horses and riders. The decrees of Haman (3:13) and Esther (8:10) will be publicized using the very same communication system.

every man . . . ruler over his own household . . . native tongue. This is the unenforceable reason, not the content of the edict. As in Nehemiah 13:23–28, bilingual homes were to use the husband's language as the default, and so Nehemiah lamented that the children of Judah "did not know how to speak the language of Judah" (13:24b). So the edict is designed to assert the husband's authority and role in his home.

Throughout Israelite history, the Israelites recognized various nationalities precisely by their various languages (cf. Deut. 3:9; Judg. 12:6; Ps. 114:1; Isa. 33:19; Ezek. 3:5–6).

Theological Insights

God routinely flips the best human intentions on their head. This is a theological point made throughout Scripture. What people label as "wise, brilliant, and ingenious" may, at times, be *foolishness* by God's reckoning. God even goes on record stating: "Once more I will astound these people . . . ; the wisdom of the wise will perish, the intelligence of the intelligent will vanish" (Isa. 29:14). The very goal of the Persian administrators—to preserve their power by publicizing their "wisdom"—falls apart. Paul develops this theological axiom in 1 Corinthians 1:19, "For it is written: 'I will destroy the wisdom of the wise; the intelligence of the intelligent I will frustrate.'" The "wise" always flaunt their own ideas, leaning on their own reasoning. Such people often prove, instead, to be foolish. In this dynamic, God lets natural consequences of evil run their course and people fall prey to their own devices.

Teaching the Text

This section is intended to construct the scenario through which God will unfold his plan. Sometimes, beyond the explicit teaching of the text, however, we can make observations about human nature that help us see ourselves and our world in a new light. Several such points can be taught appropriately from this text. First, it is helpful to note a pattern in heavy-handed leadership. One can observe (1) an ego that is wounded, (2) a crisis of personal authority, (3) an attempt to repair the façade, and (4) a reassertion of status at all costs. When any leader (like Ahasuerus) lives this way, people are harmed, because that leader has lost all "sense of proportion."[13] In 2 Samuel 24:17, David illustrates compassionate leadership when he looks out over the destruction of his own people and tells the Lord, "I have sinned; I, the shepherd, have done wrong. These are but sheep. What have they done?" Godly leadership hurts with, for, and because of others. Godly leaders don't hide behind image management.

Second, while life is full of painful ironies, we need the reminder that God is at work behind those painful ironies of life. For example, while many languages were used in the distribution of the king's edict, the actual script was really one of cunning power—the same wit and postal system Esther will use later (cf. 8:9–14). When the flexibility and creativity of systems are used to harm innocent people, God's people may need to interject just as much effort and creativity to counter destructive ideas, forces, and campaigns in society. This also helps us understand the actions of Paul and Silas, who used their legal standing to demand their rights from the city magistrates at Philippi (Acts 16:35–39). Believers must find creative ways to engage the legal system and challenge a post-Christian culture increasingly hostile to the faith community.

Illustrating the Text

Fleshly leaders hide behind image management; godly ones don't.

Popular Culture: Talk about the phenomenon of "handlers" who help famous people manage their public persona in a way that is advantageous, even if not altogether truthful. Explain that politicians, celebrities, news hosts, and so on have people to pick their clothing, write their lines, style their hair, put spin on news releases about their private lives, and even break up with their love interests for them. Focus groups are consulted, opinions are tested, and the whole point is to create a public image that will be most marketable, pleasing, and advantageous. Contrast the way a godly leader ought to care less about excellence in *public* image than conformity to *Christ's* image. There is a brilliant scene from the movie *The Adjustment Bureau* (2011) in which the main character, a politician, gets honest and tells everyone how his handlers determined the right color tie to wear and the proper amount his shoes should be scuffed.[14]

Contrasting Concept: Tell a story about a vehicle you once owned and loved that had great utility and reliability but a horrible exterior. (If you don't have a vehicle story that fits the mold, any ugly-but-dependable object or machine will do.) Explain the positive traits and benefits of the vehicle and show pictures of it if possible. Show how it may not look good on the outside, but its substance and function have been well proven. In contrast, explain that some leaders are like a car that is all polished and repaired on the surface but is rotten and unreliable when it counts—they are really just good-looking lemons. Like Ahasuerus, they are all about image but lack substance.

God helps his people to be shrewd in confronting evil systems.

History: Many have heard of Oskar Schindler, the Nazi party member who saved twelve hundred Jews from certain death in the concentration camps. When he became the owner of an enamelware and munitions factory in Krakow, Poland, in 1939, Schindler mostly saw his Jewish workers as a cheap labor force and the factory as a moneymaking opportunity. As he continued his career, however, he became a champion of their cause and spent his entire fortune on bribes and expenses aimed at protecting his workers. He was very shrewd in dealing with the evil system of the Nazi regime and spent his influence and resources to gain safety for many Jews.

Bible: The story of the Hebrew midwives in Exodus 1 is a great biblical example of shrewd women receiving help and blessing from God in their work to relieve oppression for God's people in exile under an evil system.

A Complex Identity Is Kept Hidden

Big Idea
God creatively opens doors right next to us, against all odds.

Key Themes
- God's way of securing Esther is through a timely plan from the king's personal attendants.
- God brings Esther favor in the eyes of strategic palace officials.
- Esther and Mordecai collaborate for her safety and identity.

Understanding the Text

The Text in Context

Esther 2:1–11 introduces the reader to two Diaspora Jews for the Diaspora audience: Mordecai (v. 5) and Esther (v. 7). They will serve both the Persian king and their Jewish people. In chapter 2, each receives a brief biographical note, then a scene that highlights each personality. Mordecai is portrayed as an ideal Jewish exile, considerate and loyal to the king. While Esther's beauty is known to all, her identity remains hidden. She is obedient to Mordecai but concealed in her notability.

The flowing of wine (chap. 1) is now matched by the flaunting of women (chap. 2). The king's anger links both chapters (1:12; 2:1), as do frenetic servants hatching new plans (1:13–20; 2:2–4). Both ends of the pericope concern the "beautiful young women" brought into the king's harem (2:1–4, 8–11). In the middle, the reader is introduced to the persons and backgrounds of Mordecai and Esther (vv. 5–7).

Historical and Cultural Background

Inscriptional evidence suggests that Ahasuerus (485–465 BC) was the crown prince for twelve years (498–486), holding a coregency with his father, Darius I (a relationship noted on the south doorway of Darius's private palace). Every

Persian king after Darius was busy maintaining the size and prestige of the empire. Several significant Persian wars should be noted:

- Ionian revolts against Persia (499–494 BC)
- Persian battle of Marathon (490 BC)
- Attack against Greece by a Persian fleet accompanied by Phoenicians, Egyptians, and Ionians (480 BC)
- Persians defeated by the Greek fleet at Salamis (September 480 BC)
- Persian defeat at Plataea (479 BC)
- Ongoing revolts in Egypt, prodded by the Greeks (460–454 BC)[1]

Exactly how these Persian wars form the political background of Esther is not clear. It is possible that military generals may have been summoned to the banquet of Ahasuerus (1:1–8).

Interpretive Insights

2:1 *fury had subsided, he remembered Vashti.* Regret or even positive longing replaces fury, one emotion for another (cf. Gen. 40:14). "Subsided" is like the "anger" of God diminishing when he "remembered" Noah after the flood (Gen. 8:1).

what she had done . . . what he had decreed. The time frame can be deduced. Based on the date in 2:16 (i.e., "seventh year of his reign"), we can conclude that Esther comes into the royal harem three years after Vashti's deposing. It is an additional year before her night with Ahasuerus (about December 479 BC). The ill-fated war with Greece occurs between the two queens.

2:2 *king's personal attendants proposed.* The advisers closest to the king are quick to propose a remedy for the distraught monarch, since any further brooding might be taken out on them! The theme of a search for beautiful young girls for a king, drawn from his kingdom, occurs elsewhere in the Old Testament. The selection of Abishag for David in 1 Kings 1:1–4 is another such story that shares similar plot-stages: (1) reason for search, (2) aim of search, (3) woman's obligations, (4) the main task, (5) entering the palace, (6) woman's description, (7) nature of the relationship.

beautiful young virgins. The aim of the proposal is stated up front. This advisor's plan is a pleasant diversion in another Memucan-like speech, but this one is unsolicited.

2:3 *every province . . . all these beautiful young women.* The same phrase for geography and gender was used earlier (1:20); now it operates as preparation for Esther. Age is stipulated as "young women," not girls. The prospect

The Process of Becoming a Royal Woman

In Esther 2, seven key stages can be observed in the process of developing a Persian royal woman.[a]

Stage 1. The Transport: The first stage was to collect "beautiful young women" from all over the kingdom (v. 3). With little or no regard for their will or that of their families, they were taken simply because they were beautiful and of the right age.

Stage 2. The Gathering: The second stage gathered these women in the capital of Susa (v. 3). The women were left under some form of guard.

Stage 3. The Assigning: The third stage assigned the women to the custody of Hegai (v. 3). The place they were kept is called "the house of the women," closely connected to the king's palace (v. 8, author's translation).

Stage 4. The Treatment: The fourth stage was a year of "beauty treatments"

(v. 3). Hegai was in charge of this stage and immediately initiated Esther's one-year treatment (v. 12), placing her "into the best place in the Harem" (v. 9). From this stage on, the process was personalized for each woman.

Stage 5. The Final Sorting: The fifth stage was when each woman, in turn, was summoned by the king (vv. 12–13). From jewels to articles of clothing, each woman could take what she desired. The outcome of this could shape the rest of her life in the palace.

Stage 6. The Crucial Night: The sixth stage was the young woman's special night, to please the king (v. 14a). Because of her age, she was likely a virgin.

Stage 7. The Golden Cage: The final stage was when the woman entered "the second house of women" under the care of the eunuch Shaashgaz (v. 14b), and a new season of life began.

[a] Adapted from Davidovich, *Esther*, 81–83.

of "all . . . young women" replaces the prior concern with "all the wives" (1:20 KJV). Both, however, find the king tagging along.

2:4 *who pleases the king be queen.* This is not the standard way of choosing a queen. Even the ancient historian Herodotus claims that queens were only chosen from among seven noble Persian families.[2] Herodotus seems to record official procedure, which may not reflect Esther's circumstances. It's possible that this beauty contest might only be a fresh search for a new pool of concubines (cf. 1 Kings 1:2–3) from which the new queen will be selected. Like the other women, Esther has to await "her turn" with the king. In the end, she is never said to "marry" Ahasuerus, but she is clearly made the official Persian queen.[3]

2:5 *a Jew . . . named Mordecai . . . Kish.* Beyond mere biology, Mordecai's genealogy emphasizes his station and rank "in the citadel of Susa." The fact that he sits "at the king's gate" (2:19, 21) is a strong argument that he holds a government position. The term "Jew" (*yᵉhudi*, lit. "Judean") is a rare use of a gentilic (ethnic term) rather than a patronymic (term based on a paternal ancestor) to identify a member of the Israelite community. "Jew" will be used for Mordecai numerous times (5:13; 6:10; 8:7; 9:29, 31; 10:3). Mordecai is the Babylonian form of Marduka, a common name at the time (cf. Ezra 2:2; Neh. 7:7). He presumably had a Hebrew name too, like Esther (Hadassah, Esther 2:7), but it is not given. The segmented genealogy ends with Kish, the father of Saul (cf. 1 Sam. 9:1–2).

The reader is now prepared for the connection of Haman with Agag (Esther 3:1; 9:1–10), set against Mordecai and Saul via the tribe of Benjamin. Archenemies are at war, again (cf. 1 Sam. 15).

2:6 *carried into exile . . . by Nebuchadnezzar . . . with Jehoiachin.* Kish was the person carried into exile with Jehoiachin (596 BC). This cannot be Mordecai, as he would be around 120 years old when he becomes prime minister (Esther 10:2). Mordecai's family line is given some detail for several reasons: It connects him to the tribe of Benjamin and Saul's house (cf. 1 Sam. 9:1–2), setting up ensuing conflict. The narrator also connects Babylonian-born Mordecai with "Kish" from Jerusalem, exiled with the king and nobility of Judah (cf. 2 Kings 24:14–16; 2 Chron. 36:9–10; Dan. 1:3). So by ethnic heritage, geography, and noble class, Mordecai is cast as an authentic, even superior, exile.[4]

2:7 *whom he had brought up.* The Hebrew word order of 2:7 is significant. It begins with "He was caring for," emphasizing Mordecai's role as the guardian of Esther. Even though Esther was Mordecai's cousin, she was adopted as his daughter because she was sufficiently younger.

Hadassah . . . Esther. She alone is given two names—the dual identity begins (cf. Gen. 41:45; Dan. 1:6–7). Hadassah ("myrtle") is her Hebrew name, used by the narrator. The book, however, exclusively uses the Persian Esther ("star"; 55x),[5] which the Diaspora readers could relate to.

a lovely figure and was beautiful. Following a dual-statement pattern in Esther, different terms are used to describe Esther's beauty. It seems that the former (*yepat to'ar*) presents her as objectively beautiful, while the latter term (*tobat mar'ah*) emphasizes the view of the observer. This technique is used elsewhere (cf. Gen. 29:17 [Rachel], 39:6 [Joseph]). In all such cases, the narrator and an additional character draw the same conclusion, whether the observed person is male or female—to a socially accepted or sexually exploited end.

2:9 *she won his favor.* This shows that God is at work, using strategic relationships. As with Joseph (Gen. 39:4) and Daniel (Dan. 1:9), a Hebrew exile finds favor with a court official. Jewish readers would see the presence of their covenant God.

2:10 *not revealed her nationality and family background.* Reasons could include the following: (1) to reveal her identity would prejudice her advancement; (2) the collective safety of the Jews might suffer if people knew of Esther and Mordecai's familial connection. Eating Persian food would keep

Esther hidden. Yet Mordecai's own Jewish heritage was already known (cf. 2:5; 3:4).

Theological Insights

A key theological insight comes from the *divine passives* in this text. Divine passives occur when the agent of the activity is not explicitly stated, yet God's providential hand is implied. This language occurs, for example, in phrases where the "young women were brought" (v. 8), Esther "was taken," and Esther was "entrusted to Hegai" (v. 8). The Hebrew language of "taking" (*laqah*) does not support the idea that Esther was brutalized.[6] Clearly, Esther is not in control of her own life. Edicts and emissaries are exerting their will on her. Such Hebrew phrases "portray an irresistible series of events."[7] As a writing technique, this language allowed an author to refer to God without directly naming him.[8] Even the exiles were "taken captive" (v. 6: cf. 9:1, 22). No one here has a choice. To the Jewish Diaspora, being pawns of mighty nations did not mean their God was helpless. This language links an unlikely queen with her scattered Jewish people. As one author states, "Perhaps there is a hint that providence is most active in those whose lives are shaped by God's own concerns."[9] In difficult circumstances, God pushes his particular person to the front of the line.

Teaching the Text

The *manner* of God in the book of Esther is a "behind the scenes" MO. From the opening to the closing of the story, God works through the *agency* of the characters themselves: in banquets (e.g., 1:3–4; 9:18), king's servants (1:10, 14), Esther's concealment (2:10, 20), female gatherings (2:19; 4:16), Haman's consultations (5:14; 6:13), Mordecai's recognition (6:10–11; 8:15), the king's anger (2:1; 7:10), and even letters commemorating Purim (9:20–28, 29–32). God works in the "nitty-gritty" of Persian court life. Though it is contrary to popular thought, God's apparent silence is not his absence, nor is the apparent "secularity" of the book a strike against its divine message. Actually, withholding religious expressions, rituals, or divine names only heightens the providential aid that the Jewish people receive through Esther herself. Christians must work in the *now* of life's circumstances. The nitty-gritty moments of life are really part of a larger fabric that God is weaving together. It's always easier to camp out in some extremes of, for example, deism or determinism. But God calls us to walk by faith, not seek escapes. We serve the same God that Esther did, and great faith is still required of us, every day.

Illustrating the Text

God shows up in the nitty-gritty moments of life.

Literature: *The Hiding Place*, by Corrie ten Boom. In this autobiographical book, the author tells about how God showed up in many nitty-gritty moments. It doesn't get much rougher than a Nazi concentration camp, but that is exactly the environment in which Corrie and her sister, Betsie, experienced the rescuing love of God, the power of thankfulness, and the refreshment that come through the gospel and forgiveness. Consider sharing an anecdote from the book, like the one in chapter 13 that describes how the sisters were transferred into a barracks crawling with fleas inflicting painful bites. In obedience to 1 Thessalonians 5:18, they agree to thank God for the fleas anyway. They later discover that the fleas actually kept the Nazi guards from entering the dormitory, thus giving them freedom to pray, worship, and hide a Bible.[10] God shows up when things get real and messy—there is no circumstance in which we should stop seeking, thanking, and praising him.

Quotes: Former US president Ronald Reagan once quipped, "Heroes may not be braver than anyone else. They're just braver five minutes longer."[11] Reagan was obviously not thinking about Christian faith per se when he said this; however, the quote fits. Believers may not be braver in the face of suffering and mess than other people—in fact, we are often less so. What sets us apart is the conviction that the suffering and mess are places where we can meet Jesus and experience his rescue. Sometimes, then, we just wait in that place a little longer than others and end up seeing God show up and be the Savior we've longed for.

Some of God's greatest interventions happen below the radar.

Military: Our world has seen a whole new generation of military aircraft that use stealth technology. This technology uses specially angled body panels made of composite materials arranged in shapes engineered to diffuse radar emissions. The net effect of all these nuances of shape and material is that the aircraft becomes virtually invisible to ground radar and can execute its missions without being seen or tracked. In this way, these planes can support ground troops, protect vulnerable assets, and intervene in battle without being noticed. In the same way, God often prefers to intervene off our radar, and he needs no special technology to do it; his ways are simply higher than our ways. In Esther, God's actions are in stealth mode—they are not immediately obvious to human observers, but the miraculous results are proof that he was there.

A New Queen
and a Foiled Plot

Big Idea

While we can only live one event at a time, God is often unfolding the next steps in ways we cannot see.

Key Themes

- Esther's natural qualities elevate her above all other women in the royal harem.
- Mordecai exhibits wisdom, foresight, and loyalty in his relational dealings.
- Esther capitalizes on her proximity to the king, increasingly showing an active role.

Understanding the Text

The Text in Context

Intrigue shapes the last half of chapter 2. A plot against Ahasuerus (2:19–23), communicated by Esther to the king (v. 22), anticipates a later plot against the Jews (3:1–6), also communicated by Esther to the king (7:1–7).

Esther 2:12–23 outlines the process of cosmetic treatment each harem member went through. Royal law required two increments of six-month preparation before their evening with the king (v. 12). The extensive beauty regimen sets up a contrast with Esther. She shows wisdom in how she chooses to appear before the king (v. 15). Additionally, motifs of loyalty/reward and punishment/shame are initiated for future use (vv. 21–23).

Historical and Cultural Background

The phrase describing the punishment of the plotters discovered by Mordecai, traditionally rendered as "hanged on a gallows" (Esther 2:23; cf. 7:9, 10; 9:13, 14), actually refers to impalement (lit. "hung on a tree"). Here, "tree" (Heb. *'ets*) is the wooden pole used for impaling.[1] Some ancient cultures believed this inhumane treatment impeded the body's entry into the next life.

Herodotus records that Darius I impaled three thousand Babylonians when he captured Babylon.[2] Xerxes impales the decapitated head of the Spartan king Leonidas.[3] Notice that Haman's sons were hung *after* they were killed by the sword (9:5–14). The intent of impalement was not death but the shaming of the victim and their would-be supporters through *exhibition* (cf. Gen. 40:19; Deut. 21:22; Josh. 8:29; 10:26; 2 Sam. 4:12). The body of King Saul and those of his sons are hung from the walls of Beth Shan—after the Philistines have already dismembered them (1 Sam. 31:8–12).

Interpretive Insights

2:12 *six months . . . myrrh and six . . . perfumes and cosmetics.* Myrrh is associated with purification, but it is also connected with lovemaking in the Song of Songs (4:6; 5:1; cf. Prov. 7:17). These fine products would soften the skin, lighten its color, and have a profound aromatic effect. The twelve months could have also included training in etiquette. However, some see the full year as the narrator's exaggeration of a "narcissistic and self-indulgent" culture.[4]

2:13 *Anything she wanted.* Not since the young woman was forced to leave her home and family did she have the right to ask for something in particular. What she chose was meant to enhance her appearance and affect her behavior with the king. Ironically, this is just before the king asks something in particular, as well.

2:14 *another part of the harem . . . Shaashgaz.* After one night with the king, the woman would take up residence in a second harem. Women at this stage now lived as concubines under the oversight of Shaashgaz. Even in the king's bedroom, sexuality was run by a bureaucracy of preparation, selection, recording, and deferment.[5] A domestic task force was needed.

pleased with her and summoned her by name. No woman returns unless specifically requested. Each woman "simply was a number, until she received an identity" in her summons.[6]

2:15 *daughter of his uncle Abihail.* This illustrates the formality of a woman's summons to the king—now Esther's father is mentioned for the first time.

she asked for nothing. It's worth noting a similarity: the physically perfect and handsome Daniel (Dan. 1:4) also chose the regimen of simpler vegetables and water over the king's royal food and wine (1:12, 16).

Esther won the favor of everyone. She surpasses all other women. Her undeniable beauty, and the *favor* that has come with it, has been marked out with incremental significance (1) by the narrator (Esther "had a lovely figure and was beautiful" [v. 7]), (2) by Hegai ("She pleased him and won his favor [*hesed*]" [v. 9]), (3) by the entire court ("She won the approval [*hen*] in the sight of everyone who saw her" [v. 15 HCSB]), and (4) by Ahasuerus ("She won his favor and approval [*hen whesed*]" [v. 17]). The use of the word *hesed* in verses 9 and 17 adds the element of active "devotion." So it is significant that the "approval" (*hesed*) of Hegai and "favor" (*hen*) of the court are then doubled by the "favor and approval" (*hen whesed*) of the king himself.

2:16 *in the royal residence.* The narrator's use of the same location as for Vashti's earlier banquet, the "royal palace" (*bet malkut*, 1:9), shows that Esther is now the "queen-apparent." Sure enough, her royal introduction is about to be celebrated (cf. v. 18). Historians place this around December 479 BC.

tenth month, the month of Tebeth. In the Hebrew Bible, months are typically named by their numerical order (e.g., 1 Kings 12:32). Only in the latest Hebrew books do we find both the numerical system and the more recent Mesopotamian names side by side in the same verse (cf. Esther 3:7). From this date, it appears that four years have passed since the initial gathering of the women until Esther herself was summoned to the king. Some scholars infer from this span of time that over fourteen hundred women were summoned to the king's personal chambers.[7]

2:17 *attracted . . . more than any of the other virgins.* Here is a statement of the king's feelings for Esther. The Hebrew term (*'ahaw*) can mean "loved" (ESV, NRSV, HCSB), though other translations seem to struggle with this (NIV). Even the virgins yet to sleep with the king cannot best Esther, in the king's estimate. But in this case, how long and in what manner the king loved Esther are questions not easily answered.

2:18 *king gave a great banquet.* He gives the banquet, essentially, in honor of Esther's coronation, and so it is called "Esther's banquet" (NIV) or "feast" (ESV). More significant banquets will follow (cf. 5:5–8; 7:1; 9:16–18, 22).

a holiday. This is an occasion used by Ahasuerus to garner public support. Some may have received tax relief, debt cancellation, lifting of obligatory military service, land grants or portable gifts.[8] Some of these additional elements are reflected in the Septuagint (Greek version of the Hebrew text), in verses 18 and 20: "The king made a banquet . . . for seven days, and he highly celebrated Esther's marriage; and he made a release to those who were under his dominion. . . . Mordecai had ordered her to fear God and perform his commandments." It's difficult to account for such changes, but changes such as these seem to reflect Jewish theological and moral concerns surrounding Esther's actions, so close to a pagan king.

2:19 *virgins were assembled a second time.* The phrase is difficult. Views include the following: (1) these women were another collection of virgins for the king's choosing;[9] (2) they were late arrivals from lands distant from those where the initial search had been conducted;[10] (3) this assembly was a shifting of all virgins not seen by the king to the second harem;[11] and (4) this assembly was a gathering of the king's unseen virgins to be sent back home.[12] Regardless, the fact that Esther has already been chosen as queen does not preclude other gatherings from occurring. Even Solomon held large numbers of women, accessible to his royal quarters (1 Kings 11:1–5).

Mordecai was sitting at the king's gate. This is a transitional section (vv. 19–20). Mordecai's ongoing role as a court official (v. 21) helps explain how he would have access to the schemes of the king's personal attendants (cf. Dan. 2:49).[13]

2:20 *kept secret her family background.* The syntax of the sentence (subject + participle) emphasizes synchronicity; that is, Esther remained quiet about her family, before and after becoming queen.[14]

2:21 *Bigthana and Teresh . . . conspired to assassinate.* Political conspiracies by threshold guards were not uncommon in Persian court life (cf. Gen. 40:1–3). In fact, Herodotus records that Ahasuerus is later assassinated in his own bedroom (465 BC), in a conspiracy led by his assistant, Artabanus.[15]

2:22 *told Queen Esther . . . reported it to the king.* She is called *Queen Esther* for the first time when she uses her royal status to protect against a royal threat. The king is now apt to listen to Esther, should any other assassination attempt arise (cf. 4:1–17).[16] Mediating this information not only establishes Esther as a credible court liaison; this same path of communication (i.e., Mordecai to Esther to Ahasuerus) will also later drive the plot itself, for the entire Jewish contingent. Herodotus records that the Persians were known for rewarding their benefactors (called *Orosangai*),[17] which highlights the absence of a reward for Mordecai.

2:23 *book of the annals.* The official state records. Introduced now, this book will reappear two more times (6:1; 10:2). All three references to the "book of the annals" involve Mordecai. What is now introduced as incidental will later become crucial.

Theological Insights

God's manner of operation is manifest in strategic relationships, often countering cultural expectation. God incited an attractive and pleasing quality in Esther's relationships, a relational grace.[18] God saw to the "favor" (*hen*) and "approval" (*hesed*) in Esther's relationships (vv. 9, 15, 17; cf. esp. Dan. 1:9). God's agency brought safety, distinction, and social command that Esther, in turn, would use for the benefit of others. The parallels to Joseph's life are many and intriguing, including receiving both *hen* and *hesed* (Gen. 39:21). In Joseph's case, YHWH is stated (Gen. 39:21, 23) as the active and protecting agent. These are circumstances where people could argue for God's disinterest in the lives of his people. Yet God arranged events and attitudes through strategic placement and a "relational grace" interjected into these relationships. The relational parallels to Joseph's life show that God worked this way through other biblical characters. As accounts of two people in hostile foreign courts, these narratives illustrate God's complex work where he's not even mentioned.

Teaching the Text

1. God's providential care is best observed from hindsight. From this text alone we can see how Mordecai was in the right place at the right time to hear the key facts and know the key group wanting to take Ahasuerus's life. This highlights what providence is *not*—it guarantees neither comfort nor fairness—beginning with Esther's food (compare Daniel!) and moral options, and extending to Mordecai, who foils an assassination plot, with no timely reward for it. God's providence is about his kingdom work. This always requires God's people to focus on what is central. God's love is promised; comfort and fairness are not.

2. This text shows concern for the vulnerable and shows opposition to violence. Esther is a Jewish orphan that Mordecai skillfully raises. Ahasuerus is a pagan king who was marked for death by at least two royal guards. Quite possibly, Mordecai the Jew saved the life of a narcissistic pagan king who just slept with his adopted daughter! God does not clean up the social environments he calls people to work in. This requires living amid serious tension.

3. The text distinguishes between *writing law* and *writing history*.[19] Writing is referred to sixty-three times in this book. In Esther, law functions to *disempower* people, based on their gender or race (e.g., 1:19; cf. 3:12–14; 8:9–14). History, on the other hand, is written to preserve certain people (2:23), requiring their elevation in status. The occasions of writing in Esther have *people* as the "backstory." Writing in the book of Esther is an ethical statement, not some mechanical exercise. This also includes records of courageous actions (2:23; 6:1; 10:2). But too often in the book of Esther, when official words are written, people are marked for death. In a world where blogs run like water, it is important to remember that writing can be used in dehumanizing ways. As the book illustrates, one must always know *who* is doing the writing. Writing still develops hearts and minds, but it can also be used to destroy lives. The book of Esther illustrates this well.

Illustrating the Text

Providence is best seen in the rearview mirror.

Visual Aid: Bring a car's convex, passenger-side mirror or show a picture of one. It likely says something like OBJECTS IN THE REARVIEW MIRROR ARE CLOSER THAN THEY APPEAR. This message is meant to help correct the driver's distorted view caused by the convex mirror. The curvature of the mirror is meant to give a wider view and add peripheral perspective to the picture the driver sees. The downside is that the image in the mirror ends up looking smaller and more distant than it is in reality; hence the printed warning. God's providence is often like this; when we view our stories in hindsight, we can see a much broader perspective on events and can often see God at work more clearly. However, it is easy to think of his saving acts as located only in the past. We need the same warning: The same God who showed up in one's past is also near at hand in one's present. He is far closer to us than we are able to feel in the moment.

God calls his people to be clean in the midst of messy places.

Science: Consider showing your listeners a video clip demonstrating nano-technology sprays that claim to create a water- and dirt-repellent barrier on garments. (Just do a search on the web for "hydrophobic spray," "nanotechnology spray," or "dirt repellent spray.") These videos show all kinds of dirt, sauces, and contaminants rolling right off of white garments. The technology claims to be able to make cloth materials repel water and dirt. Explain that God calls believers to function similarly, seeking to be present for others in the midst of their messes but allowing the power of God and the shed blood of Jesus to purify us and keep us pure amid the mess.

Written words can kill; God's Word gives life!

TV: Consider showing a clip of a courtroom scene (or just describe it) in which a judge reads a jury's verdict in a life-and-death trial. Point out that those words written on that tiny slip of paper have the power to kill, imprison, exonerate, or free the accused. In the same way, our name written in the Book of Life has more life-giving power than anything else that might be declared about us.

Popular Saying: Many will be familiar with the saying "The pen is mightier than the sword." This is a truism that points to the power of written words to dish out death, blessing, curse, and life. Written words start wars, heal hearts, release captives, and topple governments. This is also true of spoken words, as James recognizes: "What a great forest is set on fire by a small spark" (James 3:5b). Words have power both for blessing and cursing (3:10). We must take care with our words, spoken and written, when in positions of authority, since we will surely be "judged more strictly" (3:1).

Haman's Decision to Annihilate

Big Idea

Real honor is rooted in the fixed standards of God's character rather than the political whims of a power struggle.

Key Themes

- Power used for others furthers God's work, but when used for self, power destroys people.
- The rivalry between Haman and Mordecai continues the Agagite connection between the Amalekite king and King Saul.
- Unchecked anger becomes irrational rage, threatening to destabilize community.

Understanding the Text

The Text in Context

The main action breaks open in Esther 3. Here, a crisis is unleashed that will not be resolved until the last of the Jews' enemies are destroyed in 9:16. Haman mirrors the ego, anger (3:5; cf. 1:12), and exaggeration of King Ahasuerus (3:6; cf. 1:10–11). Like Vashti earlier, Mordecai does not comply with a command (3:2; cf. 1:12). "Retaliation escalates to dramatic proportions" as a personal affront becomes a national edict carried by Persia's best riders.[1]

Esther 3:1–6 brings to the surface an ancient ethnic rivalry (vv. 4, 6). This pericope also introduces a sharp tension, since the *unanticipated* recognition of Haman (3:1) follows the *unrewarded* loyalty of Mordecai (2:22–23). The promotion of Haman is highlighted by three phrases in the first verse: "honored Haman," "elevating him," and "giving him a seat." Because Mordecai has yet to be honored, the reader is led to ask whether honor has been denied Mordecai or whether, instead, Haman has successfully deceived Ahasuerus for it. Haman's motives are deceitful, when Mordecai has not been rewarded for his honor to the king.

Interpretive Insights

3:1 *After these events.* This refers to sometime between the seventh (cf. 2:16) and twelfth years (3:7) of Ahasuerus's reign. More precisely, it has been four years since Esther's selection (3:7; cf. 2:16–17).

honored. Haman was given some kind of promotion or treated with distinction. Related terms for "honor" or "advance" occur five times in this pericope.

Haman son of Hammedatha, the Agagite. Haman is introduced through a genealogy. Like Mordecai, who is identified as "a Jew of the tribe of Benjamin" (2:5), Haman is known as "the Agagite," and the epithet is eerily repeated throughout the book (3:1, 10; 8:3, 5; 9:24).[2] While some view Agag as a Persian province, better support can be found in the intertextual links connecting Haman with the Amalekite king Agag (1 Sam. 15:8). "Behind this curious story lies the concluding law in the Central Core of the book of Deuteronomy—to remember to hate the Amalekites (Deut. 25:17–19). The Amalekites are presented in the Torah as the paradigm of the enemy of the Jews."[3] The pericope builds toward a provocative ethnic note (cf. "Mordecai's people," v. 6 [2x]), just as Mordecai's Jewishness introduced him (2:4). To point out the fact that the Amalekites may have been killed in Hezekiah's time (1 Chron. 4:42–43) is to miss the biblical author's *archetypal* use of "Agagite" as a term for Israel's lasting enemy (Exod. 17:8–16; cf. Jude 11). Haman is at least an Agag-ish sort of person. Further, Mordecai's connection to the Benjamite king, Saul—commanded to kill the Amalekite king (1 Sam. 15:1–3)—supports the narrator's use of Haman as a *type* of Israel's enduring enemy. A modern-day example of this connection can be seen in a 1994 article in the *New York Times*, which reported an incidence of violence in Israel with the following words: "A core of militant Jews has preached a doctrine of intolerance, often with the Arab as the biblical enemy Amalek."[4] No genetic connection is needed. Hatred has fixated on one person and become its own reason: "as long as I see that Jew Mordecai" (5:13).

3:2 *All the royal officials . . . But Mordecai.* We already know Mordecai "[sits] at the king's gate" (2:19, 21). What becomes quite apparent now is that the state nobility regularly pass through this crowded area. For this reason, Haman does not even notice that one person is not acting like all the others. From Joseph to Moses, other Jewish administrators have served in foreign courts, even amid some hostility. So it is significant that both Ezra and Nehemiah were similarly in high-profile positions in Susa when they began their own stories. We can take this a step further. It was about a generation after the attempted ethnic purge in Esther that Ezra and Nehemiah headed *back* to work on Jerusalem. Perhaps the ministry of Mordecai and Esther sparked a wave of pro-Jewish activity. Perhaps the bold stand of Esther established a benchmark of written documents and Jewish purity for the equally bold ministries of both Ezra and Nehemiah. Judea may have been the outgrowth of the crisis in Susa.

knelt down and paid honor. The historian Herodotus reports that such bowing was standard protocol in the Persian court.[5] The Bible contains many examples of Israelites bowing[6] to kings, Gentiles, and countrymen: Abraham before the Hittites (Gen. 23:7), Jacob's sons before Joseph (Gen. 43:28), Moses before Jethro the Midianite (Exod. 18:7), David before Saul (1 Sam. 24:8), and Nathan before David (1 Kings 1:23).

But Mordecai would not kneel down or pay him honor. No clear reason is given, and, unlike Haman's emotion and motivations, Mordecai's remain hidden. The views of the reason for his refusal include the following: (1) Haman claimed divinity;[7] (2) Mordecai would "lose face" to a rival;[8] (3) a Jew was refusing on ethnic grounds;[9] and (4) a Jew objected on the basis of his monotheism.[10] Esther 3:2 is the earliest such refusal to bow (reflected in the Greek Addition C, part of the expanded version of Esther that appeared in the Septuagint: "I will not bow down to anyone but you, who are my Lord," 13:12–14), but ethnic and religious lines were drawn far harder during the Hellenistic Period.

Extrabiblical sources try to provide *religious* reasons, and this does have some support in the Hebrew terms used. "Kneel down" (*kara'*) and "pay honor" (*hawa*) are not the standard terms for bowing and homage (see examples above). When these two verbs are used together in biblical texts, they always describe an individual doing homage in the presence of God (Ps. 22:29; 2 Chron. 7:3; 29:29). If Mordecai's motivation appears to be ancestral (cf. 3:6; 6:10, 13; 8:7; 9:3), given the Amalekite connection, then both religious and ancestral elements may be at work here. But even earlier than Saul (1 Samuel 15), Moses had declared: "The LORD will be at war against the Amalekites from generation to generation" (Exod. 17:16). The Lord's edict trumps any other king's (Exod. 17:14). More crucial to the story of Esther than the motivation for Mordecai's refusal, however, are the results of Mordecai's refusal.

3:4 *they told Haman.* While the reader knows the "Jew Mordecai" is the focus, the "royal officials" themselves don't understand, and so they question Mordecai.

for he had told them he was a Jew. This is a rare example of indirect speech (cf. Gen. 29:12; Isa. 8:4). It is also possible to translate this clause "for it was reported to them that he was a Jew." That is, the verb ("tell, report," *higgid*) could be impersonal ("it was reported").[11] Since Mordecai had advised Esther not to reveal her ethnic identity, his own identity may not have come from his mouth. This view would create consistency with Mordecai's instructions for Esther (2:10). Regardless, the syntax emphasizes the reason: his Jewishness (see "Mordecai's people, the Jews," v. 6).

Day after day . . . but he refused. The thematic and linguistic parallels between the book of Esther and the Joseph story are many. This phraseology forms one of these connections (cf. Gen. 39:10).

3:5 *When Haman saw . . . he was enraged.* Haman did not even notice Mordecai's protest until the officials pointed it out. Were they agitating for a conflict? Haman's anger recalls the king's (1:12). For the book of Esther, the rivalry between Mordecai and Haman is a clashing of national heads in ancient hostility.[12] More than historical characters, the book presents them as a clash of forces, in literary development that spans the entire book.

3:6 *he scorned the idea of killing only Mordecai.* Haman's scorn *(bzh)* recalls the feared despising of the women (cf. 1:17): the two are different groups, but they are thematically connected. Here, the narrator directly discloses Haman's inner motivation and state of mind (cf. Gen. 34:13; Exod. 3:6). Haman's motivation drips with "perverse logic."[13]

destroy all Mordecai's people, the Jews. This would at least leave a legacy of fear in the empire, even if Haman can't achieve the honor he wants. Notice how "Jew" is now directly connected with "Mordecai's people" (cf. 3:4, 6a) into one large group targeted for death. Why Mordecai commanded Esther to keep quiet about her ethnicity becomes clearer—there seems to have been a strong undercurrent of anti-Semitism alive in the "king's gate" (3:2–3). Being Jewish now jeopardizes Mordecai's security as well as Esther's. Haman will draw on this antipathy toward the Jews. The reader has been thrust into the sadistic passion of Haman's plot, but the author uses a delayed resolution to heighten Haman's dramatic failure in the end.

Theological Insights

Haman's response to Mordecai is wildly overblown—vengeance through genocide! Vengeance is an act of power in retaliation. The classic Old Testament teaching is "eye for eye" (Exod. 21:24). Significantly, this dictum establishes a moral symmetry between offense and punishment. But this principle requires *proportionality*, limiting the punishment to the nature of the crime. Yet Mordecai's crime—if there is one—finds no match in Haman's planned genocide. Theologically, vengeance belongs to God, not people (Deut. 32:35; Rom. 12:19). Lamenting to God in speech is proper, but even these psalms never *scheme* vengeance. Instead, people of faith commit their grievances to God, as the "responsible Governor."[14] Fortunately, this God prefers mercy (Pss. 103:10; 130:3–4).

Honor is central to the biblical world: a claim to worth that is acknowledged publicly. Theologically, it is the righteous person's relationship to God and his aid that gives one honor (Isa. 43:1–7). But when leaders are unrighteous, the believer can respect the position of authority without participating in any evil program. Of course, there may be consequences for "disobeying" leaders—as

Mordecai learns from the scorn of Haman—but God's standards in Scripture supersede any human dignitary. In God's time, he rescues (Psalm 54), and he also punishes one's enemies (Pss. 35:4; 70:2; 71:13; 83:16–17).

Teaching the Text

There is a serious need to face the toxic effects of ethnic hatred in our world. How much killing is planned but not carried out? Regardless, whether it's between the Croats and Serbs, Tutsis and Hutus, Arabs and Kurds, or Palestinians and Israelis, killing vandalizes the *shalom* of nations.[15] The causes may be many and complex, but believers should hunger for peace more than vengeance (Matt. 5:9). In our world where terrorism is now "franchised," we must start teaching people how to die. The depth and determination of violence on a global scale are a reality that has changed all our lives, and there are certainly no guarantees that we won't be touched by it.

It is God's unique character that sets the standards for all human interaction, including social customs. Because the book of Esther doesn't talk explicitly about God, there's a sense of ethical "free for all" in the book. If only Mordecai had given a recorded response to the question in verse 3. Whether we appeal to ethnic custom or life's tough situations, it's necessary to be reminded of God's character. He's a living God, who gives revelation to people, is not part of nature, is always present, is compassionate, and has determined that the world should work according to his law (Exod. 34:6–7). If God were not unique, life's tough situations would be utterly impossible, with no moral compass for guidance (Jer. 10:1–16). Genuine honor is not static but relationally dynamic. Such honor tries to build others up and is dismayed when the cause of right suffers. This honor is ethically engaged; it learns and grows in its concern for "neighbor."

Illustrating the Text

Nursing bitterness leads to irrational thinking and acts.

Human Experience: Many of your listeners will be familiar with the issue of road rage. This is the phenomenon in which people become irrationally and bitterly angry over the habits of other drivers and enter into a sort of combat mode on the road. Their rage can seethe to the point where they swear, ram other cars, discharge firearms, get out of the vehicle and fight, and so on. Such behavior could lead to death and clearly illustrates how bottling up bitterness can lead to a harvest of deadly wrath. Be willing to confess if you need to—your congregants will likely know if you are describing some of your own temptations on this one.

Literature: *The Count of Monte Cristo*, by Alexandre Dumas. In Dumas's classic work,[16] the main character is wronged as a young man and imprisoned for crimes he did not commit. For years in prison, he nurses bitterness and plans for revenge. The whole of the book is devoted to his protracted and elaborate schemes for revenge. Toward the end, he finally admits that there is nothing left in him but anger. The destructive power of hatred is the same for us. While it may give us drive to escape from earthly prisons, it leaves us forever bound in bitterness, shackled with hatred and emptiness of heart.

God is our definition of right; if we ignore him, we get it wrong.

Visual Aid: Bring a plumb bob (also known as a plummet weight) along for your message. If you don't know what it is, ask any construction worker or hardware store clerk. The plumb bob is an ancient and simple tool; the Egyptians used them when building the pyramids. It is simply a weight on the end of a string—when the weight is dangled, the pull of gravity always draws the string to a perfect vertical line, thus establishing the proper plane for walls and other upright structures. If a wall is plumb, gravity works to hold it firmly together; if not, gravity works to topple it over time. Tell your listeners that the plumb line is mentioned in scripture several times as an image of God's right to measure and evaluate our works. It is a representation that he is the standard and all other things are measured against him and his laws. God is our plumb line—if actions and teachings don't line up with him, they will topple.

An Evil Scheme Is Set in Motion

Big Idea

Wicked people will manipulate one another, rewrite the facts, and then ignore the fallout on innocent people.

Key Themes

- Haman's proposal to the king is filled with distortion and deception.
- The edict of death lands on the month of Nisan, the month God delivered Israel from Egypt.
- The evil plan of Haman, stamped by the king, left the people of Susa baffled.

Understanding the Text

The Text in Context

Personal conflict between Haman and Mordecai escalates into plans for genocide. Now promoted, Haman has a new platform for talking with the king ("king" is used 12x in this pericope). Haman speaks as the defender of the empire. Haman's fabrication about "a certain people" (v. 8) really masks his hatred of one man, Mordecai (v. 5). The king gives Haman his "signet ring" (v. 10), thus in a sense "stamping" Haman's plan. Ambiguous accusations result in the giving of unlimited authority (v. 12).

Esther 3:7–15 gives us the first words from Haman, and they're pure evil (vv. 8–9). For his part, Ahasuerus proves an utter buffoon: no investigation before an entire people group in his kingdom is wiped out! The rest of the book is the process of seeking justice against an edict of death (v. 13). But Haman has tapped into cosmic forces that will actually destroy him and deliver the Jews.[1]

Historical and Cultural Background

"Pur" is a Persian loanword from Akkadian (*pūru*).[2] For this reason, the narrator explains it as "lot" each time (3:7; 9:24). The pluralized form, *purim*,

is a Hebraized word and points to a non-Jewish origin for the Festival of Purim (cf. Esther 9:24, 26, 28, 31).[3] The earliest references to Purim come from 2 Maccabees, where it is called "Mordecai's day" (2 Macc. 15:36).[4] Josephus claims that Purim was held on the 14th and 15th of Adar to commemorate the Jews' revenge on their Persian enemies.[5] A similar Hebrew practice of casting lots is found elsewhere to decide between options (cf. Josh. 18:6; Neh. 10:34; John 19:24; Acts 1:23–26). Use of the Urim and Thummim also had a similar function (cf. Lev. 16:8–10; Neh. 10:34) but never to find a "lucky day" or pursue mass killing.[6]

Ancient historians Herodotus and Xenophon both write of Persians using "lots."[7] Haman's use of *pur* also illustrates how deception was a means valued in the ancient world.[8] Casting *pur* "was not a game of chance but rather a method of pagan divination."[9] Just how *pur* was used is not clear, but clay "dice," with months or dates printed on them, may have been shaken in a bag and then tossed out.[10] The New Testament makes no reference to the Festival of Purim, though some wonder if the reference to an unnamed feast in John 5:1 is a reference to Purim. However, the Mosaic festivals of Passover, Pentecost, and Tabernacles are more likely candidates.

Interpretive Insights

3:7 *the month of Nisan.* The narrator switches from Persian calendar names (e.g., "Tebeth," 2:16) to Hebrew lunar names (e.g., "Nisan," "Adar," 3:7), a significant "heads up" for a Jewish audience. Switching to Hebrew calendar names communicates urgency, since the referenced time overlaps with the celebration of the Jewish Passover (during Nisan), when God delivered Israel from an Egyptian tyrant.

the pur *(that is, the lot) was cast.* The verse says literally "they cast pur," referring to the diviners or astrologers working with Haman.[11]

3:8 *a certain people.* Really, just one person! Here begins Haman's rationalization of personal hatred become political theory—with similarities to Memukan's earlier speech (cf. 1:16–20). The extrapolation is grotesque: as one wife involves all wives, now one Jew involves a nation. This literary technique highlights the ethical travesty in the book.

dispersed among the peoples . . . separate. Logistically, a scattered and separate people are hardly a threat, though being dispersed does make them vulnerable.

customs are different . . . not obey the king's laws. While they were culturally segregated, they were not legally indifferent—a Jew just saved the king's life (cf. 2:21–23). Haman invented the latter charge, illustrating how deception "is a strategy for establishing and protecting honor, as well as for bringing shame upon one's enemies."[12]

Shame

Mordecai's actions stem from his sense of being denied due honor. Shame and its opposite, honor, are foundational social values in the ancient Mediterranean world. Shame was a group value. Unlike people in most Western cultures today, who define shame as a psychological state, ancient people lived in "shame-based" relationships with one another. It was a matter of one's public reputation. Gaining status and esteem brings honor for the community; losing such status brings shame to the community.

This dynamic had negative and positive aspects. Negatively, when a person or group did something inappropriate, shame changed the status of that person or group. "Exposing" the dead, for example, was profoundly shameful. Positively, shame shaped a person's awareness of their obligations to the social dynamics that surrounded them.

When a psalmist cried out to God for deliverance from oppression, it was not for mere relief. Instead, God was often asked to minimize the shame and preserve the supplicant's honor: "O my God, in you I trust; let me not be put to shame; let not my enemies exult over me" (Ps. 25:2 ESV). Significantly, the honor of the supplicant and the entire Israelite nation was tied to God's honor: "Listen closely, Lord, and hear; open your eyes, Lord, and see; hear all the words . . . sent to mock the living God. . . . Now, Lord our God, save us . . . so that all the kingdoms of the earth may know that you, Lord, are God—you alone" (Isa. 37:17, 20 CSB). To the ancients, one's actions reflect on their deity.

Shame is not synonymous with the modern notion of internal guilt. Shame is external and reflects the pressure of "social norms." To contemporary sensibilities, shame can violate one's sense of self-determinism (e.g., "I don't care what anyone thinks!"). The ancients, however, tried to live shamelessly or sought vindication within the larger social order ("May the arrogant be put to shame for wronging me without cause," Ps. 119:78a).

not in the king's best interest to tolerate them. The Hebrew translated "to tolerate them" means literally "to cause them to rest." Yet Purim would bring precisely that: "rest" to the Jews (cf. 9:17–18; "relief," v. 22). Haman's tirade transitions to extermination. Where are the king's questions, addressing the people, location, examples of guilt, and so on?

3:9 *I will give ten thousand talents of silver.* Haman adds a bribe, a serious temptation for Ahasuerus, whose treasury was depleted in the war with Greece. This was about 340 metric tons.[13] Herodotus lists the entire annual Persian income at 14,560 talents. Thus Haman's offer was over half that;[14] likely it came from the seizure of Jewish property.[15] Among many errors made by the king is the lack of any investigation into Haman's claims that this "certain people" should not be tolerated (3:8). It is not because the king is wise that he critiques Haman's plot of extermination but, quite simply, because the king objects to Haman's bribe. Esther will lament that her people *have been sold* (7:4; cf. Gen. 45:4).

3:10 *signet ring . . . to Haman . . . the enemy of the Jews.* Giving the signet ring to Haman turned over political control to Haman, who was playing the king already. Now Haman also has the ancient means of notarizing, with the king's own signet ring. All that remains is to seal the "decree" (v. 9; cf. 8:8, 10). To Haman's genealogy, the narrator now adds a new descriptor: "the enemy of the Jews"! It will reappear as the fatal day draws near (cf. 7:6; 8:1; 9:10, 24).

3:12 *on the thirteenth day of the first month.* On the eve of the Jewish Passover (14th of Nisan; cf. Exod. 12:6), Haman releases the edict of death. Haman's edict is virtually the same decree that had mandated the destruction of Amalek (cf. 1 Sam. 15:3). Though they are "scattered" (3:8), this news will paralyze the gathered Jewish families. It will take the edict of Esther and Mordecai (8:9) to adequately counter the edict of Haman and the king (3:12)—text toppling text, edict dismantling edict.

written in the name of King Xerxes . . . sealed with his own ring. The decree is sent to all levels of government ("satraps," "governors," "nobles," v. 12) and citizenry, prescribing legal genocide. Some of the languages of these people would include Elamite (Persians), Babylonian cuneiform, Sanskrit (India), Aramaic (Arameans of Syria), Egyptian, Greek, Phoenician, Kassite, Vanic, and Dravidian.[16] It is the perfect ruse, since Haman is the mastermind, hiding behind the "name" and "ring" of the king.

3:13 *destroy, kill and annihilate.* The stacking of verbs is a stylistic feature of Persian legal documents,[17] and communicates thoroughness (cf. 9:5). That said, Haman had only mentioned "destroy" in his proposal to the king. But "destroy" (*shᵉmid*) enacts Haman's earlier desire to "destroy [*shᵉmid*] all Mordecai's people" (3:6).

thirteenth day of the twelfth month. The attack occurs eleven months after the edict was issued.

plunder their goods. Permission to plunder functions to bribe the death squads, garnering aid from the citizenry (v. 14b; cf. 9:10, 15–16). Haman would be sure to collect his quota for the king's treasuries. How fitting that plundering also fuels Haman's edict of death, since the Amalekites had also plundered Israel (cf. 1 Sam. 14:48).

3:15 *king and Haman sat down to drink . . . Susa was bewildered.* Using the banquet motif, the narrator sets up a stunning contrast between the authors and objects, powerful leadership and dumbfounded populace. When the king and the con artist drink together again, it will dissolve everything celebrated here (cf. 7:1–2).

Theological Insights

YHWH is Israel's deliverer. Just as he rescued his people from their suffering in the Exodus (cf. Exod. 15), so Israel's divine aid is close at hand, again! A profound theological irony is raised by the date "selected" for Haman's edict of death (3:12). By informing the Persian Empire on the 13th of Nisan—the eve of the Jewish Passover (14th of Nisan, Lev. 23:5)—Haman invokes an ancient clash of nations and deities. The Passover commemorated Israel's rescue from death in Egypt. Haman is pharaoh-like. While Haman appeals to his gods for victory,[18] YHWH is still capable of delivering his people from the death angel and the edict of death. For good reason, Israel's theological tradition celebrates: "You make my lot [goral] secure," for "the lot [goral] is cast into the lap, but its every decision is from the LORD" (Ps. 16:5b; Prov. 16:33). YHWH has delivered Israel from a tyrannical empire before; now they have a Passover and eleven months to reflect on his caring commitment that can deliver them once again.

Teaching the Text

It's hard to find a text that summarizes the "wicked person" better than Haman in Esther 3:7–15. If the "righteous person" enhances and sustains community order and well-being (cf. Pss. 12, 24, 37, 112), Haman shows how the wicked are fueled by greed and selfishness, and how they eventually destroy innocent and needy people. "Like cages full of birds, their houses are full of deceit; they have become rich and powerful. . . . Their evil deeds have no limit" (Jer. 5:27–28). It's also important to see how wicked people flaunt a disregard for the rule and reputation of God. Haman illustrates precisely this: a predatory attitude toward others follows a disregard for the one true God (cf. Deut. 10:17–18). Being "salt and light" is not just hard; it is viewed as offensive by people who lie to get ahead, tear others down by slander, scheme to advance their agenda, and steal from those who have less than they do. They have forgotten the orphans among them. In a fallen world, these are *natural* people—Christians are called to be unnatural.

Illustrating the Text

Wicked people destroy the weak and needy.

Film: In the film *There Will Be Blood* (2007), writer/director Paul Thomas Anderson gives a cinematic interpretation of Upton Sinclair's novel by the same title. The main character, Daniel Plainview, is a modern example of a Haman-like character. He is willing to do whatever it takes to build his oil empire, including destroying the lives of others who are weaker and less shrewd. Point out to your listeners how the world sadly provides us with many contemporary examples of Hamans. Invite them to think about their own experience and look for examples of the way wickedness in themselves and others always preys on the weak and needy.

Wickedness goes hand in hand with disbelief and disregard for God.

Christian Book: *The Making of an Atheist: How Immorality Leads to Unbelief,* by James Spiegel. Spiegel provides some surprising insights about unbelief. Through research and investigation, the book reveals that there is a deep connection between immorality and unbelief—but not as one might expect. Rather than atheism granting permissiveness that leads to immorality, it turns out that choices toward immorality eventually breed and reinforce an increasing disbelief in God. [19] In this chicken-versus-the egg scenario, our wickedness (behavior) degrades our theology (belief), rather than weak theology eroding our morality. Regardless of how the cycle unfolds, one thing is certain: wickedness goes hand in hand with disbelief.

Testimony: This would be a great opportunity for a strong "before and after" testimony from someone who has lived wickedly apart from belief in Christ and then was changed by a relationship to him.

Sadly, wickedness is our "normal"; believers are called to be abnormal.

Apologetics: Many people tend to fall into the trap of assuming humans are all destined for heaven as a default destination unless they choose wickedness and sin somewhere along the way and begin to lose their God-given potential. Remind your listeners of several Bible passages that point out our depravity (e.g., Rom. 3:23 and 6:23) and ask them whether the Bible then teaches that our default destination is heaven, or in fact, hell? If our default destination is hell and our wages are death, then the question is not How could a loving and compassionate God send anyone to hell? but rather How could a just and fair God invite anyone to heaven? Ask your listeners to admit (out loud, preferably) that they are sinful by nature and prone to hate both God and neighbor. Consider extending a gospel invitation based on the reality that sin is our "normal" apart from Christ and that we need to repent if we are to embrace eternal life and become blessedly "abnormal."

Mourning, Fasting, and Risking

Big Idea

Until a person declares solidarity with vulnerable people, excuses will always be found to avoid the risk.

Key Themes

- The Jews' rituals of mourning and fasting symbolize their dire situation to God and serve as a public statement for others.
- Esther's intervention for her people was practically impossible, staged from an isolated position, and could cost the queen her life.
- The faithful work of the Jews is also where God can be seen to be working faithfully—behind the scenes.

Understanding the Text

The Text in Context

Esther 4:1–17 begins with Mordecai in desperate mourning (4:1) and ends with Esther in distressed fasting (4:16). In between, the text slows down to unravel the *drama of ignorance* between the only people who can help, Esther and Mordecai. The story highlights the precarious place the Jewish people are now in. Esther is the key person who needs to act for the Jews; unfortunately, she knows nothing, while Mordecai, who lives outside the palace, knows everything but can't do much. One inside, the other outside, both Esther and Mordecai must overcome a communication barrier.[1] By the close of the chapter, it is Mordecai who is carrying out "Esther's instructions" (4:17).

Four rounds of messages structure the chapter (see table 2). Mounting desperation is evident in the *kinds of speech* that are used. Parallel actions are italicized as the speech intensifies to a veritable threat from Mordecai (4:12–14).

Royal documents are piling up, creating life-and-death tensions. In chapter 2, Mordecai intervened and saved Ahasuerus's life, and it was officially recorded (2:23). In chapter 3, Haman bamboozled the king and wrote an edict of death against all Jews, and it was published throughout the empire (3:15). Although

Table 2. Mounting Desperation in Dialogue

Setup	"Attendants *came* and *told* her [Esther]" (v. 4a) "She *sent* clothes" (v. 4b)	[Reported Speech]
Round 1 (4:6–9)	"Esther . . . *ordered/commanded* him [the eunuch Hathak]" (v. 5) "Mordecai *told* him [Hathak]" (v. 7); "to *instruct/command* her [Esther]" (v. 8) "Hathak *went back* and *reported* to Esther" (v. 9)	
Round 2 (4:10–12)	"[Esther] *instructed/commanded* him [Hathak]" (v. 10) to convey her message of explanation about her legal situation (v. 11) "Esther's words were *reported* to Mordecai" (v. 12)	
Round 3 (4:13–14)	"[Mordecai] *sent back* this answer, 'Do not think . . .'" (v. 13), his message about their desperate moral situation (vv. 13b–14)	[Direct Speech]
Round 4 (4:15–17)	"Then Esther *sent* this reply to Mordecai" (v. 15)—that is, her command, "Go, gather . . . fast for me. . . . Do not eat or drink" (v. 16) "Mordecai went away and carried out all of Esther's *instructions/commands*" (v. 17)	

Mordecai is an object in both official records, only Esther's intervention can now bring truth into this chaos. Significantly, although Esther has not previously identified with her people, now she does. It is now Esther who issues commands to Mordecai (4:16–17; cf. vv. 5, 10). Throughout the rest of the book, Esther will now act as an agent of Jewish deliverance.

Interpretive Insights

4:1 *tore his clothes . . . sackcloth and ashes . . . wailing loudly.* These are standard biblical rituals to mark catastrophe and grief. Such weeping and wailing are always a social form of communication, not a private experience (cf. Gen. 37:34; 2 Sam. 1:11; Jon. 3:6; Neh. 9:1; Dan. 9:3; Zech. 7:3). The Persians did much the same when the Greeks defeated them.[2] Mordecai understands the gravity of the situation: the end will be catastrophic if something is not done.

4:2 *king's gate.* Although Mordecai, dressed as a mourner, can advance only as far as the royal precincts to the gate, nonetheless, his wailing and mourning clothes succeed in getting Esther's attention (cf. v. 6b). Mordecai is not attempting to legally overturn the decree.[3]

4:3 *every province . . . mourning among the Jews.* As in Israel before this time, "fasting, weeping and wailing" are here a natural and collective response to tragic news and pending disaster (cf. Exod. 2:23–25; Ezra 9:5–15; Dan. 9:1–19). Mordecai represents Jewish grief and fasting at the palace where Persian glut and feasting have just occurred (3:15).

sackcloth and ashes. The Jews throughout the empire respond with the same rituals of grief that Mordecai did in Susa (cf. v. 1). The high profile given to feasting throughout the book of Esther puts these fasts (4:3, 16) in bold contrast.

4:4 *she sent clothes for him . . . would not accept them.* Mordecai was not looking for relief, access to the inner precincts, or even face-to-face conversation with Esther. Sackcloth was a provocative statement that communicated his moral dilemma, one that Esther underestimates. At this point, Mordecai's knowledge is in contrast with Esther's ignorance. But Hathak, a third eunuch to serve her (cf. 2:8, 14), will shuttle numerous messages between them (cf. vv. 6–17 and table 2 above).

4:7 *Mordecai told him everything . . . happened to him . . . amount of money.* Mordecai has access to information like the bribing money Haman promised Ahasuerus because of his high position in the Persian royal court. The substance of Mordecai's answer addresses both Esther's *what* (v. 5; i.e., not bowing) and *why* (v. 5; i.e., treasury contribution of Haman to destroy the Jews). For the first time, Esther hears Haman's name connected to the "destruction" of her people.

happened to him. The what and why (v. 5b) that Esther demands to know from Mordecai result in his three-part response: (1) the conflict between him and Haman (v. 7a), (2) Haman's donation to the treasury for the "destruction" of the Jews (v. 7b), and (3) a copy of "the edict" itself (v. 8a). This collection of information was not anything that Esther would naturally have had access to. With clarity come both Esther's grief and her resolve.

4:8 *text of the edict . . . explain it to her . . . go into the king's presence . . . her people.* Having the edict explained would give her all the necessary facts to appeal to Ahasuerus. The king does not know it is the Jews who are marked for extermination. Notice, however, that pleading "for her people" now means that Esther must reveal her nationality. This is an instruction that contradicts Mordecai's earlier order that Esther keep her identity a secret (cf. 2:10).

4:11 *the king has but one law . . . death . . . thirty days . . . since I was called.* As Herodotus also notes, law restricts access to the king for his own protection.[4] With slight condescension, Esther implies that "everyone knows this law."[5] Esther has been queen for five years, but her last conjugal visit was thirty days prior. Her initial response seeks the lowest level of vulnerability.[6] While Esther may not fully appreciate what is at stake, Mordecai doesn't fully appreciate how costly this could be for Esther.

4:13 *you . . . king's house . . . escape.* Mordecai does not tie Esther's safety to her position, since not even the royal palace will keep her safe. Mordecai's response to Esther is now quite pointed, practically a threat (i.e., "if you . . . but you . . . you have," v. 14).

4:14 *relief and deliverance for the Jews will arise from another place.* This is the most theologically "loaded" statement in the entire book. The wording "from another place" is "tantalizingly vague."[7] The Hebrew phrase that is translated "from another place" (*mimaqom 'aher*) functions as a circumlocution (i.e., indirect reference) for God.[8] The Hebrew phrase, like the English translation, is prepositional, "*from* another place" (i.e., "from God"). According to Jewish tradition, "the Place" can be used as a cipher for God's name. These are two sides of the same coin: God as the *ultimate cause* and his use of a *secondary agent*. Throughout the book, God remains "hidden," yet never better acknowledged than here. Mordecai is certain that God will intervene—if not through Esther, then through a different agent. Mordecai's logic is this: Esther's life *may be* in peril if she approaches the king uninvited, but her death *is certain* if she does not.[9]

And who knows . . . such a time as this? His question should probably be heard as one of hope, without presumption (cf. Jon. 3:9). Again, a theme and similar terms (e.g., "deliverance") vital to the Joseph story (cf. Gen. 45:5–7).

4:16 *Go, gather together . . . fast for me.* It is Esther's instructions (commands) that drive the plot now, not Mordecai's. Esther is now planning countermeasures (cf. 5:4) and clearly signals her own piety.[10] Esther is seeking to enlist God's aid and blessings as she plans to meet the king. Collective crisis is marked by collective fasting, as verses 1–3 show. Unlike the spontaneous fast of Mordecai and the other Jews in response to news of the edict (vv. 1–3), Esther's fast is a planned, three-day fast, without food or drink, and involves "all the Jews . . . in Susa" (v. 16). The standard fast lasted from morning till night (i.e., "day of fasting") and avoided only certain foods (cf. Judg. 20:26; 2 Sam. 1:12). Therefore, it is stunning to see fasting mentioned alone, especially without prayer and lament to God (cf. Neh. 9:1–3; Ezra 8:23). The phrase translated "fast for" (i.e., benefactively) can also be translated as "fast with" (i.e., as referring to accompaniment and thereby joining Mordecai and "all the Jews who are in Susa" with Esther and her "attendants"). A representative ("in/on my behalf") nuance is emphasized in more recent translations (NJPS, NRSV, CEB). Prayer and lament—evidence of relationship with YHWH—are assumed, but all religious elements are omitted in Esther.[11]

if I perish, I perish. Again, a similar phrase connects Esther to the Joseph story (cf. Gen. 43:14).

Theological Insights

The fasting mentioned in Esther 4:16 approaches an acknowledgment of faith but stops short. Throughout the Old Testament, prayer accompanies the ritual practice of fasting (cf. Jon. 3:5–9). However, a deeper look in the context of Esther reveals divine activity in the God-shaped holes.[12] Esther commands a *severe* or *absolute*[13] fast that even overrides Passover—beginning that very night (14th of Nisan)! Fasting brings symbolic expression to the repentance and humility required by YHWH.[14] The rituals expressed in Esther 4 may have been drawn from Joel 2, the only other use of the phrase translated "fasting, weeping and wailing" (cf. Joel 2:12; Esther 4:3). Mordecai, like Joel, is expressing confidence in God's deliverance, underscored by the same "who knows?" (cf. Joel 2:14; Esther 4:14). A "holy fast" then follows in both texts (Joel 2:15; Esther 4:16), a national act in the face of calamity.[15] Esther's fast is preparation for further action (cf. Ezra 8:21; Dan. 9:3).[16] Clearly, God can deliver the Jews beyond the borders of Zion.

Teaching the Text

1. When believers faithfully work, then one discovers God working *for* his people. Faithful action—as in Esther's preparation—is where God is also found acting.[17]

2. The dire issues in society today require a fuller knowledge of current events. By responding rather than reacting, we as believers can focus the power of the ethic-bearing gospel on these social concerns.[18]

3. Prayer and lament in times of crisis are entirely appropriate. But neither "magic prayers" nor some "secret ritual" can force God's hand. The book of Esther teaches that believers frequently must both trust God and take seriously their own role in advocating for those things they are praying about.[19] This distinguishes between superficial and vulnerable intervention.

4. Commitment to God always works alongside obligation to others. God calls us to join him for the sake of others. Yet "we cannot know in advance what our commitment will cost us."[20] This is difficult for Western culture, which demands predictability or limited liability. So each of us must consider the cost of discipleship (Luke 14:25–33).

5. Genocides and national disasters, by their nature, cause differing responses from people but also call for specific responses from believers: (a) They cause *mourning* from those who are directly affected by the disaster or terror. This is a normal reaction, and we should send our aid. (b) They cause *bewilderment* for those who know about it but feel powerless to help. This is a predictable reaction, and we should inform and encourage those nearby to intervene. (c) They produce only *indifference* in those whose major assets and social standing come through the suffering unscathed. This reaction is unethical and reeks of selfishness, and we should call out the indifferent for their inhuman, if not illegal, behavior. (d) They cause *delight* for those who scheme in order to gain from others' suffering and destruction. This response is evil and despised throughout the world, and we are obligated to "break the chain" of such evil by any means of justice available.

Illustrating the Text

Answered prayers include far more than we can do but almost never less than we are willing to do.

Cultural Institution: Many of your listeners will be familiar with twelve-step programs for recovery from addiction and substance abuse. Explain that the twelve steps are really way points in a process of repentance and healing that starts with helplessness and leads to victory and freedom. It is important to recognize that the first three steps (admitting powerlessness, turning to God's external power for help, and surrendering one's life to God) are essential—admitting how much you need God's help and surrendering to him are always the gateways to healing. However, steps 4 through 12 (look them up if you wish, and share as much detail as you see fit) are all action steps aimed at self-discipline, self-examination, confession, making amends, and helping others. If one started with step 4, one would have no power for transformation; if one stopped at step 3, one would find no healing and restoration. In other words, for the alcoholic, recovery is far more than we can do (so we need to depend utterly on God first, from step 1 to step 3), but almost never less than we are willing to do (so we need to take bold action in God's strength from step 4 to step 12).

Committing to God will cost more than we can know but almost never less than our whole selves.

Human Metaphor: Marriage is a wonderful picture of this concept. When a man and woman promise themselves to one another at the altar, they have no way of knowing exactly what it will take to keep their promises "for better, for worse, for richer, for poorer, in sickness and in health, till death do us part," nor do they have any concept of what specific forms the threats to their relationship will take along the way. What they do know, however, is that they cannot keep those promises without committing their whole selves to the process. One cannot pledge one's right arm, left leg, and both eyebrows to marriage and hold the rest back! Nor can one be married financially but not sexually, as parents but not as friends, or in spirit but not in deed. Marriage will always cost more than we can know, but almost never less than our whole selves. In the same way, the cost of committing to our great Bridegroom, Jesus, will certainly be higher than we can ever estimate, but it will never require less than submission of all we are and have.

Committing to God means committing to others with him.

Literature: In many fairy tales, we find a "wicked stepmother." The cruelty behind the concept is the idea that someone could commit in love to a spouse but then *not* commit in love to that person's beloved children. It is an obvious and conspicuous evil to think of saying to someone, "I love you and want to devote myself to you, but your children have to go—I can't stand the sight of them." In the same way, we sound especially wicked when we say to God, "I love you and want to devote myself to you, but your bride, the church, and your beloved widows, orphans, and lost sheep have to go—I can't stand the sight of them!" How ridiculous! When we commit to God, we commit to others, just as he did. When Christ committed to God's plan, it meant committing himself to us in the process. How can we hope to escape the same principle?

Esther Intervenes
and Haman Still Schemes

Big Idea

People are called to use their own resources, abilities, and opportunities, letting God combine their initiative with his plans.

Key Themes

- Esther draws on her authority as queen to petition Ahasuerus and "trap" Haman.
- God uses Esther's strategic banquets to pull Haman off his guard.
- The wisdom of Esther and the foolishness of Haman are brought into sharp contrast.

Understanding the Text

The Text in Context

In Esther 5:1–14, the queen starts maneuvering circumstances for a dangerous plea to Ahasuerus (5:1–7) and a daring accusation of Haman (5:4; cf. 7:1–6). Three rounds of banquets move the plot and structure of the entire book: beginning (1:1–9; 2:18; 3:15), middle (5:1–8; 7:1–9; 8:17), and end (9:17–19). Esther 5 begins the *middle round* of banquets (5:1–8; 7:1–9; 8:17). The narrator uses banquets to (1) catch key figures off guard, (2) delay vital information, and (3) perform strategic reversals (e.g., Esther for Vashti, Haman for Mordecai, enemies for Jews).[1] Esther's private banquet begins undoing what Haman achieved at the time he and the king "sat down to drink" (3:15). The feasting of chapter 5 is in sharp counterpoint to the fasting of chapter 4, bringing different people, rituals, and kinds of speech into view.

In chapters 5–7, Mordecai is silent, serving as foil for a conceited and blundering Haman (5:11–13). Esther illustrates patient wisdom next to Haman's impulsive foolishness (5:7–8). While chapter 4 simply refers to "Esther," chapter 5 emphasizes "Queen Esther," since her royal position is vital to and vulnerable in the story. Significantly, both the king and his prime minister are now following Esther's instructions (5:5). For the first time, a Jewish person hatches the plan and carries the power.

Interpretive Insights

5:1 *the third day.* This phrase may refer to the completion of Esther's *severe* fast (cf. 4:16). As an idiom, however, this is not confined to strict chronology; it's a foreboding expression of preparation for an important task or ominous event.[2] It is used of the slaughter of Hamor and the Shechemites (Gen. 34:25) and the execution of Pharaoh's baker (Gen. 40:20).

put on her royal robes . . . his royal throne. Esther is not abandoning the fast (i.e., plight) of the Jews, but in order to use her female charm and authority as Persian queen to begin interceding for her people, she must wear royal dress (cf. 4:14). With calculated tact, she keeps her word and goes to the king (4:16)—mourning in a new context. The truth is, just standing uninvited in the inner court means Esther has already violated the law. It is stunning that Esther clothes herself in such beauty during the Jewish Passover. Like Moses, she returns to the court as a deliverer.[3]

5:2 *he saw Queen Esther.* The narrator emphasizes the king's perspective, which could be rendered as "The moment the king saw Queen Esther." This captures the temporal dynamic very well. What the king sees is regal power in operation (also 5:3). Esther, the wise courtier, is immediately received by the king. Though not summoned, Esther came before the king at the risk of her life; Vashti, on the other hand, *had* been summoned, yet refused to appear. Royal authority is needed now; Esther uses it, and she is effective!

he was pleased with her. This means, literally, "[she] gained favor in his eyes" (cf. 2:17). Esther's appointment as queen and her appearing now before the king share key parallels: (1) period of preparation, (2) wearing special clothes, (3) gaining favor.[4] Seeing, favor, and banquets merge in the book (cf. 1:11; 2:9, 15; similarly, 3:5; 5:9, 13).

5:3 *What is your request?* The Hebrew *baqqashtek,* "your request," occurs seven times in Esther and once in Ezra (7:6). The question ("What is your request?") is a stereotyped phrase of royal court ceremony. Instead of hearing the request in Ezra, we have an extended letter of King Artaxerxes that itemizes "everything he asked" (vv. 12–26). This is a good illustration of a Persian-era expression.

half the kingdom. This was a rhetorical custom common to the Persian court and wasn't meant to be taken literally (cf. Mark 6:23). This "formula of generosity" follows the "ritual of acceptance" (i.e., extending "the gold scepter," v. 2).[5] Were this phrase to be taken literally, the king would be divested of his kingdom in only two uses of the phrase!

5:4 *let the king, together with Haman.* Esther shows great poise by not divulging knowledge of the edict or its architect.[6] But the reader expects Esther to plead for "her people" in some fashion. So the invitation to a banquet catches the reader off guard. Even though she is likely famished herself, Esther prepares a banquet for a would-be killer. The king is really Esther's focus, identified by her use of the masculine singular pronouns in her speech. Her use of delayed information may be intended to humanize herself and so accentuate the horror of her doomed people (see "I and my people," 7:4).

5:5 *Bring Haman at once . . . we may do.* Esther has the greatest officials of Persia doing her bidding (cf. 6:10), a reverse of 1:22. This verse ties both locations together (i.e., king's hall, Esther's banquet). This will be the sixth banquet in the book, a lead-up to her primary request, it seems. Inviting Ahasuerus will enable Esther to obligate him. Including Haman places him in her sphere of influence and neutralizes any further antics.

5:6 *what is your petition . . . your request?* As it turns out, Esther's "petition" and "request" (v. 7) is an invitation to a second banquet—her answer only appears to be anticlimactic. Two answers match two questions. She planned both ahead of time. Now that the king has responded to the "word" (*debar*, v. 5) of the queen, Esther pledges to respond to the king's "word" (*debar*, v. 8) with her request. Esther now has a guaranteed response from Ahasuerus.[7] This has piqued the curiosity of the king and stoked the pride of Haman. Esther has used court convention, with wit and wisdom.

5:9 *But when he saw Mordecai at the king's gate.* If Mordecai has returned to his position in the king's gate, then it is likely that he's heard that Esther was favorably received by King Ahasuerus. Since he has returned to his usual station, Mordecai also, it seems, has removed his garb of sackcloth and ashes.

5:11 *Haman boasted.* The narrator describes a drunken Haman (v. 9; cf. 1:10) who feels compelled to recite his status, wealth, and achievements to his friends and wife (5:10).[8] In his mind, Haman has reached the zenith of glory. Haman's language betrays his narcissism. Such reckless self-promotion is the definition of the "fool" of the book of Proverbs (cf. 29:11). Consoling the pouting noble also occurs when Jezebel tries to calm and then redirect Ahab (1 Kings 21:4–10). Only absolute power and control will do. Yet Haman's life and wealth and sons will be lost in just hours (cf. 7:9–8:1; 9:5–10)! Though infatuated with having been "honored" (v. 11), Haman is just as intoxicated with "rage" for Mordecai, who refuses him honor (v. 9).

5:13 *that Jew Mordecai sitting at the king's gate.* The participle ("sitting") shows that the customary activity of Mordecai has resumed. The fact that he's returned to the "king's gate" may indicate Mordecai's renewed confidence that Esther's audience with the king has secured some hope.

5:14 *His wife Zeresh.* The women in the book of Esther are characterized as intelligent and ready with an independent voice. The advice of Zeresh is shrewd and pragmatic.

fifty cubits. This is approximately seventy-five feet.

have Mordecai impaled. She states no capital crime (cf. 1:20–22). This is really Haman's second overture of death (cf. 3:8–9). "Haman has now twice concocted plans that will backfire. . . . The [pole], intended to single out Mordecai as first among those executed for *being* Jews, will make Haman first among those executed for *opposing* Jews."[9] The king's "elevation" (*nasa',* v. 11) of Haman is a striking echo of the fate of Pharaoh's "chief baker," who was also "elevated" (*nasa',* Gen. 40:19) by Pharaoh—both are impaled (Esther 7:10; cf. Gen. 40:22).

then go . . . and enjoy yourself. This is a stunning association of two opposite activities and quite reminiscent of the heartless drinking that Haman and Ahasuerus enjoyed earlier, after the edict of death was initially hatched (cf. 3:15).

Theological Insights

God intends wise friends to rightly represent his will and exhibit his character. God uses courageous human agents to carry out his plans. Shadrach, Meshach, and Abednego illustrate an amazing commitment to God against staggering pressure to conform (Dan. 3:8–30). Against political and ethnic antagonism—much like Esther faced—they refused to alter their devotion to God in the face of either threat of death or promise of special advancement. After all, they knew that God had rescued the Israelite nation from the rogue power of Pharaoh centuries before (Exod. 18:10). These three youths illustrate how God can use key people in horrific circumstances, even at risk of treason (Dan. 2:10–13). Life-risking action may be required to halt the march of evil that is sanctioned by national authorities (cf. Acts 4:19; Rom. 13:1–7).

Teaching the Text

Esther's actions embody Israel's wisdom theology (Prov. 13:15; 16:22; 19:11), while Haman portrays the quintessential fool of Proverbs (Prov. 12:16; 13:16; 14:8; 15:14; 16:18; 17:16; 20:3; 26:7–9; 27:3; 29:9). The wise person knows not only *how* to act, but *when* to speak. Similarly, Esther displays profound tact when working with rulers and powerful people (Prov. 14:35; 16:12–15; 19:12; 20:2; 22:11; 23:1–3; 25:3–7). Esther also shows that wisdom can require a costly effort that reaches far beyond polite words (Prov. 15:28; 17:27).[10] In the end, Esther integrates a deep commitment to God's purposes with great skill in dealing with self-centered people.[11]

Right commitments do not guarantee comfortable outcomes.[12] Believers often live with the myth that moral sincerity brings a sure reward. This mentality hungers for predictability, but what results is a dangerous perfectionism: "I did everything right! I just don't understand!" There is no theological calculus that *obligates* God or guarantees believers freedom from pain and loss, even when we are committed to the values and mission of God.[13] Again, Shadrach, Meshach, and Abednego state something quite sobering that we must take to heart: "The God we serve is able to deliver us. . . . *But even if he does not* . . . we will not serve your gods" (Dan. 3:17–18; emphasis added). While they understood that God could deliver, they also knew God could not be manipulated. Faithfulness, not controllable outcomes, is what matters. In an era of marketed expectation, this hard reality is largely unacceptable to contemporary faith.

Some of the sharpest pains in life occur precisely where we think God could/ should have "shown up" and changed the situation. *How* we should respond and *when* we should intervene to stop the harm or prevent further damage is a significant question with no simple answer. We need to help people understand two serious realities, then give them opportunity to tell their stories: (1) On many occasions God's help is needed, but God appears absent. Tragic (and angering!) stories illustrate this, time and again. In the face of extreme crisis—including fighting Ebola or inner-city poverty—people are obligated to fight evil even when God seems silent. Humans need to step up and respond, regardless of how angry or deplorable the situation may be. (2) What qualifies a person to step up and help in a dire situation is a genuine recognition of the need. Being from a royal family or having the best social platform is not a prerequisite to helping others in need. Anyone, regardless of their station in life, can find themselves in a position to intervene when a crisis occurs. The most *unlikely* person just may be the one to help. Esther and Mordecai illustrate these realities well: not only fighting evil when God hasn't "shown up" but seeing the need, even though they themselves are hated and obscure.

Illustrating the Text

The right thing is always right; it is not often comfortable.

Literature: *The Horse and His Boy,* by C. S. Lewis. In this book, in Lewis's Chronicles of Narnia series, we find a wonderful quote about this concept. The main character, Shasta, has just finished a heroic march to warn an unsuspecting king of an approaching enemy army. He believes he has finished his quest after delivering the message to a guardian hermit and collapsing on his doorstep. Instead of being given rest, he is told he must get up immediately and deliver the message to the king by running on foot. He is struck by the cruelty of the request and cannot fathom how he will have the strength to go on. The narrator explains, "He had not yet learned that if you do one good deed your reward usually is to be set to do another and harder and better one."[14] This is the way it is for us, as well—doing the right but uncomfortable thing often blesses us with a chance to do things that are even more right and even less comfortable! In the process, though, we please the Lord and receive fellowship with him as our reward.

Quote: Mark Twain, great American author, is quoted as saying, "Do the right thing. It will gratify some people and astonish the rest." The right thing has intrinsic value because it is right; it generates discomfort because in many cases it is not what people expect, laud, or reward.

If you see the problem, you may be called to help address it—especially if you are the only one and feel totally unqualified!

Church Government: Often, church members will identify a problem and bring it to the pastor or another leader. Pastors and other leaders often want to say that if you are the one seeing the problem, you may be called by God to partner with them in finding a solution. There may be a reason you are the person to whom God revealed the problem. Next time you are feeling compelled to speak up about an unaddressed need, forgotten person, unstaffed volunteer position, or logistical hiccup at your church, stop and ask yourself, "Am I willing to be part of the solution to this problem, or am I hoping to report it and make it the leaders' new problem?" Take a few extra beats to stop, pray, and attempt to bring a few solutions to go along with the problem. Offer your observations and solutions as a gift, not an ultimatum, and see what your leaders say. God might be giving you a special new ministry! Your church leaders may not be able to use all the solutions you bring, but your willingness to step up and be part of the solution is a great reflection of Christ's heart—it will bless and encourage your shepherds.

Literature: *The Lord of the Rings,* by J. R. R. Tolkien. When the fateful Ring of Power is passed on to Frodo, he realizes that the burden of undertaking the quest of its destruction must fall to him. Frodo laments over his own inadequacy to perform the task appointed him: "I wish it need not have happened in my time." The wise wizard Gandalf offers him this wisdom: "So do I, . . . and so do all who live to see such times. But that is not for them to decide. All we have to decide is what to do with the time that is given us."[15] Regardless of our talents, our age, or our resources, we may be called upon to act in times of crisis. What God requires of us above all else is faithfulness in all circumstances: to decide what to do with what he has entrusted to us.

Honor Craved
and Honor Deserved

Big Idea

People can be so blinded by pride and reckless ambition that they fail to see that their own actions are bringing their downfall.

Key Themes

- God's involvement is highlighted by both the timing and sheer quantity of coincidences.
- God orchestrates a status reversal between Haman and Mordecai: Haman into humiliation and Mordecai into honor.
- Haman's demise is signaled by various forms of "falling" in every relationship he has.

Understanding the Text

The Text in Context

Esther 6 contains an exquisite collection of "coincidences" that include (1) Ahasuerus's insomnia, (2) his reading the chronicles that record Mordecai's loyalty and lack of reward, (3) Haman's court appearance that same moment, (4) Ahasuerus's riddle-like question to Haman, (5) Mordecai being on the mind of *both* men though they do not say so, and (6) Haman's assumption that he himself is the man deserving honor. In a unique way, the narrator retreats into the background and allows the reader to experience the twists and turns of the story along with the characters themselves. Throughout the dialogue, the reader knows more than either character. Thus, a strategic twist begins to reverse the evil plot toward the Jews and, instead, "unmask" Haman.

Esther 6:1–13 functions as the structural center of the entire book, with the key phrase "That night the king could not sleep" (6:1a). Observe the following diagram.[1]

Conflict that may have seemed incidental (chaps. 1–5) now takes on a vital significance in 6:1–13 (e.g., the role of banquets, Esther's silence, and the "book of the annals/chronicles"). Haman's vanity has become his downfall.[2]

Figure 1. Plot Movement and Conflict in Esther

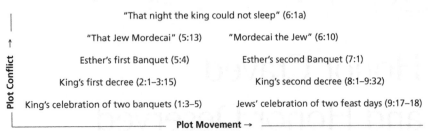

"That night the king could not sleep" (6:1a)

"That Jew Mordecai" (5:13)	"Mordecai the Jew" (6:10)
Esther's first Banquet (5:4)	Esther's second Banquet (7:1)
King's first decree (2:1–3:15)	King's second decree (8:1–9:32)
King's celebration of two banquets (1:3–5)	Jews' celebration of two feast days (9:17–18)

Plot Conflict ↑

Plot Movement →

These coincidences and reversals are a harbinger of Jewish vindication and honor. God moves the plot . . . just in time!

Interpretive Insights

6:1 *That night the king could not sleep.* The Hebrew reads, literally, "The sleep of the king fled," or, better, "The king had trouble sleeping" (NLT). The Septuagint includes more than the Hebrew text and identifies the *agency*: "The Lord kept sleep away from the king." Only hours earlier, Esther served a banquet and Ahasuerus and Haman attended, and Haman has been setting up a huge pole to impale Mordecai (5:14). "That night" also means the very night Haman finished erecting his instrument of shame and death. Neither man—Haman nor Ahasuerus, as it turns out—gets much sleep. In biblical narrative, disturbance of the sleep of monarchs sometimes indicates the hand of God at work, often resulting in the heightened profile of God's Jewish exiled servant and God's redemptive program (cf. Gen. 20:3–8; 41:1–7; Dan. 2:1; 6:18).

the book of the chronicles. Events that were recorded almost five years earlier are now read (cf. 2:16, 23; 3:7). This is the same book of royal records used before, though the narrator uses a slightly different title (similarly, the "royal archives of Babylon," Ezra 5:17).

6:2 *Mordecai had exposed . . . to assassinate King Xerxes.* The conspiracy that Mordecai had foiled was recorded in his name (2:21–23); 6:2 practically quotes 2:21. Such timing is a cipher for God's involvement.[3]

it was found recorded. The hand of God is evident when the precise passage that is read to Ahasuerus describes the unrewarded loyalty of Mordecai.

6:3 *What honor and recognition has Mordecai received?* This is a serious oversight verging on Ahasuerus "losing face," since the official chronicle should *also* have recorded Mordecai's reward/honor.[4] Persians prided themselves in their benefactors (*orosaggai*), such as Mordecai. But the lack of a record of a reward also means no reward was given to the deserving Mordecai.

6:4 *Now Haman had just entered the outer court . . . about impaling Mordecai.* More delicious ironies could hardly be found: both the king and Haman lack sleep; they have Mordecai on their mind; both wish to discuss Mordecai, but for opposite reasons—one for honor and the other for death. Haman stands in the "outer court," with plans for death; Esther stood in the more dangerous space of the "inner court" (cf. 5:1), and she came with hope for life.

6:6 *Haman thought to himself, "Who is there . . . ?"* As the narrator states Haman's motive for Mordecai's death (6:4), so now the narrator gives the internal monologue from Haman's own heart. As a literary technique, these "private-thought" statements reveal the foolish rationale or scheming of the person (cf. Gen. 20:11; 27:41; Luke 12:16–19). As Haman did earlier (3:8), the king does not name his subject, so Haman's inflated self-worth makes a conceited assumption. Only the reader sees the full scope of what's happening. G. B. Caird explains this masterful use of irony: "Dramatic irony differs from simple irony in that the contrast between what is said and what is meant is intended by the writer of the story, but there is always some character within the story, whether the speaker or another, who does not understand. The question addressed by King Xerxes to Haman is ironical, since its purpose is to make Haman think that it applies to himself, whereas in fact it applies to Mordecai."[5]

the man the king delights to honor. Haman will use this phrase of the king three times in his own "fantasy parade" that he proposes to the king.

6:8 *robe the king has worn . . . horse the king has ridden.* Wearing clothing that belongs to a king is essentially asking for that kingship. And this extends even further to the very horse that the king has ridden, what ancient historians knew was a grasp for the throne (Plutarch, *Artaxerxes* 5). Smitten with all things royal, Haman draws up his own fantasy of kingship—he already has the king's ring (3:10). But the things Haman lists must come as gifts, not power maneuvers.[6] Mired in his own words, Haman has begun to fall (cf. Ps. 59:12; Prov. 10:14; 14:3; 18:7). In fact, Haman never does get a chance to state why he came to see the king in the first place!

with a royal crest. When the king's horse also wears a royal crown or crest, Haman's intentions of a power grab couldn't be clearer (cf. 1 Kings 1:34–49). Traditional Jewish sources understand that the king's horse was his movable throne (*m. Sanh.* 2.5); therefore, neither his horse nor his scepter could be used by another person. The only high-profile element of the king's life that Haman has not mentioned is the queen. Ironically, Ahasuerus will accuse him of sexually assaulting her soon enough (cf. 7:8).

6:9 *let them robe the man . . . proclaiming before him.* Haman envisions court nobles clothing him in regal attire, proclaiming his "honor" (cf. Gen. 41:42–43), which he has now mentioned four times. Haman's ticker-tape plans mention "king" and "royal" eight times. Is there any doubt about Haman's delusions of grandeur?

6:10 *"Go at once . . . robe . . . horse . . . Mordecai the Jew."* Only at the very end of Ahasuerus's list of requirements does he identify Mordecai as the recipient. "Mordecai the Jew" was last referred to by Haman himself (5:13), including the location ("sitting at the king's gate," 5:9, 13). The king's entire description collects all those distinguishing factors of Mordecai that have so infuriated Haman all along. Haman never had a chance to voice his own agenda of death, and in fact, now he has committed himself to honoring the object of his hate: quickly, personally, and completely. Instead of nobles attending to Haman, Haman alone must clothe and attend to Mordecai—and he's mortified (cf. 6:12). That both Esther (5:1) and Mordecai are now dressed in royal robes[7] is one of many reversals and implies that the mantle of power is shifting.[8]

6:12 *Haman . . . his head covered in grief.* Actually, Haman's reasons for entering into the mourning rituals are a sham. Haman's "grief" is a mockery of the real tragedy that made Mordecai and Esther grieve in public ways and with serious personal risk.

6:13 *told Zeresh his wife and all his friends.* Described with the pathos of the Jews' mourning (cf. 4:1–3), Haman seeks comfort from his wife and "advisers" (lit. "his wise men"; cf. 5:9–14).

"Since Mordecai . . . your downfall has started . . . you will surely come to ruin!" This is cold comfort, but truer words have not been put to Haman—reality has caught up with his narcissism. Notice that his "friends" state that Haman is falling before Mordecai! With these new circumstances, his own wife sees what is coming and now wants to distance herself from Haman. This is pointedly clear when Zeresh and (lit.) "his wise men" use the second-person pronoun "you." Though the king's earlier decree attempted to confine the role of wives (1:22), Zeresh has played a determining role.

Jewish origin. It is stunning that the cause for Haman's hatred of Mordecai is now identified as the very reason for Haman's demise. Humiliation is growing. Ahasuerus and Zeresh—both Gentiles—have mentioned the Jewishness of Mordecai (cf. 6:10). The narrator is speaking through the most unlikely characters.

Theological Insights

God often shows his power by overturning human expectation. One of the most poignant expressions of God's providential hand in "reversals" comes from Zeresh and Haman's circle of "advisers" (v. 13). Here, even the reader can be caught off guard. Several observations can be made. First, their insight that Haman's "downfall has started" develops the book's theological theme of "fall" (Heb. *napal*; cf. "lot fell" [3:7]; "do not neglect" [= "let fall"; 6:10], "your downfall" [6:13]; "Haman was falling" [7:8]; "fear had seized"

[= "fallen upon"; 8:17]; "were afraid" [= "fear had fallen"; 9:2–3]). So not only does the lot "fall" (3:7); so does Haman when he "falls" on Esther's couch in desperation (7:8). At the end, a divinely induced fear "falls" on the Jews' enemies (9:2–3).

Second, Zeresh and Haman's "friends" are typical Gentiles: rational and spiritually sensitive (cf. Gen. 41:38; Jon. 1:6, 16; Dan. 2:46–47; 3:28–29). Solomon acutely understood the role of Gentiles joining in temple worship (1 Kings 8:41–43; cf. Luke 2:31–32; Matt. 28:19). Theologically, such Gentile response magnifies the glory of YHWH among the nations (cf. 1 Kings 17:24; 2 Kings 5:15–18; 6:12, 23; 8:7–15).[9] Although Esther initially identifies as a Gentile (2:10–20), the Gentiles will soon identify as Jews (8:17). So God is at work in the "big picture" reversals that shape the entire movement of the book. In the end, God's might repeals power plays, selfish ambitions, skewed advice, and ethnic distinctions.

Teaching the Text

1. Amid all the manipulation and deceit of powerful people, God's redemptive work will not be toppled. The strong hand of God continues to work in the unseen quarters of society.[10] When we understand these Bible stories, we see the caring and delivering ways that God has used. Even when human power is abused, we can put our hope in a mighty God, who will have the last say.

2. Our modern emphasis on the spontaneous, spectacular, and self-sufficient dulls our senses to the plain processes God uses in life.[11] In our culture too, God may receive a greater glory from upending our contemporary conventions. More insurance, faster internet, and larger congregations won't predispose God to our expectations. Scorned people from simple places continue to scandalize "the wise," who often build their identities on associating with "the rich and famous." In truth, we will continue to be surprised by those God picks and how he uses them. God most often works in the "mundane" ways.

3. Christian disciples face the challenge of living with a great tension: believing that God does act for his redeemed, yet realizing that it's on his timetable, not ours.[12] We can help new believers by letting them realize that faith comes with hardship, voice their frustration with God's apparent silence, ask questions that make leaders squirm, and even read prayers of lament for their painful circumstances. These teach us all, but especially young believers, that it's OK to live in some awful tension with God's ways of acting, especially when those ways don't reflect our preferred schedule. God has a peculiar providence we grow to cherish.

Illustrating the Text

God and his gospel always win, no matter how things look in the meanwhile.

Hymn: "I Heard the Bells on Christmas Day," by Henry Wadsworth Longfellow. Commend to your listeners the lyrics to this old hymn:

> And in despair I bowed my head:
> "There is no peace on earth," I said,
> "For hate is strong and mocks the song
> Of peace on earth, good will to men."
>
> Yet pealed the bells more loud and deep:
> "God is not dead, nor does he sleep.
> The wrong shall fail, the right prevail.
> With peace on earth, good will to men."[13]

Longfellow wrote this after his son was severely wounded during the Civil War, and his wife had also recently died. We desperately need the kind of reminder these words give: "God is not dead, nor does he sleep"—no matter how things look in the meanwhile.

God loves underdogs—they best reveal his glory and they best silence the proud.

Bible: 1 Corinthians 1:27–29 wonderfully illustrates this concept.

Sports: The area of sports is filled with underdog stories—consider sharing one that would resonate with your listeners. Is there a time in recent memory when the local team won against all odds? Ask your listeners a question: If you were a coach looking to bolster your reputation as a consistent winner, what teams would you want to lead? On the other hand, if you were a coach who wanted to be known for molding young players, transforming athletes, and reforming team cultures, then what teams would you want to lead? Now apply this to God: If God wants to be known as a winner who loves other winners, on whose side will he fight? On the other hand, if God wants to gain glory for himself as an amazing transformer of people who deserves all the credit in every situation, *now* on whose side will he fight? (Corrective point: Remind your listeners that God is also on the side of humble, honest winners—powerful people can also become useful vessels through willing submission and dependence on him.) The point is that God loves to reveal his strength in our weakness and to use weaklings to show his power.

God can move his ducks into a row perfectly while simultaneously receiving our laments compassionately.

Human Experience: Ask your listeners to consider times when working on manual tasks actually opened up a more intimate conversation. Maybe it was doing dishes with family while talking about life, pouring out one's heart to a knitting mother, sharing life while fixing a car with dad, or connecting with a friend while canning jams. In all of these cases, the task is completed seamlessly while conversation deepens; the manual labor doesn't need to detract from intimacy—multitasking can actually add to the rhythm of the conversation. Ask them to imagine that conversation with God is the same. He can keep the universe under control, count the hairs on billions of heads, act mysteriously to rescue us, *and* enjoy a deep conversation with us all at the same time. In the case of lament, he can fully receive and absorb our laments while simultaneously going to bat to fix them. Similarly, we can pour out our hearts to him while simultaneously serving others and being about his work. The multitasking doesn't distract from the intimacy, but rather increases it as we connect with him in the work of his harvest.

Esther Is Revealed but Haman Unmasked

Big Idea
Addressing social evil requires particular knowledge, wise dialogue, and personal risk.

Key Themes
- Esther orchestrates the second banquet to immobilize Haman with the king's aid.
- Esther's request begins with formal language, then uses personal terms to draw in the king.
- Esther quotes key portions of Haman's edict as a subtle way of telling him "she knows."

Understanding the Text

The Text in Context

The second banquet of Esther, in chapter 7, employs another comic misunderstanding just like chapter 6. Haman's assumption of honor (6:6) now gives way to the king's assumption of a rape of Esther by Haman (7:8). The anger and hatred Haman has held toward Mordecai find their resolution in profound irony—Haman is impaled on the very pole he intended for Mordecai (7:10; cf. Prov. 26:27). Chapter 6 ends with Haman covering his head in grief over Mordecai's advancement (6:12), so chapter 7 concludes with servants covering Haman's face (7:8), instead of Mordecai's.

When Esther finally states her request, it comes in wise words, royal titles, and rather personal terms. For one, Esther speaks to Ahasuerus, never to Haman. The narrator portrays Esther "cashing in" her authority as the titles of "king" (15x) and "queen" (7x) rise sharply. Haman is ultimately immobilized by the full weight of pointed questions from "King Xerxes" and informed answers from "Queen Esther" (7:5). When "my life" is "my petition" and "my people" is "my request" (7:3), her identity has merged with that of her people—Esther has the king's attention now! Haman is caught. No more edicts or alibis.

Interpretive Insights

6:14 *still talking . . . king's eunuchs arrived and hurried Haman away.* The pace of the story is quickening. Unprepared, Haman is still talking with his wife and friends when "eunuchs" arrive and hurry Haman off to Esther's second banquet (cf. 5:6–8; 7:9). Whereas the first five banquets were managed by Gentiles, the last five are by Jews. Haman is increasingly losing his control; he is cast as a recipient rather than an initiator, and being led around by others' commands (cf. 5:5; 6:5, 10, 14; 7:9). A dangerous ignorance prevents several themes from being resolved. Accurate information and understanding still elude every key character. For Esther to say anything is to drop a bombshell: (1) neither Ahasuerus nor Haman knows that Esther is a Jew; (2) Ahasuerus doesn't know the identity of an entire people group scheduled for destruction; (3) Esther doesn't know about Haman's recent humiliation; and (4) Ahasuerus doesn't know about the deep rift between Haman and Mordecai.

7:2 *"Queen Esther, what is your petition . . . What is your request?* Esther's delay in answering the king's question—also put to her at the first banquet—practically guarantees that her wish will be granted. Her patience is noteworthy, as is the king's (and the narrator's) constant use of the title *Queen.* Haman can only look up at her position.

7:3 *favor with you, Your Majesty.* Esther's language is now more relationally intimate and vulnerable, an upgrade from "If it pleases the king" (5:4). The royal relationship stands to be affected by what Ahasuerus grants (cf. 8:5).

grant me my life . . . my petition . . . spare my people . . . my request. Esther's two-part answer reflects the king's two-part question. The queen has now equated her life with the lives of "a certain people" (3:8) slated for destruction in Haman's edict. Like Haman, Esther does not identify them as "Jews," but does say "we," along with "*my* life" and "*my* people." Though she speaks only to the king, the ethnic connection in Esther's revelation is unmistakable to Haman. No less than three "unknowns" are now revealed: the queen's request is actually an intervention, Esther's ethnicity is now in the open, and the identity of the endangered people group is revealed for everyone. These are more than facts; they are earthshaking revelations.

7:4 *For I and my people have been sold.* Esther states the reason for her two-sided request—she and her people were pawned off in Haman's vindictive bribe (cf. 3:9). Showing great wisdom in revealing her knowledge of Haman's edict (4:7–8), Esther uses the passive "sold," and in this way she delicately sidesteps the king's role in sanctioning Haman's bribe.[1] Accusing a duped king would be counterproductive. This allows Haman to be identified as the real traitor, rather than an entire group of people (3:8). Moreover, Haman's scheme manipulated money and grasped at the throne, making his actions actually treasonous.

destroyed, killed and annihilated. Recalling Haman's petition to the king by using the same three verbs (cf. 3:13) of the published edict is more than a clever move; it's irrefutable. At this point, Esther has clearly revealed that she's on to Haman. Even if Ahasuerus is lost in Esther's detailed allegations (*who . . . ? where . . . ?*, v. 5), Haman has been caught and immobilized by his very own words!

7:5 *King Xerxes asked Queen Esther.* The narrator highlights the royal relationship ("King," "Queen") and, therefore, the audacity of such potential violence against Esther, her people, and the stability of the kingdom. The matter is beyond the threat of slavery, or the queen would not be speaking.

Who is he? Where is he . . . ? Esther's approach has drawn the king into a mode of sharp discovery. Like Nathan's clever approach with King David, Esther's words arouse the king's anger before identifying the culprit (cf. 2 Sam. 12:1–6).[2] Haman, who says nothing, is reduced to a topic of discussion.

7:6 *An adversary and enemy! This vile Haman!* This is the climax of the story. Esther stacks up key terms that emphasize Haman's role, threat, and character. She has aroused the king's curiosity, stoked his anger, dispelled all remaining ignorance, and thus sealed the fate of the one named at the end—"Haman."[3]

Esther's denunciation—"This vile Haman!"—is an appropriate counterpoint to Haman's original smear: "that Jew Mordecai" (5:13). By not using the formula "enemy of the Jews" (cf. 3:10; 8:1; 9:10, 24), Esther wisely casts Haman as "an . . . enemy" of both Jew and Persian, commoner and queen.[4]

7:7 *King got up . . . left his wine . . . went out.* All necessary words have been spoken. Dialogue is over. Now physical actions replace verbal statements in a sequence of cause and effect: Haman cringes, Ahasuerus leaves, Haman approaches, Ahasuerus returns, Haman falls, and so on.

But Haman . . . stayed behind to beg Queen Esther. Esther has sparked an anger in the king that can bring about change (cf. Mark 3:5; Eph. 4:26). With the king in the "palace garden," likely considering his next course of action, Haman pleads for (*baqash*) his life from his would-be victim. The ancient role of Agagite and Jew has been reversed. It is this absence of the king that now sets the stage for Haman's final mistake.

7:8 *as the king returned . . . Haman was falling on the couch.* The timing of the king's return is fatal for Haman, as the king seizes on the appearance of his queen being "molested." In Hebrew, two words (vv. 7, 8) now play off of each other. The word translated "molest" (Heb. *kabash*) is a strong word, which can be used of a stronger party or army harshly subjugating a weaker foe, "subduing" them (cf. Num. 32:22; Josh. 18:1), resulting in some translations such as "ravish" (NJPS), "attempt to rape" (NET), "molest"

(CEB) or "violate" (HCSB). If so interpreted, this is ethically complex: Haman is merely begging, but the king misunderstands what he sees (or can now redirect the charge without implicating himself in the edict). For her part, Esther withholds any clarification that could save Haman's life— she knows Haman isn't trying to rape her. In the Old Testament, political statements were regularly made by taking the wives or concubines of the leader (cf. Gen. 35:22; 2 Sam. 3:7; 16:21–22; 1 Kings 2:15–17, 22; Plutarch, *Artaxerxes* 26.2).

as the word left the king's mouth, they covered Haman's face. In this scenario, the king's declaration was Haman's death sentence. Was a violation of royal etiquette worthy of death, as a pretext to dispose of Haman for his genocidal edict? Covering Haman's face seems to signal official condemnation and mark out the guilty party.

7:9 *Harbona . . . attending the king.* Harbona's (cf. 1:10) observation really adds a further charge against Haman—namely, Haman's intention to kill an official benefactor of Ahasuerus. God is clearly working behind the scenes: (1) struggling with reason and evidence, the king observes what he needs in order to put Haman away; (2) an observant eunuch is ready with a timely solution for the king to punish Haman; (3) Esther hears about Mordecai's advance and public acclaim ("who spoke up to help the king") that occurred earlier that day; (4) Harbona has noticed the impaling pole—he knew of both the structure and its intended victim—which may be even visible from the palace window.

A pole reaching . . . fifty cubits. The height of seventy-five feet likely includes its stone base or retaining wall.

Impale him on it. Impaling was used earlier (cf. 2:23; 5:14; 6:4; also 9:13, 25). Haman intended those very words for Mordecai. Instead, Haman dies the death of a traitor, having accused the Jews of being traitors (cf. 3:8).

7:10 *the king's fury subsided.* This repeats the fury cycle of 2:1, following the Vashti debacle. But this also means that another replacement will soon be made.

Theological Insights

A core theological issue is the tension that believers face between God's sovereignty and human engagement. Esther's strategic actions and ingenious relational tact illustrate how God *partners* with people to address evil. This avoids two extremes: (1) thinking God has "fixed" every outcome already (this is ethical fatalism); (2) claiming "God has no hands but ours." While the first extreme holds no one accountable for their actions, the second creates a "puny" God and cynical disciples. We should strive for the harder balance. "Never should our confidence in God's ultimate victory dilute our own passionate involvement."[5] Strategic "wins" are important, but inevitably, further battles wait in the wings (e.g., Nehemiah's work in 5:1–6:19; Paul's warning in Acts 20:29–31).

Teaching the Text

This text raises two related issues for teaching. First, silence almost always serves the villain, rather than the victims. Esther illustrates well how speech in advocacy is a destabilizing instrument for good in an ethical dilemma. It has a prophetic impact in society. The silence of the German populace in World War II, who overwhelmingly looked the other way, allowed evil to tighten its grip by *colonizing* in the layers of German society. Naming an injustice, bringing it into the light, is an act of courage. As Miroslav Volf puts it, "If no one remembers a misdeed or names it publically, it remains invisible. To the observer, its victim is not a victim and its perpetrator is not a perpetrator; both are misperceived because the suffering of the one and the violence of the other go unseen. A double injustice occurs—the first when the original deed is done and the second when it disappears."[6] There's also a double-sided lesson: we cannot heal what we will not name; nor will we name what we are unwilling to grieve. The struggle to address sexual abuse, for example, illustrates this. Biblical stories often give us courage to speak.

Second, personal risk and pain are potential realities when evil is addressed. From the moment that Esther entered court life, she faced many risks. Eventually, using specific knowledge of a wicked plan, she risked her own life to stop the advance of an evil scheme. This principle is uniquely illustrated in the Sermon on the Mount: "Do not resist an evil person. . . . Turn to them the other cheek also. . . . Hand over your coat as well. . . . Go with them two miles" (Matt. 5:39–41). The apparent contradiction is resolved when one understands that some kinds of evil must be personally absorbed—*in order to break the chain of evil actions*. Obviously, Esther faced imminent death, not a slap. But with appropriate knowledge and some discomfort, we can slow or stop the complex cycle of evil, in its various forms.

Illustrating the Text

Brushing injustice under the carpet only creates greater injustice.

Popular Saying: When a cover-up of injustice becomes egregious, many people will say that it wasn't the problem that hurt the most, it was the *cover-up* that came *after* the problem." This taps into the irony that often covering up injustice or indiscretion becomes a crime of even greater consequence. Ask your listeners to think of times when this has happened in the news or in their own lives, and how facing the music and repenting can address injustice in far healthier ways than if it were brushed under the carpet.

If standing up against evil were easy, we would never use the word "hero."
Historical: In the face of the violence against and mass killings of Jews in World War II, the courage of Dietrich Bonhoeffer and that of the ten Boom family illustrate what some believers have done to stand for justice against powerful regimes. Bonhoeffer gave his life for his prophetic voice against the evils of Hitler, and his example illustrates the cost involved in calling out evil. The ten Boom family kept their faith in the face of evil. These men and women faced great difficulties to stand up against evil. Their heroic examples show us that we must be willing to dare greatly if we are to make a difference for others in the face of wickedness.

Quote: Former president Theodore Roosevelt commented on the grit required to stand up and fight the good fight in the face of difficulty and persecution:

> It is not the critic who counts; not the man who points out how the strong man stumbles, or where the doer of deeds could have done them better. The credit belongs to the man who is actually in the arena, whose face is marred by dust and sweat and blood; who strives valiantly; who errs, who comes short again and again, because there is no effort without error and shortcoming; but who does actually strive to do the deeds; who knows great enthusiasms, the great devotions; who spends himself in a worthy cause; who at the best knows in the end the triumph of high achievement, and who at the worst, if he fails, at least fails while daring greatly, so that his place shall never be with those cold and timid souls who neither know victory nor defeat.[7]

Sometimes, evil only stops when someone good is willing to absorb it.
Science: Share with your listeners the concept of insulators and resistors in electrical circuits. Insulators are able to stop electrical current from passing from one conductor to another—for example, touching a live wire with bare hands will give you a shock, but touching it with thick rubber gloves (insulators) on your hands will not harm you. Resistors are similar to insulators, in that they stop *some* flow of electricity, but they do not stop it all and transform some of the electrical energy into heat. If a resistor absorbs more electrical current than it is designed to withstand, it can overheat and combust. In our own strength, we can only act as resistors to evil. We can absorb some of its effects and pass on a lesser amount to others for a time, but eventually we can be overcome and melt down. Jesus is able to be an insulator, in the sense that he absorbed an infinite amount of evil on the cross without being

consumed by it. Even when he seemed to melt down into the grave, his resurrection proved that he was able to break the cycle and remain intact. When he dwells in our hearts, we can rely on him so as to become more than mere resistors—we can be insulators who use his power, grace, and forgiveness to break the cycle of evil permanently.

Neutralizing an Edict of Death

Big Idea

When God meets our individual needs, he still intends that we keep working for the needs of others.

Key Themes

- Mordecai becomes the barometer for the security and well-being of the Jews.
- "Reversals of fortune" are many, including Mordecai taking Haman's position.
- Persian laws, which cannot be revoked, are creatively *neutralized* by Esther and Mordecai.
- God brings *shalom* to the Persian kingdom when other ethnic groups identify in solidarity with the Jewish people.

Understanding the Text

The Text in Context

The architect of the edict is dead, but Haman's edict is still "active." With the backing of Persian law, the edict of death will have to be creatively defused. The only conflict that has been resolved is between Haman and Mordecai. Israel's ancient enemy, Amalek, has been dealt another blow through its representative. Now a hint of holy war is in the air. Holy war was known as *herem* warfare ("things under the ban") or YHWH war. There were distinct activities to be carried out before, during, and after such battles. For example, praise and celebration were standard responses after God brought his victory (Exod. 15; Judg. 5).

Holy war in the Bible occurred on rare occasions when God commanded the Israelites to destroy Canaan's citizens, sparing no one (cf. Deut. 7, 20; 1 Sam. 15:1–3). In the book of Esther, several elements in the Jews' fight against their enemies create a *profile* of holy war: (1) the language of "annihilation/extermination" is used, (2) nothing the Jews could value from the battle—in plunder or people—is kept, and (3) the Jews' enemy is more numerous than the Jews. Elements such as these underscore YHWH as the one who fights for Israel. Ultimately, it was his victory.

About eight months remain before the date for the Jews' slaughter. Esther 8:1–17 explains how a solution is found through a counteredict. The narrator consistently shows more than reversals in chapter 8; rather, these are enhanced states of honor that people receive.[1] Mordecai's elevation as the new prime minister at the outset of chapter 8 (vv. 1–2) is a harbinger of goodwill for all Jews throughout the empire (vv. 15–17).

Interpretive Insights

8:1 *That same day . . . gave Queen Esther the estate of Haman.* By law, Haman's "estate" becomes the property of the Persian state,[2] and Esther receives this extravagant gift (cf. 3:9; 5:11). Herodotus claims that a traitor's property went to the crown (*Hist.* 3.128–29). This is an opportune time, since Haman's death allows Esther the opportunity to bring Mordecai further into the king's service. Now Mordecai writes about significant events for his people.

the enemy of the Jews. The narrator underscores the villain in order to shift the focus back to the edict of death and away from the king.

8:2 *took off his signet ring . . . presented it to Mordecai.* Haman's loss of the ring (cf. 3:10–11) highlights Mordecai as its legitimate bearer, with royal authority. Esther extends her active role, putting Mordecai over her new "estate," and thus adds commensurate wealth to his position. Both king and queen have honored Mordecai, who is now in a position to deliver the Jews.

8:3 *Esther again pleaded . . . end to the evil plan of Haman the Agagite.* This is not "another round" of petition but a continuation of her earlier appeal to the king. This completes Mordecai's earlier instructions that Esther "plead" with the king (4:8).[3] Esther's banquets were designed for more than just Haman's removal. The "falling" and "weeping" make this exchange the most intense. Even with Haman's death, we are returned to his introduction (3:1) and the historical menace the Agagites represent.

8:5–6 *let an order be written overruling the dispatches . . . the Agagite.* Esther's new set of requests (marked by Hebrew conditional clauses ["If it please . . . if I have won . . . if I am pleasing . . . ," author's translation]; cf. 5:4, 8; 7:3) places the counteredict within the context of her relationship with the king. This is rhetorical language for making an argument. With this poetic language, Esther reminds the king of his concern for legal protocol (chap. 1), highlights Haman's complicity, and portrays herself as a horrified witness to the pending destruction of her people. She uses "dispatches" instead of the usual term for law (*dat*). This defines Haman's edict as opportunistic rather than permanent.[4] Defusing Haman's edict is Esther's concern, not defining its technical form. Also, by stating her request in the passive voice ("an order be written"), Esther outlines a course of action without indicting the king for authorizing the original edict. The combined weight of royalty is used to "overrule" the "evil" of the "Agagite" threat.

all the king's provinces . . . How can I bear to see disaster . . . to see the destruction? This is clever: by connecting the king's responsibility (i.e., "provinces") to her concerns, her interests to her own welfare, and then presenting them as questions, Esther invites the king's action for her life and her "family." The Jews are the king's people because they are Esther's.[5] This is her most complete identification with her people. Esther is the bridge to Jewish deliverance.[6]

8:7 *Mordecai the Jew.* What has been used as an ethnic slur in the book is now reversed as a designation of honor, used right next to "King" and "Queen."

Because Haman attacked the Jews. This is not quite correct, at two levels. First, Esther's attempted molestation (7:8) was the explosive pretext for Haman's immediate death. Second, were it not for the royal OK and use of resources, like the king's ring and state postal communication system, Haman's plan would not have gained traction. In fact, it's stunning how Ahasuerus basically takes no responsibility for his part in the despicable edict of death.

8:8 *write another decree in the king's name.* The "you" in verse 8 refers to both Esther and Mordecai, to whom the Ahasuerus has been speaking (v. 7). Ahasuerus recommends what they can do as compensation for what he can't do—namely, void a Persian law with his name on it. A similar situation was also faced by Darius the Mede (cf. Dan. 6:8, 12, 15), in which a counteredict was also issued (Dan. 6:25–27).

8:9 *twenty-third day of the third month, the month of Sivan.* This is the twelfth year of Ahasuerus's reign. Also, the counteredict is written seventy days after Haman's edict of death (cf. 3:12). Perhaps this signals hope for the Jews as a symbolic equivalent to the seventy-year exile.

Mordecai's orders . . . to the Jews in their own script and language. With artistic flare, the narrator mimics the format of Haman's earlier edict (cf. 3:12; also 1:22). Only this time, "the Jews" are included as a legitimate group in the empire—quite appropriate, since the danger is now formally connected to the Jewish people.

8:11 *Jews . . . the right to assemble and protect themselves.* The Jews have time to gather and prepare, but their military combat is limited to strict defensive posture or "justified retaliation" against any who attack them.[7] Haman's edict kept the Jews isolated and defenseless.

to destroy, kill and annihilate . . . and to plunder the property. Mordecai's counteredict is effective because it repeats much of the language in Haman's edict. The most poignant repetition is the three key terms of combat and the warrant to take plunder, also found in Haman's edict (3:13). And this language is virtually a repeat of the ancient directive against the Amalekites.

8:12 *thirteenth day . . . twelfth month.* About fifteen years later—fifteen years after the initial Purim festival—a trip back to Jerusalem was led by Ezra (458 BC; Ezra 7:9).

8:15 *wearing royal garments . . . large crown of gold.* These robes recall Mordecai's royal procession in chapter 6—the gold crown is one of many examples of enhanced honor (cf. Joseph, Gen. 41:42; Daniel, Dan. 5:7, 29).[8] Royal robes also recall royal tapestries (cf. 1:6). Other significant enhancements include couriers "riding [on] royal horses" carrying Mordecai's counteredict (8:14), and Haman's sadistic celebration of his edict of death (3:15) now upgraded by Jewish festivities "in every province and in every city" (8:17). Whereas Mordecai's honor was attacked in chapter 3 and previewed in chapter 6, it is established in chapter 8.[9] The court bowed to Haman, but all of Susa commends Mordecai.

the city of Susa held a joyous celebration. The last citywide impact was caused by Haman, and "Susa was bewildered" (3:15). Now Mordecai's counteredict brings "joyous celebration"! The story has come full circle.

8:16 *happiness and joy, gladness and honor.* The narrator illustrates the scope of reversal using four terms that counter the earlier grief ("mourning," "fasting," "weeping," "wailing," 4:3) and noting that the effects are felt "in every province" to which the edict has gone (8:17).

8:17 *feasting and celebrating.* Here we have yet another significant reversal of "fasting" and "mourning" (cf. 4:3), since only Persians have "feasted" to this point.

other nationalities became Jews. The Septuagint version translates this as "were circumcised," referring to the conversion of Gentiles. Rather than conversion, however, this is probably social solidarity and empathy with the plight of Jews in Persia. It does imply that the Jewish faith could be recognized as distinct from its ethnic group.[10] Hiding Jewish identity is also reversed (cf. 2:10, 20).

fear of the Jews. The social concern of Haman's "advisers" (6:13) spreads to the wider populace. This is standard Gentile reaction to YHWH's presence in holy-war contexts (cf. Exod. 15:16; Deut. 11:25; Josh. 2:9; 1 Sam. 15:3) and a powerful way God protects his people.

Theological Insights

Throughout Scripture is a vibrant theology of God's reversals. In 1 Samuel 2:1–10, Hannah celebrates a God who breaks warriors' bows, fills the hungry, and brings children to the barren (vv. 4–5). The most poignant connection to Esther is verse 8:

> He raises the poor from the dust
> and lifts the needy from the ash heap;

he seats them with princes
and has them inherit a throne of honor.

Such reversals are not just life-changing moments; they overturn expectations of the marginalized, nullify schemes of the powerful, and so bring great praise and honor back to a powerful God (cf. 2 Kings 4:32–35; John 11:41–44). Canonically, this God of reversals is exalted with the same words in Psalm 113:7–9 and Mary's Magnificat (Luke 1:46–55).

Jeremiah 33:9 encourages the Diaspora, telling them that God's renewal and *shalom* will be experienced now. The prophet uses many terms we find in Esther 8:16–17: "Then this city will bring me renown, joy [*sason*], praise and honor [*tip'eret*] before all nations on earth that hear of all the good [*tob*] things I do for it; and they will be in awe [*pahad*] and will tremble at the abundant prosperity and peace [*shalom*] I provide for it" (cf. Esther 9:30; Jer. 29:7).

Teaching the Text

1. It's a common reflex of society to use "the harm principle" (i.e., actions can be punishable only when others are hurt). This separates private from public, self from community, and intention from deed. What if Mordecai and Esther had "hedged their bets," waiting until someone was actually killed before stepping in? Instead, justice also requires punishment for what people *intend* to do, not just succeed in pulling off. This helps explain the deep tradition of disgust toward Haman. Intent itself is grounds for judgment. Defining evil only by its debris field is not only too pragmatic; it can be too late for some kinds of evil. Esther is an illustration of what preempting real evil can require of people.

2. Believers are called to meet the needs of *all groups*, precisely because Scripture roots the core of human dignity in the image of God (Gen. 1:26; James 3:9). Biblically, our vision is to be bigger than even Esther's. Unfortunately, postmodern tribalism has created "social vendors," peddling advocacy only for their concern, gender, race, or social issue. In this environment, then, it is vital to reassert biblical humanitarian concern for all. Empowering all people at the margins—not just of one's own ethnicity—enables all nations to see God's presence at work.[11] How we treat orphans (like an Esther) and the oppressed is still a barometer of genuine faith (Deut. 24:17; Esther 2:7; James 1:27).

Illustrating the Text

Humans define evil by its aftermath; God defines it from the moment of its conception.

Nature: Give the example of a mighty oak planted too near a house and over-hanging its roof. When a storm erupts and the tree drops a limb on the roof, untold damage can occur. When would people call the tree a danger? After it fell? When it grew too large? When it sprang up as a sapling too close to the foundation? Or, perhaps, should we have thought of it as a danger when the acorn first fell on the ground and began to germinate? When it comes to evil, we function as if it were an invisible oak looming over us and we never knew it existed until it falls and tears the roof from over us. In God's eyes, however, the evil is not defined by the aftermath; he saw it as evil when it was just a little acorn bouncing into the soil of human hearts. If we are to make significant progress in seeing freedom and healing, we must start to identify evil and uproot it at the acorn stage, not the ruined-roof stage.

A reliable barometer of true faith is the way one treats the foreigner, widow, orphan, prisoner, and other marginalized persons.

Popular Saying: There is a very popular and very unbiblical saying that is often repeated by people in our culture: "God helps those who help themselves." This saying is sometimes interpreted to mean that God will help you only if you are willing to participate in the process. At other times, it is meant to imply that God is on the side of the selfishly aggressive and will support whoever grabs for the glory first. According to the book of Esther, however, it seems it would be most accurate to simply say that "God helps those who risk themselves to help others." Explain to your listeners that the best plan for us is to mimic Christ and Esther by being willing to risk ourselves for the sake of saving others. When we do this, thus seeking God's kingdom first, he meets our needs abundantly.

Bible: A great cross-reference for this concept can be found in Matthew 25:31–46 or in James 1:27.

Missions: This would be a great time to highlight any mission partners of your congregation that focus on the needs of widows, orphans, prisoners, and other marginalized people.

The Jews Are Vindicated

Big Idea

God is able to upend any deceitful person, evil policy, or sinister scheme in order to further his own plan.

Key Themes

- God's "intervention" for the Jews was actually a matter of using people and resources skillfully.
- Strategic groups and political leaders side with Mordecai and promote the welfare of the Jews.
- The Jewish military conflict in Persia is cast in the language of God's holy war against Amalek.
- The Jews sought justice within their political system, not vengeance outside of it.

Understanding the Text

The Text in Context

Esther 9:1–10 describes the Jews' victory over their enemies. In fact, on Adar 13 (March 7, 473 BC)—eight months and twenty days after Haman's edict of annihilation—*both* the pro-Haman supporters and the Jews can claim that the law is on their side (cf. 3:12; 8:7–14). It is a clash of edicts. Chapter 9 resolves this tension and connects the story to the Festival of Purim.

This passage is framed by reference to "the enemy/enemies of the Jews" (9:1, 10). While Esther 9:1 states the outcome in a summary, 9:10 holds a two-part climax: (1) that all of Haman's sons died, (2) yet the Jews took no plunder (cf. 8:11). The center of the pericope develops the theme of "fear," a fear that gripped both "other nationalities" (9:2) and also the epicenter of Persian government (9:3). This fear not only prevented outlying attacks against the Jews; it also brought proactive aid for the Jews from within the government. The Jews' battle begins in the citadel, moves to the lower city, and ends in the outlying provinces. However, this conflict was not about military might but Jewish status in the Diaspora.

Interpretive Insights

9:1 *enemies of the Jews.* Haman was "the enemy of the Jews" (3:10; 7:6; 8:1), but now various ethnic groups have joined the Persians ("those who hated them [the Jews]"), out of ethnic hatred and greed (cf. 3:15). It appears that hatred of the Jews was widespread in the Persian empire.

the edict commanded by the king. Notice that the narrator now specifically acknowledges the complicity of Ahasuerus.

now the tables were turned. The narrator specifically draws the readers' attention to the counter momentum of the book. The literary elements in the first half are offset by the details and even the reversal of expectations in the second half.

9:2 *to attack those determined to destroy them.* The killing is described as an act of self-defense, not revenge (9:1, 5, 10). The force of the passage is on Mordecai's counteredict (8:11) as the actual instrument of death, not various means of massacre. Only the Jews are described as the recipients of "hate"—the reality of anti-Semitism (9:1; 3:4). The destruction that Haman had decreed under any circumstances is countered by Mordecai's edict that only applies to certain circumstances.

No one could stand against them. This expression indicates that God is fighting for the Jews (cf. Josh. 21:44; 23:9). God is seeing to his original statement to Abraham: "Whoever curses you I will curse" (Gen. 12:3a; cf. Deut. 9:14; Ezra 6:11).

9:3 *nobles . . . satraps . . . governors . . . administrators.* Significantly, this spectrum of state leadership (3:12; 8:9) also includes the "administrators" (*'osei*). They are in charge of the royal treasury (cf. Neh. 2:16; 2 Chron. 34:10). Among those who help the Jews, this is a telling group to conclude the list. The *'osei* were in charge of government projects, payments, and revenues, and Haman's original edict had specified that they be used as income officers for his proposed bribe (3:9).

helped the Jews. Driven by "fear," especially of Mordecai (9:3; cf. 8:17), the entire echelon of Persian government tries to aid the Jews. God used such fear in times of Israel's dire need for military aid and protection (cf. Deut. 11:25; 1 Sam. 11:7). Mordecai is technically "the man Mordecai" (9:4a)—not "the Jew" (8:7)—the narrator's counterpoint to Haman as "man, adversary and enemy" (7:6). Similarly, "the man Moses was very great" (Exod. 11:3 RSV). This is an astounding reversal: frightened governing classes and terrified Persian citizens.

fear of Mordecai. This phrase is used of "fear/terror" (*pahad*) produced by God (cf. 8:17; Deut. 11:25). As God has been working behind the scenes, both Mordecai's power and the Persians' fear have grown. Masses feared masses and officials feared one key official, Mordecai. It seems Mordecai had already gained significant influence during his brief tenure as prime minister. The "fear of the Jews" that already affected "other nationalities" (8:17) now reaches the halls of power and the ruling elite, with the "fear of Mordecai." Such phrases (1) imply a fear of other people (Esther 9:2–3), (2) often carry notions of holy war (Esther 9:3b; cf. Exod. 15:6; 1 Sam. 11:7), (3) can be found in the genre of oracles against enemies (Isa. 44:11; Mic. 7:17), and (4) occur in a context where the beneficiaries of this "fear/terror" experience the presence of God. Many of these thematic elements are at work in Esther 9.[1]

9:5 *killing and destroying.* These are the terms that Haman originally used in his edict of annihilation (3:13; cf. 9:6, 12). Mordecai, in turn, wrote the same language into his counteredict (8:11). The narrator stresses that the sword was used against "their enemies" and "those who hated them" (9:1, 5, 10). The Jewish response not only had imperial backing; it was confined to the limits of the counteredict (cf. Ezra 9:7–9). But now, self-defense is a moral upgrade from Mordecai's aggressive tit for tat with Haman. Because Haman's edict (3:13) had been so gruesome, Mordecai had also responded with language of massacre, the killing of women and children, as well as seizing of plunder. But ultimately, even the taking of plunder is drawn down.

they did what they pleased. The Jews fought only those who attacked them (cf. v. 1). Unless one has lived under the threat of death and persecution, it is hard to understand the desperate attempt of the Jews to neutralize their enemies in this way.

9:6 *five hundred men.* It is likely that known enemies of the Jews gathered for protection in the fortress-complex of Susa. Or, as relatives and supporters of Haman's regime, these men might have been viewed by the Jews as most dangerous. Only men are mentioned, not women and children.

9:7–10 *also killed . . . the ten sons of Haman.* In poetic justice, Haman lost the family and wealth that he flaunted before his wife and friends (5:11).[2] Haman's glory is gone, as is the last of the line of Amalek. Notice that Haman's sons are not "executed" but "killed." It appears that they joined forces with the Persian attack. His sons may even have tried to avenge their father's death. Haman's estate went to Esther (8:1), and now all ten sons are killed, a fitting counterpart to the "*ten* thousand talents of silver" he had promised the king (3:9).

In annalistic fashion, the narrative stops to name all ten of Haman's slain sons. This report may be patterned after Joshua 12:9–24, in which Israel made a list of defeated pagan kings—placing the final tally at the close (Josh. 12:24), as Esther 9:10 does. As in the case of Haman (7:10), impalement of the ten sons after death (9:14) was a practice designed for public spectacle and diminishment of status. Here, the Jews finish fulfilling the ancient instruction of God to blot out the memory of the Amalekites.

But they did not lay their hands on the plunder. Though taking plunder was standard war practice, the Jews take nothing (cf. Gen. 14:21–23). The narrator notes this three times (9:10, 15, 16) following the official death-report of Haman's sons. Mordecai's counteredict was carefully crafted to achieve complete reversal, even using Haman's terms (cf. 8:11), which allowed the taking of plunder. Though economic gain was not the goal, avoiding the plunder of their enemies showed remarkable restraint. No Gentile army in the Old Testament is ever described as having this restraint. The Jews did not need personal enrichment. God's protection in Persia was a greater asset than the gold they once took from Egypt (Exod. 11:2; 12:35). At this point in redemptive history, God has different expectations for Israel's relationship with Gentile nations. But avoiding plunder also raises the bar on how Persia's leaders treat their own people. Not surprisingly, this will create a grateful response from the surrounding people (cf. 9:20–23). Haman's intent has been neutralized (3:13).

Theological Insights

When the victorious Jews refuse their rightful plunder (8:11), a larger theological drama finds closure. If Esther 9:1–10 was just about being unselfish with material gain, then Abram already illustrated this when he rejected his portion of plunder from king Bera of Sodom (Gen. 14:21–24).

Canonically, Esther 9 adds a final step. The narrator identified Haman as an Agagite (3:1), as did Esther (8:5). Agag was king of the Amalekites (1 Sam. 15:20). It was Saul, son of Kish (1 Sam. 9:1), whom the Lord called to conduct holy war against Agag and the Amalekites by exterminating them (1 Sam. 15:3, 9), but Saul lied and kept Agag alive. The remnant of the Amalekites was destroyed later (1 Chron. 4:42–43). Mordecai is a new Saul figure. Just as Saul, son of Kish, fought against Agag, so now it falls to Mordecai, another son of Kish (Esther 2:5), to face down Haman the Agagite, once and for all.[3] In Esther 9, the Jews in Persia finally "correct" Saul's error.[4] When they leave the plunder (9:10), they avoid Saul's mistake.[5]

Just as "fear/terror" dipped into the language of holy war (9:3b; cf. 9:2b; 8:17), we find further confirmation that Mordecai's conflict with Haman is an expression of holy war. Soon after Israel left Egypt, it was the Amalekites that first attacked. The Lord was now "at war against the Amalekites from generation to generation" (Exod. 17:16). So Moses reminded Israel of the need to "blot out the name of Amalek from under heaven" (Deut. 25:19). The significance of the Jews' victory will be memorialized in the Festival of Purim (Esther 9:26).

Teaching the Text

While much of this text may sound foreign and even offensive to contemporary ears, several points should be noted. First, hate is socially taught. No one is born hating. Following Haman's life illustrates how hate can become so destructive and even contagious with other groups of people. What we can observe with Haman-type people is hatred with *propositional* intent. Such hate believes in the inferiority of the other. This descent into malice has phases people can find helpful in understanding the anatomy of hatred and its contemporary expressions: (1) It begins as encounter without relationship. An acquaintance can easily become an object. (2) Then hatred moves to an unsympathetic knowledge with no interest in *accurate* information. (3) Hatred then idolizes expressions of hostility toward these "objects," objects that feed one's irrational ideology. (4) Finally, it culminates in actively seeking to harm the other.[6] These phases resonate deeply in Esther. Such hatred and toxic divisions are painfully evident within our society today.

Second, later generations often need to complete the work of justice earlier generations started. The modern experience of the Holocaust or Shoah—as an outgrowth of government-sponsored assault against the Jews—gave rise to decades of hunting criminals and demanding restoration for caches of stolen property. The goal of equity and global justice, in courts and governments, can take generations to realize. As evil leaders are brought to justice, moral leaders and laws must be installed. Similar to Nehemiah's reforms to end misuse of the temple (Neh. 13:4–9) and mixed marriages (vv. 23–27), a bold edict was needed to complete the removal of Amalek once for all.

Third, because some of the greatest expressions of evil thrive as *social systems*, they must often be fought as social and systematic forces, too. Whether evil appears as religious terrorism (e.g., Al-Qaeda, ISIS), socialist nationalism (e.g., Third Reich), or contemporary hate crimes, people need the reminder that evil uses real faces. Dire times require Christians to take genuine risks.

Illustrating the Text

Hatred can be cultivated and taught until it becomes an all-consuming reality.

Film: *South Pacific.* The cinematic version of the Rogers and Hammerstein musical *South Pacific* (1958), based on the Pulitzer Prize–winning book *Tales of the South Pacific* (1947) by James Michener, includes the song "You Have to Be Carefully Taught." In it, a character struggling with racism and irrational hatred attempts to explain the systemic evil and cultural training that go into raising a person to hate. This song captures the chilling reality that hatred can be cultivated and taught to young people until they are consumed by it.

The process of God's justice often outlasts our attention spans.

Literature: *The Lord of the Rings*, by J. R. R. Tolkien. When we think of justice and how long a story arc it must sometimes span, we are drawn to look at epic tales with sweeping story lines. Few illustrate this idea as well as Tolkien's beloved novel.[7] These stories depict forces of good and evil in conflicts that span the rise and fall of kingdoms, the coming and going of leaders, wars and rumors of wars, and loss of memory as history passes into legend. If your listeners are familiar with these books or the movies made from them, you can reference the idea that certain stories, injustices, allegiances, or rivalries can be forgotten long before the justice and vindication they demand comes to pass. The saga of the lost ring of power and Frodo Baggins is a perfect literary example of how the whole world can give up and move on long before justice finally arrives.

Justice within the system is different from vengeance outside of it.

Ethics: Spend some time reflecting with your listeners on the difference between vigilantes, who take the law into their own hands, and those who seek justice through the legal system. While the vigilante's process seems more expedient and immediately gratifying, it leads to ethical ambiguity, since the vigilante becomes just as lawless as the original offender. Justice within the legal system is often fraught with delays, costs, and even unfair defeat; in the end, though, the person seeking justice remains on the right side of the law and retains the ethical high ground. Ask your listeners to consider which path is most appropriate for a person who wants to avoid jail. What about a person who wants to trust God's justice and wants to please him?

Further Defense and Reversals in Susa

Big Idea

God often helps mistreated people by directing the hearts of powerful leaders, bringing aid that is both spontaneous and generous.

Key Themes

- Ahasuerus shows his own "fear of the Jews" by granting Esther another day for defensive fighting.
- God brings *rest* to his people as the goal of their defensive holy war.
- The Jews mark their deliverance by the sharing of gifts within their community.

Understanding the Text

The Text in Context

The foundation for Purim is laid in this text as the Jews gain rest (9:17) from their attackers. The king grants an additional day—by decree (*dat*, vv. 12–13)—and "their enemies" are eliminated from Susa, as well. While Haman's decree was fueled by hate (ethnic) and greed (for plunder), the Jews are driven by neither, nor are animosity and greed the focus of the Purim festival. Both Adar 14 and 15 are days dedicated to Jewish celebration (vv. 17–18). Rural Jews celebrate on the 14th, and urban Jews on the 15th. With the opening two feasts of chapter 1, the closing two feasts form an envelope structure around 2:1–9:16. These are the 9th and 10th banquets in the book.

The description of fighting in Susa (vv. 11–15) parallels the report of fighting in the outlying provinces (vv. 16–17). The additional support from the king comes not from his exasperation over dead civilians but from a desire for political stability throughout the Persian Empire.

Interpretive Insights

9:12 *Jews have killed . . . five hundred men . . . ten sons of Haman in the citadel of Susa.* Two edicts are battling it out. It is unlikely that there were no

Jewish casualties, but to highlight the magnitude of the victory, the narrator mentions none. Some characteristics of holy war that are present in Esther are disproportionate matching of forces, people who are fully devoted to their cause, clever strategies, and abandonment of plunder (cf. Josh. 7). But the rules for the first day also hold true for the second day of Jewish fighting.

While some scholars view these days of slaughter as an example of mock or fabricated battles for literary flare or merely a device to explain the two-day Purim festival, a better explanation is the ongoing threat of Haman's scheme and the inflexible nature of Persian law, which necessitates further fighting.[1] In truth, if there is no attack, then none will die. The multiples of a hundred might also represent military units.[2] Haman's sons, considered loyalists to his scheme, are expected deaths in this context.

in the rest of the king's provinces. It is natural for the king to extrapolate deaths outside Susa, but his motivation for helping Esther is hardly regret over lost tax revenue; rather, he wants to bring stability to the kingdom. This requires rooting out such malice once for all.

what is your petition? . . . request? In good faith, the king asks these questions—again (cf. 5:3, 6; 7:2). While this is how Ahasuerus demonstrates his "fear of the Jews" (cf. 8:17), actual concern for his own people seems noticeably absent. "There is a force at work for [the Jews] that is greater than he has previously encountered."[3]

9:13 *Jews in Susa permission . . . Haman's ten sons be impaled.* Esther has two requests, one of substance and one of symbol: (1) that the Jews be granted an additional day of killing their enemies in the capital city (not just the citadel), (2) and that the bodies of Haman's ten sons be displayed publicly by impaling (cf. Josh. 10:26; 1 Sam. 31:10).[4] Esther's desired result is actually one of prevention. Such impaling was the height of humiliation, the ultimate degradation in warfare. While excessive and morbid to today's sensibilities, this was not torture, as the men were already dead. What Esther does amounts to securing a legal basis for additional fighting and a practical deterrent to opposition.[5]

9:15 *fourteenth day of the month of Adar . . . three hundred men.* Esther's focus on Susa implies that she is acting on particular information. The fact that three hundred are killed on the second day speaks to the wisdom of Esther's additional request, rather than some bloodthirsty attitude. The entire city yielded fewer deaths (i.e., three hundred) than the citadel (i.e., five hundred). Yet again, the Jews ignore "the plunder" (cf. 9:10, 16). Bringing vengeance on their enemy was never a basis for enriching themselves.[6]

9:16 *and get relief from their enemies.* While the description of fighting in verses 16–17 parallels verses 11–15, obtaining "relief from their enemies" is an important fact and anticipates additional rest to come (9:18, 22). By

Violence

"Human rights" seem appallingly crushed in Old Testament texts of violence—especially when seventy-five thousand lives are taken (Esther 9:16). But when religion and social hierarchies are also part of these texts, the bloodshed can seem beyond offensive to modern readers. When God sanctions such mass death (Josh. 10–12), the contemporary reader often sees a ruthless deity who patrols ancient "killing fields."

Violence consists of multifaceted destruction. Old Testament violence includes a variety of manifestations: physical violation, unethical treatment, malicious witness, violent mechanisms—and innocent suffering. Yet YHWH is a "warrior" (Exod. 15:1–3) who used brutal processes in the exodus and conquest, against brutal enemies. As Israel's root experience, God *continues* to wage war on Israel's behalf (Neh. 4:20). YHWH also calls for restraint (1 Chron. 22:8). Mass death occurs in Esther because the Persians have both God and his people as opponents.[a] The larger movement of Scripture, however, works against violence (cf. Matt. 5; Rom. 12–13).

Amid ongoing genocides and global terrorism, the combination of faith and violence is sharply distasteful today. Violence against "outsiders" (e.g., Coptic Christians) makes violence in the name of any religion a *force multiplier.*[b] As if violence was not enough, attacking because one hates another's religion only magnifies the destruction. The carnage and stigma are greater. This raises urgent questions: Is there not a real possibility of hostile force creating a spiral of violence? Does "militant righteousness" not undercut itself? Is violence justified in defense of another but not in self-defense? How should one face an implacable enemy bent on the death of others? There are no simple answers. But asking such questions admits the complexity surrounding violent actions. Violent systems may need to be taken down by opposing systems (externally) as well as by a change of values (internally). Multifaceted violence, however, requires us to relearn the role of lament. Lament is the language and cry for justice. While the sacrament of confession is offender oriented (forgiving the guilty) and needed for perpetrators of violence, the sacrament of lament is specifically victim oriented, calling Christians to share in the grief of others. Believers don't have to experience the same situation to share in the suffering. "[Remember] those who are mistreated as if you yourselves were suffering" (Heb. 13:3). Christians should also cultivate a growing thirst for the rest and peace of Christ's kingdom.

[a] Kirk-Duggan, "Violence," 1357.
[b] M. Douglas, "Violence," *DSE* 810.

identifying Mordecai and his niece, Esther, with Saul and identifying Haman with Agag (3:1), the author has placed the protagonists in the same positions once occupied by Saul and Agag in 1 Samuel 15. This time, however, the outcome has been far different. Not only are Esther and Mordecai confirmed as worthy leaders, but an entire Jewish population has been rescued from the brink of annihilation, aided by a Gentile king.

killed seventy-five thousand. The Septuagint reads 15,000, and the Aramaic Targum has 10,107. The Hebrew word for "thousand" can also mean extended family, so it might mean that seventy-five extended families were killed (cf. Exod. 12:37; Judg. 5:8). Taking the number as 75,000 makes a grand total of 75,810 enemies killed—with no Jewish deaths noted. These numbers highlight the miraculous reality of the Jews' deliverance, as well as the reality of the threat. As one scholar puts it, "The otherwise impossible victory of the Jews over their enemies (9:5–16) speaks with eloquence of the incomparability of Israel's God. Though His name is not mentioned in the book, His signature is written all over this work with redemptive grace."[7] Clearly, God's presence intervened, and the Jews' Divine Warrior acted again on Israel's behalf.

9:18 *Jews in Susa . . . they rested.* "Relief" and "rest" are significant terms from *nwh* (vv. 16, 17, 18). The narrator already used the term in referring to the king's "holiday" (*hanakhah*, 2:18). This is preparation for the Purim celebration (9:26). So it is quite telling that Haman proposed that the king not "tolerate" (*lehannikham*) the Jews, or, literally, "for us to let them rest" (cf. 3:8).

9:19 *rural Jews.* Jews have lived in walled cities since the days of Joshua. According to Jewish tradition, Jews who lived in walled cities were to celebrate Purim on Adar 15, while Jews from all other areas were to celebrate on Adar 14. In Jerusalem, Adar 15 is when Purim is celebrated.

a day for giving presents to each other. This gift giving reflects both the joy of deliverance (8:16) and its communal dynamic (8:17).[8] Such sharing was a natural expression of celebration (cf. Neh. 8:10, 12). On such an occasion, surely God was mentioned in prayers of thanksgiving and praise, which were two ancient types of psalms. Looking to God for peace from enemies is hardly a new concept for the Jewish people (cf. Deut. 25:19; Josh. 21:44; 1 Sam. 7:11–14). "Those who do not know God see only a dread power, but the Jews are able to discern the ways of God through this, and so their feasting and rejoicing already starts to point beyond itself."[9] Additionally, sending practical gifts, like food, showed that those who are sustained by God's loving hand are to extend the same care to others.

Theological Insights

God always intended to give his people rest. The motif of "relief" (9:16) and "rest" (9:17, 18, *nwh*) began in Israel's conquest under Moses and Joshua (cf. Deut. 3:20; 12:9–10; 25:19; Josh. 1:13, 15; 21:44; 22:4; 23:1). David finishes the conquest and then perceives that divine reprieve has finally arrived (2 Sam. 7:1, 11). What connects these is "rest from his/their enemies." Rest comes only after certain threats are removed.[10] God's promises of rest for his covenant people move beyond mere land, and for the Diaspora Jews, those promises stress safety, security, and political refuge.[11] Thus he commands:

"Seek the peace and prosperity of the city to which I have carried you into exile . . . because if it prospers, you too will prosper" (Jer. 29:7; cf. Ezra 6:10; 1 Macc. 7:33; Matt. 5:44). In Esther 9, the Jews find rest from legal threat and physical attack. Security is more than settlement.

Teaching the Text

1. Confronting violence can make one a violator. It is almost paradoxical how this happens, but it is worth considering how abortion doctors have too often met their end. Killing such doctors may bring a Wyatt Earp form of justice, but it hardly sends the right message. The recklessness of power works in both directions. Claiming that certain people don't deserve anything better is self-justifying and presumes God's prerogative of vengeance (cf. Rom. 12:19–21). To confront such violence, we must work within the legal system—much as Esther did, and with great creativity, too.

2. God moves in the hearts of leaders to aid people in need. Gentile leaders had a reputation of "lording it over" other people (Matt. 20:25–28). Such leadership does not bring peace to the lives of needy people. As God uses Ahasuerus, the king not only asks for practical information, but offers timely assistance for needs that he's not aware of (9:12–13). We cannot become so disgusted with a person or their office that we stop communicating or collaborating where we can. To do so eliminates any other options. Christian leadership is model-worthy, because it is willing to suffer with and for others (2 Tim. 4:1–5). This is sacrifice at its deepest levels.

Illustrating the Text

God has prepared rest for his people and will help neutralize threats to their peace.

Bible: Hebrews 4:1–13 is an incredible biblical exposition on this topic. It clearly lays out the promise of entering God's own rest, and how that rest can be threatened by unbelief. It also clearly teaches that the believer's rest is something that matters to God and is protected by his grace in salvation.

Human Metaphor: Describe a really good host or hostess preparing a hospitable and restful environment for a special guest. He or she has a goal of making the person feel loved, safe, and accepted in the home, and of giving the gifts of rest and refreshment. Talk about the kinds of things that might be distractions to that rest—phone calls, salespeople, messes, lack of provision, and so on. The good host will diligently remove obstacles and go to great lengths to ensure a proper and peaceful rest for his or her guests. How much more will God labor to remove obstacles to his people entering the eternal rest and peace he has prepared for them? He is willing to do so, even at the cost of his own Son's life on the cross!

God can move even pagan leaders to protect his chosen people.

Music: In Handel's famous oratorio *Messiah*, the words of 1 Timothy 6:15 and Revelation 19:16 (cf. 17:14) repeat over and over again: "King of kings and Lord of lords." Invite your listeners to consider what these titles really mean about Jesus; if he is, indeed, the King of all kings and the Lord over all lords, then he has the ability to rule over and through them, no matter whether they acknowledge him or not. Invite them to consider that we can infer that Jesus is sovereign over *all* presidents, rulers, and persons of power, the Judge of judges and Authority of authorities. Ask them to consider how believing this might help them pray for, submit to, and honor even pagan authorities in this world.

Medicine: Many of your listeners will have had the experience of being cared for and even healed by unbelieving doctors. Point out that even though God designed the human body, enlightened human minds to understand it, and guided the hands and skills of doctors in every cut, stitch, and prescription they give, God is not always acknowledged as the source of the healing. Just as God can fully guide the entire medical process without the doctors' consent or knowledge, so he can guide any ruler or earthly agent in his sovereignty to benefit his people!

Purim Is Established for All Jews Everywhere

Big Idea

God's blessing rests on the Jews in the Diaspora, overturning their view of exile as punishment.

Key Themes

- Celebration of Purim is formalized through written documents of Mordecai and Esther.
- Considering God's acts of deliverance requires appropriate celebration.
- God's blessing for the Jews is acknowledged apart from their return to Zion.
- The "greatness" of Mordecai is highlighted next to the "power" of Ahasuerus.

Understanding the Text

The Text in Context

At the beginning of Esther, banquets were Persian occasions; by the close of the book, they have morphed into entirely Jewish ones (9:20–32). Purim is the climax of all the feasting and festivity in Esther, which began with the king's banquet in chapter 1.

Esther 9:20–10:3 recounts the steps required to regularize the Festival of Purim. It is recorded in Esther as a legal *Persian* festival, observed by the Jews.[1] The Purim festival celebrates the end of fighting, not the days of fighting. A combination of letters by Mordecai (vv. 20–28) and Esther (vv. 29–32) makes Purim a permanent festival. In Purim, a two-day festival is established, a celebration for every Jew (v. 20), wherever they may be. As it is prescribed in the book of Esther, Purim has no religious substance.

Interpretive Insights

9:20 *Mordecai recorded these events.* Precisely what is recorded is not stated, though the stations he and Esther came to hold in Susa (i.e., prime minister, queen) and a battle report are likely information. This statement of writing led some rabbis to conclude that Mordecai wrote the entire book. Nehemiah also recounted his official position as cupbearer in Susa (Neh. 1:11b), and battle records—of defeated Amalekites(!)—are hardly new (cf. Exod. 17:14). Esther also writes, so maybe the book was cowritten, drawing from perspectives inside and outside the palace.

sent letters to all the Jews . . . near and far. This could have involved distances up to two thousand miles.[2] The phrase "near and far" places the events of Purim within the context of promised comfort: "'Peace, peace, to those far and near,' says the LORD. 'And I will heal them'" (Isa. 57:19; cf. Isa. 35:10; 51:11; 61:3; Lam. 5:15).[3]

9:22 *when the Jews got relief . . . sorrow was turned into joy.* Mordecai writes a theological summary and uses terms of God's covenant faithfulness to the Diaspora community (cf. Jer. 31:13). Mordecai's statements are significant in several ways: Not only does God's blessing operate in the Diaspora, but promises can also be realized without a physical return to Zion. Also, the use of the divine passive ("Jews got relief") involves God, once again, without making it obvious. Readers are forced to ask, How did God bring that relief to Jews in the Persian Empire?

presents of food . . . gifts to the poor. The giving has two aspects, which connect Purim to the Feasts of Weeks and Tabernacles, as they also involve sharing material provisions with dependent citizens (cf. Deut. 16:11–15; Neh. 8:10–12; Tob. 2:1–2; 1 Cor. 11:17–22). This also reverses the harm that Haman's edict of death would have brought to the weak and innocent (cf. "from the least to the greatest," Esther 1:5).

9:24 *Haman . . . the Agagite, the enemy of all the Jews.* Verses 24–25 appear to summarize Mordecai's letter, giving the background to the Festival of Purim. Haman is defined by his scheme of death and thus his identity as "the enemy." Significantly, the phrase now stipulates "all" the Jews (cf. 3:10; 7:6; 8:1). Observing Purim now means that every Jew acknowledges that their significant Amalekite enemy was finally put down in the person of Haman. "They put the final chapter of the Amalekite affair into writing."[4]

9:26 *these days were called Purim.* The earliest reference to the Festival of Purim is found in 2 Maccabees 15, when the forces of Judas defeat their enemy, Nicanor, and thirty-five thousand of his soldiers. With intriguing parallels to the book of Esther, this text reads: "Judas hung Nicanor's head from the elevated fortress in plain sight of all, as a clear sign of the Lord's help. The people decided to issue a regulation forbidding anyone to forget this day but reminding all to celebrate the thirteenth day of the twelfth month, called Adar in the Syrian language, the day before Mordecai's day" (15:35–36 CEB). Jewish tradition observed the thirteenth of Adar as Haman's dreadful day, when a fast was held—the "fast of Esther"—preceding the Festival of Purim (14th and 15th of Adar). Also recall that the rural Jewish communities celebrated on the 14th of Adar (cf. Esther 9:18–19).

9:27 *they and their descendants and all who join them.* Here, the Jews' commitment to observe Purim is expressed. The Persians (and other ethnic groups) who joined the Jews are acknowledged. "Join them" translates a word (*hannilbim*) used for proselytes (cf. Isa. 14:1; 56:3, 6). This is one of many themes from the exodus, when "many other people" joined the covenant community (cf. Exod. 12:38).

9:28 *days should be remembered and observed.* Within the Old Testament, remembrance obligates the entire community and has written content on which to reflect (cf. Deut. 6:1–25).[5]

in every generation . . . in every city. The Diaspora community is affirmed as a legitimate *post*exilic identity, without a return to Zion.[6] Enjoying the blessing of their covenant God did not depend on living in the promised land.

9:29 *Queen Esther . . . wrote with full authority . . . this second letter.* Esther's writing fixes Purim's ongoing observance (v. 32). She is the only woman in the Bible clearly said to write and establish an event.[7] Esther's royal status confirms what Mordecai wrote, granting her authority as a coauthor. Purim is the first non-Torah festival, and Queen Esther's letter contributed to the legitimacy of Purim. Additionally, Esther and Mordecai are affirmed as Jews (9:31; 10:3) and perhaps could be considered to reflect the Torah requirement of two witnesses (Num. 35:30), all in support of the Jewish observance of Purim.

9:30 *words of goodwill and assurance.* In Hebrew, this is *shalom* ("goodwill") and *'emet* ("assurance"). These same terms are used in Zechariah 8:19, when fasts are transformed into community-wide feasts in Israel. Zechariah notes that Gentiles will join, unable to resist the presence of God (Zech. 8:20–23).

9:31 *times of fasting and lamentation.* The three days of Jewish celebration (13th–15th of Adar) also commemorate the three days that Esther fasted for her people prior to interceding for them (4:16).

10:1 *throughout the empire . . . distant shores.* The Hebrew reads literally "mainland and the islands" and is a merism for the entire inhabited world. Isaiah uses the same phrases (Isa. 42:4, 10). Such an extensive realm means that Persian rule now reaches beyond the 127 provinces of 1:1.

10:2 *acts of power and might.* Such description also returns the reader to the austere profile of Ahasuerus in 1:1. The "tribute" (10:1) reflects a stable kingdom, one without the need of Haman's bribe to pad the king's treasury (3:9). With Haman's "evil scheme" (9:25) put down, Ahasuerus utilizes the tribute he receives to bring justice and peace to the empire.

book of the annals of the kings of Media and Persia. This is presumably the same book of annals already mentioned in 2:23 and 6:1. Such official

Literary Connections between Exodus and Esther

The character and activity of God richly connect the book of Exodus with Esther. What emerges is a loyal, attentive, and partnering covenant God. The links could include (1) a story of threat and deliverance revolving around a Jew who is strategically placed in a Gentile king's family and who inaugurates precedent-setting rituals (Exod. 1:1–12:42; Esther 1:1–9:19); (2) Jewish individuals who are at first unwilling to intervene (Exod. 3:11; 4:13); Esther 4:11–14); (3) the turning point of deliverance on the same day of the same month, Nisan 14 (Exod. 12:6; Esther 3:12); (4) establishment of legislation and ongoing festival observance (Exod. 12:43–13:16; Esther 9:20–32); (5) community acceptance of new legislation (Exod. 12:50; 19:8; Esther 9:27–28); and (6) the inclusion of Gentiles (Exod. 12:48–49; Esther 8:17; 9:27). God is proven to be consistent and even creative in his relationship with his people, always using agents, as the book of Esther clearly shows.

summary statements are also used to close out other historical books (cf. 1 Kings 14:19, 29; 15:31).

10:3 *Mordecai the Jew was second in rank.* Beyond achievement, Mordecai's rise to power brought stability to Persia. He basically achieved everything possible. This is reminiscent of Joseph's appointment as "second-in-command" (Gen. 41:43). These were model Israelites who brought the blessing of Abraham (Gen. 12:3) to foreign nations. A thematic link comes from Haman's wife, Zeresh, who spoke of Mordecai's "Jewish origin" (lit. "the seed of the Jews," 6:13).

worked for the good of his people . . . welfare of all the Jews. Esther and Mordecai combined to bring deliverance. While Esther intervened courageously once, Mordecai was an ongoing intermediary. Like Joseph before them, they both brought *shalom* ("welfare") to a complex international setting.

Theological Insights

God does not operate by a script that requires him to act the same way in the book of Esther as he acted in Exodus. For example, in Exodus God's visible presence could be seen by all in the fire and heard by all in thunder—his glory was palpable. In fact, entire chapters of Exodus are dedicated to God's explosive and deadly power (cf. chaps. 3, 7–11). The plagues (chaps. 7–11) and deliverance at the Red Sea (13:17–15:21) are pure "shock and awe," also designed to confront the Gentile nations with the one true God. And honor he gets! After death is visited on every Egyptian home, Pharaoh summons Moses, releases the Jews for worship (12:31), but concludes: "And also bless me" (12:32). By contrast, in Esther God's presence is not "out there." So hidden is God in Esther, the Jews are forced to draw on the faith of their ancestors and even craft new festivals. Ironically, even Esther, the great heroine of the book, is completely absent from the book's conclusion (chap. 10). Yet these books of deliverance have the same God.

Teaching the Text

1. To the Jews "throughout the provinces" (9:20), Diaspora life was a form of spiritual crisis. No sacred sites, props, or institutions were available to the Jews. But times of loss can bring fresh reflection and renewed commitment to God. For this reason, singing "the LORD's song in a foreign land" (Ps. 137:4 ESV) taught the Jews to hope in God in fresh ways, and so a new festival was to be "observed in every generation by every family" (9:28). The book of Lamentations reflects this candor in dialogue with God. Times of crisis are rich opportunities to build deeper hope in the faith community, facing its future (Rev. 2–3). Believing *through* times of crisis develops faith (Isa. 43:16–21; Jer 31:31–34; Ezek. 37:1–14).

2. Pain and praise function together. In her closing letter—an occasion of great celebration—Esther refers to "times of fasting and lamentation" (9:31). Only when we remember the pain does our thanksgiving have adequate content and perspective.[8] We must learn to worship *in* pain, not *in spite of* it. "Praise that makes sense echoes with the remembrance of suffering reversed."[9] Far and away, the contemporary reflex is to sanitize pain out of worship, removing candor and vulnerability. The gospel does not insist on joy; it welcomes a fuller arena that includes the oppressed and the broken of all ethnic groups. God's new citizenry makes one family of us all (Gal. 3:28). And God gets the glory.

Illustrating the Text

Believing through times of crisis develops faith.

Devotional Classics: *My Utmost for His Highest,* by Oswald Chambers. In this classic devotional, Chambers discusses what he calls "the unsurpassed intimacy of tested faith."[10] He asserts that faith is not sustainable or real until it has been tested by trial and suffering: "Faith must be tested, because it can only become your intimate possession through conflict."[11] When we believe *through* a time of crisis, faith flourishes in the end and we find our beliefs stronger and more resilient than when we began.

Testimony: Invite a congregant who has been through a time of severe testing to share about the ways in which believing through the struggle has increased and fortified his or her faith in Jesus.

Christian Book: *Sifted: Pursuing Growth through Trials, Challenges, and Disappointments,* by Wayne Cordeiro with Francis Chan and Larry Osborne.

This book's theses are based on Jesus's words to Peter in Luke 22:31, when Jesus tells him that Satan has asked permission to sift and test him like wheat, but that Jesus himself has prayed for Peter and his future. The authors assert that sometimes in ministry we are similarly tested and refined through struggle. They state, "Sifting happens for a reason; it's a process that leads to refinement. . . . When God is done with the sifting, our faith will thrive."[12] The believer who makes it through times of sifting and testing will find that his or her faith is refreshed and bolstered.

Pain and praise function together.

Popular Culture: McDonald's used to market a sandwich called *The McDLT*. The gimmick with this sandwich was its packaging, a Styrofoam clamshell case with two insulated halves. One was said to keep the hot side hot, while the other kept the cool side cool. In other words, the two contrasting temperatures involved maintained their differential until the last minute, so that the sandwich could be assembled and eaten in a way that accentuated both aspects of its taste. The lettuce and tomatoes were cold and crisp, and the beef and cheese were piping hot and melted. The idea was that lukewarm was unacceptable and tepid sandwiches were gross. In the same way, believers often benefit from the tension between pain and praise. Without the pain, the praise would be faint and half-hearted; without the praise, the pain would be unbearable. (For an added bonus, you might try searching these old commercials out on YouTube with the keywords "Vintage McDLT Commercial.")

Notes

Ezra 1:1-4

1. An English translation of the Cyrus Cylinder can be found in Matthews and Benjamin, *Old Testament Parallels*, 193–95.

Ezra 3:1-6

1. A. W. Tozer, *Tozer on Worship and Entertainment*, compiled by James L. Snyder (Camp Hill, PA: WingSpread Publishers, 2006), chap. 2.

Ezra 3:7-13

1. *The Simpsons*, season 6, episode 2, "Lisa's Rival," aired September 11, 1994.
2. Christopher Woolf, "A Deadly Modern Disease May Have an Unexpected Ancient Cure," *The World*, Public Radio International, March 31, 2015, https://www.pri.org/stories/2015-03-31/deadly-modern-disease-may-have-unexpected-ancient-cure.

Ezra 4:1-5

1. "A Gift of a Bible," YouTube video, 5:11, posted by "beinzee," July 8, 2010, https://www.youtube.com/watch?v=6md638smQd8.
2. George G. Hunter III, *The Celtic Way of Evangelism: How Christianity Can Reach the West . . . Again* (Nashville: Abingdon, 2000).

Ezra 4:6-24

1. E.g., Smith, *Ezra, Nehemiah, Esther*, 47–48.
2. E.g., Steinmann, *Ezra and Nehemiah*, 232–35.
3. Nelson R. Mandela, *Long Walk to Freedom* (New York: Little, Brown, 1994).

Ezra 5:1-17

1. E.g., Smith, *Ezra, Nehemiah, Esther*, 55–56.
2. Westminster Confession 1.2.

Ezra 6:1-12

1. Adapted from Throntveit, *Ezra-Nehemiah*, 32.

Ezra 7:1-28

1. "Our Story," About Us, Bible Society, accessed October 10, 2017, https://www.biblesociety.org.uk/about-us/our-history/.
2. Oswald Chambers, *"So Send I You"/ "Workmen of God": Recognizing and Answering God's Call to Service* (Grand Rapids: Discovery House, 2015), quotation from the chapter "The God of Sacramental Service."

Ezra 9:1-15

1. Davies, *Ezra & Nehemiah*, 61.

Ezra 10:1-44

1. John L. Dagg, *Manual of Church Order* (Charleston, SC: Southern Baptist Publication Society, 1858).
2. Dagg, *Manual of Church Order*, 274.

Nehemiah 1:1-11

1. A. Catherine Hankey, "I Love to Tell the Story" (1866; tune by William G. Fischer [1869]).

Nehemiah 4:1–23

1. A helpful discussion of the options may be found in Smith, *Ezra, Nehemiah, Esther*, 130–31.

Nehemiah 5:1–19

1. Charles Dickens, *The Annotated Christmas Carol: A Christmas Carol in Prose*, ed. Michael Patrick Hearn (New York: Norton, 2004), 21.

Nehemiah 9:1–37

1. The illustration comes from Ray Comfort, *Hell's Best Kept Secret* (New Kensington, PA: Whitaker House, 1989), 10–11.
2. C. S. Lewis, *The Horse and His Boy* (New York: Scholastic, 1995).

Nehemiah 12:27–47

1. Randy Frazee, *Making Room for Life* (Grand Rapids: Zondervan, 2003), chap. 1.

Introduction to Esther

1. According to the Babylonian Talmud, Esther was written by "the men of the Great Synagogue" (*b. B. Bat.* 15a), a Persian-period institution ascribed to Ezra.
2. Josephus, *Ag. Ap.* 1.40–41.
3. Josephus later identifies Artaxerxes as "Ahasuerus" (*Ant.* 11.184) and refers to Mordecai (*Ant.* 11.6.13).
4. E. Yamauchi, "Herodotus," *ABD* 3:180.
5. Herodatus, *History of the Persian Wars*, 7.205–26, 8.78–97; Yamauchi, "Herodotus," *ABD* 3:181.
6. Levenson, *Esther*, 26.
7. While Herodotus speaks of Queen Amestris, there is no convincing connection to either Esther or Vashti (*Hist.* 7.61, 114; 9.109).
8. Merrill, Rooker, and Grisanti, *World and the Word*, 355.
9. Birch et al., *Theological Introduction*, 440.
10. Beckwith, *Old Testament Canon*, 288–91.
11. L. Day, "Purim," *NIDB* 4:689.
12. Brueggemann, *Reverberations of Faith*, s.v. "Festivals."
13. L. Day, "Purim," *NIDB* 4:689.
14. Brueggemann, *Reverberations of Faith*, s.v. "Festivals."
15. Brueggemann, *Reverberations of Faith*, s.v. "Festivals."
16. Wismer, "Evil."

Esther 1:1–8

1. I will mainly use Ahasuerus (so KJV, NASB, NJPS, NRSV, ESV) throughout the commentary, but I will use the name Xerxes (so NIV, CEV, NLT) in cases of historical documentation.
2. Roop, *Ruth, Jonah, Esther*, 176.

3. Laniak, "Esther," 193.
4. Herodotus, *Hist.* 1.134.
5. Herodotus, *Hist.* 3.89.
6. Yamauchi, *Persia*, 179.
7. Smith, *Ezra, Nehemiah, Esther*, 230.
8. Jobes, *Esther*, 59.
9. Laniak, "Esther," 196.
10. Jobes, *Esther*, 60.
11. Herodotus, *Hist.* 7.8, 20.
12. Xenophon, *Cyr.* 8.8.10, 18; Herodotus, *Hist.* 1.126, 9.80.
13. Strabo, *Geography* 15.3.20.
14. Bush, *Ruth/Esther*, 347.
15. Herodotus, *Hist.* 3.95.
16. Moore, *Esther*, 7.
17. Bush, *Ruth/Esther*, 347.
18. *HALOT* (234) lists the meanings (1) "order" (1:8; 9:13) and (2) "law" (8:13; 9:1).
19. Levenson, *Esther*, 45.
20. Brueggemann, *Reverberations of Faith*, s.v. "Money."
21. Smith, *Ezra, Nehemiah, Esther*, 235.

Esther 1:9–12

1. Malina, "Feast," 82.
2. Berlin, *Esther*, 12.
3. Tomasino, *Esther*," 478.
4. Plutarch, *Moralia* 140.B.16, quoted in Berlin, *Esther*, 11.
5. Laniak, "Esther," 198.
6. Berlin, *Esther*, 15.
7. Laniak, "Esther," 197.
8. Berlin, *Esther*, 12–13.
9. Josephus, *Ant.* 11.6.1.
10. Maltbie D. Babcock, "This Is My Father's World," in *The Covenant Hymnal* (Chicago: Covenant Press, 1973), no. 82.

Esther 1:13–22

1. J. R. R. Tolkien, *The Hobbit* (London: George Allen & Unwin, 1937).
2. Crawford, "Vashti," 166–67.
3. Herodotus, *Hist.* 3.31.
4. The view of Levenson, *Esther*, 50.
5. Herodotus, *Hist.* 3.31, 118; Xenophon, *Anab.* 1.6.4; Josephus, *Ant.* 11.31.
6. Herodotus, *Hist.* 3.84.
7. Bush calls it "farcical and humorous" (*Ruth/Esther*, 350).
8. Berlin, *Esther*, 17.
9. Laniak, "Esther," 203.
10. Clines, *Esther Scroll*, 253.
11. Herodotus, *Hist.* 8.98.
12. Jobes, "Esther 2," 173.
13. Firth, *Message of Esther*, 43.
14. There is coarse language at the start of the speech.

Esther 2:1–11

1. E. Yamauchi, "Herodotus," *ABD* 3:180–81.
2. Herodotus, *Hist.* 3.84.
3. Berlin, *Esther*, 23.
4. Berlin, *Esther*, 25.
5. Standard etymology sees "Esther" coming from Babylonian *Ishtar* (*HALOT* 76). Others propose that "Esther" comes from Heb. *str*, "to be hidden" (so Laniak, "Esther," 206; cf. *HALOT* 771–72).
6. This view overinterprets the passive voice of the niphal verbs (Jobes, *Esther*, 98–99).
7. Clines, *Ezra, Nehemiah, Esther*, 288.
8. Firth, *Message of Esther*, 48.
9. Firth, *Message of Esther*, 49.
10. Corrie ten Boom with Elizabeth and John Sherrill, *The Hiding Place*, 35th anniversary ed. (Grand Rapids: Chosen, 2006), 209–10, 220.
11. Ronald Reagan, *Speaking My Mind: Selected Speeches* (New York: Simon & Schuster, 1989), 426.

Esther 2:12–23

1. Herodotus, *Hist.* 3.125, 129; 4.43.
2. Herodotus, *Hist.* 3.159. Darius I also made official record of this grand impaling in his Behistun Inscription.
3. Herodotus, *Hist.* 7.238. For the impalement of the dead, Herodotus uses *anastauroun*, but *anaskolopizein* for impaling the living (*Hist.* 9.79).
4. Levenson, *Esther*, 61.
5. Berlin, *Esther*, 29.
6. Berlin, *Esther*, 28, citing M. V. Fox, *Redaction*, 35.
7. Paton, *Critical and Exegetical Commentary*, 172.
8. See Bush, *Ruth/Esther*, 358; *Targum Esther*; Herodotus, *Hist.* 3.67.
9. Keil and Delitzsch, "Esther," in *Old Testament Commentaries*, 145–146.
10. Paton, *Critical and Exegetical Commentary*, 187.
11. Fox, *Character and Ideology*, 38.
12. Gordis, "Studies in the Esther Narrative," 47.
13. For the use of "gate" as technical language of the "court," see Xenophon, *Cyr.* 8.1.6, 16; 8.3.2; 8.8.13; *Anabasis* 1.9.3.
14. Berlin, *Poetics*, 63, 69.
15. Herodotus, *Hist.* 3.118.
16. Levenson, *Esther*, 64.
17. Herodotus, *Hist.* 3.139–41, 153; 5.11; 9.107.
18. Koehler and Baumgartner, *Hebrew and Aramaic Lexicon*, 1:332, s.v. "*hen*." A hendiadys (one concept through two words), *hen whesed* is essentially "grace and loyal love," which the translations render in various ways.
19. Laniak, "Esther," 212–13.

Esther 3:1–6

1. Laniak, "Esther," 214.
2. H. L. Bosman and C. Van Dam, "*purim*," *NIDOTTE* 3:591; cf. Exod. 17:8–16; Num. 24:7; Deut. 25:17–19; 2 Sam. 1:1–16; 1 Chron. 4:42–43.
3. Christensen, *Unity of the Bible*, 167.
4. "An Ideology Takes Up Arms against Peace," *New York Times*, February 27, 1994, sec. 4, p. 1, cited in Jobes, *Esther*, 120n6.
5. Herodotus, *Hist.* 1.134.
6. The context of Esther shows a spontaneous and intentional "kneeling" (*kr'* [+ *hwh*]) as standard protocol of respect: "kneeling down" or "genuflecting" (*HALOT* 499.1.b; H.-P. Stähli, "*hwh*," *TLOT* 1:398).
7. Religious objection is clear in *Targums Rishon* and *Sheni* ("I will not bow down, except to the living and true God"; for further discussion, see Moore, *Esther*, 36–37, 105–6).
8. Bickerman, *Four Strange Books*, 180.
9. Berlin, *Esther*, 35.
10. Similar reasoning is in Josephus (*Ag. Ap.* 2.135; cf. Acts 10:25–26).
11. A similar form used impersonally is 1 Sam. 24:1 (in Hebrew texts, v. 1 is numbered as v. 2).
12. Laniak, "Esther," 216.
13. Berlin, *Esther*, 37.
14. Brueggemann, *Reverberations of Faith*, s.v. "Vengeance."
15. Phrase from Plantinga, *Not the Way It's Supposed to Be*, 7.
16. Alexandre Dumas, *The Count of Monte Cristo*, trans. Robin Buss, Penguin Classics (London: Penguin, 2003).

Esther 3:7–15

1. Laniak, "Esther," 217.
2. *HALOT* 920. Used in the OT only in Esther, *pur* ("lot") corresponds to the Heb. word *goral* (3:7; 9:24).
3. H. L. Bosman and C. Van Dam, "*purim*," *NIDOTTE* 3:590.
4. Josephus recounts that *Phrourai* (the LXX term) was a festival observed by his contemporaries (*Ant.* 11:291–96).
5. Josephus, *Ant.* 11.6, 13.
6. Smith, *Ezra, Nehemiah, Esther*, 249.
7. Herodotus, *Hist.* 3.128; Xenophon, *Cyr.* 1.6.46; 4.5.55.
8. Neyrey, "Deception," 43.
9. Jobes, "Esther 1: Book of," 166.
10. Tomasino, *Esther*, 488.
11. Herodotus, *Hist.* 3.128.
12. Neyrey, "Deception," 43.
13. Or 333 tons (Bush, *Ruth/Esther*, 381). No wonder some see "ten thousand talents" as hyperbole (Laniak, "Esther," 222).
14. Herodotus, *Hist.* 3.95.
15. Jobes, *Esther*, 121.

16. Smith, *Ezra, Nehemiah, Esther*, 251.
17. Baldwin, *Esther*, 75.
18. Jobes, "Esther 1: Book of," 166.
19. James Spiegel, *The Making of an Atheist: How Immorality Leads to Unbelief* (Chicago: Moody, 2010).

Esther 4:1–17

1. Craig, *Reading Esther*, 76.
2. Herodotus, *Hist.* 8.99.
3. Bush, *Ruth/Esther*, 394.
4. Herodotus, *Hist.* 3.72, 77, 140.
5. Fox, *Character and Ideology*, 61.
6. Firth, *Message of Esther*, 73.
7. Webb, *Five Festal Garments*, 122.
8. S. Amsler, "*qum,*" *TLOT* 3:1140; *HALOT* 627.6.
9. Jobes, *Esther*, 134; emphasis original.
10. Laniak, "Esther," 224.
11. Boyce, *Cry to God*, 1.
12. Firth, *Message of Esther*, 70.
13. Also called an "Esther Fast." See Shields, "Fasting," 315.
14. H. D. Preuss, "*sum,*" *TDOT* 12:298.
15. Boda, *Severe Mercy*, 307.
16. Preuss, "*sum,*" 298.
17. Firth, *Message of Esther*, 70–73.
18. Firth, *Message of Esther*, 71.
19. Firth, *Message of Esther*, 72.
20. Firth, *Message of Esther*, 78.

Esther 5:1–14

1. Webb, *Five Festal Garments*, 116.
2. Other texts using the idiom include Gen. 31:22; 42:18; Exod. 3:18; 15:22; 19:11, 15, 16; Matt. 12:40; 1 Cor. 15:4; and the *Epic of Gilgamesh* 1.2.44; 1.3.48.
3. Laniak, "Esther," 231.
4. Firth, *Message of Esther*, 82.
5. Paton, *Critical and Exegetical Commentary*, 233; Herodotus, *Hist.* 9.109–11.
6. Laniak, "Esther," 234.
7. Firth, *Message of Esther*, 86.
8. Jobes, *Esther*, 145. Does this parallel imply Haman's doom? In 6:13, the same cast of characters (friends, Zeresh, and wife) all show up again, with a much different assessment!
9. Laniak, "Esther," 235.
10. Firth, *Message of Esther*, 84.
11. Firth, *Message of Esther*, 81.
12. Firth, *Message of Esther*, 80.
13. Firth, *Message of Esther*, 80.
14. C. S. Lewis, *The Horse and His Boy*, in *The Chronicles of Narnia* (New York: HarperCollins, 1995), 272.
15. J. R. R. Tolkien, *The Lord of the Rings* (Boston: Houghton Mifflin, 1994), 50.

Esther 6:1–13

1. Adapted from Jobes, *Esther*, 157, and Radday, "Chiasm in Joshua, Judges and Others."
2. Firth, *Message of Esther*, 94.
3. Clines, *Ezra, Nehemiah, Esther*, 307.
4. Herodotus, *Hist.* 3.138; 5.11; 9.107; Xenophon, *Hell.* 3.1.6.
5. Caird, *Language and Imagery of the Bible*, 134.
6. Laniak, "Esther," 242.
7. Firth, *Message of Esther*, 97.
8. Laniak, "Esther," 240.
9. Josephus notes that Gentiles regularly participated in worship in the Herodian temple (*J.W.* 2.17.412–16; 4.4.275; 5.13.563).
10. Firth, *Message of Esther*, 98.
11. Firth, *Message of Esther*, 99.
12. Firth, *Message of Esther*, 93.
13. Henry W. Longfellow, "I Heard the Bells on Christmas Day," in *The Covenant Hymnal* (Chicago: Covenant Press, 1973), no. 139.

Esther 6:14–7:10

1. Firth, *Message of Esther*, 103.
2. Laniak, "Esther," 244.
3. Smith, *Ezra, Nehemiah, Esther*, 270.
4. Levenson, *Esther*, 104.
5. Carson, *For the Love of God*, January 30 entry.
6. Volf, *End of Memory*, 29.
7. Theodore Roosevelt, "Citizenship in a Republic," speech in Paris, April 23, 1910, http://www.theodore-roosevelt.com/trsorbonnespeech.html.

Esther 8:1–17

1. Laniak, "Esther," 247.
2. Herodotus, *Hist.* 3.128–29.
3. Clines, *Ezra, Nehemiah, Esther*, 314.
4. Laniak, "Esther," 249.
5. Firth, *Message of Esther*, 114.
6. Firth, *Message of Esther*, 113–14.
7. Berlin, *Esther*, 78.
8. Laniak, "Esther," 251.
9. Laniak, "Esther," 251.
10. Baldwin, *Esther*, 99.
11. Firth, *Message of Esther*, 119.

Esther 9:1–10

1. H.-P. Müller, "*pahad,*" *TDOT* 11:522–23.
2. Fox, *Character and Ideology*, 110.
3. Waltke, *Old Testament Theology*, 770.
4. Berlin, *Esther*, 15.
5. Firth, *Message of Esther*, 124.
6. R. J. Hernández-Díaz, "Hatred," in *DSE* 349.
7. J. R. R. Tolkien, *The Lord of the Rings* (London: George Allen and Unwin, 1954–55).

Esther 9:11–19

1. Craig, *Reading Esther*, 129.
2. Firth, *Message of Esther*, 124.
3. Firth, *Message of Esther*, 126.
4. Also Herodotus, *Hist.* 3.125; 6.30.
5. Laniak, "Esther," 258.
6. Firth, *Message of Esther*, 127.
7. Merrill, "The Book of Esther," in Merrill, Rooker, and Grisanti, *World and the Word*, 360.
8. Reid, *Esther*, 146.
9. Firth, *Message of Esther*, 129.
10. Laniak, "Esther," 261.
11. J. N. Oswalt, "*nwh*," *NIDOTTE* 3:58.

Esther 9:20–10:3

1. Laniak, "Esther," 264.
2. Baldwin, *Esther*, 108.
3. Levenson, *Esther*, 126.
4. Laniak, "Esther," 262.
5. Firth, *Message of Esther*, 135.
6. Laniak, "Esther," 264.
7. Jobes, *Esther*, 224.
8. Firth, *Message of Esther*, 138.
9. Schmutzer, "Longing to Lament," 120.
10. Oswald Chambers, "The Unsurpassed Intimacy of Tested Faith," August 29 entry, in *My Utmost for His Highest* (New York: Dodd, Mead, 1935), https://utmost.org/the-unsurpassed-intimacy-of-tested-faith/.
11. Chambers, "The Unsurpassed Intimacy of Tested Faith."
12. Wayne Cordeiro with Francis Chan and Larry Osborne, *Sifted: Pursuing Growth through Trials, Challenges, and Disappointments* (Grand Rapids: Zondervan, 2012), 32.

Bibliography

Recommended Resources

Allen, Leslie C., and Timothy S. Laniak. *Ezra, Nehemiah, Esther*. New International Biblical Commentary. Peabody, MA: Hendrickson, 2003.

Breneman, Mervin. *Ezra, Nehemiah, Esther*. New American Commentary. Nashville: Broadman & Holman, 1993.

Goswell, Gregory. *A Study Commentary on Ezra-Nehemiah*. EP Study Commentaries. Darlington, UK: EP Books, 2013.

Smith, Gary V. *Ezra, Nehemiah, Esther*. Cornerstone Biblical Commentary. Carol Stream, IL: Tyndale, 2010.

Select Bibliography

Allen, Leslie C., and Timothy S. Laniak. *Ezra, Nehemiah, Esther*. New International Biblical Commentary. Peabody, MA: Hendrickson, 2003.

Arnold, Bill T., and Hugh G. M. Williamson, eds. *Dictionary of the Old Testament: Historical Books*. Downers Grove, IL: InterVarsity, 2005.

Baldwin, J. G. *Esther: An Introduction and Commentary*. Leicester: Inter-Varsity, 1984.

Beckwith, R. *The Old Testament Canon of the New Testament Church*. Grand Rapids: Eerdmans, 1985.

Berlin, A. *Esther: The Traditional Hebrew Text with the New JPS Translation*. Philadelphia: Jewish Publication Society, 2001.

———. *Poetics and Interpretation of Biblical Narrative*. Winona Lake, IN: Eisenbrauns, 1994.

Bickerman, Elias. *Four Strange Books of the Bible: Jonah, Daniel, Koheleth, Esther*. New York: Schocken Books, 1984.

Birch, B. C., W. Brueggemann, T. E. Fretheim, and D. L. Petersen. *A Theological Introduction to the Old Testament*. Nashville: Abingdon, 1999.

Boda, Mark J. *A Severe Mercy: Sin and Its Remedy in the Old Testament*. Siphrut 1, Literature and Theology of the Hebrew Scriptures. Winona Lake, IN: Eisenbrauns, 2009.

Boyce, R. N. *The Cry to God in the Old Testament*. Atlanta: Scholars Press, 1988.

Branch, Robin Gallaher. "Vashti." In *Eerdmans Dictionary of the Bible*, edited by D. N. Freedman, 1353. Grand Rapids: Eerdmans, 2002.

Breneman, Mervin. *Ezra, Nehemiah, Esther*. New American Commentary. Nashville: Broadman & Holman, 1993.

Brueggemann, Walter. *Reverberations of Faith: A Theological Handbook of Old Testament Themes*. Louisville: Westminster John Knox, 2002.

Bush, F. *Ruth/Esther*. Word Biblical Commentary. Dallas, TX: Word, 1996.

Caird, G. B. *The Language and Imagery of the Bible*. Grand Rapids: Eerdmans, 1997.

Carson, D. A. *For the Love of God: A Daily Companion for Discovering the Riches of God's Word*. Vol. 2. Wheaton, IL: Crossway, 1999.

Christensen, D. L. *The Unity of the Bible: Exploring the Beauty and Structure of the Bible.* New York: Paulist Press, 2003.

Clines, David J. A. *The Esther Scroll: The Story of the Story.* Sheffield: JSOT Press, 1984.

———. *Ezra, Nehemiah, Esther.* Grand Rapids: Eerdmans, 1984.

Craig, K. *Reading Esther: A Case for the Literary Carnivalesque.* Literary Currents in Biblical Interpretation. Louisville: Westminster John Knox, 1995.

Crawford, S. A. "Vashti." In *Women in Scripture: A Dictionary of Named and Unnamed Women in the Hebrew Bible, the Apocryphal/Deuterocanonical Books, and the New Testament,* edited by C. Meyers, 166–68. Grand Rapids: Eerdmans, 2000.

Davidovich, Tal. *Esther, Queen of the Jews: The Status and Position of Esther in the Old Testament.* Coniectanea Biblica 59. Winona Lake, IN: Eisenbrauns, 2013.

Davies, Gordon F. *Ezra and Nehemiah.* Berit Olam. Collegeville, MN: Liturgical Press, 1999.

Fensham, F. Charles. *The Books of Ezra and Nehemiah.* New International Commentary on the Old Testament. Grand Rapids: Eerdmans, 1982.

Firth, D. G. *The Message of Esther.* The Bible Speaks Today. Downers Grove, IL: InterVarsity, 2010.

Fox, M. V. *Character and Ideology in the Book of Esther.* 2nd ed. Grand Rapids: Eerdmans, 2001.

———. *The Redaction of the Books of Esther: On Reading Composite Texts.* Atlanta: Scholars Press, 1991.

Gordis, Robert. "Studies in the Esther Narrative." *Journal of Biblical Literature* 95 (1976): 43–58.

Goswell, Gregory. *A Study Commentary on Ezra-Nehemiah.* EP Study Commentaries. Darlington, UK: EP Books, 2013.

Hamilton, Victor P. *Handbook on the Historical Books: Joshua, Judges, Ruth, Samuel, Kings, Chronicles, Ezra-Nehemiah, Esther.* Grand Rapids: Baker Academic, 2001.

Haupt, P. "Critical Notes on Esther." *American Journal of Semitic Languages and Literatures* 24 (1907–8): 97–186.

Hurvitz, Avi, *A Concise Lexicon of Late Biblical Hebrew: Linguistic Innovations in the Writings of the Second Temple Period,* Supplements to Vetus Testamentum 160. Leiden: Brill, 2014.

Jobes, K. H. *Esther.* NIV Application Commentary. Grand Rapids: Zondervan, 1999.

———. "Esther 1: Book of." In *Dictionary of the Old Testament: Wisdom, Poetry & Writings,* edited by T. Longman III and P. Enns, 160–70. Downers Grove, IL: IVP Academic, 2008.

———. "Esther 2: Extrabiblical Background." In *Dictionary of the Old Testament: Wisdom, Poetry & Writings,* edited by T. Longman III and P. Enns, 170–75. Downers Grove, IL: IVP Academic, 2008.

Keil, Carl F., and Franz Delitzsch. *Old Testament Commentaries.* Vol. 3, *Nehemiah to Psalm 77.* Grand Rapids: Associated Publishers and Authors, 2000.

Kidner, Derek. *Ezra and Nehemiah: An Introduction and Commentary.* Tyndale Old Testament Commentaries. Downers Grove, IL: InterVarsity, 1979.

Kirk-Duggan, C. A. "Violence." In *Eerdmans Dictionary of the Bible,* edited by D. N. Freedman, 1357–58. Grand Rapids: Eerdmans, 2002.

Koehler, Ludwig, and Walter Baumgartner. *The Hebrew and Aramaic Lexicon of the Old Testament.* 2 vols. Leiden: Brill, 2001.

Laniak, T. S. "Esther." In *Ezra, Nehemiah, Esther,* edited by L. C. Allen and T. S. Laniak, 169–270. New International Biblical Commentary. Peabody, MA: Hendrickson, 2003.

———. *Shame and Honor in the Book of Esther.* Atlanta: Scholars Press, 1998.

Levenson, J. D. *Esther: A Commentary.* Louisville: Westminster John Knox, 1997.

Malina, B. J. "Feast." In *Handbook of Biblical Social Values,* edited by J. J. Pilch and B. J. Malina, 81–84. Peabody, MA: Hendrickson, 1998.

Manickam, J. A. "Race, Racism and Ethnicity." In *Global Dictionary of Theology,* edited by W. A. Dyrness and Veli-Matti Kärkkäinen, 718–24. Downers Grove, IL: IVP Academic, 2008.

Matthews, Victor H., and Don C. Benjamin. *Old Testament Parallels: Laws and Stories from the Ancient Near East.* New York: Paulist Press, 1997.

McConville, J. Gordon. *Ezra, Nehemiah, and Esther.* The Daily Study Bible Series. Philadelphia: Westminster, 1985.

Merrill, E. H., M. F. Rooker, and M. A. Grisanti. *The World and the Word: An Introduction to the Old Testament.* Nashville: B&H, 2011.

Moore, C. A. *Esther.* Garden City, NY: Doubleday, 1971.

Neyrey, J. H. "Deception." In *Handbook of Biblical Social Values*, edited by J. J. Pilch and B. J. Malina, 40–45. Peabody, MA: Hendrickson, 1998.

Paton, L. B. *A Critical and Exegetical Commentary on the Book of Esther*. Edinburgh: T & T Clark, 1908.

Plantinga, Cornelius, Jr., *Not the Way It's Supposed to Be: A Breviary of Sin*. Grand Rapids: Eerdmans, 1995.

Radday, Yehudah T. "Chiasm in Joshua, Judges and Others." *Linguistica Biblica* 3 (1973): 6–13.

Reid, D. *Esther: An Introduction and Commentary*. Tyndale Old Testament Commentaries 13. Downers Grove, IL: IVP Academic, 2008.

Roop, Eugene F. *Ruth, Jonah, Esther*. Believers Church Bible Commentary. Scottdale, PA: Herald Press, 2002.

Schmutzer, Andrew J. "Longing to Lament: Returning to the Language of Suffering," in *Between Pain & Grace: A Biblical Theology of Suffering*, 103–129, coauthor Gerald W. Peterman. Chicago, IL: Moody Publishers, 2016.

Shields, C. "Fasting." In *Global Dictionary of Theology*, edited by W. A. Dyrness and Veli-Matti Kärkkäinen, 314–15. Downers Grove, IL: IVP Academic, 2008.

Smith, Gary V. *Ezra, Nehemiah, Esther*. Cornerstone Biblical Commentary. Carol Stream, IL: Tyndale, 2010.

Steinmann, Andrew. *Ezra and Nehemiah*. Concordia Commentary. St. Louis: Concordia Publishing House, 2010.

Throntveit, Mark A. *Ezra-Nehemiah*. Interpretation: A Bible Commentary for Teaching and Preaching. Louisville: John Knox Press, 1992.

Tomasino, A. *Esther*. In *Zondervan Illustrated Bible Backgrounds Commentary: 1 & 2 Kings, 1 & 2 Chronicles, Ezra, Nehemiah, and Esther*, edited by John H. Walton, 467–501. Grand Rapids: Zondervan, 2009.

Volf, M. *The End of Memory: Remembering Rightly in a Violent World*. Grand Rapids: Eerdmans, 2006.

Waltke, B. K. *An Old Testament Theology: An Exegetical, Canonical, and Thematic Approach*. Grand Rapids: Zondervan, 2007.

Walton, John H., Victor H. Matthews, and Mark W. Chavalas, eds. *IVP Bible Background Commentary: Old Testament*. Downers Grove, IL: InterVarsity, 2000.

Webb, B. G. *Five Festal Garments: Christian Reflection on the Song of Songs, Ruth, Lamentations, Ecclesiastes and Esther*. New Studies in Biblical Theology. Edited by D. A. Carson. Downers Grove, IL: InterVarsity, 2000.

Williamson, Hugh G. M. *Ezra, Nehemiah*. Word Biblical Commentary. Waco: Word Books, 1985.

Wismer, P. L. "Evil." In *New and Enlarged Handbook of Christian Theology*, edited by D. W. Musser and J. S. Price, 186–88. Nashville: Abingdon, 2003.

Yamauchi, Edwin M. *Ezra and Nehemiah*. In *Zondervan Illustrated Bible Backgrounds Commentary: 1 & 2 Kings, 1 & 2 Chronicles, Ezra, Nehemiah, and Esther*, edited by John H. Walton, 395–467. Grand Rapids: Zondervan, 2009.

———. *Persia and the Bible*. Grand Rapids: Baker Academic, 1997.

———. "Vashti." In *Dictionary of the Old Testament: Wisdom, Poetry & Writings*, edited by T. Longman III and P. Enns, 826–28. Downers Grove, IL: IVP Academic, 2008.

Contributors

General Editors
Mark L. Strauss
John H. Walton

Associate Editors, Illustrating the Text
Kevin and Sherry Harney

Contributing Author, Illustrating the Text
Joshua Blunt

Series Development
Jack Kuhatschek
Brian Vos

Project Editor
James Korsmo

Interior Design
Brian Brunsting

Cover Direction
Paula Gibson
Michael Cook

Index

Christmas, 204
chronological order, disruption of, 50
church
  contributions by all members, 130
  criticism of, 155
  discipline in, 101–2
  membership, 155
  neglecting of, 176
  purity of, 100
  as temple, 68, 87
coincidences, 263
"coincidences" in Esther, 203, 263–64
command of God, 72
command of the king, 72
commitment to God, and others, 254, 256
common law, 221
community, 139
  faithfulness of, 8
  in prayer, 172
compromise, 46–47, 69
concubines, 217, 233
confession of sin, 99, 165
confidence, in God's provision, 121
conversion, of foreign women, 98
counteredict of Mordecai, 279–80, 285–86
covenant, 39, 97, 100
  blessings of, 7, 61
  corporate nature of, 91
  curses of, 7
  faithfulness, 160
  new. See new covenant
  reaffirmation of, 22
  relationship with God, 160
  renewal, 157, 165, 171–72
  restoration of, 19
creditors, 138–40
crisis, develops faith, 299
crowded loneliness, 189–90
"cry" (verb), 166
cultural systems, 218, 219
cupbearers, 104, 105–6
currency, 212, 213
curse, 173
Cush, 209
Cyrus, 6, 51
  agenda of, 29
  decree of, 9–14, 45, 54, 64–65, 153
  as polytheist, 12, 13
  restored temple vessels, 16–17
  reversed actions of Nebuchadnezzar, 60
Cyrus Cylinder, 10

Darius, 6, 58, 59, 78, 208–9, 221, 226, 233
  allows building to continue, 64
  as polytheist, 66
Darius II, 6
Darius the Mede, 279
David, 22
  leadership of, 224
  as man of God, 181, 186
  rest from enemies, 292
  tombs of, 126

Davidic descendants, 84
Davidic leader, 31, 33
Davies, Gordon F., 91
Day of Atonement, 158, 159
Dead Sea Scrolls, 204
Deioces, 221
deliverance, 167, 253
detestable practices, 90
Diaspora, 202, 281, 283
  and Festival of Purim, 297
  as spiritual crisis, 299
Diaspora community, God's faithfulness to, 296
Diaspora Jews, 203, 230, 226
discipleship, 49
  as corporate, 190
  as costly, 135, 254
discouragement, 60
  from opposition, 133–34
disgrace, 145
disobedience, 168
diversity, 127
  within the church, 130
divination, 245
divine enabling, 153–54
divine passives, 205, 230
divine sovereignty and human engagement, 273
divorce, 97, 98
doing, demands understanding, 162–63
drama of ignorance, 250
drinking, Persian, 211, 216–17

Easter, 204
"edict" (Persian loanword), 222
edict of death. See Haman: edict of
egalitarianism, 127
Egypt, 6, 78
Egyptians, 166
Eliashib, 125, 192
emotions, in worship, 40, 41
encouragement, from word of God, 61
enemies, of Judeans, 45–46, 90, 248. See also opposition
Esarhaddon, 73
Esther (biblical figure)
  absent from book's conclusion, 299
  advancement of, 226–28
  beauty of, 229
  as deliverer, 251, 258
  edict of, 247
  fasting of, 250, 253–54, 296, 297, 299
  patient wisdom of, 257–58, 260, 271
  personal risk of, 274
  as queen, 222, 227, 234–35, 257–60
  revealed as a Jew, 271
  wins favor of the king, 233–34
  wisdom of, 232
Esther (book)
  audience of, 202
  author and date, 201–2
  and Exodus, 298
  occasion of, 203

king's gate, 251, 259
kings of Media and Persia, 297
Kish, 229

lament, 254, 291, 297, 299
Lamentations, 204
languages, 223
law, reading of, 158
law at Sinai, 81
leaders, qualifications of, 154
leadership, 156, 224
Lebanon, 37
legal system, Christian use of, 224
Levites, 37–38, 40, 84–85, 181, 186
  with cymbals, 187
  faithfulness of, 187, 189
  guarding temple gates, 193
  owning land, 192
Lewis, C. S., 170, 261–62
"light to our eyes"(phrase), 92
list of returnees, 23–24, 153
lists, of priests and Levites, 183
lists of names, 4
lists of settlers, 179
loneliness, 189–90
Lord of the Rings, The (Tolkien), 262, 288
Lord's Supper, 75, 87
Lot, 216
lots, 244–45

man of God, 181
Marduk, 10, 17
marginalized persons, 281, 282
marriage, 93, 102, 183, 255
  to non-Israelite women, 90–91, 96, 99, 174, 194
Megilloth, 203–4
Memukan, 221–22, 245
men of standing, 180
Meshullam, 125
military escort, 112
mixed marriages, 158, 165
Moabites, 192
mocking, 119, 121, 131
Mordecai, 202, 205, 211, 226, 228–30, 235
  as author of Esther, 296
  as Benjaminite, 229
  counteredict of, 279–80, 285–86
  fast of, 253
  at king's gate, 259
  mourning of, 250–51, 254
  as new Saul figure, 286
  as prime minister, 278, 284–85
  rise to power, 298
  unrewarded loyalty of, 264
Mordecai's day, 245
morning and evening sacrifice, 31
Moses, 105, 258, 284
motives, 14–15
Mount Gerizim, 45
multitasking, 268–69
musical instruments, 186

musical worship, 36, 39–40
myrrh, 233

Nabal, 216
Nathan, approach to King David, 272
Nebuchadnezzar, 7, 16, 17, 23
needy, among believers, 140
Nehemiah (biblical figure), 8
  as cupbearer, 104, 105–6, 296
  faithful loyalty to God, 193
  fasting of, 105
  as governor, 138–39, 145
  grieving of, 111
  imprecatory prayer of, 131, 134–35
  leadership of, 138, 145
  prayer for strength, 144–46, 147
  prayer of confession, 103–6, 112–13, 120
  as prophet, 192
  resists attacks from enemies, 143–48
  tact of, 114
  trust in God, 146, 151
"neighboring peoples" (phrase), 90
new covenant, 7, 26, 61, 98, 100, 113, 157, 161,
  164, 169, 171, 172, 195
new exodus, 22–23, 78, 83–84
Ninth of Av, 204
Nisan, month of, 110, 245
Noah, 216, 227
northern kingdom, 7

oaths, 173, 194
obedience to God's word, 77, 81, 97, 106, 107,
  157–61, 175, 182
offerings, 31. *See also specific offerings*
Old Testament, violence in, 291
opposition
  to God's people, 54–55, 68, 116, 120–21
  misinformation campaign by, 144
  mockery of, 119
  to rebuilding Jerusalem's walls, 130–33, 154
  to rebuilding temple, 8, 43–46, 50–55, 57–61, 68
oppressed, treatment of, 281
Origen, 3
orphans, 281

pain, and praise, 300
Passover, 72, 75, 204, 205, 245, 248, 258
past, as guidance for future, 20, 21
patronymic (term), 228
Pentecost, 204
persecution, 46
Persian Empire, 6, 18, 30, 201
  edicts in, 211
  rebellions within, 144
  system of informers, 58
  taxation by, 137
Persian kings, 51, 54, 73, 202
Persian wars, 227
Pharaoh, 13, 166
Phinehas, 84
pilgrimages, 17

Printed and bound by CPI Group (UK) Ltd, Croydon, CR0 4YY

13/04/2025

14656460-0004